THIRTY FIVE YEARS IN THE PUNJAB 1858-1893

THIRTY FIVE YEARS IN THE PUNJAB 1858-1893

G.R. ELSMIE

GYAN

Published by

Gyan Publishing House
5, Ansari Road
Daryaganj, New Delhi-110002
Phone: 011-47034999, 9811692060
E-mail: books@gyanbooks.com

Distribution Network
gyanbooks.com
India, USA, Canada, UK, Australia

ISBN: 978-93-7447-281-1 (PB)

First Published, 1908

2nd Impression 2026

Printed at: Gyan Press, Delhi.

THIRTY FIVE YEARS IN THE PUNJAB 1858-1893

Author: G.R. ELSMIE

THIRTY-FIVE YEARS IN THE PUNJAB

THIRTY-FIVE YEARS IN THE PUNJAB

1858-1893

BY

G. R. ELSMIE, C.S.I., LL.D.

The last Haileybury Civilian who served in that Province

JOINT AUTHOR OF 'LUMSDEN OF THE GUIDES,' AND EDITOR OF 'THE LIFE OF SIR DONALD STEWART'

EDINBURGH

DAVID DOUGLAS

1908

DEDICATED TO THE

UNIVERSITY OF ABERDEEN

IN GRATEFUL REMEMBRANCE OF INSTRUCTION RECEIVED

BY THE AUTHOR IN 1853-55 FROM

JOHN CRUICKSHANK, LL.D.

PROFESSOR OF MATHEMATICS IN MARISCHAL COLLEGE

PREFACE

This book may be properly described as 'Notes by the way.' It consists mainly of extracts from letters and diaries written by me as I journeyed through my Indian life. I have tried to make the extracts objective rather than subjective, but they are, nevertheless, to a great extent autobiographical. This, it will be seen, from the nature of things, was inevitable. I desire, however, that readers should regard the biography merely as that of a man whose career gives a fairly good idea of the life and progress of a Civil officer in the Punjab, from the year 1858 to 1893. The narrative may be found to be of interest by old Punjabis who remember the whole or part of the time dealt with, by young men looking forward to service as Civilians in India, and by other persons who care to read about that country.

A few words will suffice to indicate the nature of my material. On retiring from the service, and on examining the papers left by my mother, who had died fourteen years before, I found that my 'letters home' relating to my Indian life had been preserved. Extracts from these letters, 1855-1878, are used freely for that period. From 1861 onwards I kept a very rough diary, from which quotations are given when the subjects seem to be sufficiently interesting and the diary contains a fairly intelligible account of them. When some expansion of the extracts from letters and diary seemed necessary, I have done a certain amount of 'tacking,' and occasionally, when an extract has been found to be very brief, I have written from memory, quickened by reading the old note. But throughout, my endeavour has been to give the impressions made upon me at the time, and not to write a retrospective account. This method causes the book to indicate growth and progress from the days of official infancy and youth to those of middle and possibly of old age. I must ask my readers to bear this in mind, and by no means to suppose that I now adhere to all the raw opinions which I formed as I went along.

The last class of material which I need notice is that of the letters of friends, mainly those of Sir Robert Montgomery and Sir Douglas Forsyth. Both of these men were my private and official friends for many years. I had the greatest regard and affection for them. No very full record of the lives of either has been made, and I doubt whether any one, save myself, possesses very many of their letters. I have given extracts from these because they throw light on many of the subjects of my notes, and also on the characters and careers of two most distinguished Punjab officers.

No very hard and fast line has been followed in the spelling of Oriental names and words. Where custom has clearly sanctioned a popular mode—as, for instance, Delhi, Cawnpore, Jullundur, Loodiana, Lahore, Cabul—that custom has been followed. Where popular modes are various, transliteration on the Jonesian system has generally been made, *e.g.* Ambala, Afridi, Muhammad. In quotations from letters, the mode of spelling used by the writers has, for the most part, been adopted. Accents have been used very sparingly, and only when it seemed that a reasonable doubt might arise as to the pronunciation of a vowel on the first occurrence of a word.

G. R. E.

TORQUAY, *June* 24, 1908.

CONTENTS

CHAPTER I

PREPARATION FOR AND LIFE AT HAILEYBURY COLLEGE

1855–1857

CHAPTER II

THE VOYAGE AND CALCUTTA

1858

CHAPTER III

ASSISTANT COMMISSIONER, LOODIANA

1858–1859

CHAPTER IV

ASSISTANT COMMISSIONER AT JHELUM, MITHUNKOTE, FEROZEPORE, AND AMRITSAR

1859–1861

CHAPTER V

ASSISTANT COMMISSIONER OF LAHORE AND MURREE

1861–1863

CHAPTER VI

JUDGE SMALL CAUSE COURT—LAHORE, DELHI, SIMLA

1863–1865

CHAPTER VII

DEPUTY COMMISSIONER, JULLUNDUR

1865–1868

CHAPTER VIII

SIMLA, CALCUTTA, AND FURLOUGH

1868–1871

CHAPTER IX

ADDITIONAL COMMISSIONER OF AMRITSAR AND JULLUNDUR

1871–1872

CHAPTER X

ADDITIONAL COMMISSIONER OF PESHAWUR

1872–1873

PAGE

CHAPTER XI

THE CRIME OF MURDER AMONGST AFGHANS

1873

CHAPTER XII

ADDITIONAL COMMISSIONER OF PESHAWUR

1874–1875

CHAPTER XIII

ADDITIONAL COMMISSIONER OF PESHAWUR

1876–1877

CHAPTER XIV

CIVIL AND SESSIONS JUDGE, PESHAWUR

1877–1878

CHAPTER XV

ACTING JUDGE OF THE CHIEF COURT

1878

CHAPTER XVI

SECOND FURLOUGH

1879–1880

CHAPTER XVII

COMMISSIONER OF THE OLD LAHORE DIVISION

1881

CHAPTER XVIII

JUDGE OF THE CHIEF COURT

1882–1884

CHAPTER XIX

COMMISSIONER OF THE NEW LAHORE DIVISION

1885–1886

CHAPTER XX

FINANCIAL COMMISSIONER AND MEMBER OF THE LEGISLATIVE COUNCIL

1887–1888

CHAPTER XXI

THE LAST YEARS

1890–1893

APPENDIX

LIST OF ILLUSTRATIONS

THIRTY-FIVE YEARS IN THE PUNJAB

CHAPTER I

PREPARATION FOR AND LIFE AT HAILEYBURY COLLEGE

1855—1857

I WAS born in Aberdeen in 1838. In the summer of 1843 my father and mother went to Southampton, which became our headquarters for many years. I was educated at private schools there till I was fourteen. From 1852 to 1855 I was a student at Marischal College and University, Aberdeen.

My going to India in the Civil Service came about in this wise. My mother's brother, John Shepherd, had been a Director of the East India Company since the thirties. I had seen several cousins, his nominees, start from Southampton to take up civil and military appointments in India, and I had become aware that, when I was old enough, I might follow their example if I felt inclined.

About 1853-54, however, the abolition of the patronage of the Directors in appointments to the Civil Service was decreed. For the future, writerships were to be awarded after competition, and no fresh admissions to the East India College at Haileybury were to be allowed after January 1856, by which time I should have attained the age of seventeen years and two months. As no one could enter Haileybury before he was seventeen, it was clear that I could only have one chance. In the autumn of 1854 I was called upon to say whether I was prepared to go to India or not. At that time I had given no serious thought to the subject of my future career. Being an only child, very happy at home, I felt little inclination to go abroad, and I was content to believe that a clerkship in the India House would suit me, for all practical purposes, well enough. I therefore declined the appointment, and not long after I was sent to Cannstatt near Stuttgart with a view to becoming proficient in German. In August 1855, however, I was disturbed by the unexpected reappearance of the proposal that I should go to India. The appointment which I had refused in the previous year had been promised to another youth, who had, almost at the eleventh hour, thrown it up. It was the last Civil appointment which my uncle had in his gift. In the end I was satisfied, chiefly by arguments used by my uncle and by the fact that certain favourable modifications had just been made in the pension rules, that it was my duty to overcome my prejudices and to agree to adopt an Indian career. By the middle of September, therefore, I had returned to England and been enrolled as a pupil of Mr. C. J. Yeatman of Westow Hill, Norwood, a well-known tutor for the entrance examination into Haileybury.

A few extracts from letters written at the time[1] will sufficiently indicate the nature of life at a crammer's and at the East India College.

[1] When I give no special description of an extract from a letter, it is to be inferred that it is taken from my 'letters home.'

WESTOW HILL, NORWOOD, *September* 19, 1855.— . . . Yeatman says that with working he has no doubt but that I shall pass. . . .

October 5.—It is fearfully hard work, such as I never experienced—from nine till nearly three in the day and from half-past six till past ten at night. . . .

October 20.—I find that in Geography and Mathematics I have little work. The four Greek Gospels, the *Medea* and the *Alcestis* of Euripides, two books of Horace with some other bit of Latin, such as one of Cicero's orations. The whole of History (English) and a lot of Paley, but not all the *Evidences*. These must be all learnt perfectly, so much so that every syllable be at your fingers' ends. . . . I have been fighting with Yeatman for a good while over *The Newcomes*,[1] which he is reading at present. He hates Thackeray,[2] reads the book with a prejudice, finds fault with everything. 'Such exposures do no good.' He knows there are plenty of Honeymen, but says it is wrong openly to ridicule them. No such London Bankers as Newcomes; Thackeray never writes for good, everything is coarse—the people are all coarse, etc. etc. Now Dickens never writes like that, he takes pleasure in displaying the good sides of human nature; Thackeray only the bad. . . . I had another controversy to-night with him: he declares that everybody doesn't change their milk-teeth, only a few in whom they are weak. I tried to convince him, but you know you can't fairly contradict such an important personage.

October 21.—Yeatman has yielded this morning as to the teeth, but is still inveterate against *The Newcomes*; never read such dreadful rubbish in all his life.

December 6.—We are working like so many horses now. It is just six weeks to the exam. However, if it will only keep fine and frosty like this, I don't mind; for then I have good spirits, which is a great thing when disagreeables have to be done.

December.—The other new fellow, by name Bernard, came

[1] Then recently published.

[2] My father and mother had taught me to be a great admirer of Thackeray.

on Thursday, has given up an Addiscombe appointment on spec. He is very clever, an excellent classic from Rugby. . . .

The preceding paragraph refers to Charles Edward Bernard, nephew of the great Lawrence brothers, who, while he was at Yeatman's, managed to exchange his Addiscombe cadetship for a Civil appointment. Bernard and I became friends at once, and our friendship, which grew with our years, lasted till his ever-to-be-lamented death in 1901.

Before going up for the examination I had to furnish certain certificates, including one from my father, who in forwarding it to me for presentation wrote the following characteristic letter:—

December 20, 1855.

MY DEAR BOY,—I enclose certificate, which, I hope, is what is needed, and, with all such documents, will help to fill the basket that holds them. As regards your examination, like all other matters where human nature is concerned, success does not always go with merit or ability, but is influenced by tact. A great influence in this sort of thing is to answer *deliberately* and *correctly*; not to appear too smart, but to think. In the other case, the examiners want to be master and puzzle. A quick answer provokes another question. Of course, this has reference to oral examination. Your disposition being impetuous requires to be checked, as the impression is that the knowledge of such persons is superficial and shallow. There is some truth in the saying that a clock, if it goes faster, runs faster out; all excitement shortens life. Fast men are short lived; they run down their persons and pockets. These principles can be applied in any position in life, and, as you say to Mama, there is a good medium. My experience is, all medium boys turn out the most useful and successful men for general life. Only one or two geniuses are wanted in an age, and they are not valued for the good they do. We are not doubtfully anxious about your examination, although we wish it well over that you may enjoy a little relaxation. However, you will find that getting ahead of work early in life saves a deal of trouble, and the well considering anything at the outset often reduces the rest to mere manual labour.

A favourite subject of warning from Mr. Yeatman in regard to the coming trial was the proper demeanour of examinees in the presence of the examiners. Glum or sulky looks might prove fatal, while a smile like that of one of his previous pupils might soften the examiner's heart and induce him to pass a badly prepared candidate. The pupil quoted was Mr. Horatio Ross (son of the well-known rifle shot, Ross of Rossie), whose smile, according to our tutor, was irresistible.

December 23.—I am going to Mansfield Street[1] to-morrow to stay till Wednesday, because I have to pass the Board, at the India House, on Wednesday afternoon. . . . I shall try and profit by my father's good advice as to coolness at the exam.

December 27.—. . . Only a week now before the exam. I ought to be quaking in my shoes.

The examination, which lasted three or four days, took place at the India House in Leadenhall Street. The number of candidates was thirty-two; the examiners were the Rev. Canon Dale of St. Pancras, the Rev. Robert Eden, and the Rev. W. Stone. Each day we had to undergo oral and written examinations. I remember being closeted with Mr. Eden and doing my best to construe a long passage in the *Medea*. Mr. Eden was

[1] My uncle lived in 7, now 13, Mansfield Street.

somewhat uncouth in manner. He moved uneasily in his chair; one of his feet was unshod; he rubbed it, evidently to soothe the pain of gout or chilblains. Canon Dale, well known for his poetical power, was a great contrast to Mr. Eden. He was most pleasant in manner, and perfectly neat in his attire. I had to translate to him a passage in the *Ars Poetica.* Mr. Stone, the examiner in the Greek Testament, was a tall and a somewhat discouraging personage. He told me to translate from the beginning of the twenty-first chapter of St. Luke, in which reference is made to the precious stones and adornments of the Temple. In verse seven I somewhat carelessly rendered the word γίνεσθαι, 'happen.' Mr. Stone solemnly pulled me up with the admonition, 'In Scripture, when translating such a passage, you should not say "happen" but "come to pass."'

Our written papers were answers to a long series of questions and problems in English History and Geography, Paley's *Evidences*, and Mathematics. Soon after the conclusion of the examination we were told to go one afternoon to the India House and hear the names of the successful candidates. The names read out were twenty-five in number, so that seven unfortunates were plucked and lost their chance of an Indian Civil career. To my relief my name was included in the twenty-five.

I shall not attempt to give a detailed description of Haileybury College and of the system pursued there. All necessary information under those heads is to be found in the *Memorials of Old Haileybury College.*[1] It must be remembered that I belonged to the last term of Directors' nominees, and that although when I entered

[1] 1894, Archibald Constable and Co.

College it contained the full number of students—about one hundred—at the end of each six months a term passed out and went on to India, and no new term took its place. The result was that during the second half of the year 1857 my term was the only term in College. It was a large one, and it eventually contained thirty-eight students, all of whom passed out in December of that year, and the East India College ceased to exist.

The subsequent careers of the following men made them the most distinguished of the last Haileybury term. I give the honours and appointments which they finally obtained.

Sir Charles Bernard, K.C.S.I., Chief Commissioner of Burma.

Sir Philip P. Hutchins, K.C.S.I., Member of the Supreme Council and now of the Home India Council.

Sir Charles Grant, K.C.S.I., Foreign Secretary to the Government of India.

Sir James B. Lyall, G.C.I.E., K.C.S.I., Lieutenant-Governor of the Punjab.

John Beames, the well-known philologist.

Richard Thomas Burney, Judge, Chief Court, Punjab.

The subjects of study included Greek and Latin, Mathematics, Political Economy, History, Law, Sanscrit, Persian, Hindustani and other Indian languages. The Principal was the Rev. Henry Melvill, Canon of St. Paul's, one of the greatest and most eloquent preachers of the day. The professor of History was Sir James Stephen, the friend of Lord Macaulay, the father of the well-known Judge, FitzJames Stephen, and of Leslie Stephen, the distinguished writer. Sir James's lectures were extremely interesting, his language and delivery perfect. The Sanscrit professor was Monier (afterwards Sir Monier) Williams. In the department of Law there had been giants before my time, Sir James Mackintosh and Mr. Empson, but I am afraid we students had not the highest enthusiasm for our professor of Law, Mr. Farley Leith, afterwards well known as M.P. for Aberdeen. His mode of instruction was wanting in clearly defined purpose, his language was involved and difficult to follow. Mr. Leith, however, could be very practical when the spirit moved him, and I recall with pleasure a piece of advice which he gave to us when urging diligence and care in preparing for and writing the papers of an important examination. He concluded his admonition somewhat as follows :—

> And, Gentlemen, don't forget your handwriting. I do not for a moment say that examiners give marks for handwriting in a Law examination, but it is well to remember that examiners are but human after all, and that their benevolent amiability is not likely to be less when they come to the end of a clearly written, easily read paper, than it would be after they had struggled through a crabbed and hardly decipherable manuscript.

The Dean of the College was the Rev. W. Buckley, a kindly man with no very decided characteristic. He was our classical professor.

The mathematical professor was the Rev. W. Heaviside, afterwards Canon of Norwich. There can be no doubt that Mr. Heaviside was a general favourite. He had many characteristics of manner, and the students showed their regard for him by calling him amongst themselves 'Old Heavy.'

Colonel Ouseley, the professor of Persian, and Mr.

Eastwick, the professor of Hindustani, were men well known for their acquirements in Oriental languages.

HAILEYBURY, *January* 26, 1856.—. . . Well, here I am sitting in my own room. It is almost 12 feet by 8, exclusive of a recess for the bed, and a large cupboard which has a chest of drawers in it, washing materials, and everything of an un-intellectual nature which belongs to my establishment. . . . All the first-term men have to call on the Principal to-day. I have just been. He is a very nice man; entertains you for a quarter of an hour; gives you good advice, and behaves in a very kind and encouraging manner. . . . Melvill preached last Sunday a sort of opening lecture, 'Whatsoever thy hand findeth to do, do it with thy might.' It was an exhortation to diligence in all daily duties, especially to be diligent in religion: 'when ye pray, pray with your might.'

We have not been troubled with many lectures as yet. Sanscrit every day; very difficult indeed. The character something quite frightful. We have a great deal of work before Easter. You must not expect a good place from me, I fear, for I think I forgot to tell you there was a second examination on the 17th January, when the appointments of the men who were plucked were filled up by seven new and successful candidates, some of them first men in Rugby, Harrow, etc., and very clever; so we are thirty-two. There have never been so many in a term before, nor so many good scholars in one.

February 4.—. . . There was what is called a tavern the other night in the next room to mine. Anybody may go, if he gives a bottle of beer. I did not patronise, but I assure you I had enough of it. The singing is very good, I believe; but the choruses not agreeable to me in my bed. I think I shall just look in some night to see the nature of it, and to hear the songs. They take place every Wednesday night, not always in the same room, thank Providence.

February 15.—Collard has sent me a piano, to my great satisfaction. . . . There is to be a concert here this week by some of the students. Young Propert[1] is a wonderful comic singer and actor, and I am very anxious to hear him. . . . I breakfasted with the Principal this morning; several other men of the first term were there. He is a very kind man, no buckram about him, puts you quite at your ease. . . .

February 21.—The concert went off last night with great éclat. Propert's comic singing is the most wonderful thing of the kind. He writes his own songs, invents the acting, and changes voice incessantly. For instance, he sang a piece called 'Othello ye Moor.' He appeared as Othello and related in song the whole play. The professors with all their glumness roar with laughter. . . .

Bernard is my greatest friend; he is a nice fellow indeed, so good-natured and good in every sense; we work a great deal together, and walk or boat together nearly every afternoon.

March 2.—The exams.[2] are all coming on. Tuesday—Greek Testament; Thursday—Law; the Tuesday after—Arithmetic; Wednesday—Euclid; and Sanscrit on the 18th. . . .

March 10.—We have at length got a little breathing time between these eternal examinations. All are done except Sanscrit, which comes next Tuesday. Mathematical exams. were yesterday and the day before. I did not do anything very wonderful, but nevertheless hope I am sure of a 'Great.'[3] You know there are no prizes, save one for the man who is head of

[1] Afterwards of the Bombay Civil Service.

[2] Before the Easter vacation.

[3] In Haileybury examinations marks were not given by ordinary numbers. A more general system was adopted. Progress or the reverse was indicated as follows:—

Great Proficiency =Gt.
Good Proficiency =G.
Proficiency =P.
Little or no Proficiency=L.

A 'Good' mark was the unit. A 'Great' was equal to two 'Goods. Medals and prizes equalled three 'Goods'; the student who scored the largest number of 'Goods' or 'G.'s' was head of the term, those below him ranked on the same principle. In languages, both European and Oriental, a 'Great' could not be obtained unless a minimum of 'extra' work over and above the pass quantum had been taken up.

the term. I think that Bernard stands a very good chance of being head. He is a steady, hard-working fellow, and good at everything.

In the result of this examination Hutchins was first, Bernard was second. To my astonishment I was fourth, bracketed equal with Charles Temple, the son of a tutor of Lord Dalhousie, who is mentioned more than once in Lee Warner's *Life of Dalhousie*.

April 10 (after Easter).—I feel on a sort of pinnacle,[1] from which many are quite able to give me a shove over. Bernard can hardly beat Hutchins this term, I think, yet he is to try it on.[2]

In the month of May the students gave a ball in college in honour of the marriage of a daughter of the Principal.

May.—The excitement is over and all is quiet again. The ball is a thing of the past. . . . The dining-hall where we danced was splendidly decorated. . . . Contrary to expectation the number of gentlemen and ladies was about equal, and in all the number present amounted to about 500. . . . 'God save the Queen' was played at five o'clock. . . . It was such fun to see all the Pros. dancing and fancying themselves beaux. . . .

Every one is going up to the peace rejoicings.[3] . . .

MANSFIELD ST., *June* 3.—We had such a crush last night outside Hyde Park; very good fireworks indeed, but very same. It was impossible to get through the crowd to see all the illuminations. . . . I went to the opera on Wednesday night at the Lyceum, heard Grisi and Mario in *Lucrezia Borgia*; enjoyed it very much, but think that Grisi's voice is a good deal fallen off. On Friday I went by myself to Her Majesty's and heard

[1] Referring to my place at the Easter examinations.

[2] Bernard eventually succeeded in taking the first place, but not till the last examination in December 1857. I was then fifth, so had fallen one step from my pinnacle.

[3] At the end of the Crimean War.

Alboni in *La Sonnambula*. What a splendid house it is. . . . I had a good seat, high up, but that did not matter; the house is so beautifully adapted for singing. . . . Alboni is a splendid singer, very fat, but far superior to Grisi as she is nowadays. . . .

October 3.—It took fourteen geese to go over us all on Michaelmas Day. I can't say they were elegantly carved, but every one had as much as he wanted.

October 8.—We had a very good sermon from the Principal on Sunday. 'Be ye mindful to entertain strangers, for thereby some have entertained angels unawares.' The practical part of which was calling all the good promptings of one's heart and little turnings after God, the angels whom we were to entertain, and that though they might look at first but commonplace suggestions, as the three men appeared to Abraham but commonplace travellers, yet entertain them and maybe you will have entertained angels. Melvill uses beautiful language and is very impressive. I only wish we had him every Sunday.

October 18.—Yesterday was the Haileybury race-day. Graham in our term took four of the prizes, and proved himself an excellent runner and jumper. . . . Bernard won a handsome silver cup for the steeplechase.

I went to a tea-fight at the Heavisides on Thursday night. These parties are certainly a change, but uncommonly slow. A clump of men stand in one part of the room like so many fools. The Pros. converse together in the middle. Their wives and daughters make up pairs at conversation, and there is always some sort of music going on which, whether it be good or bad, is not heard distinctly on account of the Babel of tongues. . . .

October 23.—We had a debate last night on whether it was expedient for a young civilian to take out a wife to India. I got upon my legs to advocate the marrying plan, and of course was in such a state of mind that I forgot all the good things I intended to say, and only remembered the foolish. However, the ice is broken, and perhaps I shall come on better some other time. The debate was carried by the non-connubialists by four votes.

October 29.—There was a boat-race here last Saturday[1] and I made a début in steering. The boat which I steered is one of the two which have to finish the match in a few days, the prize being thirty shillings to each of the crew. I was greatly delighted, for I feared to make a great mess of it.[2] . . .

The Principal is only too glad to grant exeats for the 5th November, as there is generally a row here on that night, and he is anxious to thin the College as much as possible to preserve order.

November 18.— . . . By the bye, I went in to the voluntary classical (examination) this time. There was a bit of Latin to be translated into English verse (quite a new thing) which I did in a way. It may get me a 'Great' in the subject.[3] . . . We had a most wonderful sermon from Melvill to-day. 'So Saul died for his transgressions which he committed against the Lord, even against the words of the Lord, which he kept not, also for asking counsel of one that had a familiar spirit, to inquire of it' (1 Chron. x. 13). He has certainly the finest flow of language at his command that you can imagine. Saul had previously prohibited witchcraft; he had turned from the sin, resolved against it; then his first act was to return to it. To what a double depth does one fall who has abandoned a besetting sin for a time and returns to it again. When we have fallen to the lowest abyss of remorse, would we inquire the result of the battle? Would we call from the realms of rest the spirits of the just standing before us clad in mantles like old Samuel? They would (then) say—'The Lord has called on you a thousand times and you would not hear. Go forth to battle and the Philistines shall prevail against you. . . .'

Wednesday.—The exams. are all over, I am delighted, oh! so delighted, to say. You don't know what a feeling of relief I have to-night when I think that I need not get up at some unearthly hour in the morning, and that there is no more poring over 'Rental'[4] characters in prospect, for several weeks. I

[1] On the river Lee.
[2] My boat subsequently won the final heat.
[3] It did so.
[4] Oriental.

succeeded in Persian much better than I expected. Old Wilson[1] put me on at the very place (in my extra) which, if I had had my choice, I should have chosen. With a light heart I left his presence.

LONDON, *Thursday evening.*—All has turned out exceedingly well, I am thankful to say. I have been fortunate enough to get a 'Great' in every subject including classics, at which I am in a high state of hilarity. It is what I hoped for, but not what I expected. . . . I am off to the 'Huguenots' to forget 'Greats,' etc.

Towards the end of February 1857 I took a short exeat, and went to see my friend, James Forsyth, start as a cadet for India. We had been fellow-students at Marischal College, Aberdeen. He eventually joined the Central Province Commission, and became distinguished in the Civil and in the Forest Departments. He had much of the poet in him, which he evinced, years later, in his well-known and most interesting book *The Highlands of Central India.*

HAILEYBURY, *March* 7.—The Hertford Assizes were held on Monday and Tuesday last, in consequence of which we were let off lectures on those days. Some of the criminal cases were interesting enough, but the Civil Court seemed to me a very dry proceeding. Serjeant Ballantyne conducted a case on Monday in a most wonderful manner, and though there was a good deal of difficulty about it, he soon cleared it up and gained the verdict. . . .

About this time a General Election was taking place. One day I went to Hertford to hear some of the candidates speak from the hustings. Sir Edward Bulwer Lytton, whose novels I held in ardent admiration, was a

[1] Horace Hayman Wilson, the great Orientalist, came from Oxford to Haileybury two or three times a year as visiting examiner.

prominent figure. He wore a short black velveteen coat. A large gold chain and other jewellery were conspicuous. He spoke with much emphasis and very marked action. Referring to a cautious speaker in Parliament, Sir Edward described him as never letting a cat out of the bag in the Commons without knowing beforehand to which side of the House 'that cat would jump.'

May.— . . . I am enjoying Haileybury this spring very much. Everything is so beautiful; the woods are very fine, and the clusters of chestnuts all in blossom are some of the finest I have ever seen.

June.—We had grand boat-races on Monday afternoon. An Oxford crew gave the pick of the College a downright hiding, in spite of all the trainings and dietings which they had gone through.

It was usual for some of the Directors to come down to Haileybury for the speech days at Midsummer and Christmas. This year, however, news of the outbreak of the Mutiny at Meerut and Delhi reached London at the end of June. It brought consternation to the Directors; very few came down for the speech day; proceedings were curtailed, and those who attended hurried back, if I remember rightly, to London to be present at a special Court.

In the long vacation I generally spent part of my time in Scotland. This year, in the company of a young friend, I took a short trip to Arran, Loch Lomond, and the Trossachs.

COURT HOUSE, ARRAN, *Sunday evening, August.*— . . . Left Glasgow for Arran at 2 P.M. Our journey was cheap and long;

sixty miles in five and a half hours for the sum of two shillings a head; a boat crammed with Glasgow folk 'going out,' talking the broadest of dialects. . . . On coming here we were told there were no beds, but that they could perhaps put us up in what they called—as we thought—the *coach* house. We were led forth, and came to what was to all appearances an Episcopal Chapel, with a cross on the top, within whose reverend walls we entered, and found sundry damsels preparing turn-down beds on the floor. 'This is whaur ye maun sleep,' said a wee canty body with a white mutch on her head, 'just baith the-gither in this bed.' Now, there were five other beds within these hallowed walls (as we thought), and we did not think it would be possible to sleep together with so many fellow-occupants of the room, as the heat would be something intense, so we enlightened the young lady as to how by a more skilful arrangement she might lay down another bed, which was done, and we were resigned to our fate. . . . The chamber turns out to be the *Court* House of the island, used four times in the year for the trial of criminals, and put into the hands of the inn people to do as they like with during the season. . . .

SUNNYSIDE, CULTS, ABERDEENSHIRE, *Friday.*—On Monday from Arran we went to Rowardennan and Loch Lomond. Went up Ben Lomond, the easiest ascent, all grass walks and a well-beaten path to the top. . . . On Tuesday we crossed Loch Katrine to the Trossachs; remained there all Wednesday; went to Perth yesterday. I was delighted with Loch Katrine and the Trossachs; went about with a *Lady of the Lake* in my hand and traced the places. The people there believe in Walter Scott as thoroughly as they do in their own existence; point out where FitzJames lost his gallant grey, the rock on which Allan-bane sat, and the aged oak whence the lady darted in her shallop.

August 27.—We had a most inspiriting discourse from Mr. Bain[1] on Sunday, all about the 'horrid cruelties' in the East, saying, that if the original Directors and Governors had taken

[1] A Highland Free Church minister.

such measures as to make the Indians all Christians, these horrors would have been prevented. He, of course, did not think it necessary to go into trivial details as to how any such result was to be brought about. . . . James Forsyth is safe,[1] . . . but quite a miraculous escape he had. He passed through Delhi five hours before the breaking out of the Mutiny there; had attempted to get into the dak bungalow (a sort of inn, I fancy), but found it full, and was obliged to go on. When the outbreak took place every one in it was murdered. He writes home in good spirits. They had a letter last Monday. He had lost nearly all his properties, and wrote in such a way that you could see he was not quite out of the danger In fact, he said he almost expected to lay down the pen he was writing with and snatch up the pistol that lay at his side, every moment.

The last months spent at Haileybury College were very enjoyable. The number of students in our term had increased from thirty-two to thirty-eight, the chief cause being the failure of sundry men in the previous term to pass their final examinations at Midsummer. They therefore dropped into ours. Each student now had two rooms, a sitting-room and a bedroom, so our comfort was much increased. The authorities, moreover, were more indulgent and less strict in the enforcement of rules. In the belief that small irregularities would probably be overlooked, I ventured to take to College with me a very pretty little dog, who soon became a great pet with all who knew her. This will explain my next extract, and I may add that during the interview described the dog was nestling below my coat, under my left arm.

HAILEYBURY, *October* 17, 1857.—Tinee is still an inmate

[1] See p. 14.

of my room. She was reported about ten days ago to the Registrar, Mr. Heaviside, who sent for me. I had half an hour's talk with him. He was exceedingly good-natured; said he could not give me leave to keep a dog in College; he was very sorry for me, etc. etc. However, I drew a most touching picture of the attachment existing between us, and 'stated as how' she never was to be seen unless officials pryed into my room, and at last he consented not to punish me this time, but said that if she was reported again, take away my bedroom he must. Now this was as much as to say, 'I don't want to send your dog away now that College is so empty, so you had better not get her reported; of course, I know nothing about it.' I have since heard that he has given the hint to the officials that he doesn't want to hear any more on that matter, which is very jolly of him, dear old man as he is.

Tinee duly escaped further official notice, and stayed with me till the College closed.

October 17 (*continued*).—The *Haileybury Observer* is coming out to-day, I believe. I may send you a copy to amuse you, as it is to contain some production of your son's—which it is, you must find out for yourself.

October 29.—We have had rejoicings and illuminations, etc. etc., on account of the fall of Delhi.

The foregoing extract calls for two remarks. Delhi was taken in the middle of September. The news did not apparently reach Haileybury till nearly six weeks afterwards. 'Rejoicings, illuminations, etc.,' give but a faint idea of what really occurred. Certain bold spirits carried wood, coals, and fire from their rooms to the quadrangle; a bonfire was lighted. The spirit of rejoicing spread rapidly. The meeker and milder men became abettors of the outrage on College proprieties. Old furniture, broken room-partitions were thrown into the fire. A great blaze followed. The Principal and professors rushed from their houses and scattered the offenders. I distinctly remember the figure of the Principal illumined by the flames as he laid hands on one of the ringleaders. The fire died down, but not before a large black circular spot had been burned on the grass. To the credit of the authorities, however, the greatness of the occasion blotted out the heinousness of our transgressions, and to the best of my recollection no punishments followed.

December 4.—All over for the last time. I have just come out of Hindustani *vivâ voce*, and so ends the entire performance.

MANSFIELD STREET, *December* 8.—The old College is left alone in its glory, with empty rooms and a few sad faces. To-night is the term dinner at the London Tavern; the last time we shall meet as a term. Old Heavy, the Dean, and Eastwick are coming. It will be a mingled cheerful and melancholy affair.

These notes regarding the old College of Haileybury may be appropriately closed, I think, by a transcript of the speech made by Principal Melvill on the 7th December 1857, the last Di.s' or Directors' day. At the end of the luncheon in the College Hall, Mr. Ross Mangles, M.P., Chairman of the East India Company, the father of a Bengal Civilian, who had recently distinguished himself by an act of great valour in India,[1] proposed the health of the Principal and Professors of Haileybury. Principal Melvill's reply, which I have recently found in an old *Hertford Mercury*,[2] was the following:—

I trust that I may be allowed to be brief in acknowledging

[1] For which he was afterwards decorated with the Victoria Cross.

[2] December 12, 1857.

the kindness shown to myself and the Professors. I cannot attempt, I have not the heart to attempt, to say much on an occasion which—to us, at least—is very trying and mournful. I do not at all exaggerate in using these words. For however generously we may be dealt with, and whatever other prospects in life may open before us, trying and mournful it must be, trying and mournful it ought to be, that a connection should be dissolved which has subsisted with great advantage to ourselves, and not—we venture humbly to hope—without some advantage to India. But, though I cannot say much, I may, and I must, express the deep sense of gratitude which we all entertain towards the East India Company for the great and unwearied kindness which we have received at their hands. They have been to us the most gracious and considerate masters—I only wish that we had been more deserving servants; but we have done our best; and I now ask pardon for all our deficiencies. I have also to express our earnest and unfeigned hope that the new system, whose operation sweeps this College away, may prove itself as good as the old. I ought perhaps to have said, may prove itself better than the old. And, Gentlemen, if I did not say it, it was not from any cold or niggardly feeling. But when I think what the Civil Service has been, when I remember what the Civil servants have done, amid those fearful outrages which have darkened and devastated India, indeed I feel that this is a mighty and comprehensive wish, that the system of competition may prove itself equal to the system it displaces. I shall not attempt, after what has passed in the Hall, to enumerate the deeds whether of the dead or of the living—whether of those whose names will be graven on the tablet which you, Sir, have so gracefully proposed, or of others who still survive, to render, as we may hope, yet more service to the State. But I may be permitted to make an allusion. I think that, had I been a layman, I should have felt it a high honour to rise to be Chairman of the East India Company. I think that, being that, I should have thought it much to be also a member of the British Parliament. But I believe that

I should have reckoned it better than all this to have been the father of a noble fellow who took a wounded comrade on his shoulders and bore him for miles from the field of battle till a place of safety was reached. Gentlemen, though our connection with the East India Company may now be said to terminate, our connection with the Civil Service of India does not come to an end. I think, and I believe, that for many long years to come numbers, who shall be serving their country most faithfully and most efficiently, will look back to Haileybury with gratitude and affection, and trace to some lesson received within its walls much of their usefulness as men and their consistency as Christians. We shall carry this conviction with us into our retirement. It is a conviction which will cheer that retirement; it is a conviction that will dignify that retirement. Forgive me if I do not say more. I think you must all feel that if, under circumstances like the present, I could say much, I should be utterly undeserving of being listened to at all. I bid you all an affectionate farewell. I thank you all for your warm and cordial expressions of goodwill. And with a hearty prayer that the kindness which you have shown may be returned a hundredfold to yourselves, we, the Principal and Professors of Haileybury, lay down our offices—offices which, we trust, have not been sullied in our hands. We depart to seek new homes, but never—be assured of this—to forget old friends. [1]

The tone of the speaker's voice, when referring to the signal bravery of his old student, still rings in my ears.

[1] Since this chapter was prepared for press it has come to my notice that Principal Melvill's farewell speech, as reported by the *Times*, has been printed in the *Memorials of Old Haileybury College*. I have, however, decided to let it remain, in the hope that it may prove of interest to readers who have not met with the other book.

CHAPTER II

THE VOYAGE AND CALCUTTA

1858

THE time had now come to make ready in good earnest for the start to India. It was arranged that Charles Bernard, Alexander Lawrence,[1] and I should take time by the forelock and sail from Southampton on the 4th of January. A large party, consisting of Dr. and Mrs. Bernard[2] and Mrs. Hayes (the two latter being sisters of Sir Henry and Sir John Lawrence) with numerous young people, arrived in Southampton, where my home was, on Saturday, January 2. Alexander Lawrence and Charles Tawney (afterwards Director of Public Instruction in Bengal) were our guests. The rest of the Bernard party had taken rooms in the town. The first night we all dined together in our house. The following day, Sunday, we went in a body to evening service in Portland Chapel, the minister of which was my father and mother's great friend, Alexander Maclaren, who has since become so well known as Dr. Maclaren, the eloquent preacher in Manchester. Mr. Maclaren was no doubt aware that I and others of his audience were on the

[1] Alexander Hutchinson Lawrence was the eldest son of Sir Henry. He also was going out to join the Bengal Civil Service, having been one term above Bernard and me at Haileybury.

[2] Father and mother of Charles Bernard.

point of leaving home and going forth into the world. The words of his text were, 'Ye know not what shall be on the morrow.' There was much in the sermon 'to take away with us,' as the expression is.

The next day we sailed from the Southampton docks in the P. and O. steamer *Colombo*.

AT SEA, *Friday morning*, *January* 8.—It is a most beautiful day, not a single cloud and the sea really smooth, so much so that even the *Colombo* cannot roll about as before. We are all quite well and accustomed to the motion, and competent to do great justice to the viands of the Company. You would have been surprised to see us yesterday sitting at dinner for upwards of an hour, and making up for lost time like men. I can see that if all goes well we shall enjoy this voyage very much; most probably shall arrive at Gibraltar to-night, late, and shall be able to land for a few hours to-morrow morning. There are no champagne days on board now; the Addiscombe Cadets liked it too well, I believe.

January 13.—A day before reaching Malta. . . . Since Sunday night this voyage has proved itself most abominable. A boiling sea and a strong head wind, and the ship going at the lively pace of five miles an hour minus her jibboom. . . . It was very disheartening to find that although pretty well accustomed to rolling, pitching was quite different, and we have to get used to that also. Waves like mountains, seas breaking on the deck, hatchways closed, not a breath of air in the cabin—oh, so hot and stifling. To stay down was impossible, and above it was raining torrents. . . . We had a very pleasant three hours at Gibraltar, during which we saw a great deal of the place, going through most of the excavated batteries which are cut out inside the solid rock, with loopholes every now and then for cannon.

January 16.— . . . We enjoyed our few hours at Malta very much; mounted horses and scampered all over the place. . . .

RED SEA, *January* 23.—At Alexandria we were hurried from steamer to train. About 7 A.M. we anchored in the harbour, and were welcomed by boatfuls of the most filthy-looking Arabs and Egyptians. . . . An immense barge received the baggage, which was tumbled out of the *Colombo* in a twinkling, and entrusted to the care of a horrid-looking crew, no doubt a portion of the Egyptian Administration Company. It was truly a matter of the most profound faith to believe that any article whatsoever would ever come out safe from such rascally-looking hands. . . . Landed near the railway station, and were immediately assaulted by troops of little wretches proffering donkeys for hire. . . . The boys, indignant at refusal, have a habit of making their donkeys charge at you in revenge, which is more ludicrous than agreeable.

We saw nothing of Alexandria, but got into the train almost immediately for Cairo. . . . At the stations along the line the greatest confusion and bustle prevailed; but it was great fun to see the Arabs squabbling for places in the train, and when they could not get inside, they very calmly mounted to the tops of the carriages. . . . We partook of refreshment provided by the Company at a station, where joints and fowls and oranges were supplied for us. Concerning the first-named delicacies, the general impression was that they were *chameau*—so a Frenchman said. . . . The time passed very pleasantly in a first-class carriage; we played whist at intervals, and arrived at Cairo about six, catching a very distant view of the Pyramids in the short twilight. Then we had a frantic rush to the hotel or beds. . . . We could see nothing of Cairo, as we landed just as it was getting dark, and were told that we had to start at six next morning to cross the desert. We bought Chinese lanterns, and arming ourselves with sticks went about hither and thither, and were rather amused with many things we saw. The town is not lighted, so you may imagine that we had not a very distinct idea of where we were going. There appeared to be a great many French in the town, and there were cafés and such like, but not very magnificent ones. . . . We were all up early, and rushed off to the station in order to be punctual, which we were, but the train was not. We had rather a curious scene to watch while waiting. There was a burying-ground close to the station, and in the East it is in burying-grounds that all people who have no beds elsewhere, sleep. We saw them lying in heaps, and as the sun rose, one by one emerged from amidst the sleeping mass, and giving their clothes a good shaking and adjusting their turbans, their toilet for the day was completed. They then bowed down towards the East, and as soon as their devotions were ended they marched off, one this way and another that, with the air and grace of kings, though their garments were but frieze or sacking. No sooner were we out of the town than we were in the desert, which is, as it is always described, sand—sand—as far as you can see, without a green thing to break the yellow monotony. . . . The caravans were interesting; hundreds of camels all laden, trudging along together, joined one to the other by ropes. They go single file, and are very uncomfortable-looking brutes. . . . When the railway came to an end we were refreshed with desert fare at the terminus, whence we beheld an immense number of tents, camels, and Arabs. The Arabs were engaged in lashing our baggage on the camels' backs. As soon as the inner man was revived we had a scramble for the vans, and as soon as every one was seated we set off at full gallop. Each van holds six people, and to put in half another would be an impossibility. Externally, a van is like a bathing-machine with only two wheels. Inside there are six divisions, padded and comfortable enough. Two mules and two horses draw, and an Arab coachy with a long whip hits them above, while another fellow sits on a step lower down and walks into the unfortunate beasts from below with a broad thong. . . . Over the sand like this for five hours brought us to the gate of Suez, which we were pleased enough to see. We got beds in the hotel; dined and slept as sound as tops. Suez is a most miserable place, wretched hovels of houses. We did not go to the ship till 12 or 1 P.M., so had time to have a very jolly ride in the desert on Arab ponies, and in truth we made them gallop and enjoyed the fun exceedingly. We then got on board a small steamer which was to take us to the *Candia*, lying at her moorings a few miles off.

RED SEA, *Sunday*.—The heat to-day is tremendous, not a breath of air. We have the punkahs going in the saloon all day. . . .

We enjoyed the land part of the journey exceedingly. Bernard had rather a nasty fall in Cairo when we were going to the station in the dark in the morning. He tripped in a hole in the road, sprained his ankle and cut his thumb; but he is quite accustomed to that sort of thing, and is now almost quite right.[1]

OFF GALLE, *Saturday*, *February* 6.— . . . We arrived at Aden last Monday week in the evening, and were glad to go on shore for an hour or so. We found plenty of coals and negroes who did not ruin themselves in dress, also a Parsee shop and an hotel with an old billiard-table in a very seedy state of preservation. . . . We passed a horrid night, as you can suppose, when you reflect on us four[2] in a very small cabin with the ports shut on account of the coal dust. . . .

We have been here since Thursday at twelve. After we had come out of harbour about a mile and a half, off flew some oil-box from the engine with an alarming report, disclosing a riven bearing-cap or some such thing, which prevented our further progress. So here we are making a job of it, I believe, and hoping to start some time to-night or to-morrow. . . . The delay is most provoking; said to be the fault of the 69th regiment, whom we had to take from Aden from the *Alma*, which was lying there 'broken down.' This is the sixth ship

[1] Bernard was always remarkable for his great personal activity. He used to drop from his second-story room into the quadrangle at Haileybury, and there is a legend that when he first arrived in Burma as Chief Commissioner he dropped from the steamer's bow on to the landing-place. No wonder that he bore a scar occasionally.

[2] Our party of three had become four at Alexandria by the addition of our friend Richard Burney, a fellow-termsman who had travelled with the mail *viâ* Marseilles.

they have been in on their way to Rangoon. They have broken down four already, and they have been saying all the while that they would succeed in smashing us. . . .

Tuesday.— . . . Bernard is sitting beside me writing, he is a great favourite. So are Lawrence and Burney. The latter is a great addition to our trio, he has unflagging spirits. One of his great amusements is making little sketches of blackies and other people who strike his fancy. He is a capital draughtsman.

CALCUTTA, *Sunday, February* 21.—We had a very fine run to the Sand heads. . . . The sail up the Hooghly was very beautiful; a great deal of green on each side, immense trees and compounds with villas and palaces interspersed. . . .

Bernard and Lawrence are not going up country, and we have settled to put up at Mrs. Herring's boarding-house, No. 5 Russell Street. We have got a whole floor, three nice large rooms, and we are to be boarded and lodged for one hundred rupees each per month. . . . We are not expected to pass our examinations in less than six months,[1] but of course we shall try to get out of Calcutta as soon as possible. We have got Munshis to cram us; funny old fellows with plenty of fat about them. . . . They are nice old boys withal, and can speak very good English. . . .

Calcutta is a most beautiful town and quite equals my expectations. The houses are very large and in the middle of fine gardens or compounds, as they are called, in which flowers and large-leaved shrubs abound. The drawing-rooms are handsomely furnished, more showily than in England; no carpets, but nice, cool-looking matting, and then there are always large verandahs which are generally filled with flowers. . . .

Monday.—Yesterday was a pleasant day. Bernard and I

[1] In those days young Civilians, on landing in Calcutta, were supposed to enter the College at Fort William and to remain there till they had passed a fair standard of proficiency in two Oriental languages. As we three were intended for the upper provinces, our languages for examination were Hindi and Persian. We were allowed to reside where we pleased and to employ Government Munshis or others at our discretion, provided that we presented ourselves for examination on the first of every month.

went to the Cathedral in the morning, heard the Bishop of Madras[1] preach the funeral sermon of Daniel Wilson.[2] Most people were pleased, but I thought him very long and prosy. I believe he is looking out for the vacant bishopric, but I think I have heard that Melvill has a very good chance. I don't know whether he would take it or not. . . . We hear very little about the Mutiny. The excitement was intense at one time, I am told. It could not be kept up for ever, and consequently calm has ensued. News is looked for every day from Lucknow, as an attack was expected last week. George Lawrence,[3] who used to be at Worcester Park in 1851-52, is in Calcutta just now. He has not changed in the very least; looks as young as he did then. He was in Lucknow the whole of the siege, was wounded in two places, had a bullet through the shoulder. He has recovered very fast, and is now apparently quite well. . . .

February 25.—Here we are installed in our new quarters, Mrs. Herring's boarding-house. We have a very large sitting-room and two good bedrooms. The furniture is better to look at than to feel, especially the sofas, which resemble in hardness the well-remembered couches at Ballater. . . . Alex Lawrence had an interview with Lady Canning yesterday,[4] she having sent for him. She was most kind, he said. Sir Henry must have been a splendid man. The accounts generally heard in England are nothing to what are in every one's mouth here, so universally loved and respected he was. Lawrence had seen neither father nor mother since 1848. . . .

Saturday.—Bernard and I have been out this morning for a long walk in the suburbs, through the woods. Starting soon after six, we took a revolver with us and had some mark-shooting. We were much tempted to shoot at several vultures who were sitting on the tops of cocoa trees, but restrained our

[1] Bishop Dealtry. [2] Bishop of Calcutta who had recently died.

[3] Eldest son of Sir George Lawrence. He was the first of the many Lawrences whom I have known. He was in the room with his uncle, Sir Henry, at Lucknow when the fatal shell burst, July 1857.

[4] The Governor-General, Lord Canning, had left Calcutta for a long stay at Allahabad shortly before we landed.

ardour, as all the birds of prey are protected by the law, and rather a heavy fine is the consequence of injuring them. They are the scavengers of the country, and no sooner does the odour of any offal or such like reach their nostrils than they come down in troops and soon dispose of it. The town is full of crows, who are also scavengers; the consequence is that there is a continual caw-caw all day long, a terrible din, but our ears have got accustomed to it. The crows are so impudent they think nothing of coming and perching on your venetians. Nor are the sparrows particular about flying in at the windows and picking up the crumbs from the floor. . . .

March 4.—I have to tell you of a change of plan more immediately affecting Bernard and Lawrence, but which may have some influence on me. Their uncle, Sir John Lawrence, has written saying he thinks it would be better for them to go up country and meet him at Allahabad, where he will shortly confer with the Governor-General; then study at Lahore and go to the Hills with him (Sir J. L.) in the hot season. . . .

March 17.—Lawrence and Bernard have now definitely arranged to go up country the day after to-morrow. So I am to be left solus. . . . Of course I can't stay in the rooms we have now, nor do I wish to do so. . . . They are infested with rats and cockroaches and other abominations, and besides the ground floor is very unhealthy in the rains. . . . I have found a house, just opened as a boarding-house, in which there are two vacant rooms.

7½ CHOWRINGHEE, *March* 20.—Yesterday I saw the last of Bernard and Lawrence as they were whirled away in the train. I was indeed sorry to part with them after we had been together so long. . . . The Drummonds have been very kind to me indeed. I have dined there no less than three times.[1] I was there at a large dinner party of eighteen last night. . . .

[1] Mr. and Mrs. Edmund Drummond. Mr. Drummond was at this time Accountant-General of India. I had known their son at Haileybury. Later in Lord Elgin's time Mr. Drummond became Lieutenant-Governor of the North-West Provinces. Finally he became a Member of the Council of the Secretary of State and a K.C.I.E.

COLLECTOR'S HOUSE, HOOGHLY, *Sunday*, *March* 28.—I am now staying for a few days at Hooghly, a small town about twenty-four miles from Calcutta, where Mr. Buckle, the husband of our fellow-passenger, Mrs. Buckle, is Collector. I went with Mr. Buckle to his cutcherry the other day, to see how things were carried on there. I was much amused, though of course I could not understand a word of the jargon that was going on round me. The cutcherry is a large airy house, full of native writers and assistants scribbling away all day in their different offices. There are rooms in it full of immense bales of paper containing all the accounts, history, etc., of every estate in the district, which can be referred to on an instant's notice. The Collector is king of his cutcherry. He is greeted on entering by the most profound obeisances on all sides, which, as I was with him, were extended to me also, rather to my discomfiture. . . .

A trial of a case about some land was going on. The zemindar or land-farmer of the district was trying to turn out of his estate a man who had been in possession for sixty years by special free grant from Government. . . . There was no jury; the Collector sole decider, though against his decision there is an appeal. When we were sitting there, we heard a row downstairs, which turned out to be a squabble between two natives, who were brought before Buckle and fined, both of them, for disturbance in and disrespect to the court. . . .

CALCUTTA, *April* 3.—On Monday Lang[1] and I dine at a Mr. Ritchie's,[2] a barrister, and on Tuesday I dine at the Ricketts'. Mr. Ricketts[3] is to be Member of Council in a month.

On Tuesday morning I went over the *Shannon*, now lying in the river. I enjoyed the excursion very much. I never was on board a man-of-war before. We went into every corner, down to the very keel. She is not in particularly good order, as nearly all her crew are in the Naval Brigade.

Sunday.— . . . Report says that the country is settling down

[1] George Lang, a friend, who was in my term at Haileybury.

[2] Advocate-General, Bengal. Father of Sir Richmond Ritchie, K.C.B., who married Miss Anne Thackeray.

[3] Afterwards Sir Henry Ricketts, K.C.S.I.

very fast now and that many rebels have submitted themselves, but for the truth of that I cannot vouch, as we hear the accounts of yesterday very often contradicted by those of to-day. Another parson has come to stay in this boarding-house, a Mr. Moule.[1]

Monday.—. . . The Bombay telegram arrived to-day. We have heard of Alex Lawrence being made a baronet, with £1000 a year. I suppose he will take his good fortune very calmly. . . . He must make something grander for himself, this being the fruits of his father's work. . . .

This morning I gave my horse a rest and went for a walk through the bazaar, just after all the fruit, fish, and vegetables had come in fresh. It was a very curious scene, an immense bustle, provisions of all kinds, sellers of all kinds, heaps of melons and plantains at very small prices, ducks and hens, beef, everything huddled together. Several English women, very much like boarding-house keepers, were busy at their bargains. One of them was clearing her way bravely through the crowd with the help of a strong parasol, giving every black man who happened to be in the way a sharp blow and forcing him to stand by. . . .

Wednesday.—I have received a note from Lawrence. They are living in camp with Sir John Lawrence. He wrote from Loodiana, on their way to Murree, which they hope to reach about the middle of May. . . .

April 22.—. . . A letter from Bernard yesterday, written on the day the news of the baronetcy arrived. He says that of course Lawrence is highly delighted and he did not expect anything of the kind. . . .

April 23.—The other night I experienced a nor'wester. I was about twenty yards from the house, just as it was getting dark, when in an instant I could see nothing for the pillars of dust that were being whirled about in every direction by the

[1] One of the Cathedral chaplains. Mr. Moule was well known. He was a delightful companion. He seldom spoke without amusing his hearers. In speaking of a very hot station where he had been chaplain, I remember his assuring us that his tongue remained as dry as a parrot's all the time he was there. No description could have been more graphic.

wind, which blew most violently. I could hardly find my way into the house, and when I did get inside I was almost blind with dust. After the dust-storm came the rain, pouring down in beautiful style, with thunder and lightning *ad libitum.* The result of all this was of course charming. The air was delightfully coöled, and continued fresh all night and the next morning, until the sun became strong. He soon licked up the pools, and dust was flying about again in no time. . . . I dined with the John Peter Grants on Saturday, a small party. They are very kind people indeed; live in a splendid house with immense rooms. Mr. Grant[1] will be Senior Member of Council shortly. A great big man he is, bluff and hearty, and very clever, I believe. Mrs. Grant sings remarkably well; her mother composed songs. . . . The Miss Ricketts' invited Lang and myself yesterday to a small picnic at the Botanical Gardens, on the other side of the river. We crossed together about six o'clock and were a party of twelve. . . .

Several of us have at length joined the Calcutta Volunteers. We have talked about it ever since coming out, and it is useful to know drill. So we are to be drilled every Wednesday morning; are provided with muskets and etceteras by Government. There are Cavalry, Infantry, and Rifles. We are in the Infantry. . . . I joined more as a matter of duty than for any other reason. There is little chance of our ever being called out, so there won't be much excitement for our trouble.

May 7.—I am glad to tell you that I have passed in Hindi. The papers were very easy, and if I had had them last month I should have passed, I am quite sure. *Then* the papers were much more difficult, and only two men passed, whereas this time no less than nine passed. . . . Our pay is now increased £5 per mensem. Beames has not passed in Persian, and he is much disgusted. The Persian examiner is very strict, and will let no one through in less than three months, no matter how good he may be. This examiner is a Captain Lees;[2] he has passed very

[1] Afterwards Lieutenant-Governor of Bengal and Governor of Jamaica.

[2] The well-known Captain Nassau Lees, Secretary to the Board of Examiners.

few men indeed. He told Garrett that he is not going to pass us in a hurry. . . .

May 14.—I received an invitation from Kaye,[1] who is living at Barrackpore, a military station about sixteen miles from Calcutta, to go with him to a ball, and stay a day at his house. Accordingly I started off, with two others who had also invitations, in a ghári or cab, about seven in the evening, and had a very pleasant drive of about two hours' length to the scene of the festivity. . . . The dancing was kept up very late, and we had a grand supper in a 'spacious marquée.' Before going to bed Kaye and I took a morning walk in Barrackpore Park, which reminded me more of England than anything I have seen in India. Beautiful green grass with immense spreading trees, extending for several miles along the river bank. The summer-house of the Governor-General is in the middle of it, something like a French château. . . . It was so strange, on walking through the cantonments, to see among the trees several elephants walking about with their keepers, whisking their great trunks and wagging their ears. The English appearance of the place was soon dispelled. . . .

June 8.—The thermometer in the house has been up to 98°, so you can imagine what it is outside. To go out in any conveyance is almost impossible, for the wind is so fiery that it nearly burns off the skin. On going to the door of the house, the sensation is just as if you were standing close to a mass of molten iron in a foundry. . . . There is little else to do in this fiery climate but to work, and I have already discovered that India with plenty to do may be bearable. India with idleness would be intolerable. . . . I have just had to settle a dispute between my two syces or grooms, who have had a grand fight, and, of course, mutually accuse one another. . . . There is never any reliance to be placed on the statement of witnesses (in this country). They will swear to anything for the most trifling bribe. In fact, the magistrates scarcely know how they

[1] William Kaye, a Haileybury fellow-termsman, afterwards Member of the Board of Revenue at Allahabad.

decide cases, and they say that counting the flies upon the punkah is as good a way as any. If the number be odd, then let the man off; if even, punish him. . . .

June 22.—The rains have set in, in good earnest. We have heavy showers at all hours of the day, which as yet are looked upon as a great boon, inasmuch as they cool the earth considerably. The thermometer in the house is now about 82° to 83°, a delightful change which we can well appreciate. . . . The damp is excessive; books are covered with mould in a day, so your bearer has plenty to do wiping various articles. Even books lying on the table show signs of vegetation.

July 24.—I mustered up courage the other day to write to R. S., and ask his advice as to choosing the Punjab as my destination, for really one hardly knows what to do among conflicting opinions on a subject of which one understands nothing. One says that in the Punjab there is hard work and small pay; another, that there is a good climate and plenty of scope. So I get bewildered. . . . I don't think I shall mind the hard work, for what else is there to do in this country? . . .

August 19.— . . . The Naval Brigade came down country about a week ago, and were received by all the troops now in Calcutta. It was a very pretty sight indeed. The men went in boats to the *Shannon*, and were cheered loudly as they went up the gangway. When on board, they mounted the rigging and returned the compliment, but it was so funny to see them go up, as it was quite evident that their land service had made them forget no little of their marine agility. . . .

August 27.—I went down to see Mr. Drummond off by the steamer. He goes on three months' leave. It was the first time that I had gone to see the English mail start, a scene calculated to produce the feeling of envy. . . . There are generally many Calcutta folks down on the occasion, and one man, perhaps not knowing the reason why some other has come down, rushes frantically up to him with, 'You are not going home, are you?' or some such words, which show how much he would like to be on the point of starting, despite all the terrors of sea-sickness and the heat of the Red Sea.

As old Sir James Stephen used to say at College, 'The real state of the case is simply this: India is not a colony, and no man goes to find a home there, nor does any English resident ever come to look upon it in the light of home.' . . .

A ball was given by Sir James Outram to the officers of the *Shannon* who served in the Naval Brigade. I cannot but confess to having been considerably disappointed at the personal appearance of Sir James, whom I had never seen before. Instead of being a tall grey-headed man, as I fancied, he is on the other hand quite diminutive, rather stout, with short black hair and moustache. Lady Outram is a tall old lady, very kind-looking, and of a homely appearance. . . .

September 14.— . . . I dined at the Curries'.[1] I took down Miss Grant [2] to dinner. Conversation on such subjects as music, the *Agamemnon*, the laying of the cable, and the probable lack of ice for next year. It appears that there was no frost in America last January and February; March ice won't keep. . . . After the ladies retired, it was interesting to listen to the talk of the big men; J. P. Grant himself, and Ricketts and Beadon (the Home Secretary), not to mention Mr. Currie. Opinions are not very settled as to the probable effect of this change from many masters to one mistress,[3] and these wise heads did not do much more than look profound and keep their own counsel. . . .

The preceding and other extracts relating to dinner parties in Calcutta are given mainly to show the generous hospitality which the principal Civilian and other residents lavished on strangers in the country. I arrived in Cal-

[1] Mr. Currie was at this time a Member of the Legislative Council.

[2] Afterwards Mrs., now Lady (Richard) Strachey, the editor of *A Highland Lady*.

[3] The transfer of the government of India from the Court of Directors to the Crown.

cutta without a single letter of introduction. Some of my friends at home objected to the system of sending out young Civilians armed with a sheaf of 'soup tickets,' as they were called. I soon found that I had no reason to regret the want.

September 28.—Lang starts for Bancoorah to-night, and if I pass I meet him at Ranigunj this day week. Captain Lees assures me there is no doubt of my passing, and says that he will let me know the first thing the day after the exam. Then Mr. Harington,[1] the kindest man alive, is to go with me to the Home Secretary, and make all things square for my immediate departure up country.[2] . . .

Sunday, October 3.—I have this forenoon received a private note from the examiner telling me that I have passed (in Persian) all right at last. I am not going to lose much time about leaving Calcutta. I start the first thing on Tuesday

[1] Afterwards Sir Henry Harington, K.C.S.I.

[2] Meanwhile I had decided on the Punjab as my future province. Sir John Lawrence, no doubt urged by his nephews, Bernard and Alex Lawrence, had applied for me.

More than a year after the foregoing lines of this note were written, my friend and neighbour, Mr. Lewin Bowring, C.S.I., who was Lord Canning's private secretary in 1858, called upon me holding an open letter in his hand, which he said he had just found by chance amongst his papers, and which he thought would interest me. I at once recognised the handwriting to be that of Sir John Lawrence. The greater part of the letter will probably prove of interest to other admirers of the great Ruler of the Punjab. When Mr. Bowring came in, by a strange coincidence Lady Montgomery, the widow of Sir Robert Montgomery, was paying us a morning visit.

MURREE, *August* 21, 1858.

MY DEAR BOWRING,—There is a young Civilian, by name George Elsmie, who has just passed College in Calcutta, who is anxious to be posted to the Punjab, and as I hear a good account of him I shall be glad to have him. Please arrange this.

My friend Montgomery is still making constant pulls on me for Civil Officers. He has lately asked me for three more. I have agreed to give him one, young Crommelin, who is now at Gujerat.

I hope that no more of my men will be drafted away. I have already given a great many, and am, I assure you, very hard up. Several officers, and some of them good men, are going home this cold weather. If I get

morning . . . meet Lang at the railway terminus at Ranigunj, and then go on in dak (post) carriages for four or five days to Allahabad. It is fortunate that I 'laid my dak' (as the expression is) before I heard for certain that I had passed, otherwise I should not have got away for two or three weeks, as all the carriages are engaged for I don't know how long after Tuesday. . . . My servants, like all others, at the last moment say they won't go up country.

a bad or even indifferent officer in charge of a district, all must go wrong. The mischief which may be done in six months is not cured in as many years very often.

I am afraid I must go home for a year myself. I have been gradually but surely breaking down for the last three years. I have half lost my eyesight, and suffer much from the head. The work here is excessive, and the assistance at my disposal is not sufficient. The constant grind is too great for any man. If I get better I shall come out in the cold weather of 1859, D.V. But some rest I feel I must have, to save myself from a total breakdown. I wish you would try and ascertain who will act for me. I should like Montgomery to be the man, if he can be spared. Unless my *locum tenens* is a real good workman and good fellow to boot, all will go wrong. I feel very loth to go lest anything should go wrong in my absence, but the doctors say that it is absolutely necessary.—Yours sincerely,

JOHN LAWRENCE.

L. BOWRING, Esq.

Oude ought to be settled by January next, the time when I wish to go. If necessary I could stay a month longer. There can be no question as to the superior importance of the Punjab over Oude. The work here will always be double that of Oude. And the Frontier alone makes this charge of the greatest consequence to the general interests of the Empire. Should there be any row here, or even any great danger impending, I would remain at every risk.

J. L.

CHAPTER III

ASSISTANT COMMISSIONER, LOODIANA

1858—1859

SASSERAM,[1] *Friday*, *October* 8.—We have done nothing but travel on and on since Tuesday morning, and we have only now halted at this place for breakfast and bathing. . . . On leaving Calcutta I had the pleasure of seven hours in a railway, passing through most monotonous scenery, principally rice-fields and jungle. At Ranigunj, the terminus of the line, I met Lang, and we left Ranigunj at six o'clock, having installed ourselves very comfortably for the night in our gháris.[2] . . . We put most of our luggage in one, and took possession of the other ourselves. The carriages are comfortable enough, broad seats on each side, and a board and cushion between them, so that we can lie down most comfortably, and, with the aid of pillows, sleep profoundly.

MIRZAPORE, *Sunday*, *October* 10.—For four consecutive days we have travelled day and night, resting for an hour or so twice daily. . . . Yesterday about sunrise we discovered that we had arrived at Benares, but we delayed not, changed horses at once and hurried on. . . . About the distance of forty miles from Benares there is a small town called Gopigunj. . . . On arriving at the dak bungalow we found one half inhabited, and on inquiry were told that the inmate was 'Simson, Magistrate sahib,'[3] who at that moment was administering justice in his cutcherry hard by. . . .

[1] Between Ranigunj and Benares. [2] Post-carriages.

[3] My cousin, James Simson, Joint-Magistrate of Mirzapore, who happened to be in camp at Gopigunj.

The cutcherry was merely a tent with a raised floor and a sort of dais, at one end of which a large writing-table was placed. Behind it sat, surrounded by many natives, a smiling European. Around the base of what I have called the dais a dozen or more native writers were scribbling away as fast as their fingers could go. Before the magistrate stood an unfortunate prisoner, pleaders, policemen, etc. etc. On my approach I was saluted respectfully by the assembly and shaken cordially by the hand by the European, who recognised me at once. . . . He proposed that I should not go on to Allahabad forthwith, but go with him to Mirzapore in the evening and resume my journey on Monday. . . . So having breakfasted with Lang, who went on, I remained watching the judicial proceedings conducted by my cousin until evening. It was a strange scene to my inexperienced eye. . . . After all important business had been transacted J. S. and I, girt with pistol-belts, started off in a buggy for Mirzapore, which is about fourteen miles from Gopigunj. We drove for six miles, where horses met us, and then we cantered to the Ganges, crossed in a boat just as the stars had come out. The scene was most lovely; we were silently crossing the river, which was as smooth as glass, and in the west was to be seen the most beautiful celestial trio I ever beheld; rather high up in the sky a gorgeous comet seemed to be diving down like a falling rocket with a magnificent tail of light; on the horizon the new moon, tinged with red from the last beam of the sun,[1] was about to set, and a little to the left, about as high as the comet, Venus was shining in all the glory of her silvery light. It was a truly gorgeous sight. I don't know whether this comet is visible in England, but we have seen it here for ten nights, and a worthy sight it is. . . . When we got to the other side of the river we walked to the magistrate's house, Mr. Denison's,[2] and arrived in time for

[1] I am afraid I let my imagination run away with me as to the cause of the reddish tint on the moon! Perhaps I was thinking of the third line of the second verse of *Tears, idle tears*.

[2] Mr. Christopher Denison, Magistrate and Collector of Mirzapore. A temporary inmate of Mr. Denison's house at this time was the Rev. Julian

dinner. . . . I leave here to-morrow morning, and shall arrive in Allahabad about the middle of the day.

ALLAHABAD, *October* 13.—On Monday morning James Simson and I left Mirzapore about dawn, that is to say we left the European part of the town. We had a very pleasant drive through the native quarter on our way to the ferry. The town is wonderfully clean, having been drained with great care. The natives were beginning to awake, and stood rubbing their eyes near their doors, and then started off for their morning ablutions in the holy river. Most of the houses are built of stone, and some are carved into graceful and fantastic shapes. Every now and then we came to a Hindu temple, with some sacred image inside. They are rather idols' shrines than temples, as, I fancy, the worship is carried on outside. Mirzapore is a very commercial city, a large trade of carpets and silks being carried on there. Consequently the inhabitants are as rich as Jews. I fear, however, you will think I have adopted Verdant Green's plan, and have copied a page out of the Mirzapore guide, so I had better cross the river at once. A couple of natives make a seat for me with their crossed arms, on which I sit embracing their sable necks; thus carried to the boat with dry feet through the shallow water at the edge of the river. Arrived on the opposite bank we found our horses ready; so without delay we mounted and rode for six miles at a brisk canter along a very beautiful road with trees on each side all the way. On dismounting we got into a buggy, and drove the remaining six miles to Gopigunj. . . . I soon got under way for Allahabad. I had an Irishman of the name of D'Arcy Macarthy for a companion, to whom I had offered the spare seat in my carriage. He proved himself an entertaining man enough, and told me several anecdotes of tiger-hunting and similar sports. Then I found out that my friend was a great hand at music. We discussed all the ins and outs of that subject, its composers,

Robinson, the Chaplain of Chunar, who was paying a pastoral visit to Mirzapore. He preached to us the following day, and I have never forgotten his appearance and certain of his characteristics. Subsequently he gave up the ministry, and closed his Indian career on the staff of the *Pioneer* newspaper.

performers, etc., for several hours, and so the tedium of the journey was beguiled. We arrived at the riverside about half-past three in the afternoon, and had again the disagreeable toil of crossing the Ganges, which is always intruding itself in one's way, and on this occasion we were nearly three hours in getting to the other side. However, I arrived at the house in which Robert Simson[1] was living, a short time after seven. . . . Lang is here; strange to say this house was his father's house when Judge of Allahabad, in which L. himself had passed the greater part of the first eight years of his life. It now, since the mutinies, goes by the familiar name of the 'Red Lion,' because its inhabitants are very numerous and always changing; it is, in fact, bachelors' quarters. . . . Yesterday I was taken to pay my respects to the Governor-General, which consists in writing my name in a couple of books in the hall. R. and I then called on Dr. Leckie, the G.-G.'s personal doctor, and then on Mr. Edmonstone (Foreign Secretary). I only saw Mrs. Edmonstone, who is a charming lady, whose acquaintance I had not an opportunity of making in Calcutta. However, she is most frank, and did not take long in asking me to accompany my cousin to dinner this evening. . . .

October 16.—We went to dine with the Edmonstones. It was quite a quiet affair, only one other guest besides ourselves. Mr. Edmonstone is not a very prepossessing man, rather a bahádur in his manner; some people consider him positively rude, but he did not appear so to me. . . . He seemed to like R. S., who is quite at his ease with him, and they talked a good deal together. Mrs. E. conversed with a small French artist, who has been sent out by the Queen to take portraits of celebrities. . . . I confess I am beginning to like India much better than I did. The mofussil is quite different from that mongrel place Calcutta, which is neither native nor European. . . .

AMBALA, *October* 24.—I have just been reading a book called

[1] An elder brother of the 'Joint,' who was now Under-Foreign Secretary with the Governor-General.

Oakfield, by a son[1] of Dr. Arnold, all about life and exile in India, of which he takes rather a dismal view, and hardly just, I think. However, there are many most touching bits in the book. When it came out, about four years ago, it created some sensation. . . . On Tuesday morning R. S. drove me to the railway which goes from Allahabad to Cawnpore, a distance of 120 miles . . . at present only open to those who can get tickets from Government. On entering Cawnpore I could hardly suppose it to be the same place in which all those horrors took place little more than a year ago. Everything was quite still, and nothing but several houses in ruins told the story. By five o'clock in the afternoon I had started in a dak carriage, watching the sun going down and making up my mind to three days' hard travel almost without stopping, until I should reach Ambala, where I hoped to find orders as to my future destination. . . . In the middle of the second day I drew near to Delhi. I was not, however, much in the humour to admire the wonders of that renowned place, as I had tasted no food except a biscuit since the night before. . . . Delhi is indeed a fortified city; the river flows along the south side, and we crossed over a bridge of boats. The walls are of red sandstone regularly built, and there were the gates, sure enough, which last year took such a deal of fighting to win. I only stayed long enough at the dak bungalow to eat and wash, and I started again before dark for the concluding 120 miles of my journey to Ambala. . . . I was under the impression that I should reach my destination at ten in the morning, but when ten o'clock came I found that I had to leave my comparatively comfortable carriage and get into a dooli (a sort of palanquin), and be carried eight or ten miles more. I shall not at present attempt to describe this most obnoxious and headache-giving means of transit. You will read a very good

[1] William Delafield Arnold. The father, I believe, of Mr. Arnold-Forster. My interest in the book was enhanced by the fact that a few months before leaving England I had been staying with friends at a house called 'Oakfield,' in Cumberland, where I had met Mrs. Arnold, the mother of the author and widow of Dr. Arnold of Rugby.

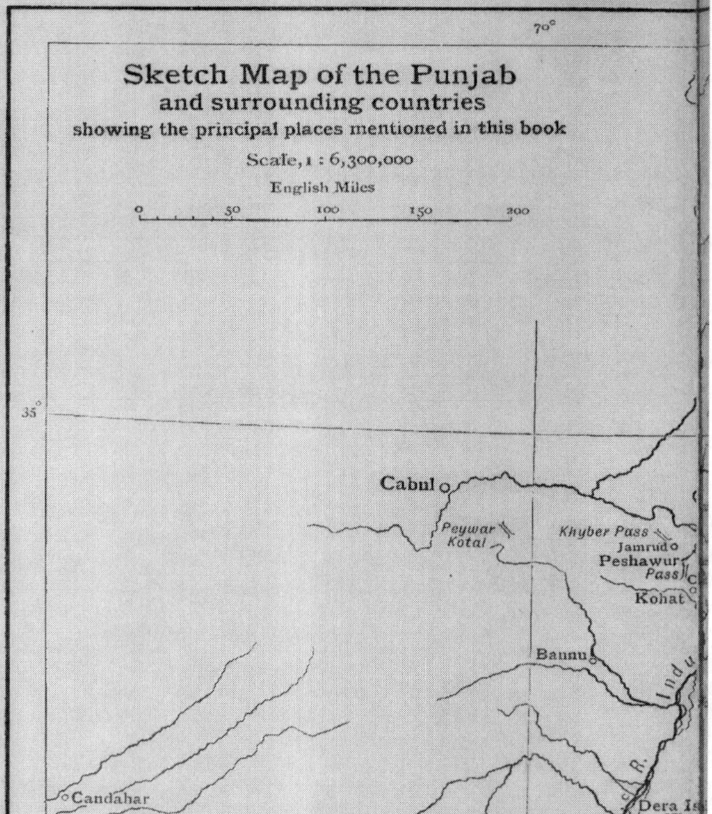

Sketch Map of the Punjab
and surrounding countries
showing the principal places mentioned in this book
Scale, 1 : 6,300,000
English Miles
0
50
100
150
200
70°
35°
30°
Cabul
Peywar
Kotal
Khyber Pass
Jamrud
Peshawur
Pass
Kohat
Bannu
R. Indus
Candahar
Dera Is
Kha
Quetta
Dera Ghazi
Khan
Muza
Fazilpore
Rajunpore
Asnee
Mithunkote
Kin
S I N D
Sukkur
70°

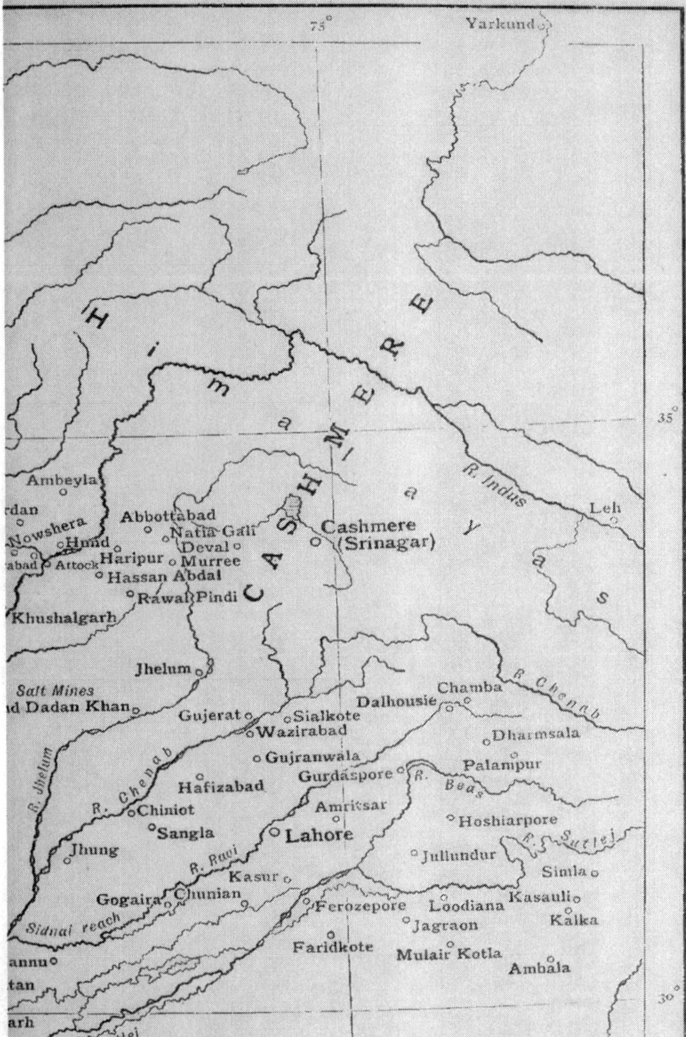

Emery Walker sc.

account of it if you can get *Oakfield.* I got to Ambala about two o'clock . . . was disappointed at not getting orders at the post-office, but this was easily accounted for, as Sir John Lawrence's camp is moving about, and the letter which I had written requesting my orders to be sent to Ambala no doubt had been unusually long in reaching its destination. . . . Ambala is very pretty; the bungalows, one-storied thatched houses, are just like English cottages, with beautiful gardens full of roses, really a charming place.

Monday.—A telegram from the Chief Commissioner's secretary telling me that I am appointed to Loodiana, and that I am to proceed at once and place myself under the orders of Captain M'Neile.[1]

LOODIANA, *Thursday, October* 28.—Here I am in the city of Loodiana, where sand prevails on every side. I arrived yesterday morning, and then started off to seek out my new master. I found him doing his morning work of reading despatches and reports in a verandah. . . . He is a tall man of about six feet, hair sandy, whiskers, beard and moustache reddish. He told me that he had just come to this station himself, having only arrived a week ago . . . is staying in the doctor's house. . . . I have all my meals there, and have slept in the dak bungalow on what you would think a very queer sort of bedstead (a charpoy, it is called), with my plaid and dressing-gown for bedclothes. However, I can sleep anywhere now. . . . I have been to look at a house this morning, with three good large rooms, bathroom, etc., and a very fair garden and compound. I shall be able to get the little furniture that is necessary from the bazaar. . . . I was introduced to the cutcherry yesterday, not that I did any work, but I was shown my room where I shall administer justice on a very small scale. . . . Of course I am as ignorant as possible about everything.

November 7.— . . . On Friday morning I moved into my new abode, which is a pretty thatched cottage or bungalow

[1] A military officer in civil employ as Deputy Commissioner of Loodiana. He was the eldest son of Dean M'Neile of Ripon.

with a nice verandah all round, a good-sized compound, and a capital fruit and flower garden, etc. . . . The garden is in very good order and has now got plenty of vegetables and some lemons and citrons, which my cook proposes to make into preserve. Then there are tall cypress trees along the walks, and ringdoves coo from their tops and parrots chase each other from branch to branch, screaming with their unmusical voices. I feel quite a householder. . . . At present I have not much more than a chair to sit on and table to eat from, a bed to sleep on, but I have enough, and that is as good as a feast. My table furniture is scanty, and will be so until my heavy luggage makes its appearance. My tablecloth is a towel, my knife loose in the handle, and my fork as ductile as lead. However, at present I only breakfast at home ; the doctor has been good enough to invite me to dine with him till I am all right, and as he lives next door, our servants make up a joint dinner between them. . . . Captain M'Neile . . . improves on acquaintance, and seems to be a very clever fellow indeed and an excellent linguist. The natives say that he gets through the work in a fifth of the time that his predecessor took. . . . He got great credit at the time of the outbreak. The senior assistant, Captain Nicolls, and his wife returned from the Hills two or three days ago. He is a Madras officer and has been three years in Loodiana. . . . He is a most gentlemanly kind fellow and she a most agreeable lady. He must be about thirty-four. . . . Mrs. Nicolls is remarkably tall and very pleasant-looking. I dined with them last night. They have a very nice house, well furnished, and seem to be a happy pair who do not grumble at the country, as nearly every one does, but make the best of it, although they would like to go home to their little boy who is in England. . . . I have not said much about the work as yet, and really I have had little experience of it. This has been a week of holidays. Monday and Tuesday, on account of the reading of her Majesty's Proclamation,[1] and Friday and Saturday, a grand Hindu festival. . . . My business

[1] Assuming the direct government of India, on the abolition of the East India Company.

is to try small civil cases not involving more than one hundred rupees, and I can punish in criminal cases by a month's imprisonment and fifty rupees fine. . . . The advantages of the Punjab seem to me to be climate, more interesting and responsible work, and not so much red tape as elsewhere. . . . We had a grand turn-out on Monday at the reading of the Proclamation. M'Neile read the English version, which was followed by the Hindustani read by a munshi (Mohun Lal). The scene was rather imposing. All the Cabul princes, who live here pensioned by Government, were assembled in their gorgeous attire, and expressed themselves highly delighted with the clemency of the Government. They think themselves no end of swells, of course, and look as regal as they can on two or three hundred rupees a month. We were all invited to dine at Munshi Mohun Lal's in the evening, and had a sort of half English, half Oriental dinner, with a native dance and fireworks after. . . . Our host was formerly Sir Alexander Burnes's munshi in Cabul.[1] . . . The town was illuminated in native fashion and looked very pretty. . . . The cutcherry work is disheartening at first, it is so difficult to understand. I have just been wading through a case which I fear I have but a vague idea of. My munshi did his best to cram it into me, but one hears such a lot of Punjabi words, quite different from Hindustani, that it requires a long time to grasp perfectly every little thing. One is obliged at first to let things take their course and look as wise as possible, whether everything is comprehended or not. . . . It all comes square in time, I suppose. Nicolls says that when he left off soldiering and commenced this life (Civil employ), what he had to learn and understand seemed an insurmountable mountain, but the way in which its acclivities and roughnesses disappeared under the influence of time was quite wonderful. . . .

Friday.—I had my first criminal case to-day. The greatest amount of criminal litigation in this country seems to be caused by fickle ladies who leave their lawful husbands. The laws of

[1] Mohun Lal had been in England, where he was well received by the Directors, who gave him a handsome pension.

marriage are endless. A Hindu betroths his child to a friend's when both are quite young. After a year or so the ceremony of the marriage takes place, and then when the parties have grown up they leave their parents' house and dwell together. They are continually suing one another for the breaking of betrothal engagements.

Sunday.—We have just come out of church. M'Neile being in camp, Nicolls read the prayers and I had to do the sermon. I read one of Kingsley's on 'The just shall live by faith,' and was not a little nervous, but there was not much occasion to be so, as the congregation did not exceed half a dozen. . . .

December 5.—I have been getting busier every day. M'Neile sends me four or five cases daily, so that I am pretty steadily employed while in cutcherry. I believe I am to have charge of the treasury shortly which will increase my responsibility. I do not grumble at the prospect of plenty to do; I rather like it. The work can't be said to be intensely interesting, but I am told that one gets more energetic in it after a month or two. . . .

Saturday.—I had a very kind letter from Mr. Harington[1] yesterday which I shall enclose. . . .

10 MIDDLETON STREET,
CHOWRINGHEE, *December* 3, 1858.

MY DEAR ELSMIE,—We were very glad to receive your letter and to hear such a good account of yourself and your doings since you left the City of Palaces and unpleasant odours. I have never been at Loodiana itself, but I have travelled through parts of the country not far from it, and thus know something of its character. You seem to have been fortunate in your station, chief, and house, and I trust that all will continue to smile upon and to prosper with you. The difficulties which you met with at the commencement of your official career have, I doubt not, already diminished considerably, and they will soon do no more than raise a smile at their recollection. . . . The great Robert Mertens Bird of the North-Western Provinces ordered a half-lame

[1] See p. 36.

buffalo into the presence, to the great consternation of a crowded court, when he thought he was directing the production of merely a bundle of dried bamboos. He had not discerned the difference between 'báns' and 'bhains.' I mention this little anecdote for your encouragement. . . . Your letter gave us the only account of Lang that we have received since you left. We are sorry to hear that he is not so well pleased, as you seem to have good reason to be, with his station. We have the authority of King Hudson's Queen for saying that those who go to Turkey must do as the Turkeys do. . . . —Believe me, yours very sincerely, H. B. HARINGTON.

Mrs. and Miss M. went to call on the chief of the Cabul princes' wives the other day. They were much amused with their reception. The mother of the Prince did the honours with great grace and embraced them at parting. The visitors reported on the beauty of the fair purdah-nashins.[1] . . . The doctor was once permitted to feel a pulse, the hand being pushed through the curtain, but he saw no face or form. The number of these princes and nobles who dwell in Loodiana may be guessed from the fact that it took me about twenty minutes yesterday to sign their pension bills.[2] . . .

December 24.—In these parts we think the two letters of Sir John Lawrence about Christianity in India are excellent. They have only just been published, so everybody is talking about them. They don't seem to have gone down very well in England, but really, what do the people know there? . . . The Hindu does not find fault with our religion. He says, 'It is yours, so keep it; we have got our own, don't interfere with that.' . . . The American missionaries here will tell you of the very scanty success that they have met with. You could count the converts made at Loodiana on the fingers of one hand, I believe, and yet the missionaries preach in an open church to a crowded

[1] Ladies who remain behind the curtain.

[2] Loodiana was full, and probably is still, of Cabul refugees, relatives, and adherents of Shah Shuja, who, on the success of the Barakzais in 1841-42, became pensioners of the British Government.

audience every Sunday. The people come to see the sight, remain perfectly quiet, get up and go away, but have no more intention of turning Christians than of flying over the moon. Now it seems to be the opinion of many hot-headed planners at home that there are a lot of poor deluded heathen out here who only want to be told and then they will believe; who are gaping for the truth and only waiting for some one to come and declare it. It is needless to say they are labouring under a false impression of what is really the case.[1]

January 12.—It has been raining the whole day, and we have had a cold, cheerless twelve hours. Cutcherry requires a sunny sky and all nature smiling to render its tedium endurable.

January 14.—It is a strange sight to see great Brahmini bulls wandering about the town quite at their ease. The beasts think nothing of helping themselves at a vegetable-stall, and the poor owner dare not drive them away; so he generally begins worshipping and entreating the creatures to go elsewhere for their breakfast. . . .

My satisfaction at being stationed at Loodiana was greatly enhanced by the fact that Charles Bernard had been appointed by Sir John Lawrence to be Assistant Commissioner of the neighbouring district of Hoshiarpore, of which my cousin Mr. David Simson[2] was the Deputy Commissioner. Simson had the reputation of being one of the best district officers in the Punjab, and Sir John paid him no small compliment in entrusting his nephew to him to be trained in his work. As I have indicated before, my interests as a learner of my business were equally regarded by Sir John when he placed me under Captain M'Neile, one of the ablest men I have ever come into contact with. Though the towns of Loodiana

[1] It must be remembered that this was written nearly fifty years ago.
[2] Afterwards Judge of the Chief Court, Punjab, 1867-70.

and Hoshiarpore were only about fifty miles apart, it was a difficult task to get from one to the other, owing to the number of streams which lay between them. Early in January I obtained a few days' leave and went to Hoshiarpore by dooli dak. There had lately been very heavy rain, and some of the streams were almost impassable. However, after a journey of some eighteen hours, I found myself in Hoshiarpore rejoicing in the companionship of Bernard, whom I had not seen since we parted in Calcutta some ten months before.

February 7.—I have not begun to work hard for the examination[1] yet, I am sorry to say, but as it takes place on the 1st April I must really begin, as it will never do to be put back for the 'little go.' I find that I have acquired a tolerable facility in speaking the language much faster than I at first anticipated. This, I hope, will do me good service in the examination, as I believe the examiners put much stress on a ready comprehension of a case when it is read out from the file. . . .

I had a delightful long letter from Bernard two days ago. We are very constant correspondents.

February 23.—Mr. Montgomery,[2] the new Lieutenant-Governor, passed through on Tuesday, wife and child with him. We all called on him at the dak bungalow about eleven in the forenoon and were received most graciously, and had a long talk with the great man. He is old-fashioned looking, with grey hair and spectacles, very mild-looking in the face and exceedingly gentle in the tone of his voice. He is very kind and polished, and kept up a most pleasant conversation for some time. He

[1] The first departmental examination in Civil, Criminal, and Revenue Law, which all Assistants had to pass before becoming eligible for higher powers and for promotion.

[2] Afterwards Sir Robert Montgomery, K.C.B., G.C.S.I. He was travelling from Oude, where he had been Chief Commissioner, to Lahore, where he was to succeed Sir John Lawrence as Lieutenant-Governor of the Punjab.

never forgot any of his visitors. Whenever he thought he had been talking to any one too long he used to turn round and commence addressing another. . . .

March 11.—Our object is to administer the Hindu and Muhammadan law so far as consistent with abstract right and wrong, not opposed to positive law and morality.

March 25.—Bernard arrived from Hoshiarpore on 16th. . . . Next morning, about six, we drove twenty-four miles to Jagraon, and rode thence—nine miles—to Bussean. There we found an immense house in the centre of a beautiful garden, full of orange and lime trees in blossom and also pomegranates. We had no idea the house was so large and in such good repair, a regular mansion. It was, I believe, formerly the Political Residency.[1] . . . Next morning came Captain and Mrs. Nicolls; we spent a day or two shooting and strolling about, and returned to Loodiana on Sunday morning.

AMBALA, *March* 29.—Yesterday I received a very kind note from Mr. P. S. Melvill,[2] Deputy Commissioner of Ambala, inviting me to stay with him during the examination.[3] . . . There are to be three candidates for examination—Lord Frederick Hay, who, you remember, was two terms ahead of me at College, and a man of the name of Johnstone.[4]

April 3.—Johnstone is Mr. Melvill's brother-in-law, and turns out to be the same Johnstone who was at the Diocesan school in Southampton with me . . . eight or nine years ago. We were both rather surprised at the meeting. He did not remember me so well as I did him, as he was a big boy when I was a little one. However, we soon struck up an alliance, and have enjoyed talking over old stories and our common difficulties about the examination. I may as well tell you what

[1] This fine house was a feature of the Loodiana district. It was used as a country-house by Sir George Clerk, Sir Claude Wade, and other Residents at the frontier station of Loodiana before the Sikh wars.

[2] Afterwards Resident at Baroda.

[3] To be held at Ambala, the headquarters of the Division of which Loodiana was one of the districts.

[4] A military man in Civil employ, afterwards Colonel Johnstone, Civil and Sessions Judge, Peshawur.

we have got through, and have to get through to-morrow. On Friday we had a set of fifteen long questions in Civil Law to write out. This took two or three hours. Then we had to dictate a plaguy police report in Hindustani, *i.e.* a police report in English was put into our hands and we were told to dictate it to a munshi in Hindustani. He wrote down word for word what we said. This, of course, had to be subjected to the criticism of the examiners. Then we had to read Persian running hand. This concluded the first day. . . . Next day we had to write a long judgment in the Persian character. Everything of course had to be done without any reference to books. To-morrow we have Revenue questions and three cases to decide.[1] This will conclude the operations. . . .

LOODIANA, *April* 12.—You will be glad to hear that I have passed the examination.[2] The news arrived very unexpectedly this afternoon. . . .

I am sitting in cutcherry, work is done, the hour is five. The munshis are sitting round preparing papers for signature and summoning parties for to-morrow. Outside, M'Neile, the Deputy Commissioner, is selling by auction the Government contracts for the sale of spirits for the ensuing year. The native auctioneer is shouting out the bids, followed by one, two, three, in Hindustani. This has been rather a pleasant day. We had a stormy night, and a good deal of rain fell. Consequently the morning air was fresh and exhilarating. Nicolls and I drove down to the jail, and then returned to chota haziri (little breakfast) with Mrs. Nicolls. I must try to describe these social little meals as enjoyed by us at this season of the year. In the Nicolls' garden there is a middle walk shaded by thick 'loquat' trees. Halfway down the walk

[1] On hearing the evidence read out in the vernacular.

[2] *i.e.* the departmental examination by the lower standard. Candidates of the present day will feel for me and others when I explain that in 1859 the examination was held only once a year, and that candidates were not allowed to present themselves for the 'higher standard' until a year had elapsed from the date of their having passed the 'lower standard.' The rules were changed the following year, 1860. The higher standard might from that time be passed by men who had never been up for the lower.

another intersects it. Turn round the corner and you will behold the breakfast party. On the left hand there is the reverse side of the 'loquat' trees, on the right a vinery and quail-house, which latter is a jolly little thatched cot built to keep these animals in during the heat. Before you is the 'duckery,' or 'tealery,' as we call it, a larger domicile than that provided for the quail, but very pretty to look at. There are two divisions, one darkened, which is the ducks' retiring chamber, the other a miniature tank surrounded by a margin. You are supposed to be standing on a path, and I have described four boundaries enclosing a square. The enclosure is divided into two portions, a grass plot and a carpet-spread plot. On the carpet is placed the tea-table, spread with toast and such like light viands. Round the table sit the party, Nicolls smoking, the doctor ditto, Mrs. Nicolls sitting without her bonnet, Mrs. B. in her riding-dress. . . . The gardener has orders to set his irrigatory processes into action, and a stream of water flows under the trees. . . .

CHAPTER IV

ASSISTANT COMMISSIONER AT JHELUM, MITHUNKOTE, FEROZEPORE, AND AMRITSAR

1859—1861

THE 'lower standard' departmental examination having been passed, investiture with increased Magisterial and Civil powers quickly followed. It was therefore no surprise to receive a gazette order transferring me to the Jhelum district, where I should be the first European Assistant, instead of the second as heretofore. I was sorry to leave Loodiana, and especially my friends Captain and Mrs. Nicolls, but I determined to act according to Punjab traditions, and to set forth for my new station without delay. My servants, horses, furniture, and luggage were forthwith prepared for the journey, and I myself started, in a dooli, within twelve hours of the arrival of orders. Bernard had, some weeks previously, been transferred from Hoshiarpore to Jullundur. To his great surprise I presented myself at his door early the next morning. The dooli journey had been uncomfortable enough. I therefore gladly accepted Bernard's offer to ride on his horses, some thirty miles by moonlight over an unmetalled road, as far as the right bank of the river Beas, from which point a metalled road ran about sixty miles to Lahore. My small amount of personal luggage was entrusted to a banghy-burdár, or fast-travelling coolie, who was to meet me at the Post-house beyond the river.

LAHORE, *Easter Sunday, April* 24.—I had a long solitary ride from Jullundur to the Beas, starting at 10 P.M. My sole companion was my pistol. . . . What was my dismay when I inquired at the Post-house whether my baggage had arrived and was replied to in the negative, the same answer being given relative to the arrival of Bernard's groom to hold the horse. There I stood, possessed of nothing but the clothes on my back, with a tired horse on my rein. . . .

After going back about four miles I fortunately met the groom. I then sent him out to search for the missing property, and waited in the middle of the road until 5 A.M., but no sign was forthcoming. There was no help but to go on to Lahore leaving instructions at the Post-house to forward the luggage whenever it appeared.[1] I therefore went on by carriage, as hard as I could pelt, over the metalled road, intending to throw myself on the bounty of Alex Lawrence[2] for a change of clothes. I found him staying with Mr. Montgomery at Government House. . . . He had tarried in Lahore on purpose to see Colonel Edwardes,[3] who is going home. Colonel Edwardes arrived an hour before me, and I had the advantage of breakfasting and conversing with that great man. He is quite young, that is to say, he is under forty, has a large beard, is good-looking, speaks very pleasantly and kindly, and appeared very fond of Alex. You know he was a great friend of his father's and is going to write his Life when in England.

I travelled from Lahore to Jhelum very uncomfortably on a high mail-cart, from which I had to dismount every half-hour when horses were changed. We reached Gujerat late at night, and rested till morning. Next day I arrived

[1] The lost packages were recovered eventually, after a great deal of trouble.

[2] Whom I had not seen since we parted in Calcutta in March 1858, but who, I knew, was at this time staying in Lahore.

[3] Commissioner of Peshawur, afterwards Sir Herbert Edwardes, K.C.B.

at Jhelum, where I was hospitably received by the Deputy Commissioner, Captain Bristow, and Mrs. Bristow. After a visit of a few days I arranged to take a house close by, on the banks of the river Jhelum, where I 'chummed' with Dr. Aitchison, the Civil surgeon, a man of considerable acquirements and of some reputation as a botanist.

JHELUM, *April* 27.—I didn't do or see very much at Lahore, but I was invited to stay with the Lieutenant-Governor, and that was something. I can't tell you what a kind man he is. I remember telling you of his appearance when he passed through Loodiana. I enjoyed staying at Government House very much, driving out with Mr. Montgomery and Major Lawrence.[1] I also came in for some useful hints and heard a good many opinions passed on the different officers. . . .

The Commissioner of Lahore drove home with us from evening church. His name is Temple,[2] and he was Secretary for a long time under Sir John; is junior to David Simson, but so clever that his seniors do not envy his luck. They say, 'Dick Temple is an exception and deserves everything he has got.' He is not unlike the French Emperor, and I fancy that is his own opinion, for he has got a beard and imperial just like his Majesty. As was to be expected in a man who is very clever and knows it, he struck me as being very conceited, but there seems to be little doubt that he has got something to be conceited of. . . . A very nice fellow has been in Jhelum for the last few days, a man named Macnabb,[3] who is the other Assistant Commissioner in the district, but who is stationed at an out-station called Pind Dadun

[1] Major Richard Lawrence, the youngest of the Lawrence brothers, familiarly known as Dick Lawrence, both by Europeans and Natives. He was at this time Military Secretary to the Punjab Government.

[2] Afterwards Sir Richard Temple, Bart., G.C.S.I., etc.

[3] Afterwards Commissioner of Peshawur, now Sir Donald Campbell Macnabb, K.C.I.E., C.S.I. His name will often appear in this book, as an officer and a private friend for whom I have retained throughout our long friendship of almost half a century the very highest admiration and esteem. I have often said that I fell at his feet the day I saw him first at Jhelum in 1859, and I have remained there ever since.

Khan. He is a man of about four or five years' standing, and seems very good at his work. . . .

The view from this house is almost too fine for description. The farthest-off object to be seen is the snowy Himalayan range, so cold and grand-looking, standing in pure relief against the blue sky behind. The snow is as yet unbroken, save by the shadows of the uneven places of the mountains. Now and then a white cloud comes down to kiss the highest peak, the consequence of which is the fall of a beautiful shadow over the snow. Descending from the high peaks I suppose we should come into a valley, the other side of which is bounded by the brown range which stands in our nearer foreground; the hills of it are nice homely little fellows, but very rugged, and apparently well wooded. At the foot of the low hills is a long expanse of level country, which ends on the banks of the river (Jhelum). . . .

May 9.—We had Macnabb staying with us for a few days. . . . I have seldom met with such a good and excellent specimen of the true Haileybury man—so gentlemanly and kind. . . . He is much liked by the natives, and Sir John Lawrence used to think very highly of him. He speaks Punjabi with great ease, and appears to understand the common people . . . a very rare accomplishment. . . .

Macnabb and I went to call on some bachelors. There are some very nice fellows among the officers,[1] especially the Major, Watson by name. He asked me to mess that evening as the band was going to play. . . . The mess is at present in a tent. After dinner the band played outside, and it was a great treat to hear some music. . . . On Sunday evening we had service in the church. The Major read prayers and a sermon, the latter a very good one, and he read with much earnestness. . . .

I rode out early to inspect a village which had been the scene of a row between rival cultivators. The cattle of one village trespassed on the fields of another. The aggrieved party retaliated with sticks and stones, the result of which, as far as I

[1] Of H.M.'s 7th Fusiliers; the regiment being at that time stationed in the cantonment of Jhelum, some two miles or more from the Civil lines.

could judge, was a general mêlée. . . . The natives have a great liking for a personal inspection on the part of the judge, so I always go out to the scene of a quarrel or claim, when within reasonable distance. . . .

May 23.—I don't know what sort of an account you have got at home of this most distressing business, the disaffection of the European troops. We have heard little enough, as of course Government has tried to suppress rumours, and the papers have been wise enough to hold their tongues. The facts that we believe here are that a regiment of European Light Cavalry who enlisted under the Company, together with the old Company's Artillery, refused to obey orders at Meerut, because they had not got bounty-money and were not bound to serve her most gracious Majesty. They say that they commenced mutiny by three cheers for the Company and three groans for the Queen; a pretty state of affairs! Well, the General in command is said to have selected one of the principal ringleaders and to have ordered him to be blown away from a gun. The men refused to carry out the order, and the 75th Queen's were told to fire on them. They refused, the consequence of which was that the officers were obliged to compromise, hear their grievances, send the man back to his lines, and promise to do all in their power to right them. Doubtless a very politic course and not altogether an unplucky one, I think, for a man to take upon himself the responsibility of letting off a soldier who had been tied up for execution. It is quite clear that much bloodshed would have followed had the sentence been carried out. However, the precedent is a bad one, and the effect of the whole on the natives must be of the very worst description. What must they think of us who dare not blow away our own men, and what will they think of a Government whose European soldiers are dissatisfied? The natives don't understand a bit, you know, what the change of government is. It is a mere name to them. The Company was a name and so is the Queen. They see no practical change. We have also heard that in Allahabad some regiments fired on their officers, but we have no particulars, and can in the meantime only hope for the best, and that the disagreeable storm will blow over.[1]

June 2.—Beames[2] and I went to church together in the evening. Major Watson[3] read to us the new Bishop's (Cotton) first pastoral letter. . . . It is especially addressed to all Christians in the enormous diocese extending from Peshawur to the Straits of Malay,[4] including Burma, Pegu, Assam, etc., a diocese about three thousand miles in length. The Bishop sympathises with the great loss of public ordinances, the impossibility of a chaplain being within reach of numerous out-stations where perhaps only one or two Civilians live, and then goes on to say that he considers it his duty to do all he can to cheer us under our privations, and intends to address us, three or four times a year through the press, some words of encouragement. . . .

June 21.—The post brought a letter this morning from the Secretary to the Lieutenant-Governor, informing me that I am to be transferred from this delightful station in August—trans Indus—away to an awful place called Mithunkote, which is an out-station in the district of Dera Ghazi Khan. . . . However, Bristow tells me that a better thing couldn't have happened to me, as I get an independent charge. . . . He says it is a proof of their good opinion of me, and he never heard of so young an Assistant being sent there; so I must look on what appeared as a reverse of fortune in a more favourable light. Of course I shall not murmur in the least. . . . If it is a proof of good opinion it is very funny, as I can't imagine what cause or reason

[1] This extract regarding the 'White Mutiny,' as it was called, must only be taken for what it professes to be, viz. a hearsay account which reached a small up-country station. For full account see *Life of Sir Henry Norman* by Lee-Warner.

[2] John Beames, a fellow-student at Haileybury; at this time Assistant Commissioner of the neighbouring district of Gujerat. Later he was transferred to Lower Bengal and became distinguished by his many works on philology, etc.

[3] I never met Major Watson again after leaving Jhelum, but thirty-five years afterwards a young artilleryman, his nephew, Captain Watson, R.A., was married to one of my daughters, one of his chief qualifications in my opinion being his relationship to my old Jhelum friend of '59.

[4] This enormous diocese is now divided into some five or six dioceses.

they have to form one of a poor young fledgling of some eight months' experience. . . .[1]

June.—Jhelum is a great boat-building district; splendid trees are floated down from Cashmere and made into boats, both native and European. For seven months of the year the river is crossed by a magnificent bridge of boats, constructed in the English fashion. They are immense barges with flush decks, anchored at the bows parallel to one another, about four or five feet apart. There are upwards of one hundred and fifty boats, I believe, required to span the Jhelum. They are splendid ones, with bows like that of the *America*.[2] The natives begin making their boats by constructing a large rectangular bottom of boards an inch or two thick; these are strengthened by transverse bands of wood. This done, the next thing is to mould the bottom, as it were; about six or ten feet at each end are moistened continually with water. This makes the wood bend upwards, props are placed underneath for support, and gradually the warping goes on. The height of the props is increased until the bend is sufficient. The sides of the boat are then nailed on and the internal arrangements completed. When all is done, a very serviceable river article is turned out. The current is so strong that they can only sail downstream; the journey up is very tedious, the motive power being coolie strength transmitted through a rope.

About this time I received a very welcome invitation from Major and Mrs. Dick Lawrence to visit them for a few days, at the hill station of Murree, prior to starting on my long journey down the river to Mithunkote. I was anxious to see an Indian hill station, and at Murree in the hot season the Lieutenant-Governor, the Com-

[1] I was afterwards told, by way of explanation—I think by Major Lawrence—that Mr. Montgomery had noticed and approved the energy I had displayed in taking measures for the recovery of my luggage which had been lost on the journey between Jullundur and the Beas!

[2] The celebrated yacht.

missioner of the Division, Mr. Charles Saunders,[1] and many interesting people were to be found. The journey to and fro was tedious and tiring, and had to be performed over bad roads by dooli and on horseback.

MURREE, *July* 3.—. . . I met the Lieutenant-Governor[2] out riding in the evening. He was most kind; turned and rode along with me a considerable way, inquired how I liked the prospect of Mithunkote. . . . I replied that when I first heard of my transfer I was rather despondent, but that Bristow told me of some of its advantages and I had begun not to mind. . . .

Sir R. M. 'Doubtless it will be lonely in Mithunkote, but never mind that. Work hard, learn all you can about the natives and your work in general, and get well up for the next examination. How do you propose going down?'

E. 'In boats; load the boats at my door in Jhelum and drop quietly down the river.'

Sir R. M. 'Of course, couldn't be better. Mind you are to take a guard of twelve men with you. Tell Bristow I say so.'

E. 'I never thought of a guard. Mrs. Bristow came up the river without one, I think.'

Sir R. M. 'Never mind that. It's always well to be prepared. I dare say eight men will be enough. We won't keep you very long in those parts.' . . .

Last night the Lieutenant-Governor and Lady M. gave a musical party, to which were invited about fifty or more. A regular programme was made out and people had been practising for some days. . . . Yesterday I went up and had a practice upon the Saunders' piano and was able to take my turn in the evening. We had a most enjoyable concert. The Deputy Commissioner of Rawulpindi, Captain Cracroft, plays magnificently on the violin, accompanied by his wife on the piano. . . . A lady who is possessed of considerable musical agility,

[1] Afterwards Resident at Hyderabad.

[2] Mr. Montgomery had now been made a K.C.B. in recognition of his great services in the Mutiny.

execution, and energy engaged in a battle with the piano, which was rather amusing to behold. She doesn't play with much taste and is fond of display. Every now and then she made a short pause, and then grabbed at the notes in a most determined manner.

PIND DADUN KHAN, *July* 16.—I left Jhelum on Thursday afternoon, sailed or rather dropped down the river, and arrived in time for breakfast with Macnabb yesterday morning. . . . My fleet consists of three boats. The one in which I travel myself has a nice little cabin built in it, covered with a thick thatch. There is room for a bed and small table, so I find it comfortable enough. . . . The second boat contains horses and buggy and numerous servants, their wives, etc. The third, furniture, boxes, piano, and guard of sepoys. . . . I hope to arrive in Mithunkote about the end of the month, if all goes well.[1] Macnabb is lonely here, of course; however, he is a capital worker and takes an immense deal of interest in all that he does. It is quite a pleasure to see him trying a case, he takes so much trouble to ferret the truth out. He talks Punjabi in a wonderful manner. . . . He worked yesterday from ten in the morning till eight at night. . . .

RIVER JHELUM, *July* 18.—Macnabb and I were eventually met by a body of men, miners and some officials, who led the way up a tortuous path to the mouth of the (Salt) mine.[2] The opening is an oval of about eight or nine feet in diameter and is the end of a long cylindrical tunnel, which bores directly into the rock. The tunnel slopes downwards. It is 'stepped'; very easy steps of about three inches in height. The other end of the tunnel opens into an immense cave—like a demon's cavern. This cave existed in the old Sikh times and was formed by the continual excavations, which were carried on in a reckless manner, without any attention to the fact that some fine day the roof might fall in. We were accompanied by a considerable number of torch-bearers who, scattering themselves about with their flaming flambeaux, caused the walls of rock-salt to glitter like

[1] The distance is roughly about four hundred miles.
[2] At Khewra in the Salt range in the Jhelum district.

diamonds. A large number of galleries led out of the centre cavern, and it is from the walls of these that the salt is dug, large natural pillars being left every twenty or thirty feet, for safety's sake. We wandered about some time and then returned to the entrance cave, where large bundles of straw were lighted, which made the scene more demoniacal than before; the half-naked miners rushing about with torches were grotesque, to say the least. . . . When we issued from the mine we recommenced our ascent on fresh horses to the higher parts of the range, having as our goal an European house built on a hill, which the Government has provided as the summer quarters of the Assistant Commissioner of Pind Dadun Khan.

July 20.—We've been making very little progress indeed, a high wind blowing directly across the stream. The boats have been obliged to lay-to a great part of the day. . . . Last night the boat in which my dinner is cooked got so far separated from this one that it did not come to anchor till half-past one in the morning. That was the hour, then, at which I dined, and, as my khitmutgar feelingly expressed it, I was 'dying of hunger.'

ASNEE,[1] near MITHUNKOTE, *July* 31.—The next day was Sunday, which I enjoyed. The calm of dropping down with the stream was pleasant and I read a good deal; began with my old friend Christiana and her children, and read about them till they were all safe over the river, or at least happily disposed of, for Bunyan says he didn't wait to see the young folks go. We anchored at sunset at a spot which seemed to me to have the warmest atmosphere I ever experienced.

On Tuesday morning early we were alongside the town of Mithunkote, and I was received by Lieutenant Minchin,[2] my predecessor, and all sorts of swell Natives on the banks. We walked

[1] A small cantonment for a cavalry regiment in the desert, about eleven miles inland from Mithunkote, where at this time the 4th Punjab Cavalry under Lieutenant Godby was stationed.

[2] Whom I was about to relieve on his appointment to officiate as Deputy Commissioner of the Dera Ghazi Khan district, of which Mithunkote was an out-station. He retired from the service as Commissioner of Lahore, in 1884.

to the house of the former, and had a small view of the town. I was rather prepossessed in its favour from the glance I had from the river, and on closer inspection it seemed to be a nice compact place, standing on a sort of promontory and surrounded by a road which might suggest the idea of Boulevard to an imaginative mind.[1] . . .

Minchin had promised all the officials, heads of tribes, police officers, etc., to introduce me to them before the day got warm; so for that purpose we went out under the largest tree, sat down on chairs stationed on a carpet, and proceeded to hold our levée. There were no end of men to attend to. They all bring a handful of rupees to be touched, that is to say, to be accepted as a present, but the receiving of the gift doesn't go beyond a very slight touch, and doubtless the donor would be very much surprised if it did. . . . The affair lasted a considerable time; much had to be said one way or another. . . .

August 5.—Minchin was very pleasant to talk to. We soon got acquainted and set to conversing on district matters. When Minchin commenced explaining how so many horsemen were stationed at such a post and so many at another I felt very bewildered, and didn't at all like the prospect of being in command of four or five hundred irregular troops.[2] However, I felt in for a penny in for a pound, and I thought it was better not to fuss myself, but quietly make up my mind that all would come right in the end somehow or other. That is a doctrine which is a consolatory one in this country, when a man has got to do work which very likely he never had to do before. . . . I am also at sea again with the language, so many words are used in these parts that I never heard before. . . . However, on the whole, I like the change. . . . The position is infinitely superior to what I held at Jhelum, and I can do pretty nearly as I like, the nearest superior authority being at a distance of ninety miles; and as that superior is Minchin, there is not much chance of being inter-

[1] A year or two later the promontory, town, and all the buildings were washed away by the river Indus.

[2] Of local Militia who had been raised after the time of the Mutiny and placed under the command of the Assistant Commissioner.

fered with. However, I am not so fond of my own way yet that I should object to having an adviser within hail. . . .

Last night there was an eclipse of the moon, and as Mr. Keelan[1] and I wanted to play our game of cribbage and watch the eclipse at the same time, we called for chairs and a lamp to be put on the roof of the house, but the light attracted all the vilest of nocturnal insects, mosquitoes, sandflies, and far more saturnine-looking objects of different shapes and varieties and sizes, so that we had positively to run for our lives and leave the eclipse to get on as well as it could. . . .

I am obliged to reconcile myself to the conviction that your letter (of July 3) has been lost . . . there has not been a failure in our correspondence until now. Of course this out-of-the-way place is the reason. It is next to a miracle that letters come at all. Most of them at this time of the year are transported over the Indus by a man swimming on an inflated skin, so there is little wonder if some portion of his freight be lost. . . .

An old Muzári chief was visiting me the other day. I rather liked the old man, so I showed him some of my possessions, played him a tune on the piano and displayed your likeness. He was much amused with the latter. . . . He highly approved of the 'arrangement,' as he expressed it, whereby when one felt any grief for absent friends, it could be at once allayed by a look at their pictures. However, I didn't quite agree with him.

Camp, Fazilpur, *August* 28.—At night sleeping near the ground would be disagreeable on account of the insects, so a high stage is erected for my bed. Six posts driven into the ground support a light roofing of sticks and straw, my bed is hoisted up and I go up after, something like a widow mounting a funeral pile, or a criminal ascending the gallows.

I had a visit yesterday morning from a Native gentleman who possesses most of the land in these parts,[2] a fine old fellow. We shook hands in a friendly manner and talked together for some

[1] An officer in the Survey who was spending a short time in camp at Mithunkote, of which I was the only permanent European resident.

[2] I forget his name, but I believe he was a relative of the Amirs of Sind.

time. He praised the Government, talked of the advantages of our rule, told me he was but as the skirt of my robe, etc., had heard that we had made an Englishman of Dulip Singh. I assured him that the young gentleman was an Englishman of his own good will, to which the old boy said, 'Of course!'

October 9.—We amused ourselves on the way home by looking at a potter making earthenware jars and dishes. The process is very curious and the ingenuity of the artificer marvellous. A circular pit of about four feet in depth is dug in the ground. In the bottom a pivot is fixed, on which a circular board revolves. From the centre of the board a wooden shaft rises perpendicularly, and is surmounted by a smaller circular board, which is the spot on which the potter works. He then takes his seat on the edge of the pit, allowing one foot to rest on the lower board. By the motion of his foot he makes the whole apparatus revolve on the pivot. He then takes a lump of moist clay and places it on the upper surface; the clay spins round and the hand of the workman fashions it as it goes. A jar is made in about a minute and is then placed in the sun to dry. The wife paints the edges and after that the whole is burnt hard. I suppose this is the process that has been used for making pots ever since pots were made. Certainly the will of the potter over his clay was exemplified, one vessel to honour, another to dishonour.

ASNEE, *October* 27.—I spent a very pleasant day yesterday. The Godbys, Hammond,[1] and I got up very early in the morning and rode out thirteen miles towards the frontier. . . . We had tents pitched in the midst of a vast plain, as flat and level as the sea, quite barren and desolate, no water near, no cultivation, dreariness on all sides, wild donkeys running in troops and an occasional deer. . . . We spent the day under canvas and rode home at night.

October 29.—Some of the Native officers of the Asnee regiment shot a wild ass. They sent the Godbys a leg, supposing it likely that we, eaters of everything, would esteem it a delicacy.

[1] The Adjutant of the 4th Punjab Cavalry. Afterwards Commandant of the 5th Punjab Cavalry.

Mrs. G. was much amused, but it is needless to say the limb was not cooked. Major Hough at Dera Ghazi Khan dabbles in photography. The other day he photographed two of his sepoys together, and offered one of them a copy to send home. The man appeared quite hurt, and refused the honour. How could he send home a picture which would be seen by women, in which a strange man was portrayed?

CAMP, DERA DILDAR, *October*.—The longer I stay in this part of the world the more loth I am, for some reasons, to leave it. . . . Until I am a Deputy Commissioner I can never have half so much power as I have now, and indeed many Deputy Commissioners haven't so much. The people of the country[1] are first-rate fellows. . . .

I enjoy this camp life very much, the constant change and plenty of employment during leisure and working hours, with a feeling of greater confidence than I had four months ago, make the time slip away very rapidly. . . . I strongly suspect I shall look back to my life here as to a golden time.[2] . . .

December 26.—Nothing has happened since yesterday except a murder. The poor man was brought in for the doctor to examine about an hour ago—killed by several deep gashes behind the ear, inflicted with an axe; cause unknown as yet, but I suppose, as usual, the unfortunate man had not kept the seventh commandment very strictly, and an irritated husband took the law into his own hands. The people of the country think it very hard that they are not allowed to be their own avengers.

December 29.—Yesterday I visited the scene of the murder I told you about. I was out all day trying to hunt up evidence, but with poor success, I fear. The man was killed in a very wild jungle, and no one could have been within hail who was not concerned in the crime. The murderer had tied his victim's hands behind his back, laid him down on the ground under a bush, and struck him deliberately with an axe. The ground was saturated with blood to a depth of several inches.

[1] For the most part Biluchis.

[2] And so it turned out.

I do hope we shall get some good clue, but at present there is but a very slight suspicion against one man.[1]

ASNEE, *January* 25, 1860.—On Wednesday I marched further south to a village called Kin. On Thursday, leaving camp at Kin, I went for a long ride to inspect the last town of the district and satisfy my eyes that the Sind frontier towers were all right. The last twelve miles contained not a human habitation, no grass, hard baked earth, out of which a very bushy tree called jâl grows every here and there. The jungle, though of the wildest description, is very beautiful. These trees spread over a large area, and their branches grow down to the ground, so that the appearance presented is of a large green ball lying on the earth. Park scenery you would call it, if there was turf. I did not get back to Kin till late at night, seven or eight. I had dinner at once, and my friend the Muzári chief[2] came in for a chat. We fell to talking about the Flood and Noah, and all those old fellows in whom the Mussulmans believe as well as we do. From that we talked of Christianity, and I asked him whether the Mussulmans think us káfirs, *i.e.* infidels. 'Oh dear no,' he said, 'we think your religion is very good, and that you keep it a great deal better than the majority of Mussulmans do theirs. We say, God is God and Jesus His prophet and Christians His disciples; also God is God and Muhammad is His prophet and the Mussulmans His disciples; so we may be all equally right.' . . .

The next morning I got a letter from Minchin saying that the Commissioner had sanctioned an exchange of appointments, and that I was to go up to Dera Ghazi Khan and he to return here once more.

Lieutenant Minchin had been relieved of his temporary

[1] An arrest was made, but the evidence was quite insufficient. The murderer was never brought to justice.

[2] Imam Bukhs Khan, afterwards created Nawáb Imam Bukhs Khan, K.C.I.E. He lived until some years after I left India, but latterly he was quite blind. He was a true Chief of his clan, and on the whole the finest native gentleman I ever knew. He sent me a farewell letter on my final departure from India in 1893. I gave him my Deringer revolver as a keepsake.

appointment of Deputy Commissioner of the Dera Ghazi Khan District by a senior officer. He thus became the first Assistant of the district, and was glad to return to Mithunkote as a subdivisional officer, while I, the junior, had to take a comparatively subordinate position at headquarters. I remained, however, only a few weeks at Dera Ghazi Khan, and I was then transferred to Ferozepore in the Lahore Division, the Commissioner of which was Mr. Douglas Forsyth. On leaving Dera Ghazi Khan I rode through the night to Mooltan ; thence, with a rest of about twenty hours at Gogaira, I travelled over a grass-spread road in a mail-cart to Lahore. At Lahore I called upon Mr. Forsyth, thus making the acquaintance of one who was to become a friend and to remain so for nearly thirty years. I then joined my new appointment at Ferozepore. Returning to Lahore a few weeks later for the 'higher standard' departmental examination, I met Bernard, Lawrence, J. B. Lyall,[1] R. T. Burney, J. G. Cordery, and others, who came up for the same ordeal. Most of us lived with Mr. Forsyth during the days of the examination, and had a very happy time. The examination was satisfactorily passed.

CAMP, FEROZEPORE DISTRICT, *April* 16.—We[2] are encamped to-day close by the riverside, under a nice little grove of trees. The march this morning was very jolly; we started at sunrise and rode from village to village through cornfields and green lanes. Some of the latter reminded us of England; pretty, tortuous little ways, with just room enough for one horse to canter and turn easily. I have been deciding a tiresome case, and have just cleared the tent of a lot of troublesome cultivators and landowners who claim some land which has been left dry

[1] Of my term at Haileybury, afterwards Lieutenant-Governor of the Punjab.
[2] Lieutenant E. Conolly of the Artillery was my companion.

by the river. There is nothing like going to the disputed place and judging for yourself. What seemed all a muddle to me yesterday was clear enough when I used my eyes and could ask all the witnesses on the spot.

Ferozepore, *May* 10.—An amusing series of entertainments was given the other day by a clerk [1] of our English office. He put forth some rare invitations, in which ladies and gentlemen were requested to witness the nuptials of his wife's sister in the church at half-past six in the morning, and afterwards to repair to his residence to partake of cake and wine, and thirdly to be present in the evening at a 'quadrille' party. The B.'s and I went to the church and partook of the cake and wine, as we thought the man might be offended if we refused. The bride, who was half black, wore a grand satin dress, and had a veil thrown over her dusky features. The bridegroom seemed well pleased with his bargain, and gave her a loud resounding kiss when the ceremony was over. The evening entertainment was unique. . . . The music consisted of an old fiddle and a triangle, and very questionable refreshments were served in a spacious tent. I was at home by half-past ten, but some enthusiasts were foolish enough to keep it up till four in the morning. . . .

At Lahore, *May* 26.—Saunders [2] came from Gujranwala soon after I arrived. The Deputy Commissioner of Lahore, Egerton, is staying with Forsyth, so we are a jolly quartett. Thursday being the Queen's birthday and a holiday . . . we sat down eighteen men to dinner, and drank H.M.'s health in a loyal manner when the cloth was removed. I sat next to Hall, my predecessor at Ferozepore, and had a long chat with him anent the district. We talk 'shop' to a great extent in the Punjab, and I really don't see why we shouldn't, considering it is the thing in which we ought to be and many are most interested. After dinner we had some very good glee singing.

[1] An Eurasian.

[2] Leslie Saunders, of my term at Haileybury. At this time he was Assistant Commissioner of Gujranwala in the Lahore Division. He and I by Mr. Forsyth's invitation had gone over to Lahore on a short visit.

Thornton,[1] Egerton,[2] and a Captain Sim[3] all have good voices and sing well together. . . . This morning the Lahore Rifle Club were drilled in the compound. It was great fun seeing such dignitaries as the Judicial[4] and Financial Commissioners and others being drilled by a little Scotch corporal of the 79th. Cust,[5] the Financial Commissioner, is a great talker, and quotes Latin during the performance. The corporal reproves him. 'Now, Mr. Cust, you must not talk.' . . .

My stay at Ferozepore only lasted a short time. Towards the end of June, I was transferred to Amritsar, where an Assistant was urgently required. At Amritsar Mr. Philip Egerton was Commissioner. He and Mrs. Egerton were charming people, and I can never forget the kindness they showed me at this time. I had suffered a good deal from fever at Ferozepore, and attacks continued after I reached Amritsar. The Deputy Commissioner was Captain Farrington, who finally retired from the service as Commissioner of Rawulpindi. He was most kind and hospitable to me, took me into his house, and kept me there for a long time, when I was more or less ailing. He was a very efficient and energetic officer, an excellent linguist, with a good deal of the manner of a grand seigneur. The Natives esteemed and feared him. Early in July I was compelled to take a month's leave in the hope of getting rid of intermittent fever. I spent the time at Dharmsala with my friend Alexander Lawrence,

[1] Mr. T. H. Thornton, afterwards Foreign Secretary to the Government of India.

[2] Mr. R. E. Egerton, at this time Deputy Commissioner of Lahore, finally Lieutenant-Governor of the Punjab.

[3] Captain George Sim, R.E., Government Consulting Engineer on the Punjab Railway.

[4] At this time Mr. Arthur Roberts. He died some years later as Resident at Hyderabad.

[5] Mr. R. N. Cust, a well-known Indian Civilian, author of many books.

who was Assistant Commissioner of the Kangra District. I greatly enjoyed being with him again. Richard Burney was Assistant at Gurdaspore, through whose district I had to pass on my way to Dharmsala.

DHARMSALA, *July* 10.—Burney is not very cheery at Gurdaspore, his Deputy Commissioner (Mr. Nasmyth) manages to throw cold water on most things B. does. Burney says the only ice in Gurdaspore is Nasmyth's smile.

July 19.—A few days ago we were all much astonished at hearing a loud report in the air, something like thunder, which was echoed to and fro among the mountains for some seconds, and was followed by the fall of some huge pieces of rock in different parts of the country. We are at a loss to imagine what really happened; whether the stones were thrown up by a distant volcano, or the crest of a mountain was struck by lightning, or an aerolite burst in the air, we cannot yet tell. The occurrence was startling, and people's minds naturally thought of Dr. Cumming's books.

July 21.—I see that Sir John Lawrence thinks a great deal depends on our judicious humouring of the native customs, *i.e.* when a native custom is not immoral, or opposed to our principles of government, by all means give in to it and conciliation will be the result. In short, respect innocent prejudices. He evidently thinks the cartridges had a great deal to do with the Mutiny, and, as far as I understand his views, he would never have given such a cause of offence. The prejudice against using greased cartridges is surely innocent, and the humouring thereof could have done no harm, but rather a great deal of good.

July 23.—The startling phenomenon I told you about seems to have been a large meteor which burst somewhere near Gurdaspore. Burney saw it. Fancy the pieces being thrown so far as this, thirty or forty miles away.[1]

[1] I myself saw a large half-buried fragment near the Gurkha lines below Dharmsala. Portions of this great aerolite are, I believe, to be seen in many museums.

AMRITSAR, *October* 11.—The event of the week was a grand entertainment given by one of the largest capitalists of the city of Amritsar on the birth of his first grandchild. About ten Englishmen were there, and an immense number of natives. When we arrived we were received by some friends of our host in the large middle courtyard of the house. Native houses are generally built round a square yard which is not roofed over. The walls, however, in this instance, were illuminated with mosaic work and such like, the dark sky with twinkling stars was our canopy, and we could spy some fair ladies peeping cautiously over the highest parapet and admiring the scene below. We were ushered into a very fine room which was lighted by candles placed in wall shades, chandeliers, etc. The floor was spread with carpet, and chairs were arranged round the room. On these we sat, and were entertained by the evolutions of dancing-girls. These creatures can hardly be said to dance. They shuffle along the ground, keeping both feet close together, and rattling their bangles. Their dancing is but an accompaniment to their singing, which goes on at the same time. Musicians beat drums and play the strangest looking guitars, and thus add to the noise. The din was awful. I amused myself talking to a very old merchant, who told me his great-grandchild was eight years old. We had a long chat about our marriages and native marriages. Here is some of our talk.

Old gentleman, by name Narsingh Das, loquitur. 'I beg your honour's forgiveness for never coming to call upon you, but the truth is I am getting old, and of late have been unable for exertion.'

Assistant Commissioner. 'Don't think of coming to see me. I am living at the top of a very long staircase[1] which will be very difficult for you to ascend; so wait, please, till I get into my new house with ground-floor rooms.'

N. D. 'Your honour is very kind.'

[1] In an old native house in the Ram Bagh at Amritsar, the only accommodation I could obtain.

A. C. 'In your country people marry so young that fathers become grandfathers at a very early age.'

N. D. 'Yes, when a child is seven or eight years old, then we commence to arrange for his marriage.'

A. C. 'But then, you don't let the bridegroom choose his bride; you just say, you must marry so and so.'

N. D. 'What can a child of nine know? We are only too glad to do what our parents wish. Perhaps your honour knows Mr. B——. When he was here, I often went to see him. One day I said, "Why don't you marry your daughter to some Sahib?" He replied, "Ask her yourself, I've nothing to do with it." So I turned round to Miss B—— and said, "When are you going to marry?" She answered, "When I meet some gentleman that suits me." The young lady was very hard to please. No less than twenty-six gentlemen sent in their cards to her, and she would have nothing to say to any one of them.[1] The custom of our country is different.'

It was great fun to listen to the old boy chattering away. He remembered when Lord Metcalfe met Ranjit Singh in 1804 at Kasúr, and I've no doubt he could tell a great many old stories which would be worth recording. Soon after we had done talking dinner was announced, and the Sahibs went downstairs to the courtyard, where dinner was laid out for us in our own fashion. We fared very well. There was beer, sherry, and champagne in abundance, and everything as it should be. Of course our servants had gone at an early hour to the house and given them some hints. The Indians contented themselves with looking on. After dinner Farrington got up and said we were much pleased with everything, and wished the youthful scion health and prosperity; whereupon we drank the grandson's health and gave him three cheers. This over, we returned to

[1] The old gentleman was confusing matters here. It is the custom in English society in India for visitors to send in their cards, rather than to trust native servants to announce their names correctly. Narsingh Das evidently thought that when gentlemen sent in their cards at a house where an unmarried daughter presided as mistress, that simple ceremony was tantamount to a proposal.

the upper room, where the dancing was still going on. When we had sat down, garlands of flowers were thrown over our heads, and rose-water (atar) sprinkled on our bodies, while servants brought trays of presents and put them down at our feet. Each tray contained a beautiful shawl, a rich piece of brocade, and a white turban; the three worth about five hundred rupees. Of course, we had to look and admire, but we went away taking only the turban, which was, perhaps, worth three or four shillings. The shawls and brocade remained behind.

December 9.—On Wednesday evening most of the station honoured a non-equestrian circus with their presence. We were not much entertained, still the novelty of seeing anything of the kind in this country amused us to a certain extent. A heavy father with daughters and sons were the sole performers. They all appeared in rotation on the tight rope, and cut very queer figures some of them. It was amusing to see the old boy, who had been busily engaged in putting up his tents all day, appear in the character of a booted cavalier with a plume of feathers. A sharp native soon detected that the smiling heroine of the rope was the identical party who had taken his rupees at the door. These people are Italian; they got a fine large tent in Calcutta, and have travelled up country. They have been twelve years away from home, and are last from California.

December 27.—I am in my assessing tent[1] just about to tax the Cashmere shawlmakers of Amritsar. About six thousand shawls are made every year, and sent to the European and Indian markets. . . . A good Amritsar shawl costs £40 here, and takes four men one year to make! It is entirely worked by the hand. Three or four men sit at a loom, one sings the pattern, and as he sings the workers ply their bobbins, two reds, two blues, three greens, etc. Patterns come out from France, and then a composer writes them out according to the stitches

[1] Among other duties at Amritsar, I had to perform that of Assessor of Income-Tax, now introduced for the first time in India by Mr. Wilson, the Finance Minister.

December 30.—Lord Canning is getting more in favour with the press than he was. The foolish outcry of the Anglo-Indians about the Arms Act is seen to have been uncalled for, and they are obliged to confess that Lord C. isn't quite so bad as he might have been. But they praise him very grudgingly, and seem rather sorry to have to say a word in his favour. I read an article the other day in the *Friend of India*, which said that Lord C. was a second or third rate peer when he came out, also everything that was bad into the bargain, but that he had now acquired a good deal of experience, and is making use of the same. I don't profess to have formed an opinion at all about Lord Canning, but one feels rather inclined to like him when the miserable Indian press heap such absurd abuse on his head.

The greater part of the year 1861 was spent in England. My father had died while I was in Ferozepore. I obtained leave on urgent private affairs, and sailed from Calcutta at the end of March. The only fact I need recall regarding the voyage is my making acquaintance with William K. Elles of the 38th regiment. He was a fellow-passenger, and we eventually became intimate friends, meeting often in later years at Simla, and elsewhere in India. He rose to be Sir W. Elles, K.C.B., Lieutenant-General of the Eastern command, but to the great distress of his many friends he died of cholera at Naini Tal in 1896.

In October I was married to the youngest daughter of the late Thomas Spears of Kirkcaldy, whom I had known from childhood.

CHAPTER V

ASSISTANT COMMISSIONER OF LAHORE AND MURREE

1861—1863

EARLY in November we sailed from Southampton in the P. and O. Company's ancient paddle-wheel steamer *Indus*. There were some interesting people on board: the Duke and Duchess of Beaufort with two fine little boys, bound for Gibraltar; the widow and daughters of Mr. Wilson, the Finance Minister of India, who left at Malta. Major and Mrs. Nicolls, my Loodiana friends, were also our fellow-passengers, and we travelled as far as Calcutta together. At Cairo, Sir James Outram was at Shepheard's Hotel. He appeared to be a mere wreck of the sprightly man whom I remembered in Calcutta in 1858. Our steamer from Suez was the *Candia*, on board of which we found Lady Montgomery and Mrs. Drummond, wife of Mr. Edmund Drummond, afterwards Lieutenant-Governor of the North-West Provinces. The voyage was uneventful, broken by landing for a few hours at Aden and Galle. Arriving in Calcutta in the middle of December, we were met by Lieutenant Hall of the Indian Navy, an old Aberdeenshire friend, then serving on the Viceroy's steam yacht *Feroze*, which was lying in the river. Hall took us ashore in one of the *Feroze's* boats. Charles Bernard, who had now become Under-Secretary in the Financial Department, also met us, and drove us to his rooms, where we abode during our fourteen days' stay in Calcutta.

Soon after landing I received a telegram saying that I had been gazetted to be Assistant Commissioner at Lahore, where Mr. Douglas Forsyth was still Commissioner. Travelling by rail and carriage we arrived at Agra, where we attended a levée of the Begum of Bhopal,[1] who had proved herself so staunchly loyal during the Mutiny. The old lady was plainly attired, wore no veil, and was most gracious and kindly in her manner.

The levée over, we started again on our way north-westwards. At Lahore we were most warmly received by Mr. and Mrs. Forsyth in their beautiful and charmingly appointed house 'New Park,' on the outskirts of the Civil station of Anarkuli. One morning I accompanied Mr. Forsyth to the newly laid out Lawrence Gardens, then little better than a barren wilderness, where Miss Forsyth, now Mrs. George Parker, planted the first tree of what was destined to become one of the most beautiful pleasure grounds of Upper India. On the 16th January I began my work at the district office as Assistant Commissioner, civil and criminal cases in abundance having been allotted to me for inquiry and decision. A great change in the manner of disposal of criminal work had taken place since I left the Punjab at the beginning of the previous year. The Indian Penal Code and the Code of Criminal Procedure had been introduced. The acting Judicial Commissioner was the keen-eyed disciplinarian, Mr. Robert Cust, whose strict supervision of the courts subordinate to him put most of us on our mettle.

[1] The Nawab Sikandar Begum, afterwards created a G.C.S.I.

LAHORE, *January* 27.— . . . We have a good deal of trouble with the new Code of Criminal Procedure. Everything has now to be done strictly according to Cocker; cases to be written out most carefully; evidence to be recorded with the utmost accuracy, and really one has enough to do in turning up chapter and verse lest any slip should be made.

February 27.— . . . The variety of work I have to do! It is quite an effort of mind to make one's senses jump from one subject to another. I am busily engaged in thinking over some dodgy excuse made by A. to get off paying his income-tax, when B. rushes in frantically with a handful of hair in his clutch, and swears he has been licked within an inch of his life and had all his hair torn out, and if he doesn't get redress he'll die on the spot. Meantime the Judicial Commissioner sends a note wanting immediately a list of all the Government house property in Lahore,[1] with names of tenants and such like. Another moment a bundle of reminders comes in from the Commissioner, drawing immediate attention to about half a dozen unanswered letters at once. You can imagine that such a grind is, to say the least, stupefying in the extreme.

After a very pleasant sojourn of some days with Mr. and Mrs. Forsyth, we went on to stay at Government House, which Sir Robert and Lady Montgomery, in their great spirit of hospitality, said must be our head-quarters until we could settle into an abode of our own. The finding of a house was a task of great difficulty. The station of Lahore was a small place in comparison to what it is now. Donaldtown[2] was unbuilt. Houses in Anarkuli were few and bad, and were moreover fully occupied. After prolonged searching we arranged to rent three-quarters of a house near the Central Jail, the

[1] The Judicial Commissioner was at this time head of the Local Fund and Government property (nazúl) departments.

[2] So called from Mr. Donald M'Leod, the President of the Lahore Improvement Committee.

property of Dr. Hathaway, the Inspector-General of Jails in the Punjab, subsequently the Private Secretary of the Viceroy, Sir John Lawrence. Dr. Hathaway retained one-quarter of the house, and managed somehow to live in it and keep his office there. The house being a well-built and healthy one, the arrangement had its advantages, but, as will be easily believed, it had many disadvantages. Our visit to Government House was enjoyable in the extreme. Nothing could exceed the kindness of our hosts and their aides-de-camp, Captains Heyland and Raikes. Colonel Richard Lawrence, the Military Secretary to Government, who had been so good to me at Murree in 1859, was a fellow-guest. He was a man whom to know was to love. Our friendship begun three years before was now cemented, my wife being included in the bond, and it continued until his death in 1896. One of Sir Robert Montgomery's great charms was that he could talk to a young subordinate about his work in the most friendly and sympathetic way and entirely without loss of dignity. 'Sat next to Sir Robert at dinner and talked shop' is an entry in my diary. Eventually in February we migrated to our own house, which became our home for more than a year. My official duties were by no means light. As Secretary to the Local Fund Committee, I was in charge of the station roads, bridges, drainage and the like. No one had a keener eye for the general tidiness of the station than the Lieutenant-Governor, regarding whom tradition related that he had been seen himself to dismount from his buggy and remove a piece of broken brick from the road, lest it should be the means of laming his own or some other person's horse. The morning inspections ended, a visit to the private swimming-bath belonging to Mr. Donald M'Leod, the Financial Commissioner, would often follow. The early forenoon found me in my room at the District Court-house, engaged in hearing police reports, general petitions, and in the trial of civil and criminal cases. Work went on till four, five, or even six o'clock. On being released, a game of racquets, a drive with my wife, or visits to friends would follow. Croquet, badminton, and tennis were then unknown in Lahore. In the evening there was often a small dinner-party at home or abroad, and in the hot weather lectures or entertainments, in the building now used as a public library in Anarkuli, were pretty frequent.

March 2.—On Thursday night we went to a ball at Mian Mir. . . . Got home about 3 A.M. . . . Up at 6 to go and meet the Raja of Faridkote (Wazir Singh), who was coming up for the railway opening (Lahore to Amritsar). Burney and I rode out some miles to meet the Raja, found him waiting for us by the side of the road, with a large retinue of riders, elephants, etc. The Raja, Burney, and I mounted on a large elephant[1] and proceeded towards the city, midst clouds of dust. The Raja is rather an agreeable man. Yesterday, at the railway opening, he wore some magnificent jewels, emeralds as big as pigeons' eggs, with large pearls and rubies. As we rounded the Lahore fort and approached the Raja's tents a salute was fired, which seemed to delight the old man. . . .

The plan for yesterday[2] was for the guests to assemble at the railway station at 10.30, and leave by train for Amritsar at 11. There was an immense concourse of natives, who shouted vociferously when the train started. . . . We made a most successful start, and ran down to Amritsar, thirty-two miles, in about an

[1] I remember the Raja told me that the beast's name was Moula Bukhs.

[2] The day of the opening of the Lahore-Amritsar section of the Punjab Railway.

hour and a half. Arrived there, we were received on a platform by the Amritsar officials, who eagerly pressed round Sir Robert,[1] and were most urgent in their congratulations. I met a great many old friends. . . . An address in English was presented to Sir Robert, also a Persian one, of which Farrington, the Deputy Commissioner,[2] read a very well-written translation. He was, as you can imagine, in his element, and made everything go off in first-rate style. When the addresses were over, we all went to a large garden close by, and had tiffin under canvas. Speeches followed; we then returned as we came.

The next extract is amusing in that it illustrates the keenness of the Judicial Commissioner, Mr. Robert Cust, to detect abuses. The Holi is a spring festival kept by the Hindus in carnival fashion, with many unedifying features. Mr. Cust did not approve of a Christian Government recognising such an occasion by allowing the Courts to be closed.

D.[3] *March* 17.—This day was a holiday for the Holi. Cust very indignant.

June 9.—We have got Lahore heat at last; 92°, 93°, 94° in the house. . . .

June 29.—Cust was saying the other day that he had advised Sir Robert to give Civilians the option of going to Bengal, for really there was nothing to expect up here; everything at a deadlock and likely to remain so for years. He is a frightful Job's comforter. . . .

August 17.—Yesterday a paragraph in the *Lahore Chronicle* said that all the civil courts in the Punjab are to be closed during September,[4] that is the courts for the decision of civil claims and actions. This will lighten our work a good deal. Of course, there will be criminal and revenue work to do as

[1] The Lieutenant-Governor.
[2] See p. 70.
[3] The letter D. prefixed to an extract stands for Diary.
[4] This was the first year in which the plan of closing the civil courts in September was introduced.

usual. I have always thought it so ridiculous to keep the civil courts open all the year round. Civil suits are not of such paramount importance that they cannot stand over. I fancy the effect of a vacation will be that half of the squabbles will settle themselves before they appear in court. . . .

M'Neile[1] gets the highest praise in the annual report. They say he is the best district officer, the best judge, etc. I believe the praise is all deserved. As far as my limited experience goes, I don't think there is a single district officer who can hold a candle to him. . . .

D. August 22.—Griffin's[2] lecture on Tennyson in the evening; enjoyed it very much; quotations first-rate.

On the 3rd September most grievous news reached Lahore. Major Nicolls, who had become Deputy Commissioner of Dera Ismail Khan on the Frontier, had died of sunstroke on his journey with his wife to the little barren hill station of Sheikh Budin.

Colonel John Becher, Commissioner, to Sir Robert Montgomery.

Sheikh Budin, *August* 30, 1862.

My dear Sir Robert,—A most melancholy event has just occurred. Poor Major Nicolls had been suffering from fever at Dera Ismail Khan, but not severely; I begged him some time ago to try a change of air, and come for a month to Sheikh Budin. He was to have been here at nine o'clock this morning, and I was waiting for him, when a man came to say he was ill on the road. A jampan was sent for him immediately, when another man of mine came in with an alarming account that he was senseless and breathing heavily, apoplectically, and that when he left he had scarcely any pulse and that his poor wife was in deep distress. Fortunately the doctor and another

[1] My Deputy Commissioner at Loodiana in 1858-59.

[2] Afterwards Sir Lepel Griffin, K.C.S.I. He was then a young unpassed Civilian, working for his preliminary language examinations at Lahore.

officer who were going out shooting met him very soon after he had been taken ill. Medicines were sent for, but in a very short time he had died of sunstroke! I have never known a more sudden and sad event,—the poor wife with him on the road. I have put her in my house, and Mrs. Campbell has kindly come over to try and soothe her. Mr. French[1] the missionary has also seen her. You know them both, it was at your house I first met them! She has insisted upon having the poor lifeless body by her, and we have only just deposited it decently in her room. I have been to arrange for his burial. I hope to prevail on her to stay here, for she has been very unwell for a long time and will be better here, and I have left the house entirely to her and Mrs. Campbell for the present. She says she has no relations in India. I am sure Lady Montgomery will be much pained to hear of the sad blow. He was coming up to enjoy a little change and rest, and lo!—I have telegraphed to you, but I also send this by post as being more full.

In a letter written to me some days later, Colonel Becher gave further details and concluded his letter by saying, 'The poor fellow was buried with military honours next day. Every one attending. Already his tomb is built. I had seen enough of him to appreciate the manliness and sterling worth of his character, and I greatly regret his loss. He worked very hard and very conscientiously.' I have given this letter and quotation not only as a memorial to Major Nicolls, but as a testimony to the great worth and charm of Colonel John Becher, a most distinguished officer. Up to this time I had never met him, but some years later Mrs. Nicolls brought us together at her house in London and we became friends.

I have been told quite recently by Sir Donald Macnabb

[1] Afterwards first Bishop of Lahore.

that the horse which Major Nicolls was riding had been lent to him by Colonel Becher. In 1864, when Colonel Becher was Commissioner of Peshawur, he lent the same animal to Major Adams, Deputy Commissioner, who was riding it at the moment of his assassination in the city of Peshawur. Sir Donald Macnabb, who succeeded Major Adams, often rode the same animal, notwithstanding that it had the reputation of being an unlucky horse.

October 12.—The rain has brought out the enormous black ants in myriads. Our floors have been black with these crawling monsters. They bite furiously, having mandibles like pincers. They are not poisonous, however. I have hardly been able to keep them off my bed. We first tried tin basins (in which were placed the bed-posts) filled with water. This was a successful preventive, till one adventurous ant forded the moat and mounted the bed-post. In his wake many of his brethren followed, to my utter disgust. So now I have been obliged to surround the water-basins with quicklime. For the present this repels invaders, but I am not over sanguine of having discovered an invulnerable defence. Our ayah quaintly remarks that the ants are a very clever people (hoshiár lóg). . . . I was rejoiced to see in the last *Lahore Chronicle* that in the beginning of next year the *actual* journey to Calcutta from Lahore may be performed in 101 hours.

Lahore to Amritsar,	1	hour rail.
Amritsar to Alighur,	52	hours carriage.
Alighur to Allahabad,	14	hours rail.
Allahabad to Benares,	11	hours carriage.
Benares to Calcutta,	23	hours rail.
	101	

1200 miles in 101 hours in India isn't bad, is it?[1]

Early in the morning of the 25th October our first child was born.

[1] The journey is now performed in a railway carriage, without change, probably in less than 48 hours!

October 26.—The Lieutenant-Governor had selected the 25th for his return to Lahore. At 6 A.M. I started off to join the party who were going to ride out to meet him. Besides, I had to see that the roads were all clear and properly watered. We met his Honour in his carriage about two miles from the city and escorted him to Government House. He was very gracious to me, and especially so when he heard of the other arrival that preceded his own by so short a time. . . . Soon after sunset I was told that the Lord Sahib (so they call the Lieutenant-Governor) had come to see me. I found his Honour walking about the garden. He was most kind; left his carriage outside the compound lest he should make a noise, and talked to me in the most paternal way possible, warned me against allowing any noise, exciting talk, interviews, etc. It was very good of him to show such an interest in us.

November 2.—Sir Robert came again on Monday, and was graciously pleased to enter our door, admire our drawing-room, and then nod benignly at baby, who was brought out to be inspected.

The year 1862 was a cholera year at Lahore, not of the worst type, but nevertheless bad enough.

November 15.—Mr. M'Leod was one of the party at dinner. He told an amusing story about ——, who had stayed a very long time at the Hills, when M'Leod was down here grilling. —— is supposed to have given his reasons for doing so thus: 'I'm keeping myself in health so that when M'Leod is down with cholera I may return to Lahore at once.'

In the last week of the year a large missionary conference was held at Lahore. The place of meeting was the American Presbyterian Church in Anarkuli. The following is from my diary of the 31st December:—

Dined at home, went to a soirée at the Forsyths, met all the missionaries and their wives. The Pollocks came home with us, and we talked the old year out and the new year in. *Sic transit* 1862.

I had served under Captain Pollock on the Frontier. He had now come to Lahore as Deputy Commissioner, and was my immediate superior at this time. In later years he became Commissioner of Lahore, and afterwards was made a K.C.S.I. for his services on the Seistan boundary commission. In the seventies, as the sequel will show, Sir Richard Pollock and I served as colleagues at Peshawur. He was a son of Chief Baron Pollock and nephew of Field-Marshal Sir George Pollock,—a man of great personal charm and of unusual quickness of perception. Sir Richard was beloved by his friends and admired for his varied talents. 'Trim' Pollock was the name by which he was known familiarly throughout the Punjab.

LAHORE, *D. January* 6, 1863.—A correspondence about trees with the Lieutenant-Governor.

The above entry, if found in an Assistant Commissioner's diary at the present day, might cause surprise; but in the early days of the Punjab the heads of the Government depended not a little on personal influence and control for getting their views carried out promptly by subordinate officers. Sir Robert Montgomery took a keen interest in the planting of trees throughout the province, in laying out station roads, in planning public gardens, and such like, and he rightly believed that a demi-official note from himself to an officer on the spot was more likely to receive immediate attention than a formal official order which had to filter through the various grades of officers before it reached the man who would actually have to carry it out. To illustrate this so-called patriarchal way of working I give the following letters about trees and the laying out of Donaldtown in Lahore in 1863 :—

SIR R. MONTGOMERY TO G. R. ELSMIE.

MY DEAR ELSMIE,—Dr. Cleghorn[1] is an authority on all matters connected with trees. I saw him, *saw* in hand, pruning away at Maclagan's[2] gate. He says he will be happy to instruct some of your men how to prune. *This* is the time for clearing the stems of trees; will you place half a dozen of the gardeners under his orders and give them *saws*? After a few days' instruction in his neighbourhood, send them out along all the highroads and prune away as fast as possible. This is all-important at this season.—Yours sincerely,

R. MONTGOMERY.

Communicate with Cleghorn. Keep me informed of the progress of the Committee. R. M.

SIR R. MONTGOMERY TO G. R. ELSMIE.

Your report is quite satisfactory. When you next write, let me know the kind of trees you propose putting in. The *cirus* tree will do in inferior ground, where the *sissoo* will not grow. The sissoo is the better tree of the two, but in kunkaree[3] spots the holes should be made extra large and some good earth from a neighbouring field put in. I have planted, or superintended the planting of, nearly all the trees now at Lahore and three generations of trees that *have died*, and have had experience.

The following letter was from my Commissioner, Mr. Forsyth. It no doubt hit a weak spot, and probably

[1] Of the Forest Department.
[2] Colonel Maclagan, R.E., brother of the present Archbishop of York.
[3] *i.e.* spots full of 'kunkar' or limestone nodules.

did good at the time and during the rest of my service. Anyhow, I never forgot the friendly advice it contained:—

T. D. Forsyth, Commissioner, to G. R. Elsmie.

Lahore, *February* 5, 1863.

My dear Elsmie,—I have just finished the Criminal Report, and in that part which touches on the character of officers have had great pleasure in recording my opinion of your merits as an officer. But lest you should be too much elated (?) I venture to offer a word of advice. . . . What I wish to say by way of counsel is, that the most trying part of our work in India is to have to listen patiently and appear to be interested in all that a native has to say when he comes to call or appears in court. Many men have acquired an immense reputation amongst natives all through this. This, in fact, has gone far to make M'Leod so revered. It is not that he grants every man's request. But they can go to him in confidence, knowing that they will never be turned hastily away, or be cut short in their story. And, after all, it is an immense relief to a man to have it out! I dare say, if you had known me as a young man, you would say, 'Physician, heal thyself,' for I was, I dare say, too apt to be hasty and imperious, and my wife thinks I am so now. But it is my daily endeavour to submit to patience. . . . *Verbum sat sapientibus.*—Yours sincerely,

T. D. Forsyth.

. . . .

February 15.—One day his Honour asked me what I thought about a hill station. 'Would you like to go to the Hills?' I replied to the effect that I supposed I should be a fool to say no, but that I would make no application to be sent there. . . . So there the matter rests. I have heard nothing more about it. I cannot say I am particularly anxious to go to a hill station. Still, of course, I would very much rather go than grind on at Lahore as an Assistant Commissioner. I would not, however, give up the slightest chance of getting a better appointment in the plains for all the hills that ever reared themselves to Heaven. If I could become officiating Deputy Commissioner of Jhung[1] on 500 Rs. a month, I would rather go there than to the Hills as an Assistant Commissioner on 700 Rs.

March 2.— . . . Towards evening an immense swarm of locusts hovered over the station. They seemed to have come from the Mooltan direction, and to be meditating where they should settle. The air for miles round was alive with them, and we feared they would do much damage to the crops. However, about midday on Sunday they took their departure, and we have seen nothing more of them. As I drove home from cutcherry they whizzed about the horses' ears. The crows seemed to have a good time of it. They made no scruple of flying into the midst of the swarm and carrying off a carcase for immediate consumption on the branch of a tree.

On the 13th March Sir Robert wrote to me saying he was 'now in a position to offer' me the subdivision of Murree, the hot weather headquarters of the Government. The offer was gratefully accepted, and it was arranged that we should take immediate steps to leave Lahore. We paid a visit of some days at Government House, and started, in a large dooli lashed to a post-office truck, on the 7th April for Murree, a distance of about 210 miles.

Rawulpindi was reached on the morning of the 9th April. During that day and the next we were received by Major and Mrs. Cracroft. Major Cracroft was my new Deputy Commissioner, the subdivision of Murree being in his district. He was a beautiful violin-player,[2] and the evening we spent in his house is chiefly to be remembered by the music which he gave us. Early in the morning of

[1] Then generally regarded as the worst and most out-of-the-way district in the province.

[2] See p. 60.

the 11th we arrived at Murree, having travelled overnight from Rawulpindi in doolies. The day was wet and miserable, and as we had to put up in a wretched hotel our spirits were at the lowest. We went to look at the very small house called 'Oak Knoll' which, *faute de mieux*, we had been obliged to take. It was destitute of all furniture, and we were unable to take possession of it till the 18th, by which time our carts had arrived from Lahore.

MURREE, *April* 12.—Sir Robert took frequent opportunities during our visit to Government House to lecture me on the duties of Assistant Commissioner of Murree. He takes the greatest interest in the station, and is very anxious that the European proprietors and residents should dwell peaceably together and not fight with the Assistant. The appointment requires a good deal of 'firmness and tact,' says Sir R. So I trust I shall not be found wanting; but, from all accounts, there are a good many conflicting elements to reconcile.

On the 27th April a somewhat unusual incident occurred. An urgent message was sent to me as Magistrate, begging me to proceed to a certain house in order to place a Mr. P. in restraint, who was vowing vengeance against his wife for unfaithful conduct. On my reaching the house I was informed that Mrs. P. had effected her escape, and had probably bolted down the hill to Rawulpindi. Having arranged for the safeguarding of Mr. P., I carried out a previously formed intention of riding down to Tret, a stage on the Rawulpindi road, on other business. On approaching Tret I saw ahead of me a jampan being hurried along by four coolies. A lady was inside. She was quite alone, barring the men who carried her. I did not doubt that the traveller was the erring Mrs. P. who was escaping from her infuriated husband. I caught up the jampan just as the lady was alighting at the Tret dâk bungalow. I accosted her and demanded her name. She turned round indignantly saying, 'I am Mrs. Pratt.' The truth flashed upon me. The lady was the wife of the well-known Archdeacon Pratt of Calcutta, whom I did not know by sight, but of whom I had heard that she intended to run up to Murree from Rawulpindi, for a few hours, in order to look at a house which the Archdeacon subsequently rented for the season. Mrs. Pratt and I became acquainted afterwards and often met, but the Tret incident was not referred to, and I never knew whether she identified me as her inquisitor.

May 13.—I heard from ——[1] the other day. He is at a place called Purneah in Bengal. He evidently despises the Punjab now; he calls it a bepraised province. This is rather amusing in a man who besought Sir Robert not to allow him to be transferred. In some jail report, written by him as Magistrate of Purneah, he scoffed at certain of the prison arrangements of the Punjab. Well, the Supreme Government wrote to the Punjab Government and requested to know what truth there was in the remarks made by Mr. ——. Can you imagine anything more delightful than H.H. the Lieutenant-Governor having to reply to this? However, Cust[2] walked into —— in fine style. After denying the truth of the allegations *in toto*, he said that Mr. —— was an officer of no experience, and if he always wrote in that way, of very little judgment. He was no specimen of the Punjab official.

Meanwhile the Lieutenant-Governor and his suite had not reached Murree. They had gone to Cashmere, direct

[1] An officer who had formerly served in the Punjab.
[2] The Judicial Commissioner.

from Lahore, on a visit to the Maharaja Ranbir Singh. Mr. Davies, the Secretary to the Government, had taken leave to England, early in the year. His *locum tenens* was Mr. Forsyth, the Commissioner of Lahore, who accompanied the Lieutenant-Governor on his trip to Cashmere.

May 28.—The great event since we last wrote is the arrival of the Lieutenant-Governor from Cashmere. Black[1] and I rode out to Dewul on Tuesday, after breakfast. Dewul is about eleven miles off, *i.e.* one march. We got there at 1.30, and in an hour's time we spied a large party of travellers approaching from Cashmere. The principal feature of the cavalcade was a number of red umbrellas, which were carried by footmen and held over the heads of the riders and of the dooli and dandy travellers. The red umbrellas were supplied by the Maharaja as a mark of respect for his guests. Sir Robert was in good spirits. He was most encouraging in every way. Forsyth was unusually frank. He said he had had great opportunities of talking to Sir Robert on things in general whilst they were in Cashmere, and that he really believed the Punjab was as good a place for young hopefuls as any other. All that was required was patience in the meanwhile. He said he believed some high prizes would shortly be added to the existing appointments. Such a thing as a High Court was not impossible.

June 28.—I find the ordinary station work very simple. . . . The Europeans are beginning to be rather annoying, however. They are generally so absurd in their requests. . . . The Indian Magistrate has to do everything, no matter what; sometimes even to look for wet nurses for young puppies.

But the ordinary work of an Assistant Commissioner at a hill station was not destined to be my sole official employment. Mr. Forsyth, writing to me in June, said:—

[1] Major Sam Black, then Military Secretary to the Punjab Government.

I have a heavy piece of work on hand; to abstract and put into clear readable form the whole correspondence regarding Cabul and Afghanistan politics since the time of annexation; in fact, it is to be a very complete history of Western Asia since 1849. I haven't time for it now; and must ask for assistance. Sir Robert told me to look out for some one, and I at once thought of you.

The work is honorary and onerous. But it is intensely interesting, and will amply repay you, in a present addition to your stock of knowledge, and in some future time will prove of real use to you. . . . What say you?

I agreed, and the result was *An Epitome of Correspondence regarding our Relations with Afghanistan and Herat*, which was printed by the Punjab Government, and became a text-book for the period 1854-63.

The following letters received by me as Assistant Commissioner of Murree show the unwearied vigilance of Sir Robert Montgomery:—

Sir R. Montgomery to G. R. Elsmie.

I want to see your havalât[1] in the bazár at the Thanah, also to take a look at the bazár. If you are not engaged, I will go down and be, say at Clark's shop, to-morrow morning at 7 A.M. and go down with you.

Ascertain if you can what damage the locusts have done, and are doing. I have had an invasion; but so far as I can tell with no bad effect.

. . . .

I think you had better *not* allow the coolies to throw earth on the roads. It makes them quite impassable. The coolies should at this season see that the side-drains are clear for the water to run freely off, that impediments are removed, and a hole in a bridge mended. Where there may be any collection of water it should be let off. But on no account put

[1] Police lock-up.

earth *on* the roads till the middle of September. From Miller's to Barstow's house and all round is in a bad state, chiefly from new earth being thrown on. And when the coolies clear out the drains, they are *not* to put the earth on the road; but on the bank side, or carry it away. I do not know whether the evil done can be remedied. Perhaps the mud might be scraped off.

6th.

If you want to immortalise your name, you can do it at small cost and with little expense.

You know the place where the picnic was yesterday—the mound near where the band plays. Walks should be made through it, and a place made level for the band. It would be then the fashionable place of meeting of an evening. There is height, pure air, *shade*, and a beautiful view. I cannot conceive why such a spot in the centre of the station should have been left so long unimproved. I happened to go there with Younghusband this morning. He will assist you in laying out the walks, and he has great taste. If you want a third opinion, ask Black to join you. Call it 'Mount Pleasant'; the walks will cost in lining out only a few rupees, and roughly made, perhaps fifty rupees. I should like you to begin at once, and I will go and meet you all, any time you fix. I am always out and disengaged from half-past seven to half-past eight of a morning.

An account of our season at Murree would be incomplete without a reference to amateur theatricals. Captains Heyland and Raikes, the Private Secretary and A.D.C. of the Lieutenant-Governor; Captain Butler, V.C., of the 101st Fusiliers; Major John Morland, the Station staff-officer; Mr. Henry Goschen, of the 2nd Punjab Cavalry (brother of the first Viscount Goschen); Lieutenant Low, (afterwards Sir Robert Low, Commander-in-Chief in Bombay); Major Elwyn, Cantonment Magistrate, Peshawur;

Lieutenant Harris (afterwards Deputy Adjutant-General of the Army), were all keen actors. Two of our chief difficulties were: first, the Lieutenant-Governor, Sir Robert Montgomery, at that time disapproved of theatricals and of dancing, and it became a question how the Assistant Commissioner of Murree and the two staff-officers of his Honour could manage to take part in theatricals without incurring the grave displeasure of their Chief; second, there was no theatre in Murree, and the only possible way to provide one was to convert a partially used barrack into a theatre. In regard to the first objection, we determined to ignore it, and impunity followed our audacity. The second difficulty was not so easily overcome. The officer commanding the station was Colonel Olpherts, V.C., a very brave but fiery man, who was said to have earned a V.C. every time he went into action. It was determined to approach him through an old friend who had served with him in the Sind campaign, and to hold out as a bait the promise to give two performances gratis to the soldiers on each change of programme. In the event Colonel Olpherts said he could not resist the solicitations of his old companion-in-arms, Major J. W. Younghusband.[1] So in time a stage was erected in the barrack, scenes were painted, a band improvised, and some six or seven plays successfully represented. In the absence of ladies,[2] the principal female characters were taken by Mr. Robert Low, who appeared in the young women's parts, while the

[1] Afterwards General J. W. Younghusband, C.S.I., the distinguished father of Sir Frank Younghusband, K.C.I.E., of Tibet fame.

[2] Up to this time ladies had not, I believe, taken to amateur acting in the Punjab.

old and the middle-aged women were played by me. The enterprise was successful, and cleared expenses. The acting of Captain Butler, Major Elwyn, and Mr. Goschen was notably good.

October 19.—Sir R. entertained me in a long conversation about my prospects, a few days ago. He began by asking me what sort of an appointment I should like, and wherein my ambition lay. . . . Sir R. said he believed there was more chance of men getting on fast on the Frontier than in other parts of the Punjab, because the Frontier appointments were exceptional, and didn't go much by seniority. He concluded by hinting that if other things failed, he might send me as a temporary measure to Peshawur, and after that make me officiating Deputy Commissioner of Kohat. . . .

The Cabul (Epitome) business is finished. I was exactly four months about it, much longer than I had expected to be, and I am not particularly satisfied with the performance. However, I think the facts are correct, and I have been particular to avoid flowery writing. . . .

Towards the end of October the Lieutenant-Governor and the principal officers of the Punjab Government left Murree for Lahore. The Umbeyla campaign began about this time, and I distinctly remember hearing, while on a short visit to Abottabad, the guns of our force firing in the direction of the Indus.

November 4.—The Governor-General, Lord Elgin, has fallen sick at Dharmsala, and his arrangements about visiting Sialkote and going on to Peshawur are all knocked on the head, they say. . . .

The expedition is now going on against some fanatic Hindustanis and ill-disposed tribes on our Frontier. The excitement about the fighting is naturally considerable. Three officers have been killed already, and as many wounded. The enemy are very staunch, and come upon our men with much boldness. Many are so much drugged that they cut down the

British soldiers who bayonet them, before the latter can draw their bayonets out again. This kind of thing :—

The gentleman on the left is the British soldier, the other individual is the Hillman, who, after he has been run through, tries to avenge himself. They say that this feat has hitherto been unknown in warfare.

CHAPTER VI

JUDGE SMALL CAUSE COURT—LAHORE, DELHI, SIMLA

1863—1865

LAHORE, *November* 18, 1863.—You will be somewhat surprised to see by the above that I am once more back again in the capital of the Punjab. On the morning of the 7th I received a letter from Sir Robert, in which he offered me the appointment of acting Judge of the Small Cause Court at Lahore, and begged me to come down at once if I accepted. . . .

It was well known that Sir Robert Montgomery laid great stress on officers travelling promptly. He had no patience with a young fellow who took 'his week to prepare' and full 'joining time' when transferred. So when I received a letter, written by his own hand, asking me to come at once, I never thought of delaying. I forthwith sent off my horses to the various stages on the road, and reached Rawulpindi the same evening. The mail-cart, on which I travelled one hundred and seventy miles from Rawulpindi to Lahore in twenty hours, was a most uncomfortable, high, two-wheeled gig. Horses were changed twice an hour, and at every stage the passenger was obliged to descend, a most fatiguing process.

I began work in the Small Cause Court, Lahore, on Monday the 9th November, *i.e.* within forty-eight hours of receiving the Lieutenant-Governor's letter, and during that day I was the guest of Mr. Forsyth, the Commissioner.

The next day I went to Government House and was put up in a tent in the compound. The camp of the Commander-in-Chief, Sir Hugh Rose, was at Mian Mir, also the Governor-General's camp, the latter waiting in vain for poor Lord Elgin. Many guests dined at Government House, among whom I specially remember Colonel, afterwards Sir Henry, Durand, and Colonel, afterwards Sir Richard, Strachey. On the 18th my wife arrived from Murree and joined me as a guest at Government House. We had great difficulty in finding quarters of our own. All houses in Lahore were occupied. However, Mr. Cust, the Judicial Commissioner, came to the rescue and allowed us to take shelter in his office tents as a temporary measure. Meanwhile my friend Sir Alexander Lawrence had been transferred to Lahore from Sialkote as Assistant Commissioner. He and Lady Lawrence put up in a miserable hovel near the Anarkuli bazaar. We dined with them on the 25th, and during the evening I propounded an idea which had suddenly flashed upon me. Mr. Forsyth was sending his family to England during the cold weather, intending to follow himself in spring. His house, New Park, was a particularly fine one. It had been originally built by Sir Robert Montgomery when he was Judicial Commissioner. The idea was that the Lawrences and ourselves should determine to live together and boldly offer to buy Mr. Forsyth's beautiful house. The proposal was received with acclamation, and in a few weeks we were all comfortably established in New Park.

November 20.—What a ridiculous report seems to have

reached England about the invasion of the Punjab by seven thousand troops. Of course it was a canard. This disturbance on the Frontier may have given rise to it. The expedition is going on, but I grieve to say we have lost a great many men and officers already, and no one seems to know when the fighting will end. . . . We have lost about eleven officers. This morning very bad news arrived. Our poor friend Chapman, the Adjutant of the 101st, has been killed. E.[1] received a letter from him this morning, and to Sir Robert came a telegram to say he is dead. Poor E. is much cut up, as she was very fond of him. He was a good man and a true friend; we feel his loss most acutely. . . . This is only a part of the sad news we have to tell. Poor Lord Elgin is not expected to live.[2] In fact, his case was pronounced hopeless nearly a fortnight ago. . . . He is now lying at Dharmsala on the verge of the grave. I believe the place for his burial has been chosen, the steamer ordered to be in readiness for Lady Elgin, and the *pro-tem.* Governor appointed. . . .

December 20.—. . . We have had some great successes on the Frontier; on the 15th and 16th we at last advanced and killed about five hundred of the enemy. Our losses were trifling. The whole affair will be over in a short time. Sir Robert's face is recovering its calm look. He was much harassed, poor man, when the Governor-General was dying on one side and our troops were being cut up on the other.

LAHORE, *January* 3, 1864.—You are not far wrong in your estimate of Sir Robert's character. He is thoroughly kind and good. The way to gain his goodwill is to attend to your duty and let him see that you are doing so without parading the fact. He is pleased when he finds out that you admire men whom he admires, or approve of plans that he has approved. He doesn't like opposition or obstructiveness. He cannot bear a man who gives reasons why orders cannot be carried out. He likes promptness and perfect obedience. He is not an original man, but

[1] E. = my wife.

[2] Lord Elgin died at Dharmsala on the 20th November 1863, the day on which I was writing.

is very practical, and if he doesn't know how to do a thing himself he won't be long in finding some one who does know. He is not jealous of his subordinates. On the contrary, he encourages them and consults them on all manner of subjects. He is not above talking of the gravest political matters with a third-class Assistant. Sir Robert's kindness or friendliness often misleads people and makes them think he has a special regard for them. . . . Davies [1] was lunching with us to-day and talking of Sir John (Lawrence). Sir John always had a capital answer for men who howled for promotion. 'I was for six years an Assistant on four hundred rupees a month.' . . . A native merchant was comparing Sir John and Sir Robert when talking to me yesterday. He said Sir John was a 'lion man,' Sir Robert an 'angel man'; at heart both are out and out good.

The chief public event at Lahore in the early part of the year 1864 was the opening of an Industrial Exhibition, in a building specially built for the purpose in Anarkuli. This Exhibition imposed much extra work on the local Civil officers, who were placed in charge of the different departments. I am afraid I did not feel very much enthusiasm in the matter, having inherited a prejudice against 'Exhibitions' as savouring of humbug to a considerable extent. An indirect advantage was that the opening ceremony brought the principal Punjab officers to Lahore, and helped to no small extent to promote better acquaintance among them.

January 17.— . . . The State opening of the Exhibition takes place on Wednesday next, the 20th. This week is to be a regular week of tamashas.[2] A large number of Commissioners and Deputy Commissioners are collected in Lahore, with Rajas and Nawabs *ad lib.* The European visitors are principally located in a large camp in Anarkuli. The native

[1] Mr., afterwards Sir Henry, Davies.

[2] *i.e.* sights and ceremonies of various kinds.

grandees are on the plain on the north of the city. To-morrow is fixed for the grand durbar or levée for the reception of the Native Princes, etc. The Civilians have to appear in evening dress at twelve noon! A terrible go, is it not, for those whose dress suits have had much wear and tear? However, there is no help for it. Sir Robert will no doubt be resplendent in diplomatic uniform, cocked hat, gold lace, orders, etc. On Tuesday H.H. the Lieutenant-Governor gives a grand fête at Shalamár to all residents and visitors. On Wednesday the Exhibition is to be opened with all possible pomp. On Thursday come a grand review and ball. Friday, State visit to the city. Saturday, Amritsar will be illuminated. . . . Of course, cutcherry is entirely suspended, but I would rather spend the holidays shooting in the jungles than at the monster fêtes and revelries. . . .

January 20.—The Exhibition excitement is at its height. This is the opening day. The Lieutenant-Governor proceeds in grand procession from Government House at twelve o'clock, receives our address, and replies to the same from a magnificent velvet dais, marches round the building, and finally declares the Exhibition open. . . . As for the Exhibition, it is a very mild affair.

. . . To Exhibition soon after eleven; opened at twelve. Sir Robert read a good speech. . . .

Meanwhile Sir John Lawrence had arrived in India, and assumed the office of Viceroy at Calcutta.

February 5.—There seems to be no delay in filling up vacancies. Sir John knows whom to appoint, and is independent of the advice of secretaries. The papers say that Sir John looks as though he could say to every one with whom he comes in contact, 'I have the advantage of you,' and no doubt he has.

A brief summary will suffice to indicate the general current of our life at Lahore during the first four months of the year. We continued to live in New Park. Lady Montgomery left Lahore for England, for the last time, on the 8th of February—a serious loss to us and many others to whom she had been invariably most kind and hospitable. On the 26th February an heir to the Henry Lawrence baronetcy was born in New Park, who was christened Henry Hayes on the 4th April. Sad to say, he inherited his title before the year was over. He died in Ireland a few years ago, leaving several daughters but no son, and was succeeded by his uncle, Henry Waldemar Lawrence, Deputy Treasurer of the Inner Temple. Our happy home at New Park was broken up early in April. Sir Alexander and Lady Lawrence left Lahore to join their uncle, the Viceroy, at Simla. It was understood that Sir Alexander was to receive a better appointment than that of Assistant Commissioner. He was either to be an Under-Secretary in the Government of India or Superintendent of Coorg, but as his health was not of the best at the time, a long rest in the Hills was to be taken in the first instance.

The permanent Judge of the Small Cause Court at Lahore, Mr. Berkeley, was on his way out from England, and I was transferred to a similar appointment at Delhi. Major Pollock,[1] who had succeeded Mr. Forsyth as Commissioner of Lahore a few weeks previously, took New Park and its contents off our hands.

On the 5th May we left Lahore, and reached Delhi four days later, where the Deputy Commissioner, Mr. T. H. Thornton, afterwards Secretary to the Government of the Punjab and Foreign Secretary to the Government of India, gave us shelter. After a day or two we moved

[1] See p. 86.

into a somewhat gloomy-looking house just inside the Cashmere gate and close to St. James's Church. We forthwith did our best to settle down, but the task was not an easy one, as the dirt and dust of ages had been allowed to accumulate, and most of our servants and heavy baggage had still to arrive from Lahore.

I began my work in the Small Cause Court the day after reaching Delhi. It was child's play in comparison to that of the Lahore court, the people being far less given to petty litigation than in the Punjab proper. My colleague for the disposal of retrial cases heard *in banco* was the Commissioner, Colonel Hamilton, a fine old officer of notable service as Commissioner of Mooltan and elsewhere. His health was not robust, however, and he died not very long after this time. On the whole, we felt depressed enough during these early days at Delhi. Our house was indeed a sorry contrast to that which we had left behind. The heat was considerable, and increased daily. The prospect of the hot weather in Delhi was anything but cheering, and the warnings given by old inhabitants regarding possible Delhi boils did not help to lift the cloud. The congestion was, however, soon relieved in a most unexpected manner. On the tenth day from our arrival at Delhi I received a telegram from the Secretary of the Government offering me the Small Cause Court at Simla, which had suddenly fallen vacant owing to the serious illness of the Judge, Mr. Murphy. This changed the aspect of affairs. It filled us with energy; we immediately set about the packing of our effects, and after gigantic efforts we managed to leave Delhi for Simla the following evening.

SIR R. MONTGOMERY TO G. R. ELSMIE.

LAHORE, *May* 22.

MY DEAR ELSMIE,—I doubt not you were much surprised to get an offer of Simla. But when I went over the list with Davies[1] I could not find any name who I thought would do the work of the Small Cause Court so well as yourself. You combine firmness and a knowledge of the law with consideration, and that is required at Simla, also *tact*, which you showed at Murree. And I am glad for your sake and Mrs. Elsmie's that the turn of the wheel has taken you there. But you are to consider that your merits alone get you the place. Simla is full of important people, and there is none so *shrewd* amongst them all as Sir John Lawrence. I do not think he would like you to take part in theatricals. They are hardly fitting the grave sobriety of a Judge, and I shall be glad to hear you eschew them as an actor.[2] . . .—Yours sincerely,

R. MONTGOMERY.

P.S.—I should like occasionally to hear how you get on with your work.

Apparently I must have thought that the Financial Commissioner, Mr. Donald M'Leod, had helped to bring about my transfer to Simla, as I find a letter from him of 27th May in which he says:—

'I was rejoiced to hear of your appointment, but beyond partially prophesying it I had nothing to say to it. You will find it a troublesome post, I fancy, in some respects. But I believe that nothing is required but strict impartiality and a conciliatory demeanour to ensure success, and I shall confidently look forward to your fully attaining it.'

The journey from Delhi to Simla in 1864 was a tedious

[1] The Secretary to Government.

[2] This expression of opinion, after what had taken place at Murree in the previous year, was far from a pleasant surprise. However, I refused, as in duty bound, all invitations to take part in theatricals at Simla.

process as compared to that of to-day, when it can be done by rail in less than twenty-four hours. Two nights of hard travel in a carriage brought us to Kalka at the foot of the Hills. Thence we were carried in jampans four long stages, arriving at our destination on the morning of the fourth day. Simla hotels were then of the most miserable kind. One night in a wretched tumble-down building in the heart of the bazaar sufficed to drive us into the first vacant house we heard of. This was Annandale Lodge, on Peterhof Hill, not far from the Viceroy's. Immediately on getting into Annandale Lodge I had to hurry over to Peterhof[1] to attend a Viceregal levée. Three or four days later we were invited to dine with the Governor-General.

SIMLA, *May* 30.—We dined at Government House on Saturday evening. We were the only guests. The Governor-General, the Lawrences,[2] the Impeys,[3] two A.D.C.'s and ourselves and Dr. Hathaway made the party. Sir John is a fine-looking man.[4] . . . His large frame gives him a most commanding appearance. Judging from what I saw the other night, I perceive in him a supreme indifference for the conventionalities of society. . . . He wanted to read the newspapers, and that nothing should interrupt him. This seems to be combined with great kindness all the same. . . . Sir Charles Trevelyan[5] is a complete contrast to Sir John. E. and I were looking at a cricket match last night. Sir Charles came up and asked Captain Impey to introduce me to him. He at once commenced a conversation which lasted nearly an hour, for we rode home together. He begged me to introduce him to E., to

[1] The residence of the Viceroy.

[2] *i.e.* our co-sharers in New Park, Sir Alexander and Lady Lawrence.

[3] The Military Secretary and his wife.

[4] I had never seen Sir John Lawrence before.

[5] Then Finance Minister.

whom he was very civil. He talked on all manner of subjects from Haileybury to the Christianising of India. He regrets the abolition, though he would have been glad to see the improvement of Haileybury. Sir Charles began his career in the Civil Service, and I believe Sir John was his Assistant at Delhi thirty years ago. Lady Trevelyan is rather formidable in appearance and manner. She is a sister of Lord Macaulay.

My immediate superior at Simla was Colonel Richard Lawrence, youngest brother of the Viceroy, who had resigned the office of Military Secretary to the Punjab Government in order to become Deputy Commissioner of the favourite hill station and Superintendent of the neighbouring Hill States. The pleasure of serving under Colonel Lawrence was to me one of the chief attractions of my change of appointment. My work was troublesome but not very hard: much of it consisted of the trial of Civil suits in which European residents were involved. One of the first cases which I remember having to deal with was a claim for damages brought by a Simla house proprietor against Mr. (afterwards Sir Clive) Bayley, the Home Secretary, who had taken a house called Ellerslie on the strength of written descriptions forwarded to him in Calcutta. On reaching Simla Mr. Bayley found the house to have many defects and to come greatly short of what he had been led to expect. He declined to occupy it, or to be in any way responsible. The case was tried with the aid of a small body of assessors, of whom Colonel (afterwards General Sir Richard) Strachey and General Tytler (previously Superintendent of the Andamans) were members, and the claim was dismissed.

On the 30th July my predecessor in office, Mr. Murphy,

who had been ill for many weeks, died. In former times he had served as a clerk under Sir John Lawrence when Collector of Delhi. Sir John took much interest in his old subordinate. A few days before the death, by the Viceroy's special request, I was deputed to go to the dying man's bedside and to make his will. The document was submitted to Sir John for approval, who thought a codicil should be added. This was accordingly done, the Viceroy's private surgeon, Dr. Farquhar, going with me to Mr. Murphy's house. Sir John Lawrence himself attended the funeral on the 31st.

Towards the end of August Sir Alexander Lawrence accompanied his uncle, Colonel Richard Lawrence, on a trip into the interior. Lady Lawrence remained behind at Government House. On the 29th August I was under orders to proceed a short way out of Simla to meet the Raja of Nábha, who was coming from the plains to pay his respects to the Viceroy. According to custom, the Nabha vakil[1] was to call at my house to go with me to meet his master. The vakil was late in arrival. When at length he came into our verandah, he said there could be no official reception of the Raja that day as a great calamity had occurred, viz. the death by accident of the Viceroy's nephew, Sir Alexander Lawrence. Alas! the news was too true. Two days previously, at a distance of several marches from Simla, Sir Alexander had ridden on ahead of his uncle, along the narrow hill-path. When Colonel Lawrence reached a certain point in the road, he saw his nephew's little dog sitting transfixed, as it were, on the brink of a chasm. A wooden gallery which

[1] Agent.

had run along the face of a rock had been carried away. At the bottom of a deep abyss lay the motionless bodies of the rider and his horse. Sir Alexander's body was recovered, not without much difficulty. An Armenian wood-merchant, Mr. Arathoon, well known at the time in the Punjab, happened to be in the neighbourhood. He did all he could to help Colonel Lawrence in the most trying and difficult task he had before him. Eventually, after a series of forced marches, Colonel Lawrence arrived in Simla with the body of his nephew. No news of what had happened had preceded him. Colonel Lawrence broke the intelligence to his brother, the Viceroy. The latter broke it to the widow. In the forenoon Captain Impey and I went to the cemetery to choose a place for the grave, and at 4 P.M. the burial took place. I was asked to be one of the pall-bearers, and to help to carry the poor fellow from the gate of the cemetery to the grave. A more trying day I never passed through. Thus I lost one of my dearest friends and companions, a man of a most gentle and loving nature, who had troops of friends, and, I am sure, not a single enemy in the world.

On Sunday, the 4th September, Bishop Cotton, preaching in Christ Church, Simla, referred to the 'sudden plunge' which had brought so much sorrow to many of his congregation. A year or two later the preacher was destined to perish himself by a sudden fall into the river Ganges.

Sir Herbert Edwardes was Commissioner of the Ambala Division in 1864. He lived for most of the summer with the Governor-General at Simla. Sir Herbert was an eminently satisfactory officer to serve under.

Appeals from my orders in important civil and criminal cases lay to him, and I cannot remember any instance in which he did not take a highly sensible and a broad view of the points in dispute. Sir Herbert had been Commissioner of Peshawur when the treaties of 1855 and 1857 were made with the Amir Dost Muhammad Khan, and to him was mainly due the credit of those important agreements. I was naturally anxious to learn whether the account of the origin and completion of the treaties which I had given in my little book had met with the approval of Sir Herbert.

Sir Herbert Edwardes to G. R. Elsmie.

Kussowlie, *November* 14, 1864.

. . . I have never seen the Epitome of Cabul correspondence of which you speak! If you have a copy to spare I should like one much, as I keep up my interest in our alliance, which I proposed in 1854, and brought about in 1855, a fact which, perhaps, you, like most officers in the Punjab and a portion of the public, know not of.[1] It was quite against the opinion of Sir John even, who declared it *would never do any good to us.* But Lord Dalhousie adopted my views and authorised me to carry them out; which I did, and the *Treaty was the result*, with what benefit to India let 1857-58 declare! Now see if you can find anything of this in Aitchison's Treaties; and then learn a lesson in the truth of history from practical life. Not that it is much of Aitchison's fault, for the Punjab Government Office told him no better. When I told this to Sir Robert at Lahore in 1862-63, he (the Lieutenant-Governor) said, 'You don't say so!' However, I *do* say so; and I hold the proof in my possession under the handwriting of Lords Dalhousie and Canning,

[1] I knew it well, for had I not read all the original documents, which showed in the clearest way that Sir Herbert was the real author of the treaties.

and Sir John Lawrence. . . . If you will refer to the Punjab Reports of the period, you will find the Treaty spoken of impersonally, as a policy, which was thought of and conceived and brought about, but apparently it fell from the clouds, for it is not said *who* did it. Excuse this dissertation; but wrongs bubble up long after they have been forgiven.—With kind regards, believe me, yours sincerely,

HERBERT B. EDWARDES.

SIR HERBERT EDWARDES TO G. R. ELSMIE.

KUSSOWLEE, *December* 30, 1864.

I have despatched the little book you lent me this day to you at Simla, and hope it will reach you safely. It is excellently done, and shows a just discrimination of the comparative worth of items of political intelligence. . . . It interested me greatly by recalling past events, and I wish I had got a copy of it. I will try and get one from Lahore. . . .—With our united kind regards and sincere Xmas and New Year wishes for you both, I am, yours sincerely,

HERBERT B. EDWARDES.

Towards the end of October the Viceroy and the principal members of the Government of India, the Commander-in-Chief, and his staff returned to the plains. We gradually settled down to a very quiet winter life in a hill station. Very few of our friends remained, but I may mention some of them, Colonel and Mrs. Dick Lawrence, Captain (afterwards Sir William) and Mrs. Elles, Mrs. Scott, a venerable widow lady with a wonderful talent for music. Mrs. Scott was sister of Colonel Ouseley, our professor of Persian at Haileybury. Her piano playing was most charming, her power of improvising quite unrivalled. During the winter, I don't suppose that more than one house in twenty was occupied;

public and private entertainments practically ceased. The monotony was varied by one or two short shooting excursions into the interior. It was a very happy time. Work was light, the days short, and there was much leisure for reading.

CHAPTER VII

DEPUTY COMMISSIONER, JULLUNDUR

1865—1868

IN the beginning of 1865 Sir Robert Montgomery was succeeded as Lieutenant-Governor by his son-in-law, Mr. Donald M'Leod. The year is a memorable one in the history of my official career, in that, after having been seven years in India, I found myself appointed to the charge of a district. I was far from being very fortunate in this matter. Many officers in the Punjab had become acting Deputy Commissioners in three or four years after entering the Commission, but, by the time I joined, promotion had been blocked, and advancement was slow.

During the winter months we had had the unexpected excitement of a possible transfer to the Central Provinces. Charles Bernard had become Secretary to Mr. Temple, the Chief Commissioner at Nagpore. Mr. Temple, no doubt at Bernard's instance, applied for my services, but, after great delay, his application was refused by the Viceroy, who thought the 'drain on the Punjab staff had already been too great.' My disappointment was keen at the time, but consolation followed on the receipt in the month of March of the following telegram from the Secretary to the Punjab Government:—

You are to officiate as Deputy Commissioner of Jullundur; join as soon as possible without waiting to be relieved.

The contrast between the work of a Judge of a Small Cause Court and of a Deputy Commissioner of a district was very great in 1865. In the former post the business was almost entirely judicial, and consisted mainly in disposing of the civil suits set down for trial each day. Before and after office hours, which seldom exceeded four or five, I was my own master. But at Jullundur, in charge of a territory of, say, one thousand square miles in extent, and containing more than half a million of inhabitants, the threads of the administration of every department met in my hands [1] as the head of the district. Judicial work (criminal, civil, and revenue) was overwhelming. I found that my predecessor had left about three months of judicial work in arrears. I had forthwith to attempt the delivery of a lock-up containing many prisoners accused of dacoity, robbery, theft, etc., of the graver descriptions of which none of my subordinates had jurisdiction to dispose. A file of some two or three hundred civil appeals from Native judges throughout the district had to be faced, while new

[1] The following sketch of the duties of a district officer in the Punjab in the sixties, written by me a few years ago, is perhaps worthy of reproduction, as indicating the system of government then prevailing:—

The chief representative of Government in each district was, and still is, a Civil officer called the Deputy Commissioner, a man of all trades in very truth. He was the Head Magistrate with power to imprison for two years, the principal Civil Judge with power to decide Civil claims of unlimited value. He was the Collector of all the Government revenue, the rent of the village lands, the excise duties on spirits and opium, and all taxes and cesses, the controller of the stamp duties, the custodian of all Government cash, the paymaster of all salaries, pensions, and such like, throughout his district, the Superintendent of all Government schools, the chief Jailer, responsible for the safe custody and proper treatment of some three or four hundred prisoners, the maker and repairer of roads and bridges and Government buildings, the head of the Municipal Councils in the larger towns, the chief manager of poorhouses and dispensaries, the conductor of public worship on Sundays at headquarters, where the European community was too small to warrant the appointment of a Government chaplain! This is but a mere

appeals were presented daily. Revenue appeals relating to tenancy, rent, etc., were almost equally numerous. The Police department was under the District Superintendent of Police, but he was bound to report all serious occurrences to the Deputy Commissioner daily by word of mouth, and to give him a detail of the measures he proposed to adopt. The Educational department was heavy. There were many village schools throughout the district, with larger and more important schools in the big towns. My predecessor had been one of the pioneers of female education in the Punjab, a branch which required very delicate handling. Borne down as I was by heavy judicial arrears, I fear I had little energy to spare for this, at that time somewhat unpromising field. Another department deserves mention, that of the charge of the Municipalities throughout the district, which included the improvement, the cleansing, the watering, the taxing of the chief towns. Again, with

outline of a Deputy Commissioner's duties, but sufficient perhaps to give an idea of their variety and scope.

As a staff of assistants, a Deputy Commissioner had an European Assistant of some years' experience, and a young Civilian 'learning his business.' Besides these he had a large native staff, native magistrates, sub-collectors, writers, and clerks, police officers without number, schoolmasters, village officers, and such like, scattered throughout the district.

The immediate superior of a Deputy Commissioner or district officer was the Commissioner, who controlled three or four districts. As a Court of original jurisdiction, a Commissioner tried all heavy criminal cases, murders, highway robberies, and the like. Then as an Appellate Judge, appeals lay to him from orders passed by the Deputy Commissioners in all criminal, civil, revenue, and other cases. There were ten Commissioners, the headquarters of the principal of them being Delhi, Ambala, Amritsar, Lahore, Peshawur. Over the Commissioners were two high officers stationed at Lahore: the Judicial Commissioner (nowadays represented by a Chief Court of five or six judges), the final court of appeal in all criminal and civil cases; the Financial Commissioner, the controlling and appellate authority in all matters connected with revenue, taxation, and such like.

At the head of all was the Lieutenant-Governor.

the exception of the Grand Trunk Road, between the Sutlej and Beas rivers, all the district roads and bridges were under the charge of a local committee of which the Deputy Commissioner was the President. The collection of land revenue, the excise revenue, the income-tax, was managed by the Deputy Commissioner, under whose supervision the cash was kept and the accounts supervised. I need not enlarge further on the subject of the cares of a Deputy Commissioner in 1865. It is sufficient to say, that at the present day the holders of that office have been relieved of a great portion of their appellate work, District Judges and Judicial Assistants having been appointed. Notwithstanding the weight of the burden, however, I have no doubt that, during the whole of my Indian career, no work which has fallen to my lot has interested me more than that of a District officer.

JULLUNDUR, *April* 20.—I shall have to give up attempting to write letters till I have got my work properly in hand. Somehow or other the days slip by, and I find no time even to write my diary. My hand is so out of practice at district work that I cannot please myself at all. I am at office all day, and I come home feeling that I ought to have stayed there all night.

July 16.—My days are all alike. I get up in the morning as soon after five as I can tear myself out of bed. I then go out for a short ride to the city or jail and come home about seven. I then open my English official letters and do odds and ends of work till half-past eight, and during this hour and a half I am almost sure to be interrupted by a visit from some native who wants something. At half-past eight I betake myself to my bath, and at nine we breakfast. At ten I am in office; there I remain always till six, sometimes till half-past six or seven. After that I come home and go for a drive. At eight we dine, and we go to bed between nine and ten pretty well tired out. Now, you will admit that it is almost impossible for any one who is not a Hercules to be fit for much after dinner, after a day of grind and worry. . . . The heat has a great deal to do with it, of course. We have had a very long, trying hot weather. The first tolerable fall of rain came down two nights ago and has refreshed us considerably. Before that we were roasted. . . .

Q. still rules over us from an elevation of 6000 feet above the sea-level. He is a man whom it is impossible to help liking to a certain extent. He is very good, very conscientious, very hard-working, and, I should say, clever in a sense. He has, however, spent most of his time in one station, and there he got into a groove from which it is impossible seemingly for him to get out again. He is decidedly old school and behind the age, and I don't think he is a good lawyer or a judge. Moreover, he will take nothing for granted, and in his extreme desire to do everything perfectly he suspects flaws where he does not see them and where none exist. The consequence is that he gives a good deal of trouble and useless work. The Deputy Commissioner of Hoshiarpore is a little ball of fire and pepper, who generally makes a point of fighting with his superiors. He is furious at Q. He wrote me a letter the other day, detailing his grievances, and finished it by saying that 'a more gentlemanly man he had never seen, but a more incompetent officer he had never served under.' . . . We all want wisdom and knowledge. Every day do I feel the truth of the maxim that 'Knowledge is power.'

July 30.—Q. is a very good hard-working man, very anxious to do what is right, but not very well versed in law. He prefers deciding a case according to what he thinks ought to be the law rather than according to what is in reality the law. A predilection to eccentricity of that sort is, as you can imagine, sometimes productive of a good deal of annoyance to his subordinates who have attempted, as they are bound to do, to stick to beaten tracks. Colonel Lake (his predecessor) was rather fond of amateur legislation. On one occasion he had made some proposal to Cust (who was at that time officiating

Judicial Commissioner) involving a departure from the law. Cust began his reply in something like the following strain: 'Sir, I have the honour to inform you that neither you nor I nor the Lieutenant-Governor have the power to make the law, that function is vested in the Legislative Council of the Governor-General.'

September 19.—This is the month of September. Civil courts closed. I do not find that it is a month of rest as I hoped it would be. I begin to think that I was a fool to wish to be a Deputy Commissioner. The post is one in which, work as you like, you will always find that plenty remains to be done. In truth the field is unlimited, and its extent sometimes makes my head reel when I contemplate my own inability to cope with the task. I am somewhat in the blues, however, and indeed I have been greatly dissatisfied and disappointed with myself ever since I came to Jullundur. I did not begin fair, and I have allowed the heat and the (for me) extraordinary work to break my spirit somewhat. . . . I had a letter from Forsyth dated Ballater, August 10, by last mail. He says he believes the Punjab system of overwork is a great mistake. I don't know whether I have been overworked or not, but this I know, that since I came to Jullundur I have done nothing else. I have not read a single book. I have written the most miserable scraps of letters. I have not played racquets. I have not ridden about as I used to do. I think I have miscalculated my powers. I thought I could soon get a district into order, but I find the task an impossibility, and I begin to agree with Forsyth and to vote the Punjab system a miserable economical dodge and a gigantic mistake.

I have put in these desponding extracts to show the state of things which in those days used sometimes to produce what was called 'a Punjab head.'

October 5.—I have got rid of my arrears at last, but I still find that I have more to do than I can well manage. I fancy I should make better speed of it if I took things in a quieter way.

Unfortunately I cannot help taking on at times. I am therefore often discomfited.

October 22.—At last I really have got my work under control. I can hardly understand the sensation of rising from my chair at 4 P.M., feeling that I have a clear file. Ever since the first of this month I have been actually able to play racquets for an hour almost every evening. Throughout the whole of the hot weather I took hardly any exercise at all, the consequence of which was that I got flabby in mind and body.

Towards the end of October, just as I had cleared off the heavy arrears left by my predecessor, I received an intimation from Government that I should soon be called upon to give up the officiating Deputy Commissionership to Major Edward Paske, a senior officer who was expected to return from furlough shortly. This was a great and unexpected blow, but it had to be borne with due meekness. Major Paske arrived and took over charge on the 14th November. The prospect brightened somewhat on the 23rd November, when Mr. Forsyth also arrived from England. He had been transferred as Commissioner from Lahore to Jullundur, and he forthwith took over charge from his *locum tenens*. Mr. Forsyth took up his abode with us, as there was no house available for him in the station. Soon after this I was appointed to be his personal assistant in order to help him in clearing off heavy arrears in the Commissioner's Appellate Court My chief work consisted in preparing English abstracts of civil appeals which had been tried by Native judges. As personal assistant I accompanied the Commissioner on a pleasant march through part of the Jullundur and Hoshiarpore districts. And so the year came to an end.

The beginning of 1866 found us at Jullundur waiting

developments. In February, in consequence of the transfer to another district of Major Paske and also that of another senior officer who succeeded him, I again became officiating Deputy Commissioner. The district work was now in order, and merely required steady daily attention to prevent the accumulation of arrears. Mr. Forsyth continued as Commissioner. He and I thoroughly understood each other and each other's ways of working; so no friction arose.

As I had had no leave of any sort for upwards of four years, it was determined that I should take three months' privilege leave to Simla during the worst part of the hot weather. We accordingly secured a small house called Pine Cottage situated in Native territory at the extreme end of Chota Simla. My wife and children started from Jullundur for Simla in the middle of May. I followed a fortnight later.

We went a good deal into society. The Viceroy, Sir John Lawrence, had now been joined by Lady Lawrence and his two eldest daughters. Mr. Maine was the Legal Member of Council. Mr. Massey had succeeded Sir Charles Trevelyan as Finance Member. Mr. Noble Taylor was Member for Madras. The Commander-in-Chief was Sir William Mansfield, who, with Lady Mansfield, lived at Woodville in Chota Simla. Colonel Richard Lawrence, after having acted for a time as Resident at Nepal, had returned to Simla as Deputy Commissioner. Colonel Stewart, afterwards Field-Marshal Sir Donald Stewart, was Deputy Adjutant-General of the Army. Captain W. K. Elles was a Deputy Assistant Adjutant-General. He and Mrs. Elles lived in Westfield, the house immediately above ours. We saw them almost daily. It was during the summer of 1866 that the trial by court-martial of a military officer, who had been aide-de-camp to the Commander-in-Chief, took place. The case created a great sensation. The President of the General Court-Martial was Sir James Brind, a distinguished Artillery officer. The scene of the trial was the old theatre, close to the racquet-court, below the church and bazaar. I attended the proceedings with considerable regularity. The official prosecutor was Captain Elles, while the accused was defended by Mr. W. Tayler, formerly Commissioner of Patna, and Major Malleson, author of *The Red Pamphlet* and many other books.

Some account may be given of the recreations of Simla society at this time. Racquets were played in the old court, which was subsequently turned into a market. Croquet had become very popular, and was played for the most part on earthen or gravel courts. Enthusiasts would go down to Annandale and play without boundaries on the turf there. As a general rule, three players played on each side. Mallets and balls were heavy, but hoops were wide, seven or eight inches at least. Sir John Lawrence, Sir William Mansfield, Dr. John Murray, Mr. Alex. Monteath, Colonel Donald Stewart, were all keen players. Badminton and tennis were unknown.

Amateur theatricals flourished. As I had gone to Simla on leave, I was under no restrictions in regard to acting. My début took place at a private charade party given at the Mythe by Mr. and Mrs. Whitley Stokes. One of the words to be acted was Nelson. For the first syllable the scene from *The Old Curiosity Shop*, in which Mrs. Jarley instructs little Nell to describe the figures, was chosen. The part of Mrs. Jarley was allotted to Major Allen Johnson,[1] an inimitable actor, but at the last moment he received bad news from home and was obliged to give it up. I was called upon to take Major Johnson's place. The part of little Nell was taken by Miss Agnes Norman, afterwards Lady Newmarch, who was certainly one of the very best actresses of impromptu charades I have ever seen. The 'Waxworks' seemed to bring down the house. The 'figures' were represented by some of the best known ladies and gentlemen in Simla. Mr. Edward Lushington, the Financial Secretary, was 'Jasper Packlemerton.' One of the Miss Durands, 'Charlotte Corday'; Mrs. Grey, 'Mary, Queen of Scots,' and so on. Mr. Maine, the Legal member, was one of the audience. He was so much impressed by the success of the waxwork scene, that he determined to give an entertainment at his house, consisting of a succession of scenes from Dickens. A conference of sympathisers was held, with the result that a few weeks later 'Bob Sawyer's Supper-party,' 'A Scene in the Portsmouth Theatre,' from *Nicholas Nickleby*; 'Pickwick and the Middle-aged Lady,' 'Dick Swiveller and the Marchioness,' and others were given most successfully at Mr. Maine's house.

Subsequently a similar performance took place at Woodville, the residence of Sir William and Lady Mansfield, 'Mrs. Gamp's Tea-party' being substituted for the 'Scene in the Portsmouth Theatre.' The part of Mrs. Gamp was taken by Mrs. Jim Harris, a splendid actress of middle-aged parts. Her performance of Mrs. Raddle, Mrs. Vincent Crummles, and Mrs. Gamp are indelibly

[1] Afterwards General Sir Allen Johnson, K.C.B., Military Secretary at the India Office.

impressed on my memory. In the 'Tea-party' scene I had the honour, as Mrs. Prig, of supporting Mrs. Harris, as Sarah Gamp, and I well remember the sensation caused in the audience when I snapped my fingers in Mrs. Gamp's face, and, notwithstanding her ample proportions, declared that I didn't believe there was 'no such a person as Mrs. 'Arris.'

The end of the season brought a temporary change in my official life. I was appointed to act for two or three weeks as Under-Secretary to the Government of India in the Home Department, to take the place of Mr. Monteath, who had been appointed to officiate as Postmaster-General. My first impressions of secretariat work, as written down at the time, are of somewhat roseate hue, but further experience convinced me that the charge of a district, with all its varied responsibilities, was far more satisfying as a sphere of work than the preparation of notes on files of papers for submission for the orders of higher authorities.

Meanwhile Colonel M'Neile,[1] the permanent Deputy Commissioner of Jullundur, had returned to his district from the Central Provinces, where he had been officiating as Commissioner for nearly two years. Early in November the Government asked me whether I was prepared to go to the Frontier as Deputy Commissioner of Bannu. The journey was a formidable one in those days for a man with a wife and four young children. However, I accepted the offer and we made a start from Simla. We halted at Jullundur, which lay in our route, but we hadn't been there more than an hour when a telegram reached me saying that the then Deputy Commissioner of Bannu

[1] My former master at Loodiana.

had changed his mind, had given up his leave, and the district would not be available for me. The Commissioner of Jullundur, Mr. Forsyth, applied for my services as Assistant Commissioner there, and Government agreed. We were obliged to take a house in cantonments, none being available in the Civil lines. Very early in the following year Colonel M'Neile was appointed to be Commissioner of Delhi, and I became for the fourth time officiating Deputy Commissioner of Jullundur. I well remember the hearty way in which Colonel M'Neile wished me good-bye and every kind of success. He was what the world would call an austere man, but he evoked a strong personal regard on my part. I never saw him again, and in many respects I have never met his equal. He died prematurely at Dalhousie in 1870, the loss to the service being very great.

That the Deputy Commissioner should live in cantonments three and a half miles distant from his cutcherry was not an ideal arrangement. However, there was no help for it. We had a good many useful horses, and when necessary I went to the Civil lines three times a day. Moreover, proximity to the Military authorities was advantageous in many respects. Troublesome questions could often be settled verbally. We lived next door to Captain Jerome, the Brigade-Major. We were intimate friends, and when cholera made its appearance later in the year, there was no friction between the Civil and Military authorities in regard to quarantine regulations, location of cholera camps, and such like knotty matters. The monotony of station life was often varied by trips into camp, *e.g.* early in February I accompanied the Commissioner on a march to Philour, where we met the Lieutenant-Governor's camp and with it marched back into Jullundur

Thence we went on to Kapurthala and to the west bank of the Beas at Wazirbholar, the latter place being the boundary of my district.

March 20.—. . . In India everything and every person requires constant supervision. If you do not watch your clothes, they will become moth-eaten. If you do not look after your furniture, it will be eaten by white ants. If you do not look after your servants, they will rob you and cheat you and lie to you. Sometimes we get quite disheartened. There are crises of disagreeables. Things seem to go on straight for a week or two and then everything takes a cross turn. Your cook spoils everything he touches. The cowman steals or waters the milk; the washerman beats your English table-linen into shreds, and makes you cold with anger. Your bearer breaks your lamp chimneys by the dozen; the horses go lame, the tailor strikes for more wages, and every servant becomes more or less cross-grained and irritating. You will imagine from this that we are passing through a crisis. I am glad to say, however, we are not.

On the 22nd March, Ranbir Singh, the Maharaja of Cashmere, encamped in the Jullundur cantonment, on his way to the Kumbh Mela at Hurdwar. The duty of receiving his Highness fell on me, the Commissioner being absent.

D.—Got up as soon as it was light. Went out to meet the Maharaja. The big man came in about 7.30. Arrangements were fairly satisfactory The military turned out in great force. Major Mercer, Deputy Commissioner of Sialkote, was the British officer in personal attendance on the Maharaja. In the evening to the Maharaja's durbar. The Maharaja improves on acquaintance; he can be very pleasant. He seemed very pleased to see Major Grant,[1] asked him all manner of questions.

[1] Major James Augustus Grant, of African fame, who at that time was stationed in Jullundur with his Gurkha regiment.

About a month later it was reported to me one morning that the Maharaja had driven rapidly in a post-carriage through the Jullundur district during the night, fleeing from the outbreak of cholera among the pilgrims on the banks of the Ganges.

D. April 19, *Good Friday.*—At 6 A.M. went to church, came home, received a note from Kelly (a police officer) telling me of the outbreak of cholera among the Hurdwar pilgrims. Went down to the Civil lines at once and made arrangements regarding quarantine, etc. Met Jerome (the Brigade-Major) on my return, went to a meeting of the Cantonment Committee. Wrote letters to Forsyth (the Commissioner) and Thornton (the Secretary to Government) about the cholera.

D. April 20.—A day of telegrams and interruptions and notes. All manner of arrangements necessary to stem the tide of cholera rushing up from Hurdwar.

D. Sunday, April 21.—Jerome and I to the quarantine camp on the Hoshiarpore road.

D. April 22.—Before breakfast went to camp on Hoshiar pore road and to jail. Cholera increasing at former. In the evening Jerome and I to the camp on the Beyn river.

D. April 24.—Cholera still all-engrossing.

T. H. THORNTON, SECRETARY TO GOVERNMENT, PUNJAB, TO G. R. ELSMIE.

LAHORE, *April* 23.

Many thanks for your letter informing us of the arrangements made for the prevention of the spread of cholera. They appear to have been excellent, and, as yet, attended with the best results, all seem to have done their duty well. Up to last night not a single case had occurred on this side of the Beas, but all arrangements have been made at Amritsar and Lahore to protect the city and cantonments from the introduction of the disease. This is the first occasion in India, I believe, in which cholera has been generally recognised as a contagious and infectious disease, and it will be a great triumph if we succeed in grappling with it on this principle. I am glad to say that, from accounts received this morning by telegram, the number of deaths of pilgrims in the Ambala *district* is decreasing. . . .

April 27.—We have had a regular fight with cholera. Fancy about three millions of people (the population of London or of Scotland) meeting together at the great Ganges fair at Hurdwar; imagine their hatching cholera and then dispersing in living streams to the four winds. Our task has been to weed out the sick from the crowd, and to cure them, if possible. The curing, however, has been a secondary consideration; the important part of the task has been to destroy everything connected with the disease, by burning bodies and clothes. The first cholera case in this district occurred on Saturday last, just a week ago. Since then we have had about one hundred deaths among the pilgrims. As yet we have kept the pestilence out of the city and cantonments, and I trust the worst is over. The worst has not been very bad, but sufficiently so to show that it might have been very serious. . . . The rush of pilgrims is now abated. In a few days more the last of them will have passed through the district. You can understand that I have felt a good deal hunted. Telegrams and letters coming in constantly. Throughout all, the uncomfortable feeling that perhaps we might have done something more and taken more precautions.[1]

Promotion in the Punjab was at this time almost at a deadlock. The pay of district officers was very poor in comparison to that in the Regulation provinces. Many of my contemporaries in Lower Bengal and the North-Western Provinces were infinitely better off in respect to salary than I was. I had been made a second-class Assistant Commissioner on 600 rupees per

[1] See p. 134.

mensem in 1863, a first-class Assistant Commissioner on 700 rupees in the following year. There I stuck with many others for years. With acting allowance as Deputy Commissioner I only drew a little over 800 rupees per mensem net, and it was almost impossible to make ends meet. I mention this partly in order that Punjab officers of the present day may be thankful for the improvement which has since taken place.

Though the Commissioner, Mr. Forsyth, and I were great friends, both privately and officially, we by no means agreed on every point. On the contrary, Mr. Forsyth often thought I was too much the slave of strict legal procedure in some departments of my work. His official youth had been passed at a time when the Punjab was governed in a more patriarchal system than had prevailed since the introduction of the codes. During the hot weather of 1867 Mr. Forsyth ruled his division from Dharmsala, the headquarters of the Kangra district.

T. D. FORSYTH, COMMISSIONER, TO G. R. ELSMIE.

DHARMSALA, *June* 30.

. . . You must not *worrit* yourself too much because your Commissioner gives you a mild touch up now and then. I don't think I am ever very severe, and certainly am far less so than I used to be, or than some other Commissioners are. But as regards Amla,[1] I feel it very necessary to keep a tight hand myself over them, and advise others to do the same. That legal precision which in judicial matters is most commendable, and which very properly would lead one to acquit nine guilty men rather than convict one innocent man, does not apply to the executive side. The Chief Court have lately called upon me

[1] Native vernacular clerks.

to explain the delay in transmission of cases. I have, therefore, come down heavily on my own office. It is very true that if I would listen to them I could always get one hundred excellent excuses why such and such a thing is not done. But my answer is, 'I want the order obeyed and not excuses.' . . . A Commissioner, and a Deputy Commissioner too, should be a bit of a tiger. I have acquired confidence in overcoming obstacles by experience, and have sometimes been surprised at my own success. . . . I recollect last year C—— raised a perfect mountain of difficulty on one subject, till at last I could stand it no longer, and got savage, and then I found his mountain melt away. Similarly with native Amla. They have one hundred objections and two hundred good reasons for not doing a thing when ordered. But if they see you are determined, and are not inclined to be too lenient, they will take good care to obey orders. There is evil in becoming *too* legal or inelastic, and whatever one may be on the bench, certainly on the executive side a degree of sukhti[1] is necessary to be a vigorous and efficient ruler. If you won't think me very irreverent, I should exemplify —— as the pattern of a gentle, good, kind, and *fearfully inefficient* ruler.

I don't mean to pay you such a bad compliment as to liken you to him, and have merely instanced him as the extreme of excellence and ——!![2] M—— had more of the shaitán[3] about him, and got his work done far better. This is a long homily, more given in self-defence than as a lesson to others; perhaps, too, it has been prompted by your presenting the legal aspect for my inspection. Law is all very well, but often 'summum jus summa injuria.'

However, I will end as I began. Don't think too much of the patriarchal warnings of your ancient Commissioner. You are never likely to be told, as I have been, that 'I was a d——d Assistant,' or that 'I was not worth my salt.' On the whole, I think Commissioners are much to be pitied. Their acts and orders are mercilessly criticised by their juniors, and generally

[1] Hardness. [2] *Sic* in original. [3] Devil.

they are voted to be unfit for their post! It's the penalty we all pay for enjoying a good position.—Yours very sincerely,

T. D. Forsyth.

Our quiet life at Jullundur in the hot weather of 1867 was unexpectedly broken in the middle of July by the arrival of the following telegram: 'You have been appointed by the Viceroy a member of the Commission of inquiry on railway management, of which Colonel Hodgson is President. Proceed to Lahore at once, making over charge to Mr. Harcourt.' I started the same night, and sat the following day at the preliminary meeting of the Commission. Colonel Hodgson was an officer of the Engineers, holding at that time the appointment of Public Works Secretary to the North-West Government. The second member was myself. The third was Captain Filgate, an Engineer from Madras. Both officers were strangers to me. The subject of the inquiry was the many alleged cases of mismanagement, amounting in some instances to dishonesty and fraud on the part of the Agent of the Sind, Punjab, and Delhi Railway Company. The line was guaranteed by Government to pay its shareholders at least 5 per cent. Roughly, some £50,000 per annum represented a 5 per cent. dividend on the shareholders' capital. The line at this time was making about a ½ per cent. profit, so that Government had to find some £45,000 to make up the 5 per cent. A condition of the guarantee was, that if the profits exceeded the amount necessary for the payment of a 5 per cent. dividend, the excess should be divided equally between the shareholders and the Government. But in 1867, no matter how good and careful the management of the railway should be, there was not the least chance of the profits amounting to more than a small portion of the required 5 per cent. dividend. It was alleged that the Agent, and some of his subordinates, seeing how hopeless it was to attempt to increase the dividend of their shareholders above the 5 per cent., were guilty of reckless and fraudulent mismanagement, knowing that the Government could be the only loser. For instance, if first-class management could produce £10,000 profit, the Government contribution would be reduced to 4 per cent. instead of 4½, but the shareholders would get nothing more than their 5 per cent. The inquiry was expected to last some three or four weeks at the outside, but alas, it dragged its weary length along till the 25th October, on which day I at last got back to Jullundur. The delay was due to many causes, the chief being the peculiar temperament of the President of the Commission, who was quite inexperienced in the conduct of a quasi-judicial inquiry. Nothing could have been more trying than those months at Lahore proved to be. Heat was excessive, cholera was raging in the city. The Commission sat from day to day in a miserable ill-ventilated room in the Lahore railway station, the thermometer verging on 100°. I can never forget the discomfort and annoyance endured. Daily reports of progress were forwarded to the Government of India, and by Government to the Railway Directors at home, the result being that before our final report was submitted, the Directors had dispensed with the Agent's services, on the ground that his incapacity for his office had been made abundantly manifest, irrespectively of whether he had been guilty of fraud or not.

The Government of Sir John Lawrence eventually

expressed their opinion in full on the state of affairs disclosed by our report, agreeing in our view that there had been much mismanagement and laxity, but that there was no proof of dishonesty.

For the first seven and a half months of 1868 I continued to be Deputy Commissioner of Jullundur. In August I went to Simla on privilege leave. From the 1st October I was again appointed to officiate in a temporary vacancy as Under-Secretary in the Home Department of the Government of India, and in that capacity I worked at Simla and Calcutta until I went home on furlough early in 1869.

My work in every department at Jullundur being thoroughly up to date, and for the most part in grooves laid down by myself, I found that steady daily disposal of my various files, judicial and administrative, involved no great strain. The contrast was great when I remembered the struggle against piles of arrears which had wellnigh exhausted me in 1865. Indeed, in 1868, I was oppressed by the fear that the ease with which I kept my work up to date indicated some occult slackness and a failure to initiate new developments. In the spring I made several tours in camp, one chief object being to appoint for the first time Municipal Committees for some of the minor towns of the district. A free hand was given by Government as to the mode of selection of members, but as a general rule I was much guided by the votes of the principal inhabitants. I found that the people took a keen interest in the matter. I received the votes in my tent, men who paid Income or Licence tax being held entitled to exercise the suffrage. Early in March we paid a short visit to Lahore, my object being to confer with Mr. (afterwards Sir) C. U. Aitchison and other Civil officers there, regarding the feasibility of the introduction of a bonus scheme calculated to counteract the great stagnation of promotion in the Province. The general lines of our scheme were simple enough, and met with approval by the higher Provincial officers, including the Lieutenant-Governor, Sir Donald M'Leod. The proposals were afterwards submitted to the Viceroy, who declined to support them, and made some ot us gnash our teeth and repeat the rhyme written a year or two before by a distinguished officer when suffering from cold water poured by the Viceroy on one of his schemes.

A certain old Delhi Collector
By luck got the Viceregal sceptre,
In progress he'd falter
And swore he'd ne'er alter
His views as a Delhi Collector.

It will be remembered that Sir John Lawrence, at an early period of his career, was Magistrate and Collector of the Delhi district. His serishtadar or court-reader was a Cashmeri Pundit called Moti Lal. When I was Deputy Commissioner of Jullundur, Pundit Moti Lal, a fine-looking old man, was one of the Native subordinate judges. I gave him leave on one occasion to go up to Simla to pay his respects to the Viceroy, his old master: Moti Lal returned much pleased with his reception, and he called on me to report himself. In the course of conversation, I said, 'Is it true, Pundit Sahib, that Sir John Lawrence's temper was somewhat quick in early days?' 'Very much so, very much so,' was the reply; 'but gradually, just as promotion came to him step by step, so his temper grew softer and softer.'

CAMP, BEAS RIVER, *February* 6, 1868.—My tents are pitched on the bank of the uninteresting Beas. You can hardly imagine a more dreary scene than the one I have peeped at once or twice during the day. Wind and rain have been going on since an early hour in the morning; I have been sitting shivering, wrapped up in coats. I have been obliged to have my stove removed, for the wind blew all the smoke into my face, and made the tent unbearable. I am about twenty-five miles from home in the territory of the Kapurthala Raja. The business that brings me here is the charge of a very troublesome bridge of boats, which is one of the plagues of the life of all Deputy Commissioners of Jullundur. Fortunately it is in a good condition now, and I can go back to the station with an easy conscience.

On the 23rd March I presided in the Jullundur City at a public meeting assembled for the distribution of rewards to officials and others who had done good service in the previous year during the conflict with cholera. For the first time I attempted to make a speech in Hindustani. The English draft of what I said has survived, and may be quoted here as a sequel to what has been already written on the subject, and as illustrating the semi-quarantine system which was then in vogue in cholera outbreaks, which I understand has now been abandoned:—

You all remember that in the month of April last year, the great Kumbh Mela took place at Hurdwár. Thousands and thousands of pilgrims passed through this Doáb[1] on their way to the Ganges. Two or three millions of men and women assembled near the sacred bathing ghát. There were Maharajas, Rajas, Sirdars of the highest rank; there were opulent merchants, and there were the poorest of the poor. On the 10th April the pilgrims bathed in the river. The Government arrangements

[1] Territory between the two rivers Sutlej and Beas.

were excellent. Every one was happy. There was no crowding at the ghát, no deaths by drowning as in former days, when no trouble was taken to secure the safety of the bathers. When the bathing ceremony was finished, every one prepared to return home. A terrible enemy, however, had been lurking unseen in the midst of the great crowd. As the people began to leave the banks of the river, the cold hand of cholera arrested them. The retreat homewards became precipitate. The people ran, the enemy followed. Man after man, woman after woman, child after child, fell by the roadside and died. On the 19th April, we who remained at home heard what had happened, heard that the pilgrims were flying back from the Ganges, terror-stricken. The way in which the news reached me was this. Mr. Kelly, who was then District Superintendent of Police at Ambala, wrote to me a private letter in which he said, 'The pilgrims are taking cholera back to the Punjab, do all you can to protect the district.' You all know what happened then. We were bound to do all that we could to keep the enemy away from us. The pilgrims were not allowed to enter the towns until we were certain that they had been purified from all taint of the disease. Those of them who were sick were taken care of in the roadside hospitals; those who were very poor were fed. Through God's mercy it would seem that some benefit resulted from what was done. In the city of Jullundur and in the Cantonments there was hardly any trace of the cholera. In the other towns and in the villages some persons did die. Altogether, some 700 or 800 persons fell victims.[1] But this number was very small, and it is believed that if precautions had not been taken, instead of 700 or 800 there would have been 7000 or 8000. Of course these precautions could not be taken without exposing many Government servants and others to great risk of infection from the disease. The Native doctors and their hospital servants had to attend personally on the sick. Many of the Amla of the District office, and the Tehsils, had to work among the infected

[1] This number included cholera deaths in the autumn, when the disease appeared in many villages.

band of pilgrims. Many shopkeepers and others had to go out of the city and supply food to the travellers. The Lieutenant-Governor, having heard all this, has been pleased to direct me to give rewards to those persons who were most conspicuous in their exertions to benefit their fellow-men. We have met this morning to distribute the rewards which the Government has sanctioned, and I trust that all present will join with me in the prayer that a disaster similar to that which I have now described may through the goodness of Providence be averted in the present year. If, however, such a calamity should be permitted to come upon us, let us fervently trust that the rewards now bestowed may have the effect of stimulating every inhabitant of this district, be he Government servant or not, to do his utmost to quell the violence of the disease and to protect the mass of the people. We all know that the preventive measures which we were obliged to take were very harassing to many persons, but we must remember that they were highly beneficial to a very vast number. In all matters of this kind, the few persons who suffer inconvenience must be consoled by the thought that their hardships have contributed to the happiness and safety of the majority.

On the 25th March we were in tents at Giréna, near the Beas. Sir Donald M'Leod, the Lieutenant-Governor, had come from Lahore to the other side of the river with a large camp. In the afternoon, in the presence of a large assemblage, the first girder of the railway bridge over the Beas was raised. The following day the Lieutenant-Governor's camp crossed the river on its march towards Jullundur. Sir Donald M'Leod himself was suffering from illness, so all arrangements for his official reception had to be given up. He remained in camp in the Jullundur cantonment for some weeks until he was able to march on towards Kangra. On the 29th March a fair-haired young boy, who belonged to the 92nd Gordon Highlanders, then on their march from Kurrachee to Jullundur, drove into our compound in an ekka.[1] He was a day ahead of his regiment. His name was James Alexander Lawrence Montgomery, son of Sir Robert and Lady Montgomery. The young fellow stayed with us for some time and became our fast friend, and has remained so till the present moment, when, having filled the responsible position of Financial Commissioner of the Punjab and retired from India, he has been appointed Land Commissioner of the East African Protectorate.

SIR R. MONTGOMERY TO G. R. ELSMIE.

7 CORNWALL GARDENS, QUEEN'S GATE, W., *May* 6.

I have to thank you and Mrs. Elsmie very much for your kindness to our Jamie and for receiving him on his arrival, and I would much prefer his arriving in an ekka to a coach-in-four. It is well he should begin his career in a humble way. . . . He has a good deal of quiet resolution, and I think has the foundation of a good officer. My great wish eventually is to get him into the Commission or Political Department. . . .

The presence of the 92nd regiment gave fresh life to Jullundur. The commanding-officer was Colonel Hamilton, father of Sir Ian Hamilton and of Mr. Vereker Hamilton, the artist. We saw much of Colonel Hamilton, a fact which increased the pleasure of our acquaintance with his brother, Mr. George Hamilton of Skene House, Aberdeenshire, in the years 1879-80. The second in command was Major Forbes Macbean, a very interesting and accomplished man, with a splendid singing voice. Other officers in the regiment were Harry Brooke, Henry Gordon (of Manar, Aberdeenshire), the Honourable John Napier, etc. I believe it has been the fate of some civil

[1] An uncomfortable two-wheeled native pony-cart.

officers to live in a state of semi-warfare, or at all events of armed neutrality, with the military officers quartered in their districts. Such, I am thankful to say, was never my fate. I always regarded military society as a relief from that of the Civil lines, and I cannot recall any misunderstanding with commanding-officers, of the smallest importance. This fact is, I dare say, attributable to the clearly expressed warning by Sir Robert Montgomery, when he sent me to Murree in 1863, to take care to avoid rows with the military. If we had differences of opinion we settled them by conference, and did not let them go up to higher authority.

In May, Bishop Milman of Calcutta and his sister, Miss Milman, visited our station.

D. May 10, *Sunday.*—Church at 5.30 A.M., Bishop Milman preached and took part of the service. He preached from the chancel step, saying he did so because there was no pulpit. His sermon was decidedly good, 'Whither goest thou?' Extempore from beginning to end. In the evening there was a confirmation service; decidedly impressive.

D. May 11.—The Bishop had a lay meeting in the Artillery mess, which I attended. One or two matters such as Missions, Sunday-schools were discussed. The Bishop is evidently a man of business, who has no intention of letting the grass grow under his feet.

May 11.—About Sunday-schools, the Bishop said, they were very desirable indeed, provided they were made pleasant to the scholars and not wearisome. In regard to Missions, he was much puzzled by the fact that Mission schools produced so few converts. Boys went there, learned the Bible perfectly, but went away and had not the remotest notion of being converted. He said that many missionaries were beginning to doubt whether it was worth while to keep their schools open. The secular education imparted by Government schools seemed to do as much good as the religious education given by the missionaries. After the meeting the Bishop started for Hoshiarpore. I decidedly liked what I saw of him. He is evidently High Church, in the Bishop of Oxford's style, but is a very far way removed from Mr. Maconachie and such like.

June 24.—Dined at our next door neighbour's. Afterwards went with them to the soldiers' (92nd regt.) theatricals. We went as a matter of duty and expected to be bored frightfully. However, the men had the good sense to act a Scotch piece called 'Cramond Brig,' in which James v., in disguise, has dinner in a farmhouse, and then brings his entertainers to Court and floors them by the announcement that he is the king. The farmer is thereupon made a knight, and his wife, Tibbie Howieson, puts up the family umbrella to protect herself from the falling honours. We laughed a good deal and thought we had got off cheaply.

The following entry refers to a notable change in regard to the administrative charge of jails. It relieved district officers greatly, and no doubt was of much benefit to prison management.

July 6.—At last my jail is likely to get into good order, as they have allowed me to put the Civil surgeon into executive charge. He is a fixture here. The old practice was to put Assistant Commissioners in charge, but as they are constantly being changed, the jails did not get justice.

August 6.—I was particularly delighted with an Italian proverb quoted by Lord Carnarvon: 'May God keep me from those in whom I put my trust, my own right hand will keep me from those whom I distrust.'

CHAPTER VIII

SIMLA, CALCUTTA, AND FURLOUGH

1868—1871

ON the 20th August we arrived at Simla on two months' leave, having taken Courteen Hall in Boileau Gunj, a house belonging to our old friend Mrs. Scott. We saw a good deal of Sir John Lawrence during his last season at Simla. Lady Lawrence and one of her daughters had already gone home. Croquet was still a very popular game, and the Viceroy preferred that form of recreation to solemn rides along the Mall. We were very frequently asked to make up Sir John's match in the afternoon. His Excellency played with great keenness.

SIMLA, *August* 27.—In the afternoon we went to play croquet at Government House. . . . The Governor-General took E. for his partner, and fortunately they won the game. E. came in for a good deal of praise and dispraise; whenever she did a good stroke she was lauded, and *vice versâ*. . . . Once when she had the misfortune to miss an easy shot, H. E. exclaimed, 'I can't understand how your husband ever married such a woman.' . . .

September 14.—Immediately after dinner we all went to the Assembly Rooms to hear Babu Keshub Chundur, a Bengalee, give an account of the rise of the Brahmo Somaj religion. The Governor-General and the Commander-in-Chief were both there. The Babu speaks English remarkably well, and he delivered a very good and very earnest lecture; Brahmos are Hindus of all classes, who have entirely thrown off their own religion and caste and have become pure Theists. Their faith, as far as it goes, coincides with ours, but it stops short of revelation. They regard the Bible as the best of books, but they do not regard it as inspired in the orthodox sense. The Brahmos now number some thousands, and the lecturer said he believed Brahmoism would sooner or later be the religion of India.

A day or two later Mr. James Gordon, Private Secretary to the Viceroy, asked me to call upon him, and then offered me a three months' acting vacancy as Under-Secretary in the Home Department. I accepted the appointment, taking over charge of the duties on the 1st October. My chief reason was that I had practically determined on taking furlough to England in the beginning of the following year.

As Under-Secretary I should in ordinary course go down to Calcutta with the Government in November, and sail for home at the end of my three months in January.

It was about this time that, after dining at Peterhof, I found myself sitting next to Mr. Gordon. We talked among other things about the work of a Private Secretary to the Viceroy. Mr. Gordon said that one of the most disagreeable of his duties was dealing with written and personal applications for honours preferred by men who thought themselves entitled to decorations!

D. October 19.—At 11 A.M. went to Government House to hear the debate in Legislative Council on the Punjab Tenancy Bill. It lasted nearly seven hours. The fight was worth seeing and hearing. The only men, however, who can speak well are Mr. Maine and the Commander-in-Chief. Sir John was determined to carry his pet bill. . . . He seemed to say, 'I am the Governor-General and I mean to have my own way. . . .'

I may add to the preceding note that I distinctly remember that, at the close of the debate, Sir John arose from his seat, and, looking round on the Punjabis present, said, 'There, you've got the Act, see that you work it properly.'

In the middle of November the Government of India returned to Calcutta. As an Under-Secretary I was permitted to travel in a special train from Ambala to Howrah. The whole line had just been completed, but was not open to the general public. The contrast between the journey from Calcutta in 1862 and that as now performed by rail in about forty-eight hours was very great. My wife and family followed a few weeks later. We had great difficulty in finding satisfactory accommodation in Calcutta, and had to make more than one change. A bright feature in our life at this time was our Sunday evenings at the Fort Church, where the Rev. Henry Matthew was chaplain. We were much struck by his eloquent and most impressive preaching. In after years we made his acquaintance as Chaplain of Simla. Later Mr. Matthew became Archdeacon and finally Bishop of Lahore. The memory of his friendship will always be cherished as that of one of our most valued possessions.

The last note of 1868 illustrates the kindness of Sir John Lawrence:—

D. December 30.—E. and I went to the monster ball at Belvedere, the Lieutenant-Governor's; a regular crush. We were only there an hour, for the Governor-General very kindly offered to drive us home. So we arrived in state at our hotel in a carriage and four, the companions of our drive being the Viceroy and his A.D.C.

Our New Year's Day treat was a long visit from Colonel Richard Lawrence, now the Resident of Nepal. He had come to Calcutta in order that he might travel as far as Ceylon with his brother, Sir John. On the evening of that day we were present at a most enjoyable vocal concert given by Mr., afterwards Sir John, Strachey. The performers were the artistes from the Italian opera. The music selected was almost entirely chosen from the works of Rossini, who had died a short time before. On the 8th January my time at the Home Office came to an end. Again, as in 1866, I cannot say that I gave up the work as Under-Secretary with regret. No doubt I had fancied that freedom from the daily grind and perpetual interruptions to which a District officer is subject would be congenial, but I am disposed to think that a man who had been accustomed for several years to be the administrative head of half a million of people must feel the loss of power and of the general interest of his work when he finds himself limited to serving up files for the orders of others. My advice to young Civilians anxious to try their hands at secretariat work would be, 'Let your time as Under-Secretary precede, not follow, your time as Head of a district.'

On the 18th January Lord Mayo arrived in Calcutta to assume the office of Viceroy. He was received in the usual manner by Sir John Lawrence, the Members of Council, Chief Secretaries, etc., at the top of the grand flight of steps on the north side of Government House. On the same afternoon we took possession of our cabins on board the *Candia* at Garden Reach, deposited the children and nurses there, returning ourselves to dine with friends. Later, we attended a great 'At Home' at Government House, given in honour of Lord Mayo. Finally, between twelve and one in the morning, we went on board the *Candia*, being rowed in a small dinghy from the shore. Early the next morning our ship started on her voyage. Sir John Lawrence, Colonel Richard Lawrence, and their party joined the *Candia* by a quick steamer some distance down the river. On the 21st we were well out at sea. On the 26th we reached Galle, where Sir John Lawrence and his brother landed, intending to spend a fortnight in Ceylon.

We rested a day and a half at Alexandria, and while there visited Pompey's Pillar and Cleopatra's Needle in company with our fellow-passengers, Mrs. Burge and her son Hubert. Mrs. Burge was the wife of the Archdeacon of Calcutta. The boy is now Headmaster of Winchester College.

Soon after reaching London I was enrolled as a student at Lincoln's Inn with a view to passing the necessary examinations and being called to the Bar before my return to India. Rightly or wrongly, in common with other Punjab Civilians, *e.g.* Messrs. J. W. and T. W. Smyth, Mr. D. G. Barkley, I was impressed with the belief that the status of an English barrister would tend to advancement in the judicial line in India. Subsequent experience showed that it probably did do so. I was greatly helped and encouraged at my start and afterwards by Mr. John Winder of Lincoln's Inn. He invited me to his chambers on many occasions, and did his best to initiate me in the mysteries of 'Real property' law, a field on which I had never previously ventured. My second helper was Mr. (afterwards Sir) Fitzjames Stephen, to whom I had taken a letter of introduction from his brother-in-law, Mr. (now Sir) Henry Cunningham, who was at that time Government Advocate at Lahore. Mr. Stephen invited me to walk with him from his house in Cornwall Gardens to his chambers in the Temple. During our walk he mastered my 'case,' and gave me much valuable advice regarding my studies. In his chambers he showed me a table covered with his pending briefs, and told me I might go there at any time and read any paper which might appear to be of interest. This permission I often availed myself of, and so became conversant with the inner history of some of the most important cases then before the courts.

In 1869 Mr. Forsyth also came home on furlough, and we met very often. He had for long taken a keen interest in all Central Asian questions, and he set himself to do his utmost to bring about a better understanding between Russia and England on boundary and commercial questions. To explain the situation more clearly I quote from the *Autobiography of Sir Douglas Forsyth*[1] published after his death :—

On leaving India for Cabul, Shere Ali[2] wrote me a letter . . . expressing a wish to see me in Cabul at some future period. The idea of establishing amicable relations with the Central Asiatics and with the Russians having been so fully approved of by Lord Mayo, he authorised me to go to England, and thence, if possible, to St. Petersburg, to endeavour to effect

[1] Richard Bentley and Son, 1887, pp. 46, 47, etc.

[2] The Amir of Cabul, who had been received by Lord Mayo at Ambala.

some practical arrangement. Unfortunately, his own party were not at that time in power. The Duke of Argyll was Secretary of State for India, and threw cold water on the proceedings of Lord Mayo. . . . When I reached England I found the Duke turned a deaf ear to all the proposals I put before him. Curiously enough, when all hope of success seemed denied me, I found a very useful friend in Sir Roderick Murchison, then President of the Geographical Society. He listened carefully and attentively to all I had to say, and at once introduced me to Baron Brunow, the Russian Ambassador, who caught the idea which was put forward and spoke to Lord Clarendon[1] on the subject, and he suggested that I should go to Baden-Baden to see Prince Gortschakoff. I met with the utmost courtesy and consideration from Lord Clarendon, who thoroughly approved of Lord Mayo's views. Armed with letters of introduction from Lord Clarendon and Baron Brunow, I went to Baden-Baden and spent a week in very pleasant interviews with Prince Gortschakoff, at the end of which time he informed me that he had received a telegram from the Emperor, inviting me to pay him a visit.

I returned to London highly pleased with my success, so far only to find my hopes once more damped by the lukewarmness of the Duke of Argyll, who could not see any advantage from my proposed acceptance of the Emperor's invitation, and refused to accredit me, and as my leave was about to expire there seemed no help for it but for me to return to India. But Lord Clarendon was my good angel in this matter. He, in the meantime, had gone abroad and met Prince Gortschakoff, with whom he had conversations which have since become historically famous, one result of which was to advise me to apply for extra leave on private affairs; and then, taking me into his own department, properly accredited me to visit Russia. He first of all sent me to Constantinople to see our Ambassador there, and General Ignatieff, the Russian Minister, after which I travelled by Odessa, Kief, and Moscow to St. Petersburg, and

[1] Then Foreign Secretary.

with the aid of Sir Andrew Buchanan's counsel I had long interviews with Prince Gortschakoff, General Milutin, Minister of War, M. de Reuter, Minister of Finance, M. de Stremououkoff, head of the Asiatic Department. One great object which Lord Mayo had in view was to define with some approach to exactitude the territories of the Amir, Shere Ali's possessions, for the Russians had distinctly declared that they had nothing whatever to say to Shere Ali's dominions, but what those dominions were they professed to be in some doubt. . . .

At an interview which I had with the Emperor . . . his Majesty said that all that had hitherto passed between his Ministers and myself had been reported to him, and he was perfectly satisfied and hoped that I was too.

I may here remark that in 1872 or 1873, when the subject was again brought forward, the Emperor referred to that conversation, and said that he believed the matter to have been really settled then in concert with me. This will be found in the Blue Book. . . .

Mr. Forsyth invited me to accompany him on his travels in Europe, and to act, as occasion might require, as his Private Secretary. On the evening of the 2nd July I went with him to the House of Commons, expecting a debate on a Central Asian question. On reaching the lobby, however, we met Mr. Grant Duff, the Under-Secretary for India, who told us that the House had been counted out. 'Well, then,' said Forsyth, 'you must get us into the House of Lords to hear the Irish Church Debate which is going on.'—'I have no power to get you in,' was the reply; 'you had better come with me and look as much like Members of the House of Commons as you can.' We followed the advice and soon found ourselves in the desired haven. A most interesting debate on the question of concurrent endowment was taking place. I listened to it, leaning against the side of what looked like a small pew, in which sat a venerable lady by herself. I soon recognised her as Lady Trevelyan, whom I had met in Simla five years before. I stood a patient listener for four hours, and was thoroughly well rewarded by hearing a debate in which the Archbishop of Canterbury (Tait), the Bishop of Oxford (Wilberforce), the Bishop of Gloucester, Earl Russell, the Duke of Marlborough, Lords Salisbury, Athlumney, Hardwicke, Kimberley, Carnarvon, Granville, Denbigh and others took part. On the whole, with the exception of the Archbishop and the Bishop of Oxford, I was disappointed in the powers of eloquence displayed by the noble lords, some of whom, notably Earl Russell, were more or less inaudible; but I went home thankful that the Central Asian debate had collapsed and that I had had the good luck to spend many hours in the House of Lords, under the best possible auspices.

Brief diary extracts will give a sufficient outline of the journeyings with Mr. Forsyth, both at home and abroad, in the latter half of 1869. I refrain purposely from reproducing many descriptions of places seen or visited, as no doubt much better accounts of them are to be found elsewhere. What I aim at is to give some idea of Mr. Forsyth's energy and success in attempting to improve our relations with Russia on Central Asian questions.

D. July 23.—Met Forsyth at the Victoria Station; started together for Dover and Brussels.

D. 24.—Reached Brussels soon after 7 A.M. . . . In the afternoon we called on Mr. Lumley, the English Minister. I was much interested in the conversation. . . .

D. 26.—Reached Cologne early. After travelling along the

Rhine, past Mayence, Heidelberg, etc., we got to Baden-Baden about 3.30. . . .

D. BADEN-BADEN, 27.—Forsyth went to see Prince Gortschakoff, came back much pleased. . . .

D. PARIS, *August* 1.—Forsyth went to see Monsieur Khanikoff.

D. EXETER, *August* 20.—British Association; went to the Geographical section. Heard two Russians, one of whom was Mons. Khanikoff, speak. The Russophobia question was discussed, but Forsyth with wisdom abstained from taking part.

D. *August* 24.—To the Geographical section. Heard Forsyth and Mr. T. Saunders read their Central Asian papers. F.'s paper seemed to take. . . . Sir Stafford Northcote's speech was good. . . .

D. LONDON, *September* 13.—E. and I went out to pay some visits, called on . . . Lady Lawrence. . . . Lord Lawrence gave E. his carte.

To the best of my recollection this was the last occasion on which I ever saw the great John Lawrence. The carte de visite, on which he signed his name, is still carefully preserved. It is placed in an album next to a photograph of Lord Lytton, but both of the ex-Viceroys are looking away from each other in opposite directions. Many years afterwards, in 1881 I think, I showed the pictures to Rai Mul Singh, a native gentleman of Lahore, of the old school, who had known John Lawrence well and who fully appreciated the different views held by him and Lord Lytton on the subject of Afghanistan. Pointing to the opposite lines of vision in the subjects of the photographs, I said, 'Maghrib, masharik (East and West), as you may perceive, Sáhib.'—'Bé shak, bé shak' (no doubt, no doubt), said the Rai Sahib, 'bilkul mukhtilaf,' *i.e.* altogether different.

But I find that Charles Bernard wrote to me as follows

on the 27th January 1876: 'Lord Lawrence, with whom I am staying, is very kind. He says Lord Lytton is a clever, pleasant man, who will make a good G.-G.' It is needless to say that Lord Lawrence did not remain very long of that opinion.

D. PARIS, *September* 17.—Forsyth has just returned from his interview with Lord Clarendon and appears in high spirits. . . . Left Paris 8.35 P.M.

D. September 18.—Baden about 10 A.M. . . .

D. September 27.—At Pesth. After breakfast the two Forsyths[1] and I went to call on Arminius Vambéry, the Central Asian traveller. He is a shortish man with a lame leg, very small eyes. He appeared exceedingly glad to see the Forsyths and acted as our Cicerone all day, showed us what there was to be seen.

D. September 30.— . . . Arrived at Varna, about 8 P.M., in the dark. We were conveyed to the pier in carriages, driven over the roughest of roads. From the pier we were bundled into boats and carried to the Austrian steamer. Started about 10 P.M. for Constantinople,—we were just a day late.

D. CONSTANTINOPLE, *October* 1.—About noon we entered the Bosphorus, and the sight of it rewarded us for all our toil. . . .

D. October 2.—. . . Got rooms at the Hotel d'Angleterre in Therapia. Called at the English and Russian embassies. . . .

D. October 9.—A storm (which has been going on for some days) continued. Didn't go out all day. Forsyth and I dined at the English Embassy (at Therapia). We had to grope our way along the shore from the hotel. Darkness was considerable and the weather tempestuous (no vehicles available). . . . The Ambassador is the Hon. Henry Elliot, a son of Lord Minto, I believe. A very pleasant, gentlemanly man. . . . On Friday

[1] *i.e.* Mr. Douglas Forsyth, and his elder brother, Mr. William Forsyth, Q.C., author of *The Life of Cicero*, etc., who was to travel with us as far as Constantinople.

Mr. Elliot took Forsyth to see the Grand Vizier. They went to his palace in the English Stationaire, a small war steamer in attendance at the Embassy. The Russian Ambassador[1] here promises us all manner of attention in Russia, so I hope we shall not find the journey very tedious. They say the Russian railway carriages are the most comfortable in the world, and that you can go to bed in them in a most satisfactory manner.[2]

D. October 12.—Last day at Therapia. . . .

D. October 14.—Reached Odessa after a smooth and satisfactory passage about 9.30 A.M. . . .

D. October 15.—Started in the railway at 6 P.M. . . .

It must be remembered that at this time the railway from Odessa to Kief was not open to the public, and it was only through the special favour of the Russian officials that we were permitted to travel the whole way from Odessa to St. Petersburg by train.

October 18.—At Kief. A very fine old town. Mr. Nethersole, the English tutor of the Russian Governor-General's son, came for us and took us to see the various monasteries, churches, etc. They were well worth seeing. We called on M. Moravief, to whom Forsyth had an introduction. He is a brother of the Moravief of Kars; a very quaint old Russian gentleman, living by himself evidently, in a comfortable house. We called on the Governor-General, a good-looking man, pleasant enough, but appeared busy and did not even ask us to sit down.[3]

We went to see the catacombs of St. Anthony—very curious, in perfect preservation—bodies in niches.

At 4 P.M. we embarked on a small steamer on the Dnieper

[1] Ignatieff.

[2] This was in 1869, when sleeping carriages for ordinary travellers were unknown in England.

[3] His Excellency, however, invited us to dinner that night, but we were obliged to continue our journey at once. The mode of our reception was probably due to Russian etiquette, the Governor-General assuming the regal manner.

and after a short journey got into the railway and proceeded towards Kursk.

D. October 20.—In the railway till past 10 A.M. A very cold night, arrived in Moscow in the midst of mud, gloom, and the remains of a snowstorm. . . .

D. October 21.—Spent the greater part of the day in the Kremlin. . . . Much struck by the barbaric splendour of Moscow. . . .

D. October 22.—Afternoon went to the Sparrow hills and had a magnificent view of the city.

D. October 23.—Plumer [1] and I went to the Foundling Hospital and were very much interested in it. It receives any number of babies and asks no questions. At 2 we left Moscow for St. Petersburg.

D. October 24, *Sunday*.—Reached St. Petersburg about 9 A.M. The night had been passed most satisfactorily in a sleeping-carriage.[2] . . .

Called at the English Embassy and were very kindly received by Sir Andrew Buchanan. . . . Walked down the Nevski Prospect. . . .

October 26.—The political interest of Forsyth's visit begins. He received letters from Lord Mayo and Sir Donald M'Leod yesterday of a most satisfactory description. The Governor-General (of India) fully recognises Forsyth's position. Sir Andrew Buchanan, the Ambassador here, seems to think there is much to be done. . . . There is a Bokhara Ambassador here, and it is clear that Forsyth's work will be interesting. In the evening we dined with Sir Andrew Buchanan at the Embassy, a very fine house, everything in A1 style. There was not a large party. The Asiatic Minister and the Prussian Ambassador, Prince Henry VII. of Reuss, a cousin of the King of Prussia. I sat next to a niece of Sir Andrew's. . . .

D. October 28.—Left St. Petersburg with Plumer at 1 P.M., travelled all night. Forsyth to follow. . . .

[1] Mr. Hall Plumer, brother-in-law of Mr. Forsyth, who had joined us.

[2] The first I had ever seen.

D. November 2.—Reached London.

D. Sunday, November 14.—Went to see Forsyth, heard from him a full account of his last week in St. Petersburg. He certainly accomplished much.

Mr. Forsyth gave me full particulars of the private interview which had been accorded to him by the Emperor Alexander, who spoke in French, suggesting that Mr. Forsyth should reply in English.

D. November 26.—. . . Saw the Forsyths for the last time before their departure (for India).

Soon after reaching India Mr. Forsyth was deputed by Lord Mayo on a mission to Yarkund.

During the early months of 1870 much time was given to studying for my law examination,[1] which was finally passed at Lincoln's Inn in the end of May.

D. January 18, 1870.—To Lincoln's Inn, dined and was introduced. . . .

D. June 16.—Heard from India of my promotion to be a Deputy Commissioner of the Third Class in the Punjab (*i.e.* in more than twelve years after I had joined the service).

SIR ROBERT MONTGOMERY TO G. R. ELSMIE.

I remember now the pleasurable sensation I experienced when first made permanently a district officer. I had not then, as you have, some eight children (or is it ten?).[2] My wife tells me you have got your promotion, and I write a few lines heartily to congratulate you both; and now your career, if health and strength be continued to you, is easy and certain, and I expect and feel sure you will get on rapidly, and you deserve it for pluck and determination in working at home amid all the distractions. . . .

[1] The subjects were Real Property, Common Law, Equity, Roman Law, Constitutional Law, Indian Codes.

[2] It was only six!

D. Friday, August 26.—Decided on going to Eastbourne for the croquet match with 'Cavendish.' We took all day about it. However, I managed to come off victorious and brought home the cup in triumph. 'Cavendish' beat me the first game easily, and then I managed to pull off the second and third games.

D. October 26.—I dined at the Montgomerys', where I met Sir Donald Macleod (who had just come home from the Punjab at the end of his Lieutenant-Governorship).

The time for our return to India was now drawing near, but an extension of two or three weeks' leave was necessary in order that I might be called to the Bar in Hilary term 1871. At that time, however, there seemed to be a prejudice at the India Office against Civilians making any attempt to compete with Barristers pure and simple in the struggle for high judicial office.

D. November 18.—Got an answer from the Secretary of State declining to give an extension. Went straight to Sir Robert Montgomery, but it was no go, so I have to make up my mind to start next month.

D. November 23.—To the India Office, saw Mr. Seccombe,[1] Financial Secretary, and managed to tell him that I had another reason[2] for wishing to stay some extra weeks at home. He encouraged me to plead it, and I believe I shall not have to go in December after all.

D. December 2.—Evening post brought letter from the India Office giving me my leave.

Sir Robert Montgomery to G. R. Elsmie.

I got your letter just as I was coming to office, and have not had a moment till now to write and say I congratulate you on your success. You deserve a *silk gown* as well as being called to the Bar. All I can say is it is marvellous to me, and increases

[1] Afterwards Sir Thomas Seccombe, K.C.S.I., etc.

[2] My wife's health.

the opinion I have always had of the *power* of *Secretaries*. I believe *they* are, under all Governments, most *powerful*, from *Bismarck* to *Seccombe*!

The last week or two of January 1871 were busily occupied. On the 21st James Forsyth[1] lunched with us. I never saw him again; he died in London of a violent attack of jungle fever within about two months of this time, while engaged in passing *The Highlands of Central India* through the press. On the 25th Sir Donald M'Leod came to see us. He was as kind as ever. Alas! we never saw *him* again. The hurry of the last few days will best be described by an extract or two from my diary.

D. January 26, 1871.— . . . At five reached Lincoln's Inn for the purpose of being called. The various processes lasted till seven, when I was shaken hands with by Vice-Chancellor Malins and one or two other grandees; then I rushed home as fast as I could to do what was possible in the matter of packing.

January 27.— . . . To the Court of Queen's Bench and in company with many others enrolled myself as a Barrister. Said enrolment consisted of signing my name twice and paying two and sixpence; no swearing or anything of that sort. On to the P. and O. office, got passage tickets. . . .

January 28.—We sailed from Southampton for Egypt in the *Massilia*.

[1] See pp. 14, 17.

CHAPTER IX

ADDITIONAL COMMISSIONER OF AMRITSAR AND JULLUNDUR

1871—1872

IN the beginning of 1871 the war between France and Germany was going on, and it was impossible to take any other route than the old one *viâ* Southampton. The rate of progress at sea was very slow, seldom exceeding 250 miles a day; a very small amount of contrary wind reducing us to about 180. At Suez, for the first time in my experience, the railway carriages were run alongside of the Bombay steamer.

We were much struck by the beauty of Bombay. We rested for a day or two at our old station, Jullundur, where I received an order appointing me to be Deputy Commissioner of Gujranwala; but we had not been at Gujranwala more than two or three weeks when I was directed to take up the duties of Additional Commissioner of the Amritsar and Jullundur divisions. My few weeks at Gujranwala were my last term of office as a district officer. For the next fourteen years I was, for the most part, engaged in judicial work.

The appointment of Additional Commissioner was nominally a temporary one, the practice of the Government being to send the extra hand to assist Commissioners who had fallen into deep judicial arrears.

Additional Commissioners were popularly known as 'donkey engines.' On arriving at Amritsar an arrear file of about seven hundred appeals, Criminal, Civil, and Revenue, was made over to me; and so anxious was the new Lieutenant-Governor, Mr. Henry Davies,[1] to see these old cases cleared off, that I was ordered to submit a weekly return showing the progress made.

AMRITSAR, *May* 22, 1871.—The thermometer has been at 90° in the house for the last few days. Yesterday the heat was frantic and we felt no energy. So oppressive was the air that we knew a storm must be coming. Well, a thunderstorm did come about 6 P.M., wind and rain, but the air was loaded with dust. This gave us a bearable evening, but the storm returned at intervals during the night and kept us awake and on the move. The moment the wind ceased, we opened our doors to let the cool air in. We went to sleep, only to be woke up again by the return of the wind and the banging of every door in the house. Then we had to shut the doors, the result of which was closeness and stuffiness to a degree. This morning we are reaping the benefit, for the thermometer has gone down to 85° and life is endurable once more.

Towards the middle of June a good deal of excitement prevailed among the Sikhs in the city of Amritsar regarding the slaughter of kine by Muhammadan butchers. On the night of the 14th–15th June an attack was made on the butchers' quarter, and four men were killed. The police exhausted their ingenuity in their endeavours to discover the criminals. Eventually a large batch of men were committed for trial, and they were brought before me on the 9th of August. The police, however, admitting that they had been on

[1] Who had succeeded to the post on the death by accident, a few months before, of Sir Henry Durand, Sir Donald M'Leod's successor.

the wrong tack, were permitted to withdraw from the prosecution. All the accused were released, and I cannot now remember whether the real criminals were ever traced. The Amritsar butcher murders were comparatively forgotten early in the following year, when their importance was eclipsed by the more serious outrages connected with kine killing which took place in the Native State of Mulair Kotla.

About this time I received a letter, of which I give an extract, from a young Civilian who had been my Assistant at Jullundur a few years before. I had found him somewhat impatient of control occasionally, and apt to jib against my attempts to induce him to follow the law, where clearly laid down, rather than his own supposed common-sense. Meanwhile he had become a Magistrate on the Frontier. The frequent disregard of the law which he saw there had led him to modify his former somewhat crude views.

. . . I recollect after coming here writing you a very wild sort of letter, saying how I liked the rough and ready sort of way things were done, legality being little regarded, but I have now quite come round to the opinion you expressed in your reply that if a man knew his work, the laws were quite elastic enough to enable him to act legally and yet quickly. . . .

SIR ROBERT MONTGOMERY TO G. R. ELSMIE.

NEWPARK, MOVILLE,
CO. DONEGAL, *August* 23.

. . . I learn there is a great onset on Prinsep[1] for *under* assessing.[2] It is a good fault, and I hope he may be able to show he has not gone unnecessarily low. A country prospers under a light assessment. Large communities with small hold-

[1] Mr. Edward Prinsep, at that time Settlement Commissioner of the Punjab.

[2] The land revenue.

ings, if called upon to pay high assessment rates, suffer terribly. They do not gain by high prices, as they have only sufficient to feed their own families.

I was sorry to see an account of the *beef* rows. I dare say some laxity has crept in, in the matter of slaughtering kine and selling beef. The police must be terribly out of heart. Since 1861 there have been annual reductions and changes; no body of men could work under it; much better break all up and have any new police force that the authorities for the time being think best. Nothing is so bewildering and disheartening to a service as constant changes. . . .

By the middle of August, having practically cleared off the Amritsar arrears, I moved over to Jullundur to undertake a similar task there. The civil courts being closed during the month of September, I held my court for the disposal of other work at Dharmsala. In the Jullundur Division the acting Commissioner was Mr. Arthur Brandreth. There, also, was Mr. Edward Prinsep, the Settlement Commissioner of the Province. Both officers were highly clever men, thoroughly conversant with native character. To work more or less in close contact with them was of great advantage. By the middle of October we were settled in Jullundur for the cold weather. In November Mr. Brandreth marched down the Kangra Valley with the Viceroy, Lord Mayo, who, amongst other great qualities, was noted for his personal activity.

JULLUNDUR, *November* 15.—The Brandreths gave us a long account of the Viceroy's march. The pace at which the Viceregal party seemed to have travelled takes away one's breath to think about. Lord Mayo, a man of fifty, thinks nothing of riding fifty miles. One day at Palumpore he had a durbar and reception in the forenoon, then a huge entertainment in the evening, dinner, fireworks, supper. Next morning he went out bear-shooting and was absent till 3 P.M. Then on his returning he immediately mounted his horse and rode twenty-two miles to the next stage, where he dined. Everything, however, seems to have passed off capitally.

Towards the end of the year Mr. Clive Bayley, Home Secretary to the Government of India, under whom I had worked at Simla, passed through Jullundur, making a short stay. According to his wont, he was anxious to lose no opportunity of antiquarian research. Early one morning I drove him to the city of Jullundur and to the Devi tank, his object being to discover a likely spot where, by digging, a lât or pillar of Asoka might be unearthed.

JULLUNDUR, *December* 20.—Our life is exceedingly monotonous, and though not unpleasant it does not afford much material for talking or writing. Conversational powers get very rusty in India. There are no subjects for light conversation out here. No music, no pictures, no popular preachers, nothing going on of any sort. I miss music very much.

Early in 1872 I was again unexpectedly appointed to sit on a Commission at Lahore to investigate many alleged cases of gross mismanagement on the part of the Agent of the Sind, Punjab, and Delhi Railway. The nature of the inquiry, however, differed from that of 1867, in that no bad faith or fraudulent intention was alleged. Generally speaking, the charge was that the Railway Company had appointed an Agent altogether incompetent for the work. This gentleman, when originally nominated, had proclaimed his technical unfitness for the post, but he had eventually yielded to the persuasion of his friends in England and undertaken a task for which he had no qualification save that of strict personal integrity. My colleague in the Commission was Colonel O'Connell of the Madras Engineers. It will be remembered that the shareholders of the Railway were guaranteed by Government a minimum return of 5 per cent. on the original value of their shares. It was popularly supposed that the Viceroy, Lord Mayo, took a great personal interest in railway administration, that he viewed with extreme displeasure the laxity of management displayed by the Company for many years, and it was thought to be not unlikely that, if our report confirmed the Viceroy's view, opportunity would be taken, in pursuance of the terms of the original contract between Government and the Company, to put an end to the management by the latter, and to assume, on the part of Government, direct control of the railway. Be that as it may, the assassination of the Viceroy while on a visit to the Andaman Islands occurred before our inquiry was complete, and was probably not without its effect in determining the final view of the Government of India.

Our report was signed on the 7th of March, and on the following day I returned to my ordinary duties at Jullundur. I never saw the detailed opinion of the Government of India on our findings and recommendations. The Railway Company was, I believe, allowed to continue its management for many years, but the assumption of direct control by the Government is now a matter of ancient history. Colonel O'Connell, writing to me from Calcutta, said:—

I have not yet seen the despatch to the Secretary of State on the subject. I believe the question was discussed as to whether the Secretary of State should not be advised to take over the line, and that there was considerable difference of opinion on the subject, even with reference to the point whether he had the power to do so. I do not expect, therefore, that our report will bear fruit immediately, but I am satisfied that it cannot be shelved altogether.

The matter was closed, so far as I was personally concerned, by the receipt of an official letter from the Government of India conveying their thanks to the Commission for their 'lucid and judicious report.'

During my stay at Lahore two distressing events occurred. I have already mentioned one of them, the murder of Lord Mayo. The other was the murder by a large band of Kookas, a sect of fanatical Sikhs, of certain butchers in the Native State of Mulair Kotla, near Loodiana.

The first British officer to reach the spot was Mr. Cowan, the Deputy Commissioner of Loodiana. In his opinion the crisis was so grave that, although he had no legal authority, yet, as representing the British Government, he felt himself bound to sanction the execution, by blowing from guns, of many of the riotous murderers who had been condemned by the Court of the Native State. Mr. Forsyth, who, having completed his first mission to Yarkund, had become Commissioner of Ambala, arrived later. *He* had legal authority to confirm the procedure of the Native State, and in virtue of that authority he sanctioned further executions, there being no doubt as to the guilt of the prisoners. In the result, what might have grown into a rebellion was stamped out, but the action of Mr. Cowan and Mr. Forsyth was disapproved by Government.

T. D. Forsyth to G. R. Elsmie.

Ambala, *January* 21, 1872.

. . . I arranged for troops and then went straight to Loodiana. Cowan had rushed off energetically, and was in too great a hurry . . . as now, I fear, he will find to his cost. . . . He proposed to execute captured Kookas on his own authority. . . I wrote officially and demi-officially to Cowan warning him not to abandon all procedure. I pointed out that the offences committed by the Kookas were of two kinds, those in British territory and those in a Native State. As regards the latter, I pointed out that the procedure was simple and rapid. He had only to get the Názim,[1] or himself in the emergency, to prepare the case and send it up for my sanction, which I should give at once, and then the men could be executed. But my orders arrived too late, or were attended to, too late, and Cowan blew away forty-nine men, and one was cut to pieces while attacking him. I went out at once and saw that the proceedings as regards the rest were properly conducted, and sentenced sixteen men to death. I should have merely transported them, had I not feared that anything like disavowal of Cowan's act or sudden leniency might have a bad effect on the native mind. For unquestionably we were very nearly in for a great outbreak. We know now that it had been arranged at Bhainee[2] that a party of one hundred *mustánas*[3] should make a rush on Kotla. Had they been successful, it is difficult to say what would have been the end of it all. When, however, the band of mustánas was so suddenly blown into the air, the others who came up thought it best to beat a retreat. . . . I could not get positive orders to arrest and deport Ram Singh, but did so on my own responsibility. I got him in quietly at 1 A.M., and without saying a word to any one but Menzies,[4] started him off by the morning train at 4 A.M. to Allahabad. There is quite enough,

[1] An official of the Mulair Kotla State.

[2] The headquarters of Ram Singh, the leader or Guru of the Kookas.

[3] Drugged desperadoes.

[4] The Deputy Inspector General of Police.

I think, to show his complicity, so far as knowledge of the proceedings of his followers go, and this ought to be a sufficient warrant to Lord Mayo to act. But we shall see.[1] . . .

LAHORE, *February* 8.—. . . There are all sorts of rumours afloat about the view taken by Government in regard to the Kooka row. . . . Forsyth believes he has saved the province from a great outbreak, but, of course, it is difficult to satisfy a Government at a distance that such is the case. People in Lahore say he has been suspended, but I do not believe this. I think he will pull through without much unfavourable comment from Government. . . . I have this moment had another letter from Forsyth. As I thought, *he* has not been suspended, but Mr. Cowan has. . . . All Forsyth's conduct was strictly legal . . .

February 22.— . . . In common with every one in India we have been mourning very deeply for poor Lord Mayo. . . . The newspapers are unanimous in lamenting him, and there is no doubt that his loss is a very grievous one for the country. The assassination has no political significance. The assassin is a man steeped in murder who ought to have been hanged long ago. Unfortunately he seems to have been an excellent fellow, save when tempted to exercise his skill in murdering. Hence his getting a ticket of leave and being allowed to be almost at large in the colony. . . . The Government seems to have admitted that Forsyth's action in regard to the Kookas was legal. . . .

JULLUNDUR, *April* 18.—I have been reading *James* Forsyth's book[2] and envying the opportunities for sport afforded by a life in the Central Provinces. The book is exceedingly well worth reading. J. F. had a very decided spark of genius in him. Genius, that wonderful thing which is totally different from talent, ability, cleverness, power of acquirement, etc.

Charles Bernard, who, as Secretary to the Government of the Central Provinces, had known James Forsyth, and

[1] Ram Singh was afterwards deported to Burma under the same law as Lájpat Rai was deported in 1907.

[2] *The Highlands of Central India.* See pp. 14, 17, 155.

who also knew that he was an old friend of mine, wrote: 'I have just been reading Forsyth's book; it was very sad his dying like that in his youth and in apparent health. He certainly was a very clever fellow and a capital writer. He was the cleverest of the young men in the Central Provinces by a long way.'

May 10.—The decision of Government [1] in the Kooka case has been published in the *Gazette* of India. Mr. Cowan has been dismissed, and Mr. Forsyth, blamed for supporting Mr. C., but expressly declared to have acted legally throughout, is transferred to Oude, and debarred from employment in a position where he will have the control of Native States. The orders have been published in the *Gazette.* Forsyth is shown to have deprecated any rash action in the strongest way before Mr. Cowan did the fatal deed. . . . Eventually I think the sentence may be modified or forgotten. . . .

During this year the proposed Punjab Laws Act of 1872, a somewhat crude measure, to say the least, was under the consideration of the Legislative Council. I had some correspondence on the subject with Sir Robert Montgomery, who wrote as follows:—

. . . Changes are so numerous nowadays and legislation so rapid, that I do not wonder at the amazement of a people who twenty years ago had never heard of a law. It will take a good deal of reasoning to make them understand *compulsory irrigation* and the *metric* system. This last, not even the English nation can tolerate.

In June, judicial work took me again to Amritsar. I put up with General Reynell Taylor, who had lately been appointed Commissioner there and with whom it was now my privilege to work as Additional Com-

[1] Cf. chap. iii. of the *Autobiography of Sir Douglas Forsyth.*

missioner. General Taylor was Commissioner of the Derajat Division when I was Assistant Commissioner of Mithunkote in 1859-60. At that time, however, we never personally met, Dera Ismail Khan, the Commissioner's headquarters, being over two hundred miles from my little station. We had met, however, officially, on paper, and I had a keen recollection of the charm of his style of writing, and of the consideration he showed towards his subordinates. He had the reputation with Europeans of being a perfect English gentleman; with Natives of being an 'angel.' My acquaintance with him entirely confirmed these opinions. It was a pleasure to be in his company.

DHARMSALA, *August* 31.—Yesterday's *Pioneer* contained the Secretary of State's despatch on the Kooka affair. There were only four short paras. expressing concurrence in the views of the Government of India and granting Mr. Cowan a pension. . . . I still think, however, that Forsyth's subsequent representation, which brings forward fresh matter, may have a good effect. . . .

At the beginning of September I was sent down to Lahore to investigate the circumstances of the suicide of an European prisoner in the Central Jail. The result of my inquiry was to acquit the jail officials of all serious blame, and I made a full report of the case to the Punjab Government. Some weeks later my report was acknowledged, and I was informed that the Lieutenant-Governor entirely agreed with my conclusions. At the beginning of the following year the case was re-opened at the instance of the Supreme Government, and I was called upon to supplement my report with some additional particulars. I was surprised that so clear a case should have given rise to any doubt on the part of the Viceroy and his colleagues. On opportunity arising, I mentioned the fact of my surprise to the Assistant Secretary to the Punjab Government. He said he thought it probable that the order for further report had been suggested by Lord Northbrook's Private Secretary, who had the reputation of being disposed to find flaws in the reports of Local Governments. However that may be, I never heard of the case again, so I presume that my return to the demand for further particulars had satisfied what appeared to me to be somewhat captious criticism. If the Assistant Secretary was correct in his surmise, the critic was no less a personage than Captain Baring, R.A., who has now become the Earl of Cromer, the builder of the present system of administration in Egypt.

Charles Bernard had lately been appointed Secretary to the Government of Bengal under Sir George Campbell, the Lieutenant-Governor. I had, apparently, asked him to give me an account of Bengal and its system of administration. In reply he wrote describing a state of things which has now culminated in the division of the immense unwieldy province into two Lieutenant-Governorships. I have never seen the official papers about the much criticised 'partition of Bengal,' but I have little doubt that Bernard's account of the state of things in 1872 prepared my mind to believe that the old maxim of *divide et impera* must sooner or later be acted upon.

C. E. Bernard to G. R. Elsmie.

CALCUTTA, *August* 4, 1872.

. . . About Bengal I hardly know what to say. It is an enormous province, or rather set of provinces. One district has 3,900,000 souls, and others are some few above 2,000,000;

and several between 1,500,000 and 2,000,000. There are no Tahsildars;[1] and only during the last few years have there been subdivisional officers. Some out-divisions contain 600,000 souls or so. There is a great deal of work to be done; no one knows anything of his district, because the district is so large, because a Magistrate has no hands or feet on his district except the new police; and then for seventy years the Board of Revenue have adopted, enjoined and enforced on all officers, abstention from inquiry into rural affairs of all kinds. You would hardly believe it, but in one district when the Survey came there were twenty-three whole pergunnahs which could not even be found. They had been annexed by the neighbouring big estate-holders, and the people could not, or would not, give information about them. When I first came down I was astonished to find that 'adum-ool-nishân' villages[2] were a recognised institution, and there were ever so many in some districts. All the Collector cares for is his rent roll; if an estate is one day in arrears it is sold up promptly. And the purchaser has to search it out. It often happens, or did happen, that an estate-holder agrees with his neighbours that they shall annex his estate until it is entirely whittled away. He then defaults; the estate is put up to sale, no bidders come forward, and the estate when looked for cannot be found.

Of course there are no statistics, or none reliable, of area and cultivation. Last year the Board reported that only three officers in the whole of Bengal had been more than two years in their districts. I think Campbell is trying to remedy much that is wrong; he is not much supported by his officers. But if he stays, he'll leave a great deal of good behind him.

There is another fact, one from another province hardly realises, and that is the enormous differences between the different provinces which make up Bengal. Behar is just a slice of the North-West Hindustanee country, with an enormous population, immensely rich soil, and fearfully rack-rented. The

[1] Sub-Deputy Collectors and Magistrates.

[2] Villages of which there was no trace.

C. E. Bernard

Patna Commissionership alone contains as large a population as, pays more revenue than, and is about equal in area to the whole of the Oudh Chief Commissionership. One estate in Behar alone, the Durbhanga property, has a net income after paying the land revenue of about thirteen lakhs. Then the Bengalees are as different as possible from the Beharees: they live in a moist climate, have very small holdings, raise enormous crops to the acre; the ryots are mainly Muhammadans, they unite and have strikes against their landlords, and live pretty happily. Every ryot has his boat or two instead of his carts, like an up-country ryot. You can't go ten miles without coming across a large river. There is one big district near the sea, in the delta of the Brahmaputra and Ganges, where not one officer keeps a horse or pony, but all have their boats. The Magistrate is to have a steam-launch to take him about.

Last year in the floods you could have set sail in a flat-bottomed boat and gone clean across country, probably for two hundred miles, in Eastern Bengal. The luxuriance of the vegetable growth here surpasses anything in Northern, or Western, or Southern India. The cost of living, too, is cheaper than in most parts of India; firewood is cheaper in Calcutta than in any big town of Northern or Central India. Over the whole country rice averages cheaper than wheat in the Punjab or N.-W. P., and of course is immensely cheaper than in Bombay or Central India. In some out-of-the-way districts clean rice still keeps on an average of the year at twenty-eight or thirty-two seers a rupee. Yet the population is immensely dense. Denser far than the N.-W. P. districts, north-west of Allahabad.

Of course, with all these rivers and streams, the supply of fish is prodigious. Even on the Calcutta maidan, after heavy rain, fish appear in the ditches and surface drains. I can't conceive whence they come.

The Zemindars, after being left undisturbed for seventy or eighty years, after raising their rents for the last twenty years, are an immense power in the country; they oppose tooth and nail any measures which tend to inquire into the condition of their estates, or anything that is proposed to make villages or villagers more independent of the big landlords.

Then there are such gradations of landlords; you really often meet four or five gradations of landlords, tenure below tenure, before you get to the actual ryots. This is, of course, so much the worse for the ryots, as all these landlords have to be fed and to pay for their luxuries out of the profit of the land. But in the long-run it has tended greatly to mitigate the evils of the permanent settlement, for it has diffused the enormous profits of the land in Bengal over all these grades of landlords, instead of leaving all the profits to a few great landlords and the work to a nation of rack-rented ryots.

Then, besides Bengal, we have Orissa, with a people who are cut off by hills and rivers and seas and lakes from the rest of India; a people who write the strange curly characters of the south; who are very timid and quiet, but yet are on the whole better educated, and possess more schools and habits of reading and writing than any race in India. Of course, all over India there is a higher class, who go by different names in different parts, but who do the writing and reading for the whole country. But in Orissa nearly every man reads or writes a little; or at any rate, if this be an exaggeration, it is safe to say that the majority of men of the ryot class have learned something in the way of reading and writing.

Then there is Assam, the upper valley of the Brahmaputra, peopled by Indo-Chinese people; very fertile but very much neglected, and surrounded on all sides by hills; and hill tribes also raid down upon the plains when so disposed. The tea-planting interest has done an immense deal for Assam and Cachar; about £1,500,000 sterling worth of tea is produced yearly, and more than three-quarters of the price is spent in the districts where the tea is grown. Last year I saw a show patch of tea-bushes on a small plantation, the patch was only an acre or so; it had yielded 19½ maunds of dry tea-leaf that year; and the average price of the produce had been 14 annas a pound;

so that the acre of land yielded a crop worth 1370 rupees or so in one year. The cultivation and picking cost, perhaps, two coolies to the acre all the year round, or say 120 rupees.

The Darjeeling Hills are full of tea-planters, and they are most lovely; but the tea yield per acre is not generally so heavy as it is in Assam. Then there is the province of Chota Nagpore, a country of petty chiefships and wild tribes, where the land revenue is now barely a twentieth part of the rental. The Sonthal pergunnahs are a little group of hilly tracts, where Bengalee Zemindars are the owners, and Sonthals, or other hill people, are the ryots. Of course there can't be much accord between them; the Bengalee Zemindar carries his case home to the Privy Council, but daren't show his face in Sonthalia. The Sonthal has to rebel, or to kill the Zemindar's agent, or to burn the bunniah's shops. Meanwhile we have to deregulationise the country periodically when affairs get warm. When matters cool down, Bengalees creep back and regulations with them.

It is Sunday to-day. So I have inflicted on you a long essay, instead of writing a resolution on Muhammadan education. . . .

Early in October Bishop Milman and his sister visited Dharmsala.

D. DHARMSALA, *Sunday*, *October* 6.— . . . Consecration of the cemetery by the Bishop. . . .

The cemetery at Dharmsala surrounds the church. It contains Lord Elgin's grave and monument, and has, with the church, been greatly injured by the earthquake of April 4, 1905.

We returned to Jullundur in the middle of October. On the 23rd, just as we were settling down for the cold weather, I received the following letter from Mr. Lepel Griffin, Secretary to the Government of the Punjab:—

The Lieutenant-Governor desires me to say that he has decided upon transferring you to Peshawur. . . . Your transfer is made for the reason that the Lieutenant-Governor has heard very favourable opinions of your judgment and ability as a judicial officer; and as he is particularly anxious that the judicial administration of the Peshawur Division may be brought into a more satisfactory condition than at present, and the great murders and crimes of violence reduced, he has selected you for this post.

The work of the Additional Commissioner, or Civil and Sessions Judge, at Peshawur was notoriously difficult. Moreover, the vernacular language of the Peshawur Division, comprising the three districts of Kohat, Peshawur, and Hazara, was for the most part Pashtu, a language of which I was ignorant. This fact must necessarily add greatly to the difficulty of the task of trying heavy criminal cases. Then Peshawur had a bad name for unhealthiness, and it seemed doubtful whether I was justified in allowing my wife and family to run the risk of contact with the malaria of the Peshawur valley. There was much to be said in favour of sending them home. Altogether, a move to Peshawur seemed a risky proceeding at the best, but Mr. Griffin's letter gave me no choice, and after a few days it seemed to us the right thing to pack up our goods and start for the Frontier. This determination was confirmed by the reflection that Mr. Donald Macnabb was at that time the Commissioner of the Peshawur Division, and that I should work as his colleague in the judicial department. So, early in November, we left Jullundur *en route* for Peshawur. Our first halt was with General Taylor at Amritsar, where I remained for several days in order to clear off as many as possible of the cases which remained on my appeal file.

JULLUNDUR, *November* 1.—The Government of India has published a letter to Mr. Forsyth, which acknowledges two mistakes in their resolutions, and adopts a much more conciliatory tone towards him. . . . The Governor-General says a further report has been made to the Secretary of State, so I am still hopeful that a modification of the original order may be made. Every one speaks most highly of Lord Northbrook.

D. AMRITSAR, *November* 8.—General Taylor and I went to the railway station, met the Commander-in-Chief and his party. Lord Napier, Colonel Roberts,[1] and one or two others came to stay at the General's. . . . Evening, a good many men were invited to meet the Commander-in-Chief. . . .

D. November 9.—The Chief's party left by the morning train, the General and I went down to the station. I drove with Captain FitzGeorge, an A.D.C. I am told he is a son of the Duke of Cambridge.

D. November 19.—A farewell walk with General Taylor. It is a great matter of regret bidding him good-bye. He is one in a thousand. . . .

[1] Now Field-Marshal Earl Roberts, V.C., etc.

CHAPTER X

ADDITIONAL COMMISSIONER OF PESHAWUR

1872—1873

AFTER resting at Lahore we travelled for five days in a post carriage to Peshawur, where we were received by Mr. Donald Macnabb. In order to prepare my mind for the chief kind of work which would occupy me on the Frontier, I had procured from the Commissioner's office at Peshawur many packets containing the English records of criminal trials which had been held by Mr. Macnabb while Additional Commissioner some years before. During the journey I read these records with great interest. They filled me with admiration of Mr. Macnabb's power as a judge and his great knowledge of and sympathy with native character. Many years afterwards I endeavoured to give expression to this feeling in dedicating to him a book on *Crime and Criminals in the Peshawur Division.* The dedication ran as follows: 'Dedicated to Donald Campbell Macnabb, C.S.I., late Commissioner of Peshawur, in grateful acknowledgment of the help, sympathy, and instruction received from him during my service on the Frontier, and in token of my profound admiration of his unrivalled ability as a Ruler and a Judge of Afghans.'

PESHAWUR, *December* 10.—I have been very busy in court. The work is new, the cases difficult, and I am utterly ignorant of the language of the people, Pashtu. Every word has to be interpreted to me. This causes a great waste of time, and it is particularly unsatisfactory not to be able to speak directly to the witnesses. The work is principally criminal—murder cases to any extent. I believe that one hundred murders have been reported in this district (Peshawur) alone, this year. The people, though well disposed towards us, are very lawless, and they have blood-feuds which last for generations. . . .

We have been grievously shocked by the news of Sir Donald M'Leod's death.[1] The bare announcement has reached us. There was no resisting his influence when you were brought into personal contact with him. His death is indeed a terrible end to his career. . . .

Some weeks afterwards a letter containing full details of the accident and of Sir Donald's last moments reached us from England. The letter is too painful to be reproduced even at this distance of time. It was a comfort, however, to learn from it that, notwithstanding his grievously maimed state, there is good ground for believing that he suffered no pain. His last words were 'Glory to God in the Highest,' and the final passing away was described as 'almost like a translation.'

December 24.—Murder here is a profession. Last year there were ninety-three murders committed in this district alone, and I believe only about ten men were punished. A man is sleeping outside in the hot weather. His enemy steals up to him and stabs him, and is off in the darkness in a moment. The wounded man awakes, has seen no one, but he immediately declares that certain persons, his enemies, have killed him. These men, say three or four, are arrested, and a lot of false evidence is immediately hatched against them, the truth being that *one* of these probably hired an assassin to do the deed, the name of the real assassin being known to no one but the hirer.

[1] By an accident on the underground railway in London.

When the case comes into court, the falsehood of a great many of the witnesses becomes manifest, and one's first impulse is to let every one off. The difficulty is to weed out the few grains of truth that are mixed up with the falsehood. It is most perplexing, but interesting in spite of the difficulties. I like the work much better than the Civil appeals, which formed my principal occupation at Jullundur and Amritsar.

Good news from Mr. Forsyth. One day I had a letter from him written in the lowest spirits. The next, a note came saying he had just heard from Sir Robert (Montgomery) that the Governor-General, in forwarding Forsyth's statement, had said that the Government of India saw no reason to withdraw the censure they had passed, but they gladly took the opportunity of acknowledging Mr. Forsyth's previous services, and they did not see why he should not be employed in another field if the Public Service seemed to require it. His Grace of Argyll re-echoes these sentiments, so, as Sir Robert remarks, the ban has been removed. This is all that could have been expected. I always thought this would be brought about. . . . I am longing to hear more particulars.

Towards the end of January I went into camp with the Commissioner, Mr. Macnabb, trying cases during our halts in or near the villages where the crimes had occurred. On the 27th January we arrived, a large riding-party, at the out-station of Murdan, the headquarters of the celebrated regiment of 'Guides.'

D. Murdan, *January* 27, 1873.—Just as we sat down to breakfast in the Assistant Commissioner's house, a hue-and-cry was raised that a thief had bolted with a horse. It appeared that one of the sowars'[1] horses was being held by a coolie, who mounted it and bolted across the plain. A hot pursuit followed. Mr. Macnabb, the Assistant Commissioner, many native gentlemen, and others galloped after the thief. The sowar had

[1] Native horsemen.

meanwhile mounted my horse and started in pursuit of his own. The thief was eventually caught by the sowar, who cut him over the head with a sword. It seems he is an old hand, and had previously carried off one or two horses in a similar manner.[1]

MURDAN, *January* 28.— . . . The collection of Buddhist sculptures excavated from the old mounds in the neighbourhood is very interesting. The Muhammadans hereabouts are such iconoclasts that even the coolies chip the figures as they dig them up.

From Murdan we marched in almost a direct line, crossing the Indus *en route* to Hassan Abdál, where we arrived on the 1st of February. Preparations were being made there for a large Military Camp of Exercise. The following day Mr. Davies, the Lieutenant-Governor, arrived with his camp.

On the 24th January Mr. Forsyth wrote from Fyzabad: 'My release from purgatory has come sooner than I expected. I am ordered to proceed at once to the Punjab to take charge of the Yarkund Envoy, and within ten days I hope to be at Pindi! My special deputation is expected to last about three or four months. . . . Wonders will never cease. . . .'

CAMP OF EXERCISE, HASSAN ABDÁL, *February* 3.—While I was in R.'s tent, I was surprised and delighted to hear a familiar voice outside. It was Forsyth, arrived from Fyzabad. He hadn't taken long to come; it was most pleasant meeting him again, and at last he seems in good spirits.

HASSAN ABDÁL, *February* 4.— . . . An Envoy from Yarkund arrived in British territory a few weeks ago. He turned out to be an uncle of the Ruler of Yarkund and one of the men who accompanied Forsyth on his previous mission. When this news reached Calcutta, the Governor-General forth-

[1] He was soon after brought to trial and heavily punished.

with appointed Forsyth to attend the Envoy and to escort him to Calcutta. Of course, there is no one in India who understands more about the subject than Forsyth does, and in appointing him the Government has consulted its own and Forsyth's interest. . . .

Mr. Macnabb and I dined with the Lieutenant-Governor and Mrs. Davies in their camp at Hassan Abdal. This was the first opportunity I had had of meeting Mr. Davies since he had become Head of the Province. After dinner he came up to me at once and began talking in a very friendly way. On the whole, however, I had little or no personal communication with Mr. Davies during his Lieutenant-Governorship: the main cause, no doubt, being that my work at that time was purely judicial, and I seldom left the Frontier. Moreover, Mr. Davies, when he assumed office at the beginning of 1871, issued a circular in which demi-official correspondence between himself and his officers was to a great extent forbidden. This order was very unpopular at the time, and was, in my opinion, afterwards proved to have done harm in several ways. It certainly had the effect of doing away with much of the personal influence previously exercised by Lieutenant-Governors over their subordinates.

The 7th February was the great day of the military manœuvres at Hassan Abdal, Lord Napier, the Commander-in-Chief, being present. Mr. Forsyth, who accompanied the Yarkund Envoy to Calcutta, subsequently received orders to proceed with him on his return journey to his own country. Meanwhile, however, the Envoy went to Constantinople and tarried there some time. During this interval Mr. Forsyth was engaged at Calcutta and Simla in organising his Mission. I give some extracts from his letters from time to time, in the hope that they may be found interesting.

T. D. FORSYTH TO G. R. ELSMIE.

CALCUTTA, *March* 14, 1873.

. . . The Envoy leaves this to-morrow for Bombay and Constantinople. . . . He returns in June and the Embassy will start in July. . . .

D. PESHAWUR, *March* 22.—Got up early in order to go out with the Commissioner for a drive, but he did not come as expected, and it turned out that the cause of his detention was the murder of Major Macdonald[1] at Michni[2] by some border men. A wretched affair apparently. In the evening the poor fellow was buried (in Peshawur) with military honours; funeral decidedly imposing. The weather lowering and inclined to burst into a storm.

On the 27th of May we started for Abbottabad, the headquarters of the Hazara district. We were charmed with the beauty of Abbottabad, which is some 4000 feet high, situated in a basin formed by low hills. Wild roses and other flowers were in abundance. The place was very un-Indian in appearance and somewhat reminded me of Bridge of Allan in Scotland. My work at Abbottabad occupied about four or five days. We then marched on to Natia Gali, which at that time consisted of a single wooden Government rest-house. It is now a fairly large hill station, the headquarters in summer of the Chief Commissioner of the Frontier Province.

NATIA GALI, HAZARA DISTRICT, *June* 6.—This is a lovely place in the hills, some 8500 feet high, half way between Abbott-

[1] Cf. p. 140, *Lord Lytton's Indian Administration.*

[2] Fort Michni on the Mohmand border.

abad and Murree. We are in a small wooden hut, which was put up last year; very rough, a stone wall in the middle with fireplace, no plaster, the outer walls and roof just rough planking. However, we are by no means uncomfortable. There are some chairs and tables and carpets in the hut. The climate is simply delightful, almost cold at night. During the day, however, the sun is strong and the thermometer not so low as we expected. The house is entirely by itself. There are a few European troops encamped about three miles off, towards Abbottabad. . . . Hazara must be the finest district in the Punjab. It has every variety of scenery and climate. It reaches from the plains to the snows, and is of enormous extent. Some 3000 square miles. The wood here is most luxuriant. Horse-chestnuts, firs, larches, oaks in great variety and profusion. Round about, the hills are literally clothed with wood, and on that account are even finer than those of Simla and Dharmsala.

T. D. Forsyth to G. R. Elsmie.

MAHÁSU,[1] *June* 17, 1873.

. . . I am in a state of suspended animation, very much as a lady is who has prepared her dinner and finds the guests won't arrive in proper time to eat it before it is spoilt. I have everything ready for a start, and am only waiting for the Envoy. He isn't exactly due yet, and there is no good ground for doubting his turning up to time, but somehow I should be happier if I had him here. Job's comforters abound everywhere, and there are plenty of kind friends to predict that he won't come, and that my second Mission is sure to be a failure. I had rather begin with abuse and end with praise; and, in fact, I look with great distrust on all expeditions that are started with too much *éclat*. They generally come to grief, so that I am rather thankful to hear a good croak now and then. I believe I shall have an uncommonly hard time of it, diplomatically; for the Russians are very much offended at our interfering, as they say

[1] Near Simla.

they have taken the Atalik[1] under their protection, so I may expect all kinds of difficulties. But I suppose you will say that is what I am paid for. . . .

NATIA GALI, *June* 19.—G. acknowledges by present mail £50, 4s. 6d., which left me in April in the form of 545 rupees. So you see our rupees are no longer anything like two-shilling pieces, and never will be again, I believe.

The above extract relates to an early stage of the fall in the value of the rupee. Twenty years later, when I retired from the service, my 545 rupees would have realised at the outside £30 in London.

NATIA GALI, *June* 19.—We leave this hill on Monday if all is well. I should have enjoyed the place more had I not been worried by disagreeable cases. Murders, murders, till I feel I have got swords, daggers, and pistols on the brain. It is bloody work sentencing people to be hanged, and hoping the Chief Court will sanction the executions.

In July I held another large jail delivery at Peshawur. The heat was very great. On the 11th July the temperature in my court-room was 102°. On the 2nd of August I went to Kohat to hold a jail delivery there, travelling from Peshawur with the Rev. J. W. Adams, who was afterwards made a V.C. for his gallant conduct in the Afghan campaign of 1879-80. He was a man of great personal activity, most vigorous and efficient as a military chaplain. During this visit to Kohat I saw much of Captain (afterwards Sir Louis) Cavagnari, the Deputy Commissioner. I find that I noted down at the time that I was disposed to think that he was the best district officer in the Peshawur Division. His subsequent brilliant career fully confirmed that view.

[1] The Ruler of Yarkund.

T. D. Forsyth to G. R. Elsmie.

Simla, *August* 10, 1873.

. . . The Envoy is to leave Constantinople on Tuesday, and I start from this on Monday the 18th. . . . I have a long journey before me; and not altogether an easy task. . . . By the bye, it would not be altogether unamusing if I published all the applications I received and still *daily* receive to accompany me. One man, determined to clench the matter by flattery, wrote, 'Under Providence I hope, but under your guidance I am sure, success must be awarded to your expedition.' Poor Providence! I quite felt for it. . . .

Cherat,[1] *August* 29.—The view is certainly glorious here on clear days. The nearest point on the Indus is said to be twenty miles off, and yet we can see the ripples on the water with my binoculars. We are on the very ridge of the range, so that on one side we can see the whole of the Peshawur valley, and on the other the plains in Jhelum and Shahpore and the valley of the Indus.

T. D. Forsyth to G. R. Elsmie.

Camp Nooralla,
Ladak, *September* 16, 1873.

. . . We have got on, so far, famously. I left Murree in pelting rain and rode out three marches, and kept on at that rate every day till I reached Srinagar, where I found Gordon[2] and Chapman[3] and Bellew[4] very comfortable in one camp, which is arranged in proper military order, that is to say, instead of being pitched anyhow *à la* Commissioner fashion, they are arranged in proper order with the Envoy's flagstaff opposite my shamiána! Then the hundred mules, which form our chief baggage support, are picketed in two lines behind, and the escort on

[1] A small sanatorium for troops on the range of hills between the Kohat Pass and the Indus.

[2] Now General Sir Thomas Gordon, K.C.B., etc.

[3] Now General Sir Edward Chapman, K.C.B.

[4] The late Dr. H. W. Bellew, C.S.I.

one side with the guard over the treasure. The kitchen department was rather weak, not to say awful, till Munirudin[1] arrived, and then the change was instantaneous and complete. You know, of old, M.'s powers, and I have only to say that he is now distinguishing himself in his usual brilliant manner: the more apparently difficult the situation only calling forth from him additional vigour, so that Bellew is lost in admiration, and declares he never ate such dinners on any expedition.

We were right royally entertained by the Maharaja,[2] and he and I met frequently, and vowed eternal friendship, and our parting was as that of lovers! We are now within a march or two of Leh, having come along at a good pace, making twenty-one regular marches in fifteen, without giving a sore back to our mules or suffering any inconvenience. I, being an old stager, fare somewhat better personally than my companions, for whereas they are greasing and oiling their noses and lamenting the likeness of their cheeks to raw beefsteak, I have preserved the pristine beauty of my proboscis by completely shading my face from the sun. We shall halt a week at Leh, and then begins the hard work to cross the Kara Korum. We have heard that the Yarkundees are waiting with supplies and ponies for us on the other side, and I expect Syad Yakub Khan to catch us up before we actually reach Yarkund territory, so that as supplies have been laid out and the weather seems settled, I hope we shall get on without mishap. Biddulph has gone off with Trotter and Stoliczka[3] by the Panjory Lake and Changchemno, and is to join me at Shahdulla on the 20th October. I suppose we shall make our entry into Yarkund about the 10th November.

I like my companions exceedingly. Bellew is a first-rate man in every way, and with all his attainments and knowledge charms me by his modesty. Chapman makes a good secretary, and Gordon, as second in command, relieves me of all details in

[1] The native butler.
[2] Ranbir Singh of Cashmere. See pp. 125, 126.
[3] All members of the Mission.

camp arrangement, so that I am quite a gentleman, I can assure you, and am utterly ruined for all routine work in future! By the bye, I haven't mentioned perhaps the most important member of my staff, Sergeant Rhind, Piper H.M. 92nd Highlanders, who is entertained as Camp Sergeant, but who also delights my Scotch feelings by making the hills resound to the tones of his bagpipes. Surely I have enlisted the sympathies of all Scotchmen in the success of this expedition by thus bravely subjecting myself to such torture! I hope you will not fail to make your mother acquainted with my heroism.

Of course, while passing over such beaten tracks, I have nothing interesting to tell. We had only one sad accident, and it was indeed sad. Crossing the *Zoji la* we had the inexpressible grief of seeing a mule miss his footing and send two precious casks of Whisky and Brandy down a precipice some hundreds of feet, and for a while the river ran brandy, whisky, and water. You may imagine our feelings. This morning we had nearly another accident, for Chapman's mule bolted with his photographic apparatus and everything seemed a complete smash. However, to our great relief, only one bottle was broken, and he has just taken the best picture he has managed to get since he started. . . .

T. D. Forsyth to G. R. Elsmie.

SHAHDULLA, *October* 22.

We have got over all the difficult part of the journey now, and are on the threshold of the promised land, not sorry, I assure you, to have nearly done with the heights for a time. There is one pass between this and the plains of Yarkund, but it is only one day's journey up and down, 17,500 feet. You will probably read enough about our journey, for three at least of my party are sending contributions to the 'local prints,' so I am spared the necessity of description. Everything goes by comparison. If you were suddenly transported here from Peshawur, I dare say you would howl at the cold, whereas we consider ourselves fortunate in getting into a milder climate, the difference being that water only freezes the moment it is poured out, whereas a few days ago we couldn't get water at all. Everything was hard ice, and even ink by the fire would freeze before it could be put upon paper. It is evidently very healthy work though, for we are all remarkably well and jolly. Everything has gone *perfectly* smoothly with us, and there have been no *contretemps* of any kind. I have a first-rate set of officers, who pull well together, and have exalted ideas of the importance of their mission, which is of course quite proper. The Yarkund authorities are determined there shall be nothing wanting on their part, and are stuffing us like turkeys; not to be killed at Xmas, I hope! Their conduct is a curious comment on the predictions of the Cashmere quidnuncs, and on the evil reports spread by the scribbler from Pathánpore. Some of the Government bigwigs, too, who were afraid to give me much support before starting, may now perhaps think it safe to express approval. Temple gave as a reason for opposing the grant of an adequate salary to me, that he didn't feel sure that the Mission would be a success! This principle, if applied to the Finance Minister's salary, would rather astonish him, I think.

I think we shall reach Yarkund about 10th November; remain there a week or so, and then go on to Kashgár, after which we shall see what we shall see. I hear there is splendid sport of every kind to be had in an enormous jungle about seven days' journey north of Yarkund, where I hope to distinguish myself. I never was in better health or trim for sport, and if I have only got the Treaty signed by that time I shall blaze away with a will. . . .

I have just heard that eight hundred horses have come in for my camp in addition to some three hundred already arrived, so I am not in want of carriage at all events. Gordon and three others have gone on to Sanju. I am awaiting the arrival of the Syad from Constantinople. He is to be in to-day. . . .

. . . .

PESHAWUR, *November*.—The October number of *Fraser* came in from the library yesterday. . . . Read the article on the Indian

Civil Service. It gives a very good idea of the financial possibilities of the members. Among other things it says that the men who, thirty years ago, could, according to Macaulay, have saved £30,000 in their term of service cannot now save more than £3000, and that very few ever succeed in saving more than £5000 or £7000 nowadays. I verily believe this to be strictly true of all save the few who come in for the prizes. About 5 per cent. get prizes, according to this writer, the vast majority never rising above £3000 per annum, which they draw for the last few years of service.

By the time that my service came to an end I found that, for an Indian Civilian with a large family to educate in England, saving anything at all was out of the question.

December 24.—Mr. ——, Judge of the Chief Court, arrived two days ago on inspection. He has been staying with Mr. Macnabb, and goes over to Kohat to-day. On his return he comes to us for a day or two. He is a very handsome, kind, gentlemanly sort of a man, about fifty I should say. Very peculiar in some of his opinions, but evidently anxious to do right. He and I very often differ about cases, and his peculiarities exasperate me, but I hope to have one or two things out with him when he is here. It is fortunate he is nice personally, otherwise one would be inclined to sulk and say nothing. He has never been here before. I expect he will be rather astonished as he rides through the Afridi Pass to-day and meets a matchlockman at every turn. I think he ought to be kidnapped into the hills, just a little way, in order to harden his heart against these delightful Afghans.

CHAPTER XI

THE CRIME OF MURDER AMONGST AFGHANS

1873

DURING my stay at Cherat I wrote an official report on the prevalence of the crime of murder in the Peshawur Division. I doubted whether much fruit would follow my remarks and suggestions, but I felt that I had brought the subject up to date, and thereby relieved my mind of some heavy responsibility. The importance of the subject was fully admitted on all hands, and many were the minutes by higher authorities which my report called forth. Great delay occurred, however, before the matter was taken up by Government in real earnest. Eventually, as will be seen, results of far-reaching effect followed, which could hardly have been anticipated in 1873. Some extracts from my report will show the nature of the chief difficulties with which the criminal administration of the Peshawur frontier was beset at this time.

The heaviest and most important part of my work as Additional Commissioner of this division consists of the trial of persons accused of murder. The extraordinary prevalence of this crime in the Peshawur district and the remarkable features of individual cases could not have failed to create a deep impression on my mind, even had I been ignorant of the facts that the Government regards with the utmost concern the continued frequency of murders, and that the prevention of their occurrence and the due punishment of their perpetrators are the objects of the greatest anxiety. . . . The information which I possess on the subject has been for the most part derived from trials in my own court, from conversations with many respectable natives of the district, from the perusal of the criminal reports of the Judicial Commissioner, Chief Court, and the Inspector-General of Police, and from the examination of the records of a very large number of sessions trials held at Peshawur during the last twenty years. . . . In 1849-50, murders or crimes accompanied by murder are said to have been committed at the rate of one per diem in the Peshawur district. . . . The first annual returns of crime for the Peshawur Division were those for 1853. The Judicial Commissioner,[1] in his annual report for that year, wrote: '. . . The amount of crime exhibited is quite appalling, and shows that in the Peshawur valley every species of crime is perpetrated on an extended scale.' . . .

It appears that a considerable improvement had taken place in 1859. The Commissioner, Major James, then wrote: 'The number of violent crimes has annually decreased as much as can be reasonably expected on this border.'

The number of murders had fallen from 83 in 1853 to 43 in 1859. In 1868, however, the number rose to 80; in 1869 it fell to 73; but during 1870, 1871, and 1872 the number of murders was 92, 93, and 103 respectively. It would seem, therefore, that the crime at present, though much less prevalent than in 1849-50, is more so than it was in 1853. . . .

Peshawur is one of thirty-two districts in the Punjab, and its population may be roughly taken to be one thirty-second of that of the whole Province. Nevertheless, it has to account for at least one-third of the murders committed within the whole of the provincial area. . . .

The population belongs chiefly to the Pathan or Afghan race. This fact is of course the main root of the evil.

'Brave, independent, but of a turbulent, vindictive character,

[1] Mr. Robert Montgomery.

their very existence seemed to depend upon a constant succession of internal feuds. . . . They knew no happiness in anything but strife. It was their delight to live in a state of chronic warfare. . . . Blood is always crying aloud for blood. Revenge was a virtue among them; the heritage of retribution passed from father to son, and murder became a solemn duty.'[1]

Such was the character of the people when the Peshawur Valley formed part of the kingdom of Afghanistan. During the time of Sikh rule 'the maintenance of internal order (in the Peshawur Valley) was scarcely attempted; blood-feuds between districts, villages, and families were unchecked, or followed only by the levy of fine when the Government officers deemed it prudent to interfere. In fact, the Pathans continued to govern themselves by the same rude and sanguinary laws which had been handed down to them by their forefathers, and which offered to their wild nature a more congenial mode of avenging wrongs and adjusting disputes than the courts of infidels. . . . The Sikhs were unable to adopt any systematic restraint of those deep-rooted habits and feelings which filled the district with crime and blood.'

Subsequent to British annexation, I find the people of the valley described as a 'race of men accustomed from their youth to murder and revenge, and to appeal to the sword for the settlement of every dispute.' . . .

It may be said, however, that the whole of the people are not Pathans, for they only represent 46 per cent. of the population. But, in the opinion of the late Sir Herbert Edwardes, 'there is evidently something in the air of the Frontier which rouses brutality in every Muhammadan.' My short experience fully confirms that view. It is indeed no matter for surprise that the inferior tribes should have followed the example of the dominant race, and that Afghan customs and the Afghan code of honour should have become the fashion.

Foremost amongst the causes which excite the Pathan to revenge are wrongs and jealousies in regard to women. Husbands

[1] Kaye's *War in Afghanistan*, vol. i. p. 11.

however, are not the only persons who consider themselves bound to avenge injuries of this description. Brothers will seek to destroy the seducers of their sisters or sisters-in-law; parents will murder daughters who have been dishonoured before marriage; disappointed lovers will from spite kill innocent girls whom they have been unable to obtain in marriage. I have been assured that when a Pathan discovers that his dishonour is generally known, he decides deliberately that it is better to die than to live, so long as he can avenge himself. Transportation and hanging are said to involve no disgrace whatever, so long as they are incurred in what is considered a righteous cause. Marauding expeditions and disputes regarding land and water are fertile sources of blood-shedding. So long as the population is armed, thieves are not likely to set forth without weapons. When quarrels arise between two factions in the fields it is not difficult for them to call out armed adherents from the villages. Murders attributable to any of these causes become in their turn the sources of others—the relatives of the victims being bound to avenge their death. Hence arise the blood-feuds which are handed down from father to son. . . .

A standing source of difficulty with which both the village and regular police must contend is the proximity of independent territory. Escape across the border is generally easy, and is frequently resorted to by murderers, who know that their guilt would certainly be discovered if they remained behind, and who can depend on finding an asylum with a society which approves of murder and welcomes murderers. . . .

I may appropriately notice one of the principal causes which tend to baffle justice at each stage of the inquiry. It is admitted to be a custom of this valley for the friends of murdered men to add to a true accusation against the real assassin an utterly false one against his relatives. It is also a daily practice to try to improve a true case by false evidence. I have had repeated instances of this abominable and embarrassing system in my own court, but I prefer to make quotations from better authorities than my own experience in proof of its existence: 'A society where the ruin of rivals or opponents by any means is regarded as merely a natural proceeding.'

Again, 'If one could believe that Watmeer and his brother did take the names of the accused in good faith the matter could be simple enough, but the unfortunate thing is that one cannot believe these names were taken in good faith, as it is the constant practice in this country for wounded men not to take the names of those who actually wound them and whom they distinctly recognise, but to denounce the persons whom they feel sure were the instigators of the attack, thereby defeating their own object and the ends of justice.'

The practice was also admitted as notorious by the Chief Court in the case of the Crown *versus* Sirbuland Khán, Dilawur Khán, dated 12th February 1869: 'It is impossible, in dealing with evidence from the Peshawur district, to disregard altogether the custom among the Pathans of that district, which is a matter of notoriety, to accuse all the members of a family when one or more of them commit an offence of this kind. . . .' It is interesting to compare these extracts with what was written in regard to a similar matter in the Lower Provinces so long ago as 1803:[1] 'In the course of trials the guilty, very often, according to the best of my observation, escape conviction. . . . Very frequently the witnesses . . . swear to facts in themselves utterly incredible for the purpose of fully convicting the accused, when, if they had simply stated what they saw and knew, their testimony would have been sufficient. They frequently, under an idea that the proof may be thought defective by those who judge according to the regulations, and that the accused will escape and wreak their vengeance upon the witnesses who appear against them, exaggerate the facts in such a manner that their credit is utterly destroyed. Witnesses have generally each a long story to tell (they are seldom few in number, and often widely differ in character, caste, habits, and education) thrice over, namely, to the Darogah, the Magistrate, the Court of

[1] Report by H. Strachey, Esq., at p. 741, vol. i., of the fifth report on the *Affairs of the East India Company*. Madras, 1866.

Circuit; they relate tediously and minutely, but not accurately, a variety of things done and said; numerous variations and contradictions occur, and are regarded with cautious jealousy, though in reality they seldom furnish a reasonable presumption of falsehood.

'But who shall distinguish between mistake and imposture? What judge can distinguish the exact truth, among the numerous inconsistencies of the natives he examines? How often do these inconsistencies proceed from causes very different from those suspected by us; how often from simplicity, fear, embarrassment, in the witness; how often from our own ignorance and impatience? . . .'

I do not think it will be denied that all these difficulties exist in connection with trials in Peshawur at the present day.[1] . . . The whole matter must be treated as a special case. . . . The careful working of Section 6 of the new Frontier rules as recently amended, whereby any person or persons accused of any offence, notwithstanding any proceedings short of actual conviction or acquittal, may be tried and sentenced to fine by a council of elders or jirgah, affords probably the best check against false accusations and false evidence which could be devised. Whenever there is reason to suppose that a false accusation has been made, the case should ordinarily be referred to a council. The falsehood would almost certainly be detected, and the council should have power to punish the false accuser. . . .

In cases of homicide or attempts, it should, however, be competent to a council of elders to sentence the accused to rigorous imprisonment for a term not exceeding five years in addition to fine, such sentences to be subject to confirmation by the Deputy Commissioner. I cannot think that a fine is in any way an adequate punishment for murder. . . .

The report concluded with the recommendation that:

in respect to all cases arising from murders, culpable homicide,

[1] As an illustration I give in the Appendix my judgment in a typical Peshawur trial of the year 1876, reprinted from *Crime and Criminals in the Peshawur Division*.

and attempts to commit these offences, the local courts should be removed from the jurisdiction of the Chief Court (at Lahore). . . .

It is with much hesitation that I have adopted this opinion, but a very careful examination of the Chief Court's appeal statistics, and of the files of every case in which the orders of the Sessions Court have been altered since 1866, has convinced me that it is impossible for any Sessions Judge at Peshawur to guard against the reversal or modification of a very large percentage of his orders. In 1870 the percentage of interference on appeal alone was 31, in 1871 it was about 25, and in 1872 it was 29. I do not of course presume to criticise the justice of these orders, but when it is remembered that in former years the great majority of the sentences passed by the Commissioner were practically final, that the increase of crime has steadily kept pace with the increased percentage of interference by the Chief Court, I come to the conclusion that one of the remedies to be adopted must be that of strengthening the local courts. Such a measure can, I admit, be only justified by the existence of most exceptional causes, but I think I have shown that they do exist, and that the general good of the community demands that they should be counteracted by every reasonable means in our power. That the means should be severe is justified by the character of the Afghan nation. 'Rigour is inseparable from the government of such a people: we cannot rein wild horses with silken braids.'[1] . . .

[1] Kaye's *Afghanistan*, vol. i. p. 120.

CHAPTER XII

ADDITIONAL COMMISSIONER OF PESHAWUR

1874—1875

T. D. Forsyth to G. R. Elsmie.

KASHGAR, *January* 2, 1874.

I SENT you a letter from Shahdulla in October, but have not yet favoured you with any account from Eastern Turkestan; so I may as well remind you that I am still in the land of the living and not altogether sunk in barbarism. . . . You will probably have seen quite enough in print of our doings, so I won't attempt to repeat what has been told so well by the *I. P. O.*[1] special correspondent. We have been getting on most successfully in every way, and I find everything running most smoothly. Perhaps not the least pleasant part of my life is being rid of the servile feeling which attaches to life in India. I am my own master, at all events, here, and can treat with the contempt they deserve all young bumptious secretaries. There is something delicious, too, in the feeling that I have got through my term of service,[2] and can make my bow whenever it suits me to do so. I have a charming set of officers with me, all pull well together, and I have no insubordinate and inefficient Colonels or Majors to ruffle my placid temper. . . . It is intensely cold, but fortunately there is no wind or damp, and as we have skates and any quantity of ice, it is a pleasant amusement of an afternoon to try and keep on one's legs on skates. I can't rate my performance at any higher figure, for not having had skates on for thirty years, and not having hit off the exact point of centre of gravity, the operation of skating is a kind of

[1] *Indian Public Opinion*—a Lahore newspaper. [2] For pension.

fearful pleasure. By way of amusement we are teaching the Yarkundees the science or art, whichever it may be called. Another science I have to acquire is how to get outside, as a Yankee would put it, all the dishes with which we are overwhelmed whenever we call upon our hospitable friends. The Kashgarees are determined to blow us out, to show their love for us, and though all their cookery is excellent, it is possible to have too much of a good thing. In spite of the thermometer having retired for the winter to zero, the enthusiastic sportsmen of my party have gone off to shoot tigers, wolves, ovis Poli, and all kinds of game. I am forced to remain behind for affairs of State, and so dub myself a martyr, but am not altogether sorry to be comfortably housed with good fires. When spring breaks, I hope to commence a long tour towards the north. We have perfect liberty of action and motion, so that we ought to see a good deal of the country. Fortunately the officers on my staff are all of a most industrious, inquiring turn of mind, so that no end of information will be accumulated, without the burden falling on me. This is certainly the land for sport. At Yarkund we had snipe, ducks, pheasants, hares, deer. Here we have all these and double chikor and ovis Poli, morul, a fine large stag, keek or lyre-shaped deer brought in to us constantly, and I am starting a regular zoological garden.

The Amir, Yakub Khan, is exceedingly friendly. I have a great respect for his administrative powers, for he keeps everybody in perfect order, and is a very just man, though severe in his punishments. The Queen in *Alice in Wonderland* would make the Amir a good wife, or, perhaps, between them both the order 'off with their heads' would be repeated rather too often to be pleasant. . . .

PESHAWUR, *February* 18.—I have a very heavy case on hand which is bothering me a good deal, and I cannot get my thoughts off it. These abominable murder trials worry me greatly at times. The ruffianism and lying are of such gigantic proportions. The fear lest one should believe a liar, and the dread of disbelieving a truthful witness, 'harrow' one. I can use no better or more forcible expression. I often feel inclined to have done with the whole thing, and beg to be sent to some quiet district where murders are extraordinary events, and not things of daily occurrence. There is a fascination about Peshawur, nevertheless. The climate at this season is, for the most part, lovely. The surrounding hills are magnificent. The English society is certainly as good, if not better than you will find in any other Punjab station. Then the work, though very harassing at times, is not so tremendously heavy that one can't get through it.

March 4.—It is rather amusing to compare the remarks of A. and B.[1] on the dissolution of Parliament and Mr. Gladstone, the one hoping he may be allowed to grapple with the question of reform, the other wondering whether the country will ever recover from the treatment received at his hands. Well, judging from the telegrams, the country seems determined to have done with him for a time, at all events. We have only newspapers up to the 5th February, when the elections were about two-thirds concluded. By telegraph, however, we know all about the new Ministry, Ashantee battle, etc. I am afraid the Liberals must have deserved their fate, or have fallen victims in an attempt to please all parties. Of course they haven't gone far enough for their radical section, and they have gone a great deal too far for those who are on the borders between the two parties. For myself, I care very little which party is in power, and I sympathise not at all with the abuse which one party hurls at the other. I suppose it is 'constitutional' and necessary, but I am thankful that one may be loyal to the existing Government without any charge of being a turncoat. The policy of the country is for progress and advance, no matter which party is in power, and I doubt not we shall do very well with either. The new Ministry strikes me as a very strong one, as far as its members are concerned, and I heartily wish them every success.

I haven't finished my big case yet, I am sorry to say; had to

[1] Friends at home.

adjourn it for more evidence. I rode out to the village where the murder occurred a few days ago, but the people were in such an excited state that it wasn't possible to make much of them. I am afraid the case is ruined by the addition of false accusations to true ones. . . . This often ruins the case altogether, and makes you feel unable to punish any one, because you can't discover which of all the prisoners is the guilty one.

In March, Sir Richard and Lady Pollock arrived from England in Peshawur. Sir Richard was the permanent Commissioner for whom Mr. Macnabb had been officiating. Sir Richard was an old friend under whom I had served both in the Dera Ghazi Khan and Lahore districts.[1] I was glad to welcome him at Peshawur, though much grieved to say good-bye to his *locum tenens*, Mr. Macnabb, who was proceeding on leave to England.

April 1.—The mail that came yesterday brought us the papers with the close of the Chief Justice's summing-up in the Tichborne case. I am delighted with Sir Alexander Cockburn's remarks on the duties of a judge, and should like to illuminate some of his sentences, and hang them up round the Chief Court. Mr. Justice Lindsay's idea is that a judge should be an 'icicle,' but I do not in the least agree with him. A judge should be a sensible man who knows truth, or what is likely to be truth, when he sees it.

Apropos to the preceding opinion, I may note that Sir Donald Macnabb, many years after his retirement, and many years after I had left the Frontier, revisited the Peshawur district. In talking to one of the Chiefs, Sir Donald asked him if he remembered me. The Chief hesitated a moment, and then said, 'Oh yes, he was the Sahib who, when examining a witness, used to put his

[1] See p. 86.

eyeglass in his eye, and was at once able to see whether truth was being spoken or not.' I am afraid the Chief overestimated the power of my glass as an alethometer, but I was glad to know that I had been regarded as, at all events, a seeker after truth.

T. D. Forsyth to G. R. Elsmie.

YANGI HISSAR, *March* 27.

I hope I am to your 'memory dear,' for I certainly have been long lost to sight, and haven't had a letter from you for a long time. . . . You will probably have seen in the papers that my mission this time has been an entire success. The Treaty was signed two months ago, and I have sent off a party to explore the Pamir, so that I shall have done as much as Politics or Science can rightfully demand. Our relations with the Amir of Kashgar have been of the most friendly kind, and there has been no *contretemps* of any sort to mar the triumph. My officers have pulled well with me. . . . We have had a long spell of cold weather, and it is only now at the end of March that we are emerging from winter. But we have been made most comfortable, and have nothing to complain of. The people are most friendly and pleasant to deal with, very different to the native of India. I find Bellew a capital companion and invaluable officially, as he is working hard at translating histories and collecting information which is to swell the report or record of 'the second mission' to Yarkund and Kashgar.

T. D. Forsyth to G. R. Elsmie.

LEH, *June* 21.

Your last letter gives me a hope, that if you only get timely notice I may have the pleasure of seeing you at Murree as I pass by. I expect to be there about the 12th July, and shall probably stay two or three days. . . . I leave this to-morrow for Cashmere, not at all sorry to have done with the *high* travelling, which I feel doesn't at all suit my old bones and broken wind. . . .

During the next month or two I was fully occupied in holding Sessions trials at Peshawur, Kohat, and Hazara. At intervals news came from Mr. Forsyth reporting progress on his homeward journey from Yarkund. In July, when we were at Cherat, a letter unexpectedly arrived from him dated Srinagar, Cashmere, giving me probable dates of his arrival at Murree and Rawul Pindi. This letter caused me to set out at once, in the hope of a meeting. In the afternoon I rode down the hill some eighteen miles or more to the Grand Trunk Road, whence I travelled by carriage, arriving at Rawul Pindi about seven the next morning. There I ascertained that Mr. Forsyth was travelling that day down the hill from Murree, and would rest at Barakao, about twelve miles from Rawul Pindi, in the afternoon. I hired a post-office cart, and drove to Barakao. Mr. Forsyth arrived between one and two.

CHERAT, *July* 18.— . . . We had a most satisfactory talk at the rest-house for two hours, and then drove to Rawul Pindi together. We parted at 5.30 P.M. I had to travel back here, and Forsyth to dine at the General's. . . . He was a good deal taken aback by his grand reception on entering the Punjab and Murree. The Commissioner, Secretaries, and a host of others came out to receive him, and when he got to the house where he was to stay, he found a guard of honour drawn up. . . . It was a curious contrast to his departure from the Punjab in 1872. . . .

August 2.—Yesterday's paper contained a telegram telling of Mr. Forsyth being made an extra Knight of the Star of India. So he is Sir Douglas after all. Of course it was absolutely certain that this would come, but the quickness with which the honour has been bestowed, and the fact of their having made him an extra Knight, there being no regular vacancy, is very complimentary.

PESHAWUR, *December* 9.—A member of Parliament, Mr. ——, and his wife have been visiting Peshawur. They stayed with General ——, who is a bluff Yorkshireman. When Mrs. —— said she was delighted with India, the General remarked that he didn't wonder at it, seeing they were passed from place to place, from one comfortable house to another. 'In a year or two,' he went on to say, 'I expect there will be hotels in every place, and then we shan't see so many of you travellers. I wonder whether, when I come home, the Lords-Lieutenant of Counties will look after my comforts? I trow not.' The General rather prides himself on the utterance of these home truths. . . .

I may close the record of the year 1874 by the following note written at the time, which shows that some substantial progress had been made in meeting the tendency of the Chief Court to interfere in criminal appeals:—

This year the percentage of interference is much less. The reversals, instead of being slightly over 15 per cent. on convictions in my court, are only just over 3 per cent.

At the beginning of 1875 our home at Peshawur was temporarily broken up. Owing to the serious illness of one of our children it was decided that my wife and family should at once go to England. I received permission to escort the party as far as Jullundur. On my return journey I spent a night at Amritsar with General Taylor. It was a great pleasure to meet again, but it was the last time that I ever saw him.

I conclude my references to General Taylor, who, within a year or two from this time, retired from the service, by two characteristic extracts from his letters. The first was written to my wife at Peshawur soon after our arrival there, and illustrates, *inter alia*, his spirit of quiet humour and power of friendly sympathy. The second extract is from a letter addressed to his own wife, which has already been published in the *Life* by Gambier Parry. Friends who admired and loved Reynell Taylor will not object to reading again his touching disclaimer of official ambition.

AMRITSAR, *January* 12, 1873.

MY DEAR MRS. ELSMIE,— . . . I am so glad that you like Peshawur better than you expected to do. I think I promised you this, or at any rate meant to do so, but in truth I felt much for you, as the distance was great and the change of scene certainly considerable. I felt sure, however, that with the good spirit in which you were both going, you would very soon find alleviations, and begin to feel a more comfortable grasp of the new position. Here we have fallen into the dumps altogether . . . the place seems quite deserted. I am all alone in my big house with four plated dishes, purchased for 180 Rs.; so you will, I hope, allow that the extravagance has not been startling, and there are now receptacles for the food, and the muffin-plates retire on their legitimate duties. . . . I have had very heavy sessions cases, some of considerable difficulty, and I have one left, a heavy one, the open slaughtering of a zaildar[1] by his brother and his own son! Even Peshawur does not often afford anything so bad. There are about sixty witnesses for and against. . . . Give my love to your husband and to Donald Macnabb when you see him. You don't mention how you like your own house, but I suppose, as you do not speak unfavourably of it, it is bearable. I should like to feel clear of its exact position. I know the house Macnabb is in, and the Commissioner's cutcherry, and the District cutcherry, and the Artillery mess. To which of the above establishments is it nearest? Ask Elsmie to mention in his next letter, whenever that may come off. I hope your children flourish in the Peshawur air.—Believe me, yours very sincerely,

REYNELL TAYLOR.

[1] A rural police-officer.

General Reynell Taylor to his Wife.

I feel the pinnacles are not for me, and without any sour-grape feeling I can honestly say that I can get on very comfortably, thank God, without them. My pinnacle is a competency to live at home and among my children. If this is granted me, others may perch on the icy peaks of fortune, and I will not grudge them the success. They are icy in the main, though they glitter so in the sunlight, and sympathy fails to a great extent when they are reached. The individual has then to fly or fall alone, and the peaks themselves have sharp points and edges which make them less charming as resting-places than they appeared below.

February 17, 1875.— . . . I have very nearly given up troubling my head about doctrines, which appear to me to be for the most part the invention of ecclesiastics . . . and which cannot possibly be understood and grasped by the vast majority of plain and simple people. . . . The world will soon see religion simplified, I expect. Unless it becomes so, the conversion of India is a very far-off thing indeed. . . .

Fancy my meeting the Rev. F. Glover here, father of the Ashantee Captain Glover. I had seen him once before at home. . . . He is travelling in India as the privileged representative of Professor Piazzi Smith, in order to reveal to people the mystery of the Great Pyramid! He is upwards of seventy, I believe, and evidently has a bee in his bonnet, but is a kindly old man. It is marvellous the number of people who get this length nowadays.

During the early part of this year, I find that I occasionally played whist with Colonel Cobbe of the 17th Regiment. He had the reputation of being an extremely fine player, and so far as I was able to judge, the reputation was thoroughly well deserved. I certainly am not conscious of ever having played with such a complete master of the game. He seemed able to grasp the whole situation after a few tricks had been turned, and from that time to perceive infallibly where the rest of the cards lay. He had a perfect temper and never showed annoyance at the mistakes of inferior players, but at the end of the hand he would gently indicate how those mistakes might have been avoided. He did this with such perfect tact that his criticisms were received on all hands with gratitude and full acceptation.

In the middle of April Colonel James Hills, V.C., of the Artillery, came to share my house. We had much in common, and the hot weather which we spent together will always be remembered by me with great pleasure. In the autumn, to my sorrow, Colonel Hills left Peshawur to take up the appointment of Assistant Adjutant-General of the Lahore Division. Subsequently his career was a most distinguished one. His services on the staff of Sir Donald Stewart during the second Afghan war and at Cabul as Governor of the city were most marked, and he is now General Sir James Hills Johnes, V.C., G.C.B., with, I hope, many years of life before him.

SIR DOUGLAS FORSYTH TO G. R. ELSMIE.

CALCUTTA, *March* 23.

The Fates are very capricious and now have sent me to quite a new country. I am off to Burma on a special mission to bring the King of that country to his senses. You will doubtless have seen this announced in the papers. It is rather a violent plunge into a new sea just at this time of year, but I don't at all object, as it establishes one fact, viz. that when work is to be done I am not forgotten, and there is a certain amount of pride in feeling that one is of use. . . .

May 2.—I never thought it possible that the Gaikwár[1] could

[1] The trial of the Gaikwár of Baroda on a charge of attempting to poison the Resident had just taken place.

be reinstated. I think the Government have got out of the difficulty very successfully, considering all things. They will not be in a hurry to appoint a mixed Commission again. The experiment of giving Natives a really difficult case to investigate will show that they are not up to such a task. Anyhow, according to my experience, it is quite enough for a criminal case to be really difficult for a Native to shirk giving an opinion on the issue. The failure of these Native Commissioners may check for a time the absurd desire manifested in some quarters to put them wholesale into high judicial appointments. In this way good may be done.

SIR DOUGLAS FORSYTH TO G. R. ELSMIE.

SIMLA, *May* 6.

. . . I leave this on Saturday, and *hope* to be back in July. I can scarcely believe the King will fight; anyhow, he will have to give in, and had better do it with a good grace. . . . Perhaps you shall have a voice from the cage in Mandalay.[1]

The month of May 1875 is memorable in the annals of the city of Peshawur, on account of the great fire which broke out on the 13th and lasted till the 16th of the month.

D. May 13.—Towards evening heard that a large fire was raging in the city. Immediately after dinner I rode down to the Hushtnagar gate to see whether I could be of any assistance. The fire seemed quite unmanageable, wind very high. A whole bazaar, with an immense number of houses behind it, seemed on fire. . . . Superintended the blowing up of some houses by a Sapper sergeant. . . . I remained till past 3 A.M., when I came home, feeling I could do nothing.

D. May 14.—Went down to the fire between 7 and 8 A.M. Nicholson[2] and others continuing the mining and blowing.

[1] For a detailed account of the Mission to Burma, see chap. xi. of the *Autobiography of Sir Douglas Forsyth*. I have found no further letters from him on the subject.

[2] Now General Sir W. G. Nicholson, R.E., K.C.B., etc.

We thought progress had almost been arrested. Anyhow, when Hills and I returned, we were full of hope. I telegraphed to the Commissioner at Abbottabad, saying I thought matters were mending; however, the wind sprang up afresh by evening; the fire was making immense strides. Hills and I went down about 6 P.M., came back to dinner, and then went down again and remained till between 2 and 3 A.M. We supervised a great deal of blowing-up by the Engineers, and thought we had done fairly good work, but nothing would stay the wind! Fortunately no casualties seemed to take place.

D. May 15.—Fire continues violently. Went down about 8 and remained two or three hours. Not able to do much good. Fire attempting to cross the gaps made the previous night. Every one is almost exhausted, and it is extremely difficult to work. Came home about 11 A.M. and rested during the day. Went down again in the evening. Great mining going on all day. At night a body of Europeans, under Hills, wrestled with the fire and frustrated its attempt to cross the stream near the Kotwáli (principal police-station of the city). Evening, drove down to the Gorkutra, whence had a splendid though fearful view of the fire. The sight, as a sight, was certainly magnificent.

D. May 16, *Sunday.*—Got up at 5 and went down to the city. Matters much improved. The engines were able to play on the last burning house, and there seems every chance of an end having come at last.

May 17.—Fire seems now finally extinguished.

Towards the end of May I held a long jail delivery at Abbottabad. My work detained me there till the 15th of June. During that time I paid a visit of several days to General (afterwards General Sir Charles) and Mrs. Keyes. General Keyes was at this time commanding the Punjab Frontier Force. Mrs. Keyes was a sister of Sir Henry (afterwards Field-Marshal Sir Henry) Norman. At Natia Gali, my next stage, I was the guest of Sir

Richard and Lady Pollock. One evening the record of a criminal trial held by me at Kohat was received back from the Chief Court. The case was a very difficult one, and I fully expected that the Judges would reverse the conviction and cancel the sentence, but I was not prepared for certain very severe and, as I thought, undeserved criticisms which the Judges were pleased to record in regard to the mode in which I had conducted the proceedings in the case. After careful reconsideration of the whole file, I came to the conclusion that the criticisms were highly unjust. I laid the papers before Sir Richard Pollock, who thought that the remarks I objected to were quite uncalled for. A week or two later, on passing through Murree, I sought an interview with Sir Henry Davies, the Lieutenant-Governor. I stated the facts fully to his Honour and to his Secretary, and I added that, if the remarks were justified, I thought I was unfit to retain my office. Both of these gentlemen were clearly of opinion that I could not accept the censure in silence. Sir Henry Davies gave a touch of humour to the matter by bidding me remember that the remarks to which I took exception had been written at Lahore in the month of June, when the thermometer indoors was well up in the nineties. Then followed a somewhat prolonged correspondence with the Chief Court, into the details of which it is not necessary to enter. Suffice it to say that in the end, on the 20th December, I received a copy of an order from the Judge of the Chief Court who had written the remarks, directing me to erase every word of them from the record. I have always regarded this controversy as the greatest, if not the only, official 'row' which I had to encounter during the whole of my service. It was only in my mind finally disposed of when, some two years later, I found myself appointed to a seat on the Bench of the Chief Court on the recommendation of the Punjab Government.

July 25.—The Chief Court have been bullying me a good deal lately, and saying that I put things too strongly for the prosecution in cases which come before them. You know they never see the cases in which I acquit. I deny their charge *in toto*, but I admit that I am very anxious not to let off guilty men in a community where one out of every five thousand of the people is murdered per annum; that is to say, murder is about twenty times as prevalent here as in other districts. It is not in human nature to disregard that fact altogether, even when one is acting judicially. I have told the Government of my difficulty, and said that my own impulse is to take a year's furlough, and not to attempt to struggle on under a Court which is prejudiced against me. The truth is, I have never scrupled to speak out my mind about the Chief Court, and I came here determined to do so, and from the first I proclaimed my intention to make a stand. . . . No one in my position can be expected to work well without much support. One of my faults is that I do not *reverse enough of my subordinate's orders*.[1] I do my utmost to support when it is possible to do so, just as the Government at home does its best to support the Indian Government, and not to cavil at every petty flaw. . . . I have had more worry and vexation here than in all my previous service put together, and yet I like the place and appointment, and should be sorry to give them up.

In September I left Peshawur on three months' privilege leave to England. Trains were now running on the

[1] Cf. p. 397 of Sir Theodore Martin's *Life of Lord Lyndhurst*, where it is said that a charge against Lord Lyndhurst was that he almost always affirmed: 'And why not, if the judgment appealed from was sound.' In contrast to this, Lord Cottenham is said to have always presumed the decree to be wrong till the contrary was clearly proved!

North-Western line between Lahore and the Chenab; so that from Wazirabad I was able to travel the remaining sixty miles by rail to Lahore.

During my few weeks at home I frequently saw Sir Robert Montgomery at the India Office and at his own house. We had many long talks regarding North-West Frontier politics, and my own difficulties in the attempt to repress serious crime in the Peshawur Division. On one occasion I called on Mr. Fitzjames Stephen[1] at his Chambers in the Temple. He allowed me to talk fully to him and show him papers about Peshawur crime.

Mr. Fitzjames Stephen to G. R. Elsmie.

4 Paper Buildings,
Temple, *November* 13, 1875.

My dear Mr. Elsmie,—I have read the enclosed with much interest. I am by no means sure that you have not made out a *primâ facie* case for some special action on the part of the Government. It might, for instance, be possible to let the appeal in cases of murder in the Peshawur Division go to a special court consisting of Sir R. Pollock and yourself, or some other Commissioner on the spot. I should not have hesitated to advise some such measure to check such an increase of crime.
—Ever sincerely yours, J. F. Stephen.

Sir Robert Montgomery to G. R. Elsmie.

My dear Elsmie,—Your visit to Sir H. Maine yesterday made a great impression, and he has suggested that he and I should go to Lord Salisbury and get him to initiate a despatch which may lead to your views being carried out. I will do this *con amore*. So your visit will not be in vain if we can have

[1] Who had by this time resigned his seat as the Legal Member of the Viceroy's Council.

something done. . . . It will be well for you occasionally to correspond with Mr. Stephen and Sir H. Maine. R. M.

These are only a few farewell lines, my good wishes for your journey.

On the 17th of November we left London on our return to India, and arrived at Peshawur on the 18th December.

CHAPTER XIII

ADDITIONAL COMMISSIONER OF PESHAWUR

1876-1877

NEW elements will be introduced into the record of 1876. Early in the year Lord Lytton succeeded Lord Northbrook as Viceroy, and soon after it seemed to be in the air that a more decided Central Asian policy was about to be adopted by the Government of India. Lord Lytton's action in regard to Afghanistan, and the Frontier generally, will be noticed from time to time, but it must be remembered that I had no official connection with these subjects. The fact that I was the colleague of the Commissioner in the Judicial department accounts, however, for my being brought into daily contact with him, and it would have been strange had I not become aware of much that was causing him anxiety in the Political and other departments of his work. Apart from questions relating to Afghanistan, the conduct of the Afridis, which led to the closure of the pass between Kohat and Peshawur during this year, caused much trouble to the Commissioner and his subordinate, Captain Cavagnari, the Deputy Commissioner of Kohat.

D. PESHAWUR, *February* 12, 1876.—We dined quietly with the Pollocks to meet Sir Bartle Frere, who has returned to India on the Prince of Wales's staff. He was as bland as could be, but not very amusing.

D. February 15.—Day of Pollock's picnic to the Khyber. E. and I drove out to Jamrud, and thence went by pony and elephant to the Khyber. Day decidedly successful. Sir Bartle Frere and Canon Duckworth were the principal guests. The question was propounded as to what the Afridis would do with the Canon if they carried him off. The reply was hazarded that of course they would rifle him.

February 22.—We have just come back from dining with the Pollocks to meet the Bishop (Milman) and his chaplain, who arrived on an inspection tour. The chaplain is a Mr. Jacob,[1] son of one of the old Winchester Archdeacons. . . . We are looking forward to hearing the Bishop preach on Sunday. He is really an eloquent man; always preaches extempore. . . .

D. Sunday, February 27.—The Bishop preached at the evening service, but not with his usual force, evidently suffering. . . .

March 2.—The Bishop very ill, little improvement manifest.

D. March 15.—Heard of the death of Bishop Milman at Rawul Pindi, to which place he had been moved in the hope of benefit from change of air. In common with others we regret him much.

About this time Sir Douglas Forsyth left India on furlough with little or no intention of returning. He made an extended tour on his way to England.

SIR DOUGLAS FORSYTH TO G. R. ELSMIE.

CALCUTTA, *February* 14, 1876.

I start on my travels this day week, and expect to come to a standstill some time in August. I am afraid you will be tempted to put aside your pen till then in the matter of corresponding with me, but there is no reason why you should *not* send a letter to America to cheer me on first arrival in that country. . . . I am already beginning to look down on Indian official life as a passing scene which has no personal interest for

[1] Now Bishop of St. Albans.

me. The idea is prevalent that there will be a great change in our policy when Lord Lytton comes out. . . . Probably you, like all of us, feel that the most important question of the day is the fearfully ruinous rate of exchange, and there is unfortunately no prospect of improvement. It is very hard upon small incomes, and makes the problem of living comfortably on next to nothing, all the harder. I don't know where we shall finally settle. But a workhouse appears the most suitable place. . . .

March 7.—The Kohat Pass closed. I have to go to Kohat on duty at the end of the month. E. will probably go with me, but the journey is a great grind, as we have to go down the Trunk Road to Attock, then for eight hours in a small boat on the Indus, and after that have a four hours' drive over a bad road. I fear the Pass will not be open for a long time, as the Afridis do not seem inclined to come to terms. We have quarrelled with them about their not repairing the road in the Pass. The Pass is in foreign territory, and we have hitherto paid the tribes 10,000 rupees per annum for the use of it, but pressure has been put on them to make it a good drivable road. This they consider beneath their dignity, so we have stopped the allowance, and blockaded the tribe, *i.e.* we allow none of their members to appear in British territory. The effect is that they are cut off from their trade with Peshawur, on which they almost entirely depend. It is supposed that they will give in and come to terms in a month or two. Meanwhile it is very aggravating to have to go a round of one hundred and twenty miles instead of forty miles by the direct road.

My wife and I left Peshawur late at night. We reached Attock before dawn, where we found a boat ready for us, with a thatched covering to protect us from the sun. We dropped down the Indus rapidly and satisfactorily. By 2 P.M. we were at Khushálgurh, some forty miles from Attock. Here we put up at a rest-house till early the following morning, when we started soon after 6 A.M. for Kohat. We drove three stages in a dogcart. For the fourth stage Captain Cavagnari had sent out his own carriage to meet us. Kohat was reached shortly before 11 A.M. We were most kindly received by Captain and Mrs. Cavagnari in their new house, 'Octagon Hall,' during our stay. Outside the station the country was in a somewhat disturbed state. Ill-disposed tribesmen trespassed at night within cantonment limits, and special precautions were taken when we drove to the houses of friends after dark, Captain Cavagnari having heard of Afridi plots against him and of 500 rupees having been offered as the price of his assassination. My work being finished, we set out for Peshawur on the 3rd of April. It was, of course, impossible to return by the river up stream, so it was arranged that we should drive in dog-carts and such like, straight from Kohat to Attock through the Khwarra range. The first day, after travelling some thirty or forty miles, we put up in a rough police-station at Lukhar Talao, where we spent the night. Khairabad on the Indus, opposite Attock, was reached in the evening of the following day. Khairabad is about forty miles from Peshawur on the Grand Trunk Road, so from thence we were able to reach home by post-carriage none the worse for our adventures, which were nevertheless attended with a certain amount of risk. On the 21st of April, early in the morning, I heard from Sir Richard Pollock that he had been summoned to meet the Viceroy, Lord Lytton, at Ambala on the 24th. During the day Sir Richard made over charge of the Division to me and left Peshawur. On his return he told me that he had been well received by Lord Lytton, but that he was full of secrets and his mouth was closed. I gathered, however, that some startling disclosures had been made to him with regard to our future relations with Afghanistan.

SIR DOUGLAS FORSYTH TO G. R. ELSMIE.

YEDO, JAPAN, *May* 12, 1876.

I dare say you haven't had many correspondents in Japan, and perhaps you are wondering where I have got to, so I will send you a few lines to let you know my opinion of this part of the world. I have had a most delightful trip so far, and am only sorry that I did not take it at an earlier period of my life. I am astonished at the ease with which it is possible to compass nearly all that I have done within the three months' privilege leave which Civilians can get without loss of pay. The journey to Hong-Kong can be performed from Calcutta by a direct opium steamer in thirteen days, and the journey thence to Yokohama occupies seven days more, so that in three weeks you can be landed in Japan. I have made a more extended journey, but I will just sketch what might be done by a Civilian on a holiday. Suppose you reached Yokohama in three weeks, and spent four days there and at Yedo, and then travelled in eight days across country to Kioto, the ancient capital of Japan, thence by rail one day to the seaport of Kobe, thence by steamer to Shanghai, passing through the inland Japan sea. This would occupy four days more. Shanghai would not occupy more than one day. Thence to Hong-Kong five days, and thirteen or fourteen more back to Calcutta. Thus the whole journey might be accomplished in sixty-six days, leaving twenty-four days for delays on the road and for accidents. Steamers go two or three times a week between Hong-Kong and Yokohama, and almost as often to Shanghai; from this and between Shanghai and Hong-Kong the communication is daily or nearly so.

Thus I show you that a three months' trip to Japan is quite

possible and it is well worth doing. I never enjoyed anything so much in my life. Penang and Singapore are places worth seeing, but they can be easily done in the time the steamer usually stays at each place. Hong-Kong pleased me greatly: it is thoroughly English and the people live in English houses and are quite civilised! I found Sir Arthur Kennedy a model Governor, most hospitable and genial and ready to give information on all matters connected with his small Government, and withal sociable and free from official pride. There is a marked difference between these Colonial and Foreign Governors and Ministers who have to deal with free and independent Britons and Europeans, and our Indian officials of the general class. From Hong-Kong I took a run over to Canton. The steamer goes every day and the journey only occupies five or six hours. Canton is a good specimen of a Chinese city. It is the commercial capital of Southern China. The streets are very narrow and there is scarce room for two chairs (or jampans) to pass. They are filthily dirty and the odours are severe. But it is well worth going through the town to see Chinese life. I spent three days with Sir Brooke Robertson, our Consul, who showed me the principal objects of interest. I was surprised to find so few fine buildings, and was disappointed in the chief Pagoda. In fact, I have seen finer buildings in Burma than I have met with anywhere in China, except at Peking. I went over the arsenal at Canton and found them making Gatling guns. They have a good supply of Krupp's heaviest guns, and take care of them. My first impression, on seeing the arsenal and their fortifications and their war steamers, etc., was that they were becoming a formidable power, but further inquiry and acquaintance lead me to a totally different conclusion, and I should say that China is the sick man of the East, just as, if you remember, we saw ironclads at Constantinople and observed an appearance of military grandeur, yet we know that all is rottenness within.

I took the direct steamer to Shanghai, though by so doing I believe I missed the prettiest part of China. Shanghai is a purely European settlement on the banks of a river twelve miles from the sea, and is just like a neat country or seaport town at home. Every Englishman in China lives most comfortably, so far as I have seen. Food is cheap and the devil hasn't sent the cooks, though perhaps he takes them when their work is done! From Shanghai magnificent steamers ply up and down the Yangtsze Kiang as far as Hankow, 600 miles off. I hadn't time to go so far, but instead took steamer to Tientsin going by Chefoo, a pretty little watering-place, and then across the gulf of Pe-cheli. I saw the celebrated Taku forts, which have been entirely rebuilt and refortified since our last war. Tientsin lies eighty miles up the river Peiho and is a town of considerable importance. The Viceroy of Upper China, Li Hung Chang, lives there. He is by far the most influential and intelligent officer in China, and is said even to aspire to usurp the throne. Having been at Kashgar and Burma I was an object of curiosity to his Excellency, who sent a message to say he wished to see me, and we had a very interesting interview. I was much struck with his fine appearance and open, frank manner. By some he is considered to be brusque, but I did not find him offensively so. From Tientsin to Peking the distance, ninety miles, has to be travelled in country carts over the vilest road imaginable. The carts are somewhat better than hackeries,[1] but have no springs and are drawn by mules, who now and then indulge in a trot so as to give an extra scrunch to one's bones. We did the journey in one spell of twenty-six hours, and arrived at the Peking Legation more dead than alive. Here we stayed a week, and I found Sir T. Wade most hospitable and kind. He coached me up in Chinese Politics, and of course we had a good deal in common to talk about, as Kashgar and Burmese or rather Margary's affairs occupy the chief attention of the Chinese at present. I visited the Summer Palace and the chief objects of interest in and near Peking. It is quite a Tartar city, and the country around, the bazaars and inhabitants, reminded me greatly of Yarkund. But the city of Yarkund is Paradise compared to Peking in the matter of odours. It is the

[1] Indian country carts.

most pestilential city in the world, and as the Legation is situated in the heart of the city, you may fancy the delights of living in Peking. The Emperor is a mere child and never seen. The Empress-Mothers form a Regency, Prince Kung and others being Councillors, and there are boards presiding over each department. All seem to be in a state of collapse, and the very offices are in an advanced stage of decay. The only two boards showing any signs of vitality were the Board of Punishments and the Board of Education. I think the population of Peking has been greatly overrated. It is true that the walls round the Tartar and Chinese city together measure twenty-four miles, but there are vast vacant spaces inside. The wall is tumbling to pieces in places, and there doesn't seem to be much care to repair it. In fact, if Peking were in the Punjab, the Commissioner, Deputy, and all the municipality would receive severe wiggings from H. H. the L.-G. for the disgraceful state of neglect manifest. But Chinamen are happy in their Viceroy, happier still in their filth. I visited the Summer Palace, and could form an idèa from the ruins of the beauty of the place before we committed an act of vandalism, which might have been avoided had Napier been Commander instead of Hope Grant. It is too long a story to go into now, but it is the opinion of men best able to judge, that had we only had a more competent General in China at the time, our campaign at Peking might have produced much more beneficial results. But this is a long matter. I returned from Peking to Tientsin by boat, and found a journey down the Peiho about as interesting as going down the Jhelum or Ravi in a dust-storm. The cold during our visit was considerable, and I was glad to buy a good stout fur at Tientsin and to wear it all the time. I got back to Shanghai on 13th April and found spring just bursting the leaves. A run of thirty-six hours took me across to Nagasaki, which has the loveliest little bay I ever saw, studded with prettily wooded islets, and the hillsides of the mainland clothed with fir forests, tea plantations, and luxuriant crops. The steamer took us thence through the Straits of Simosaki and by the inland sea to Kobe, and more exquisite scenery it is impossible to enjoy. The Bosphorus, Adriatic, and Lake Maggiore are all rolled up into one day's journey. Kobe or Hiogo is one of the Treaty ports of Japan where Europeans have settled but find very little business to do. Here I landed and went by Japanese rail to Osaka, twenty miles off, and thence travelled by jinrickshah to Kioto, the rail not being open just yet the whole way. Jinrickshah is a miniature buggy drawn by a man or men, who go at the rate of five or six miles an hour and keep it up for forty miles! I came over from Kioto to Yokohama in eight days. The distance is three hundred miles, and for each day one set of men performed the whole distance, merely stopping a few minutes every hour or so to eat rice or drink tea.

Japan is certainly the most lovely country I have seen, the scenery is charming. We pass over hills and along valleys, beautifully wooded or covered with luxurious crops, every field the pattern of neatness. At times we found the whole country-side covered with azaleas, camellias grown into large trees, and the wistaria is trained to grow like vines over trellis-work. The people are as friendly as possible and very merry. At every village there are tea-houses or inns which are patterns of neatness and cleanliness. Kioto, the Mikado's ancient capital, is situated in a lovely valley, which reminded me somewhat of Cashmere. The streets are broad and marvellously clean. The Japanese keep everything in perfect order and are the most civilised nation that I have seen in the East. An Exhibition of Arts and Manufactures was held at the Palace in Kioto; and I saw some lovely specimens of Keramic ware. But I haven't time or space to write as I should like, or I would give you a dose of Japanese and Chinese politics with a few sentiments of my own about India. One thing I may say, however, *i.e.* that I wish much that I had undertaken this journey before I visited either Yarkund or Burma, and as regards the latter country, Sir T. Wade told me things which make me less charitable towards Lord Northbrook than I was. But I must conclude this. I leave on the 25th for San Francisco, and after visiting the

Yosemite Valley and Niagara hope to reach London by 15th July,—shall be glad to find a letter from you addressed to London. Give me all your news. . . .

P.S.—Please remember me kindly to Pollock, and tell him that the political secrets entrusted to him in Calcutta, which he guarded so carefully, have been revealed to me. I may have something to say about them when I get home.

In June we left Peshawur for the Hazara district, travelling *viâ* Rawal Pindi and Murree. I held jail deliveries at Natia Gali and Abbottabad, returning to Peshawur and Cherat at the beginning of August. There is little of interest to record regarding this tour, but I find the following amusing note regarding Mr. Donald Macnabb, who meanwhile had returned from England and had been appointed temporarily to be Commissioner of Lahore. Up to this time pleaders, barristers, and advocates were very rarely seen in our courts at Peshawur, indeed no professional lawyers had their headquarters in the Peshawur Division. Mr. Macnabb, however, found himself surrounded by a very different legal atmosphere.

NATIA GALI, *July* 14.—Macnabb wrote from Lahore that he feels as though he was fighting with beasts at Ephesus while surrounded by all the pleaders and barristers who congregate in his court.

SIR ROBERT MONTGOMERY TO G. R. ELSMIE.

INDIA OFFICE, *July* 13.— . . . Frontier matters are engaging my thoughts much, and I greatly fear some fiasco. There seems to be a feeling of the need for some great change, viz. to separate off the whole frontier and make it a separate charge! The present system is said *not* to work well and a better is needed! I cannot agree with you about the Kohat Pass road. To my thinking it is a terrible blunder, and if the past history of the

Pass had been looked to, could not have occurred. The Afridis will *never* make the road. I said this six months ago, and told Sir Henry[1] that it is the only mistake he made in six years. Cavagnari and Pollock should never have proposed it, and it would be a very large ingredient in the hands of those who advocate a change, for a change. We old Punjabis are greatly troubled about it. As to any question of altering the law at Peshawur to make it more workable, all is hung up for the present. The idea is, I believe, to *revolutionise* the whole Frontier! Perhaps put you all under Pelly or Merewether! But I am in hopes that, after all, there will not be great changes. I deprecate any except what *you* want. But when we know that all will stand firm, I will see about your reforms.

I see of course all the papers about the Kohat Pass, and have also many private letters. There is but one opinion about the whole matter here, viz. *that it is a great political blunder*.

Forsyth has come home looking very well. He had a long interview with Lord Salisbury yesterday. I dare say he will rise again to the top somewhere. I must close this. I wish I could have written more. Keep me informed of all that goes on Politically and Civilly. . . .

Sir Robert Montgomery had evidently taken alarm on hearing, as a Member of Council, of Lord Lytton's proposals regarding Afghan policy and the separation of the Frontier.

SIR DOUGLAS FORSYTH TO G. R. ELSMIE.

LONDON, *August* 3.

. . . I strongly advise you to start round the world; it freshens one's ideas and quite changes one's nature. My only regret is that I didn't do it at an earlier stage of my career. Perhaps, though, *then* it would have had a bad effect, for it certainly causes one to think very much less of India and the

[1] Sir Henry Davies, the Lieutenant-Governor.

humdrum life of an official in an up-country station, even though he may have the exciting work of an Additional Commissioner at Peshawur. . . .

The year 1876 was a cholera year, not of the gravest type, but there was much apprehension lest a serious outbreak should take place in the Peshawur city and cantonments. The disease had for some time been slowly creeping up country, and the precaution of quarantine was enforced at various places on the Grand Trunk Road.

September 25.—E. came down from Cherat on Wednesday last, the 20th. It was somewhat difficult to decide whether she should come or stay. At Cherat there were nightly alarms of Afridis, thieves, and such like, shots being fired close to the house. Down here there is the usual risk of fever, and at present there has been a good deal of fuss about some few cases of cholera in the city. . . . I agreed to let E. come down as the best thing to be done under the circumstances.

October 3.—I have been detained by the unexpected arrival of Ata Muhammad Khan, our agent at Cabul, who has been summoned post-haste to Simla. He came to me in the Commissioner's absence. I have had to receive and talk to him, telegraph for orders, etc.

Cholera . . . was confined to the city for upwards of a fortnight. Last Thursday night it suddenly broke out amongst the European troops. A good deal of mischief was done in two days, but a violent dust-storm seems to have cleared the air, and there have been no fresh European cases in cantonments since Sunday. Those which have occurred have been among the men only. Type of a very bad kind, doctors quite unable to do anything. All the affected regiments and batteries have hurried out into camp, and there seems every reason to hope that the outbreak in cantonments was the crisis in the district. . . . The European soldier goes out like a candle in a few hours.

Donald Macnabb hopes to be here about the middle of the month.[1]

November 15.—Sir Lewis Pelly is coming up to Peshawur in the bigwigs' train, and the papers are saying he is to be the next Lieutenant-Governor . . . but I believe he has had no personal experience of the North-West Frontier. He has the reputation of being plausible. He will hardly be welcomed at first. It is impossible to say what will be the result of the Viceroy's visit here. The secret of its object has been thoroughly well kept, and no one seems to know whether even the Afridi question will be much considered.

November 29.— . . . The Viceregal party arrived on Wednesday the 22nd and left on the following Sunday, all well, to Mr. Macnabb's intense relief. His hands were so full, poor man, that he hardly had a moment to eat, far less to sleep. Every corner of his house and adjoining office was full, and there was a long line of tents in the garden. The entry into Peshawur was a success. The party drove in carriages from Attock at a great pace, and reached the dressing and refreshment tents, some five miles from the city, about 3 P.M. There they shook the dust off, while the staff put on their gorgeous uniforms. The procession of carriages being formed, the start was made. About a mile further on the Lieutenant-Governor and Mr. Macnabb met the Viceroy, and the former was taken into his carriage. Near the city Major Ommanney (the Deputy Commissioner) with the Native Chiefs were drawn up. Then the procession turned into the city and drove through some of the principal streets, a royal salute being fired from the old fort. All Military and Civil officers, including myself, who had no special part in the proceedings, were on the steps of Macnabb's house to receive his Excellency. So we had a first-rate view of the arrival, and of the big people as they alighted and walked up the long stone staircase. Lord L. . . . with the Star of India on his left side, was the only one of the arriving party in plain

[1] To act as Commissioner for Sir Richard Pollock, proceeding to England on short leave.

civilian dress. The Lieutenant-Governor, Commissioner, and Deputy Commissioners, being political officers, have to wear diplomatic or political uniforms on such occasions. It is much the same, I believe, as English court-dress, dark-blue coat with gold lace, sword, cocked hat, etc. Lady L. is very tall, decidedly handsome—very pleasant looking when she smiles. . . . The reception being over I carried off my two guests, Mr. Thornton[1] and Colonel Allen Johnson.[2] . . . Macnabb had a dinner-party for eighteen in his house every night, and a supplementary one presided over by the Cavagnaris in the adjacent house for ten or twelve. My guests and I dined the first night. . . . Lord L. is supposed to take no interest in questions of general internal administration, and the Lieutenant-Governor's term of office having so nearly expired, he is only anxious to keep things quiet and get away. So a long time will have to elapse before I see any of the reforms which I have advocated introduced. Mr. Thornton, who was very pleasant and kind, said the Government of India would probably sanction anything sent up by the Local Government, but at present Frontier affairs were in such a transition state, changes of a most radical kind being quite possible within a short time, that nothing small was likely to be taken up just now. A prolonged conference took place on Friday afternoon, when a good many big questions were decided, but only those within a certain charmed circle know the particulars. Apparently there is to be no expedition against the Afridis, but Cavagnari's proposal of having a thoroughly good road for military stores direct from Rawul Pindi to Kohat is to be adopted, as indeed it should have been months and months ago. A very heavy fall of rain spoiled the visit a good deal. The officers (military) had got up a theatrical performance for Friday, which was a great success as far as the acting went, but all the illuminations and decorations outside the theatre were drenched, and it was with the greatest difficulty that people could get there at all. Rain fell

[1] Foreign Secretary to the Government of India.

[2] Deputy Military Secretary. See p. 122.

in torrents and the roads were deep in mud. Lord and Lady Lytton, having promised to go, made a point of keeping their engagement and seemed well pleased. . . . One of the pieces was Sullivan's musical operetta on the subject of 'Box and Cox.' The music extremely pretty; the duets, trios, etc., are very effective. On Thursday forenoon there was a levée for all officers, European and Native, and on Saturday there was a parade of all the troops in the garrison. . . .

SIR DOUGLAS FORSYTH TO G. R. ELSMIE.

44 ONSLOW SQUARE, *November* 22.

. . . Lord Lytton seems to be very restless and given to change. Old Lord Lawrence, whom I saw yesterday, and who is now almost totally blind, deplored to me the craze for alterations. The idea is that Lord Lytton will announce all at once, at the Empress Durbar, the absorption of Sind into the Punjab, creation of a Frontier Chief Commissionership, Oudh absorbed into North-West Provinces, and Central Provinces transferred to Bombay. Norman,[1] I dare say, will be Lieutenant-Governor, Punjab; Pelly, Chief Commissioner on the Frontier. Pollock is to be offered to Amir Sher Ali, who will refuse to have him. Somebody is to be sent to Balkh, and of course Quetta is to be occupied! Such is the India Office gup. The Quetta business is a revival of Rawlinson's oft-mooted and as often rejected scheme. It reminds me of a saying in the play of the *Brothers* by a rejected lover: 'She will accept me erelong, for I have been refused seven times, and of course this can't go on for ever.' . . .

December 13.— . . . There is not much to tell you. The Pollocks came back a week ago, both well. Macnabb is still here clearing up arrears of work. All sorts of secrets and mysteries are in the air, and the general impression is that the clouds will be dispelled on the 1st January at Delhi. Pollock says it is certain that Sind is to be annexed to the Punjab.

[1] Sir Henry Norman.

Some say Oude will be annexed to the North-West Provinces. The new Lieutenant-Governorship will doubtless be announced. Forsyth sends me a message that Sir Richard Meade will probably be the man. I am strongly tempted to go down to Delhi. We have long talked of spending Xmas with the Brandreths at Jullundur, and they are most anxious for us to come. . . . Now that the railway is open to Jhelum, the undertaking isn't very formidable. Bernard is to be at Delhi, so the temptation to go is strong. The courts have a fortnight's holiday from 24th December to 8th January, and all officers, who can be spared, are permitted to go. . . .

Accordingly at Christmas we were the guests of Mr. and Mrs. Brandreth in the Baraduri in the Civil lines at Jullundur. The house party consisted amongst others of Mr. and Mrs. James Lyall, Mr. Burney, and Mr. Cordery (afterwards Resident at Hyderabad). One evening the chief amusement was the starting of a private lottery in regard to the succession to Sir Henry Davies as Lieutenant-Governor in the following spring. As a general rule it is not difficult to foretell who will be the next Lieutenant-Governor. At this time, however, there happened to be a multitude of possible candidates. Among them were Sir Lewis Pelly, Mr. Philip Melvill, Mr. Scarlett Campbell, Sir Douglas Forsyth, Mr. Robert Egerton, Sir Richard Meade, Sir Henry Norman, etc. etc., thirteen in all. The drawing of the lottery and the sale of the thirteen horses gave rise to much fun and laughter. My wife drew Mr. Robert Egerton, but had to sell him at the auction for a fair price. A few days later I went on to Delhi alone, arriving at dawn on Sunday morning the 31st of December. I was met at the railway station by Charles Bernard, who took me to the camp of Mr. Morris, Chief Commissioner of the Central Provinces, whose guest I remained during my visit. Bernard was at this time one of the Commissioners of the Central Provinces. Though we had kept up a steady correspondence, we had only met once for a day or two during the long interval between 1861 and 1877.

I shall not attempt to describe the ceremonies of the 1st of January 1877, of which many full accounts have been published. The reading of the Proclamation and the delivery of the Viceroy's speech took place on a large plain to the north-west of the city of Delhi. An elaborately decorated dais was erected for the Viceroy, who, in speaking, faced an immense grand-stand filled with Native Princes and Chiefs and Political officers in attendance. Behind the Viceroy were two large blocks of seats for European and other visitors who had no official position in the proceedings. The distance between the Viceroy's rostrum and his would-be auditors was so great that it was futile to attempt to hear more than a few words of his speech. I was much struck by the beauty of the music of the Grand March, played by massed bands at important points of the ceremony. The music was new to me, and no one in my neighbourhood could tell me its name or that of its composer. It was not until long afterwards that I discovered that the composer was Wagner, and that the march was that which he wrote to accompany the entrance of the nobles and other guests into the 'Hall of Song' in *Tannhäuser*. More impressive to my mind than the Proclamation scene was the extraordinary and wonderful collection of camps which were pitched outside the city of Delhi. Any one of these camps was, to say the least, unusual and striking to eyes which had never before seen camp life in India on a really large scale. The camps of the Viceroy, the Commander-in-Chief, the Governors of Bombay and Madras, of the Lieutenant-Governors of Bengal, the North-West Provinces, and of the Punjab were each a marvel in itself. But, when to these were added the camps of the great Princes of India, a city of canvas arose from the Delhi plains unrivalled for extent, such as I had never seen before and shall certainly never see again. One of the most enjoyable features of the great gathering was the unexpected meetings with old friends from all parts of India.

On leaving Delhi I returned to Jullundur, and we reached Peshawur on the 9th January, thankful to be at home once more.

CHAPTER XIV

CIVIL AND SESSIONS JUDGE, PESHAWUR

1877-1878

AFFAIRS at Peshawur were far from being in a tranquil state at the beginning of 1877. On the 11th of January news reached the Commissioner that the Jowaki Afridis, whose country is in the spur of hills between Cherat and the Kohat Pass, had made a raid on Nowshera, killing certain policemen. From that time, Sir Richard Pollock was of opinion that an expedition would probably be necessary before the Kohat Pass could be reopened and tranquillity restored on that part of the Border. Considerable excitement was aroused by the rumour, daily increasing in strength, that Lord Lytton was intent on separating the whole of the Frontier districts, from Peshawur to Karachi, and forming them into a new Province. The scheme appeared to most Frontier officers to be practically impossible, one of the chief reasons being the immense length of the proposed Province and the great variety of race elements in the Frontier tribes.

D. January 15, 1877.—Government seems disinclined to make any decided move. What with the Eastern question at home, tribes, and Afghanistan, and impending separation of the Frontier, affairs seem to be in a somewhat ticklish state; much mystery prevailing.

January 24.—Sir Lewis Pelly arrives here to-day, as the Viceroy's Envoy and Plenipotentiary, to confer with the Cabul Prime Minister, who is expected in a day or two. No one, I believe, knows what Sir L. P.'s instructions are, not even the Lieutenant-Governor. . . . All that seems certain is that Lord Lytton and his private secretary, Burne, are charged to carry out a certain policy in defiance of all contrary opinions, and there are said to be tremendous splits in the Councils in London and Calcutta in consequence. . . .

The view expressed in the preceding extract was strengthened by the curious fact that Sir Lewis Pelly, on arrival in Peshawur, did not become the guest of the Commissioner. Arrangements had been made for him to live in the headquarters of the Church Missionary Society, whose principal representative was the Rev. Mr. Hughes, a man of considerable linguistic acquirements and of some influence with Pathans. The Civil officers of the station, as in duty bound, called on Sir Lewis, and some of us were invited to dine at the Mission-house to meet him. Mr. W. Jenkyns, a young Assistant Commissioner, was placed on special duty in attendance on the Cabul Envoy, but in the first instance no local officer was taken into confidence on the subject of the negotiations. Sir Lewis had the reputation of being a first-rate Persian scholar. His Secretary was Dr. Bellew, famed, amongst other things, for his great knowledge of the Afghan language.

D. February 3.—Everything seems in a state of unsettlement. Sir Richard very anxious, not knowing what is going to happen, with the Cabul Envoy and Sir Lewis Pelly conferring together all day long. I believe Sir Richard has at last been taken into confidence, as Sir Lewis does not find things going as smoothly as he could wish. Meanwhile the Lieutenant-Governor is at Rawul Pindi, quite in the dark as to Cabul affairs, but supposed to be busying himself on Afridi matters.

February 7.—Sir Richard came in between 10 and 11 P.M., bringing a long telegram from Cavagnari giving very satisfactory accounts of the negotiations. Some sections of the Afridis appear to have given in, to have left twenty-five hostages at Kohat, and to have promised compensation for raids and such like. Those sections which have yielded are expected to work on those which are still recusant. Doubtless they must be very tired of being locked into their hills all this time, any man who shows his face on our plains being liable to seizure and imprisonment under the rules of the blockade. The telegram put us all into good spirits; it was very long, some six or seven sheets, and gave full particulars. It certainly will be a great triumph for Cavagnari and Pollock if the objects are attained without fighting.

D. February 8.—Big day at the Mission school in the Peshawur city. We went to the Mission premises about 12; there was a great gathering. Sir Lewis Pelly, the Cabul Envoy, etc. etc. Some of the scholars recited, Pollock made a speech in English, Captain Plowden in Pashtu; very well I thought. I followed in Urdu. . . .

I remember that I touched on the great progress in inventions made in recent years, saying that I was quite prepared for the day to come when we should be able to fly in the air like birds. The old Cabul Envoy, Nur Muhammad Khan, who sat a few seats in front of me, became alert immediately, turned round and stared as though he thought me more or less of a lunatic.

February 21.—The Lieutenant-Governor mystery is at last solved by Mr. Egerton's appointment. There is no doubt whatever about it, for Pollock had a letter from him last night in reply to a congratulatory telegram. It seems that Mr.

Egerton knew himself on Xmas Day, but was sworn to secrecy. He says the Frontier is not to be separated, meanwhile, at all events. Well, I think we are safe from the whims of an outsider for the next five years at least. I don't suppose there will be a single dissentient voice. Pollock telegraphed to him, 'Congratulate you, ourselves, and the Punjab,' and in doing so he undoubtedly expressed the general feeling. . . . He is an exceedingly just, genial, kind-hearted man, without a petty feeling of any sort, and in appearance he is a very fine specimen of an English gentleman. He is thoroughly acquainted with the Natives and their language, has a marvellous memory for things and men, but he has never been supposed to be very brilliant or fond of change. Anyhow, I feel the interests of the province and of the officers are safer than they would have been in any one else's hands. . . . A correspondent in the *Pioneer* says: 'Although every one agrees that a better appointment could not have been made, yet after all the mystery there is just a feeling of disappointment that the bag being opened, a most proper tabby cat walked out. People who expected a surprise are disappointed.'

D. March 10.—On opening the *Punjab Gazette*, discovered that I had been confirmed in the new appointment of Civil and Sessions Judge of Peshawur. Nothing could have been more unexpected than this order coming out at a time when there is so much uncertainty about the future of the Division. However, I am well pleased by what seems to be a mark of satisfaction from the retiring Lieutenant-Governor.[1] . . .

March 21.—Sir Richard received a letter a few days ago from the Viceroy himself, saying that the report that the Frontier was not to be separated was entirely erroneous, that it had been fully determined on, would be brought into force in a few months as soon as details could be worked out. Sir R. was told to supply every kind of information to Sir Lewis

[1] The work of the permanent Civil and Sessions Judge was practically the same as that of the temporary Additional Commissioner, the pay of the former being slightly better.

Pelly, the officer charged with the introduction of the scheme. This was the first intimation of Sir Lewis Pelly being anything but Envoy on the Cabul question, and poor Sir Richard is much taken aback, and feels himself in a very uncomfortable and awkward position. . . .

The opening of the Kohat Pass is a great triumph for him and Cavagnari. They have said from the first that nothing but patience was required, that the blockade must reduce the people to straits. It has done so, and now trade is going through the Pass again and the road is to be made, compensation given by the Afridis for outrages, etc.

D. March 23.—Pollock rather delighted with a letter from Griffin, in which he throws doubt on the separation scheme, and virtually says Viceroys and Secretaries of State may propose, but Councils dispose. We shall see; anyhow I can hardly believe in the very rapid introduction of the new scheme.[1]

D. March 26.—The Cabul Envoy died of an internal disease about 2 A.M.[2] Jenkyns[3] came to tell me and to ask that the Civil Courts might be closed, so I did not go to Office. . . . The Lieutenant-Governor and Lady Davies arrived from Kohat *viâ* the Pass.

D. March 27.—Had a long talk to Cavagnari about Pelly, etc. We are all feeling that it is more or less likely that Pelly will disappear, and the separation scheme burst up.

D. March 31.—Went over to the Pollocks', and was not altogether surprised by hearing that telegrams had come from the Viceroy recalling Pelly and ordering Pollock to go on as before, reporting everything to the Viceroy. The Viceroy had decided to await the Amir's pleasure no longer.

D. April 2.—Sir Lewis Pelly sent his P.P.C. cards round the

[1] Nothing was done until some twenty-five years later, when the present small North-Western Frontier Province was separated from the Punjab in 1901 during the Viceroyalty of Lord Curzon.

[2] The old man had been ailing for some time since his arrival in Peshawur.

[3] The English officer in attendance, see p. 229. Later on he was one of Cavagnari's staff at Cabul, and perished in the massacre.

station and left Peshawur; as far as I can judge, never to return, but he gives out the reverse.[1]

Extract from a letter (author unknown) which appeared in the *Civil and Military Gazette*, Lahore, on March 27, 1877:—

One argument I have heard within the last few days in favour of the separation of the Frontier is worth considerable attention. It is stated that it will be a gain to the Frontier to remove it from the jurisdiction of the Chief Court; I confess there is a great deal in this. I feel all the responsibility of the expression when I write that the Chief Court, as at present constituted, possesses neither the confidence of the Judicial tribunals nor of the people of the Province. Records partially perused, vernacular documents misunderstood, the words of Acts twisted into strange meaning, just judgments reversed, thieves let loose on society, vicious customs perpetuated by judicial sanction, and unmerited censure of officers often couched in extreme acerbity of language, mark and mar the labours of the gentlemen who at present preside over that august Tribunal, the Chief Court of the Province. It is no wonder that it is as unpopular on the Frontier as elsewhere, and it is quite natural that Frontier tribunals should endeavour to free themselves from subjection to it.

Most of them were eventually freed from it when the Frontier Province was separated from the Punjab in 1901.

April 1.—. . . The abuse of Disraeli (in the Edinburgh *Daily Review*) is ridiculously childish. D. could never have become what he is if he is as bad as you and the Editor paint him. He knows the art of managing men, at all events, and he is marvellously clever, and he has the great art of keeping his temper, an essential in a leader. However, I am far from being

[1] We never saw him again. For a full and most interesting account of the conference between Sir Lewis Pelly and the Cabul Envoy, see chap. v. of *Lord Lytton's Indian Administration*. Longmans, 1899.

a warm admirer of him, but I might be one if I were brought into personal contact with him. Lord Lytton, too, may be extremely foolish about some things, but it is impossible to read any of his speeches or letters without seeing that he has a large gift of genius, though it may not be of the kind most requisite for a Governor-General. . . . I cannot help being a great admirer of natural gifts, and I cannot abuse their possessors unless I believe them to be evil-minded and dishonest. Now, I suppose that Disraeli is just as anxious to do well for the country and the people as most men in his position would be. It is a difficult thing to be a Prime Minister and please all. As far as I can see, the higher up a man goes, the more abuse he receives. Sir Henry Davies was telling Pollock the other day, he had had to fight hard, and had got abused for every measure of importance he has carried out in the Punjab. I fancy he is truly thankful to give up the struggle meanwhile.

Mr. Robert Egerton took over charge as Lieutenant-Governor from Sir Henry Davies early in April, and on the 11th of the month arrived at Peshawur, where he was the guest of Sir Richard Pollock. He must have had many difficult points of Frontier politics to discuss with the Commissioner. On the 16th Mr. Egerton held his first levée. On the 19th he came to a small party in our house, when a performance of the old comedy of *Perfection* took place. Charles Paragon was acted with much success by Mr. Lepel Griffin.

April 18.—. . . Colonel Black has a letter this morning from ——, one of the Members of Council,[1] . . . saying that Lord Lytton is the most eccentric Viceroy since Lord Ellenborough.

May 2.—. . . Pollock says he longs to get out of the whole business, and has no heart to work under the present Viceroy. . . . Of course, Lord Lytton is shockingly ignorant, but there

[1] At the India Office.

are some flaws in our system which he has spotted. However, he rushes off at a tangent and thinks everything wrong, and sneers at local traditions. The said traditions are the outcome of the past policy of the Government of India, and many of them would be gladly abandoned by the Frontier officers if Government would issue clear instructions. Mr. Egerton seems perfectly ready to hold his own with the Government of India, and I think better times are in store.

SIR DOUGLAS FORSYTH TO G. R. ELSMIE.

44 ONSLOW SQUARE, *May* 27.

. . . Syad Yakub Khan[1] is gaining great popularity here. I went with him to Liverpool. I little thought in my youthful days that I should ever be talking Persian on the river Mersey. The authorities have not yet made up their mind what treatment politically to subject him to. But in all matters of hospitality he is thoroughly well looked after, and the Queen has sent special orders for him to be well cared for.

Pelly's failure with reference to Afghanistan has been much commented on in the newspapers, and Lord Lytton does not win enthusiastic applause for his measures. In the India Office I believe Lord Salisbury[2] to be supreme, and everybody else is nowhere at all. He scarcely consults any one. . . .

MURREE, *July* 7.—We hear from Simla that Lord Lytton's unpopularity is something amazing, and the last piece of gossip is that Lord Salisbury is all for Russia and Lord L. all the other way. Our last telegrams tell of the passage of the Danube and of several Turkish victories in Asia Minor.[3] All this points to a satisfactory conclusion. The harder the struggle the Russians have, the more chance there is of England taking a less exaggerated view of their strength. I have very little Russophobia in my constitution. I fancy that sooner or later we must be established as the owners or protectors of Egypt,

[1] The Yarkund Envoy of 1873.
[2] At this time Secretary of State for India.
[3] The beginning of the Russo-Turkish War of 1877.

and I don't suppose that even the Khedive would object very much, provided we made things comfortable for him. I trust he will pay our July coupons.

August 4.—A Calcutta paper professes to give the real secret of Pelly's mission, which may very possibly be correct.

From the *Statesman and Friend of India*, July 25, 1877:—

The true history of Sir Lewis Pelly's mission is, we believe, this. Mr. Disraeli had fully resolved upon war with Russia, and she was to be attacked simultaneously by us in Europe and Central Asia. Sir Lewis Pelly was sent out to persuade the Amir to allow us to make Afghanistan the real base of our operations, by permitting us to occupy certain of the Afghan fortresses. A large force was massed upon the Frontier in hope that Sir Lewis Pelly's persuasions would be successful, and upon the declaration of war the Russians would have found two powerful British columns advancing towards Herat *viâ* Quetta and Cabul with the intention of rousing Bokhara, Khiva, Khokand, Kashgar, and all Central Asia against them. That some expedition of this kind was not only contemplated, but actually resolved upon, we have no doubt. The project was thwarted by the refusal of the Amir to allow the occupation of Afghanistan for the purpose, and had to be abandoned altogether when the English nation became fairly awakened to the guilt into which the nation was so nearly betrayed. All danger of any such expedition was long since, we believe, at an end, but it is the fact, we are told, that members of the Viceroy's staff in Calcutta last season were speaking freely of the certainty of war in a few weeks. The nation has escaped a great peril, and Parliament ought not to be satisfied without a full disclosure of what Mr. Disraeli's purpose was, and the arrangements which were being made to carry it into execution.

September 16.— . . . These five years of Peshawur cases have involved more strain, more annoyance and vexation than all the other years of my service put together. No one can be in Peshawur and not suffer in some way. I have been fortunate not to suffer physically. I have the greatest difficulty, day by day, in holding myself to my work. Sometimes I feel so exasperated that the temptation is to spring from my chair and declare that nothing will induce me to toil on through these mazes of lies. No one has ever done as much of this peculiar Peshawur work as I have done. Every one has had some sort of relief after two or three years. But it is no use my going on about it, for the peculiar nature of the mental strain cannot be realised by any one who has not suffered from it. . . .

October 3.—Sir Richard returned to Peshawur a few days ago, having been ordered down with General Keyes to hold a conference with Colonel Colley, the Viceroy's Military Secretary, in regard to a campaign against the Jowakis. The Viceroy's idea is that all the old system is wrong, and doubtless Colonel Colley is the principal private Military adviser. He has gone over to Kohat with General Keyes to see the Pass and the hills for himself, and it is to be hoped that something good will come of it. But Sir Richard trusts the Viceroy's wisdom as little as the Viceroy trusts his. Cavagnari thinks Lord Lytton is anxious to understand the situation, and that he has many sound views. Anyhow, Cavagnari is in great favour and in daily correspondence with Lord Lytton about Cabul and such like, and Sir R. is merely kept on for appearance's sake. Fortunately Cavagnari and Pollock are the best of friends and thoroughly loyal to each other, so there is no bad feeling between them. . . . C., being so much younger than P., finds it less difficult to humour the big man. The situation is, to say the least, interesting, and to watch it helps to distract our attention from ourselves. C. and P., when I am on the spot with them, tell me everything that is worth knowing.

D. October 4.—Evening, dined at the 7th N. I. mess, of which I am an honorary member. Colonel Colley, Lord William Beresford, Pollock, and others were there. I sat next to Colley, and he was pleasant enough, but of course I could not pump him. . . .

G. R. Elsmie to Sir Robert Montgomery.

October 10.

My dear Sir Robert,—I have just received your son's letter of 12th September, in which he mentions the fact of the separation scheme having been discussed in Council. We are all naturally very anxious to know the final decision, which I suppose must, to a certain extent, be in accordance with the Viceroy's views. Lord Lytton has not received much help from Frontier officers in drawing up his scheme, whatever it may be. Opinions may have been asked from a very few, but I doubt whether they were freely given. And yet, from all that I can gather, most Frontier officers are far from thinking the present system perfect, and would be glad to see some change which would lead to greater vigour being introduced into the administration generally. I have heard that the Viceroy complains greatly of the attitude of Frontier officers, considering that they have shown no desire to help him. Very possibly they have held back, but if they did so it was because they did not know that they were expected to come forward. They imagined, wrongly no doubt, that all the changes had been cut and dried when Sir Lewis Pelly appeared on the scene as the chosen Apostle of the new policy. They felt themselves to be condemned unheard for having humbly obeyed their former masters. All this could not but be very trying, and in selecting an unpopular man like Sir Lewis Pelly to go up to Peshawur and set everything right, a very great mistake in tactics was made. It may be said that Frontier officers had no right to take offence. Possibly not. But any one acquainted with the antecedents and with human nature must have known that they would. I could write a good deal to show you how Sir Lewis Pelly's attitude at Peshawur tended to confirm the prejudice against him. Suffice it to say, however, that the Viceroy's assumption of superior wisdom, accompanied by an ignorance of detail which manifested itself constantly, together with the unfortunate selection of Sir Lewis Pelly, generated more opposition than his actual policy did. The local Government was not regarded with any great degree of respect. Sir Henry Davies had the reputation of being afraid of displeasing the Government of India, and he had irritated a good many officers by finding constant fault with the criminal administration and such like, and yet taking no thorough measure for its improvement. For example, the Commissioners and Deputy Commissioners of this Division have been arguing against the Chief Court for seven or eight years, and declaring it to have been the cause of incredible mischief. Yet in Griffin's memorandum in defence of the Frontier administration, he had the face to say the Chief Court had never been hypercritical! The whole of the memo. was painted *couleur de rose*, and I do not know one Frontier officer who would have endorsed one half of what was said. Before I ever came to the Frontier, Macnabb wrote to me as follows (he was then acting as Commissioner for Pollock): 'When I held this district one really could get something done and keep the ruffians in order a bit, but it is heartbreaking to try and do anything now. Any effort you make is rendered nugatory by the new-fashioned ingenious arrangement of how not to do it. I am sick of it, and wish I could go to sleep for five years, and cut the whole concern.' This was written in May 1872, and yet Sir Henry Davies and Griffin write in '76, '77 as though everybody concerned had been perfectly delighted with the system. Doubtless that system worked grandly in old days, when the Punjab Government had power and authority, and the Judicial Courts trusted the local officers; but in these days of railways, telegraphs, and Chief Courts, no subordinate authority is trusted, and intermediate authorities like the Punjab Government seem to live only to keep things quiet till there is a grand explosion. I hope you will not misunderstand me, but I believe I am right in saying that the best Frontier officers would be glad to see *some* change; they would be glad to have their powers extended, and to be in immediate communication with the Government, which has the power of supporting them, and finally sanctioning their proposals. But they are very far from thinking they require a *complete* outsider like Sir Lewis Pelly to teach them, and they are quite unable to see how it can be possible to administer *as one province* the long and narrow strip of territory from Karachi to Peshawur. I believe that plan to be a physical impossibility if there is to be only one local head through whom everything is to pass, but I do not see why there should not be two Commissioners, one of the Afghan, the other of the Biluch frontier, working in direct communication with the Government of India. I believe that a change of this sort accompanied by freedom from the Chief Court would be welcomed by the best of our Frontier officers, and they need not on that account be in any way credited with a desire to advance beyond our present border, and get into Central Asian difficulties.

Of course I write as a mere onlooker, with very imperfect sources of information, but it is impossible to help being intensely interested in what is going on. When I read your son's letter the spirit moved me to put before you what may, perhaps, be in some way a new view of matters. In haste to catch to-day's post, etc. etc. . . .

Sir Robert Montgomery to G. R. Elsmie.

November 16.

My dear Elsmie,—I am much obliged to you for your letter of the 10th October. I wish you had written to me *before*, and more *frequently*. The fact is, that though Peshawur is a point of great importance, and much depends on what is going on there and the feeling that prevails, for almost *years* I have never had a line from *any one*, and it would greatly strengthen my position here if I knew the local politics and feeling of the place. Pollock never writes. I suppose he is tongue-tied, and you must be the most independent man on the Frontier! As a rule you are in bondage to no man! The attitude assumed by the Government of India since the arrival of the new Viceroy, *quoad* the Frontier, has been a source of great regret to me and to others. Had it been founded on experience I would have had nothing to say. But this could not have been the case in the first few months of his Viceroyalty. I doubt not, as time goes on, he is learning that everything that was done before was not wrong, and that the Frontier question is a *real* difficulty, that it has engaged the attention of the best officers for many years, and that there is no royal road to success. It is far better to amend a system than destroy an old one and start a new one. I think there can be no doubt but that the Frontier requires strengthening in officers, and that the same, or nearly the same, staff that existed when there were no codes and very simple law, could never efficiently or satisfactorily work the great additional load imposed. I am in great hopes that any change will in the main be in *improving* the position and not destroying it, and a few weeks will probably announce what is to be done.

From time to time evidence creeps out of the great want of vigour and foresight on the part of the Frontier officers, and I have had my face *blackened* by the way the Peshawur Civil officer allowed the young Engineer officer to go up alone to Abazai, and left him to invite the attack that was made on his men. Even in the Lahore circle I would not have allowed a *road* to be marked off without sending some one. But the officiating Commissioner refers *Jacob*[1] to the Deputy Commissioner, who says 'all is right, go out and begin.' No one is sent, not even a Tehsildar, or a police-officer, and the result we know. I could not have believed such utter want of care and foresight on such a border, and there are two Bombay Frontier officers on our Political Committee, who say, 'Is this your Punjab management?' I think there is the evidence of great weakness at Peshawur and elsewhere; some change is needed. . . .—Believe me, yours very sincerely,

R. MONTGOMERY.

D. October 14.—Reading Jowaki papers which Pollock has given me. There seems a clear case made out for an expedi-

[1] An Engineer officer.

tion. The J.'s are utterly in the wrong, and must be smashed, I should say. I trust it may be well done.

D. October 21.—Read a very interesting memo. by Colonel Colley, on his visit to the Frontier. During the day Cavagnari sent me the Viceroy's scheme for formation of a Frontier Province. Very interesting; I went to Cavagnari in the afternoon and talked it over.

October 31.—Things much as they were a week ago. The local authorities, Pollock and Cavagnari, very much bothered by Jowakis on the one side, and a Government which either cannot or will not understand on the other. . . . The Jowakis committed an abominable raid the other day—surprised a sepoy guard at the foot of the Cherat hill and cut them to pieces. Some seven or eight killed and the rest wounded; a nice business. 'Who would have thought it?' etc. The Viceroy is so engrossed with Cabul and Central Asia and Imperial questions that he seems to care very little for these border tribes, who are waxing fat and kicking. I believe, however, that things will come pretty straight by the end of the cold weather, if Government can only be induced to be properly energetic. They don't want a row at present, and that seems to be the very reason why the Afridis are giving trouble.

D. November 2.—Pollock troubled and anxious about Jowakis. Government playing at cross purposes.

D. November 7.—The squeezing of the Jowakis is now to begin, and it is to be hoped it will be done well.

November 7.— . . . General Keyes goes against the Afridis' (Jowakis') principal village *to-morrow*. This is not generally known. I fancy misunderstandings are now at an end, and probably the result will be good. The Lieutenant-Governor starts on his march on the 29th and will be here about the 12th prox.

D. November 10.—News of the advance into the Jowaki country. Paiah occupied. Six Jowakis killed. Terms to be demanded by order of the Viceroy very stringent—so much the better if they can be enforced.

November 11.—All has gone well as yet with the expedition.

The advance was made on the 9th. They have killed some twelve Jowakis and wounded a lot. *They* did us hardly any damage. Our long-range rifles keep them at a respectful distance, but they never come forward and fight. They scramble about amongst the rocks and take shots at our men when they can. If we could get at them they would be doubled up in a very short space. Lord Lytton seems very determined that they shall have their spirit broken, and has ordered terms to be demanded of such stringency that Pollock does not believe they will ever be obtained. However, I don't see why, if Government is determined and is prepared to use a sufficient number of men, a more severe example should not be made than has ever been attempted before.

SIR DOUGLAS FORSYTH TO G. R. ELSMIE.

76 ONSLOW GARDENS, *November* 9.

. . . If I had my life over again, with my present experience, I can truly say that no appointment I have ever held equalled that of Commissioner of Jullundur. . . . If ever I get into Parliament and become a busy politician, then, possibly, I may change my opinion, but as things go at present I look upon the position I have just mentioned as one of the finest in the world. . . . You say that in two or three years' time you will be a Commissioner. If so, then take my advice, come home now for two years, have a good fling of England, and then go back, strong, well, and penniless, I dare say, but that won't matter, and enjoy life as a Commissioner. As to your setting up at home and picking up a few hundreds a year, it is a delusion and a snare, unless you have exceptional luck, which I hope you may have, but it is not safe to speculate on. . . . It appears to me that Lord Lytton is doing his very utmost to get up a big Frontier war, and he was very properly described in the India Council, not long ago, by a bold but truthful member, as the very worst Viceroy that ever went to India, at which speech Lord Salisbury looked aghast. . . . I am gradually becoming a City man, and shall be very glad if I get enough to occupy me there six days in the week. Idleness in England is bad for a man. . . .

. . . .

November 28.—Government has at last sanctioned something more than a blockade, and there is to be a double attack on the Jowakis, from the Kohat and Peshawur sides. The troops were to have moved out from here on Friday but the rain made it impossible. They will go in a day or two, and I suppose the simultaneous attack will take place about this day week or earlier. General Ross commands on this side and will have about three thousand men, viz. one thousand Europeans, two batteries of artillery, four native regiments. . . . Major Wilson's Elephant battery with forty-pounders is to go, and they hope to be able to shell the principal village from a distance of two or three miles. I think the Afridis will be astonished, but I doubt whether we shall do them much damage in the matter of life, for they will not come out and fight, merely shoot from behind rocks and such like. Lord Lytton has declared, I believe, that he is determined to humble them, and he will not allow the troops to withdraw until most stringent terms have been enforced. Sir R. thinks the Afridis will never give in to the terms as proposed, but I expect Government will authorise some modifications when the time comes.

On the 13th of December the Lieutenant-Governor, Mr. Egerton, arrived in Peshawur and put up in his own camp, which had been pitched within cantonment limits.

D. December 17.—A day to be marked with a white stone if events turn out as we hope. . . . At 3.30 P.M. I had an interview with the Lieutenant-Governor, to whom I was anxious to state my reasons for applying to leave Peshawur on furlough to England. Mr. Egerton heard my story, and replied that he had just recommended me to the Viceroy to officiate as Judge of the Chief Court in place of Mr. Justice Lindsay, who was proceeding on leave. It was very satisfactory to find that the recommendation had actually been made. Nothing could have been pleasanter than Mr. Egerton's manner. . . . I feel that nothing but this can atone for the past.

The month of January 1878 was our last at Peshawur. A good deal of time was spent in preparation for the move to Lahore, as on the 2nd of the month I had received a telegram from Calcutta telling me that my appointment to act as Judge of the Chief Court had been sanctioned. The expedition against the Jowakis drew to a close, and before the end of the month negotiations with a view to peace were begun. I find the following in a letter written on the 24th of January:—

Jowaki elders are at Kohat and there is hope of a settlement, but the Viceroy's demand that certain ringleaders should be given up is the knotty point which there seems to be no getting over. It is difficult to make a band of robbers give up their chiefs. The chiefs object.

February 6.—Just starting (for Lahore), carriages at the door, luggage being packed. . . . Thankful to be leaving Peshawur, sorry to bid good-bye to friends.

CHAPTER XV

ACTING JUDGE OF THE CHIEF COURT

1878

THE closing words of the last chapter indicate, but do not fully describe, the mingled feelings with which we left Peshawur. The relief was chiefly on my part, and had reference to the nature of the work with which I had contended for more than five years. The burden of trying more than a hundred difficult criminal cases every year, most of them involving charges of murder,[1] to say nothing of criminal and civil appeals from subordinate courts, was a heavy one indeed. I doubt whether I ever really recovered from the strain. Socially, life at Peshawur was most enjoyable. Our house was a good one, surrounded by a delightful garden. It was in the heart of cantonments, where the garrison consisted of a Brigadier-General and his staff, two British regiments, several batteries of Artillery, two Native Cavalry and four Native Infantry regiments. We made many lasting friendships. The Natives of the district, notably the Pathan chiefs, apart from their enmities and their sympathies with wrongdoers of divers descriptions, were highly interesting and attractive. Notwithstanding the fact that my duty compelled me to pass a great number of capital and other severe sentences, I was never con-

[1] As an exemplar case, see Appendix.

scious of arousing the personal ill-feeling of any accused persons or witnesses who came before me in court. Prisoners seemed to feel, whether they were innocent or guilty, that the responsibility for their position rested with their enemies, who had either justly charged them or who bore false witness against them. Government, however, thought it necessary to take special precautions for the safety of the Sessions Judge, and a guard of policemen, who mounted a double sentry over our house at night, had their living quarters in our compound.

The journey to Lahore had now become easier, the railway having been opened as far as Jhelum. We reached the Lahore station at dawn on the 10th February, and immediately drove to Mian Mir, where for some days we were the guests of old friends, General Donald Stewart, commanding the Lahore Division, and his Assistant Adjutant-General, Colonel James Hills.[1] I had many long and interesting conversations with General Stewart on Afghanistan politics and his experiences as Governor of the Andamans, but I little thought that, more than twenty years afterwards, I should be intrusted with editing his *Life*.

A few days later I took over charge of my new duties from Mr. Justice Lindsay. Judges of the Chief Court were few in number in 1878. We were only three: Mr. Henry Meredyth Plowden,[2] Mr. John Watt Smyth, and myself, all recently appointed. A bench of two Judges sat every working day in the large court-room, hearing cases which required the decision of more than

[1] See p. 203.

[2] An English barrister, who had previously been Government Advocate in the Punjab.

one Judge. The third Judge sat in chambers, disposing of work within his competence. The cases being mainly Criminal and Civil appeals, in which judgment was given after going through the records of the lower courts and hearing the arguments of Counsel, the work seemed to me far less trying and exhausting than the conduct of heavy Criminal trials involving the examination of witnesses and accused persons, and making a record of their statements. The house in which we settled in Lahore was, strange to say, the same as that in which we had made our first Indian home in 1862. It had now become the property of Mr. Justice Lindsay, and we had agreed to rent it during his absence in England, and to keep up the beautiful grounds with which it was surrounded.

SIR DOUGLAS FORSYTH TO G. R. ELSMIE.

76 ONSLOW GARDENS, *February* 8, 1878.

I must send a few lines to congratulate you heartily on your appointment to the Chief Court, which, though only temporary as yet, is certain to become permanent erelong. . . . I lead a very *English* life now. . . . I have been much interested in the debates on the vote of credit, and have been to the House of Commons two nights. There is an immense amount of poor speaking, very little real eloquence, except, of course, from Bright and Gladstone, that most mischievous and *un*patriotic politician, as one of his party calls him. It certainly is very humiliating to think how the real interests of the country are sacrificed to party feeling. I think Gladstone has a great deal to answer for in the way he has allowed himself to be led away by his feelings. How the Russians must inwardly smile at our divided Councils and our gullibility. . . .

D. March 2.—About noon a most disagreeable earthquake and trembling took place. It lasted about three or four minutes.

. . . Evening, dined at the S.'s; met the newly appointed Bishop, Dr. French, of the Church Missionary Society.

D. Sunday, March 3.—At eleven to church (St. James's, Anarkuli), where the Bishop was installed. Rather an imposing ceremony; many of the clergy there.

Dr. French, the first Bishop of Lahore, was a remarkable personality, not easily forgotten. He was an enthusiastic missionary, manifesting the fact very clearly by laying down his office after ten years, and dying as a working evangelist in Arabia. He was held to be a difficult man to deal with in ordinary business matters. His firmness of purpose, however, was often a grand feature in his character, and to it is mainly to be attributed the fact that the Lahore Cathedral was completed and dedicated during his short episcopate.

D. March 10.—Work here takes a long time. . . . Eight hours' grind yesterday, but fortunately the mental strain is nil compared to the anxiety caused by Sessions trials at Peshawur. . . . My colleagues are both very hard-working, and I find we pull well together. I don't anticipate any serious differences of opinion. . . .

With reference to the foregoing remark, I may add that in no subsequent year did I find work in the Chief Court was disposed of more satisfactorily than in 1878. It was certainly very heavy, but we were just able to prevent the accumulation of arrears. I have no hesitation in saying that Mr. Plowden was the ablest and most talented judge with whom I have ever been associated. Mr. Smyth was a man of infinite patience, good temper, industry, and common-sense, with great knowledge and experience of the people of the country.

D. March 10.— . . . The Jowaki business has been settled. . . . Altogether Lord Lytton's policy of thrashing them well when we were about it has paid, and I think, as I have all along, that the general result will be excellent.

SIR DOUGLAS FORSYTH TO G. R. ELSMIE.

76 ONSLOW GARDENS, *April* 12.

. . . Sir Henry Davies and Edward Prinsep are living together and have forgotten their official differences. It is wonderful to see how *small* the biggest Indian swells become when once they struggle in the London crowd. There is but one thing needful here, money; with it you can do anything, without it life isn't worth living. . . . The Eastern question absorbs the chief part of our thoughts and conversation. I have always firmly maintained that we shall not go to war with Russia, and I don't think Dizzy ever really *wished* to do so, but he very properly prepares for such a contingency, and is quite ready to do so rather than see England abandon all her principles and sink into a nonentity. And he must have been terribly hampered by the insane and unpatriotic action of Gladstone, who has quite lost his following. I know numbers of out and out Liberals, who a year ago were his staunchest supporters, now declare their bitter disappointment at his conduct. I am not at all rabid against Russia, *i.e.* I don't feel so very vicious against her for grasping all she can get in Turkey, because I always expected she would do so, but I *am* rabid and disgusted with the pro-Russian party here for being such perfect idiots as to believe every word Russia said, and who allow themselves to be so gulled. George Campbell has been somewhat eccentric in his utterances and expressed pious horror at the 'undisguised perfidy of Russia,' which he ought to have been prepared for. I was quite prepared for Lord Salisbury's circular, or at least for some such expression of his views, for from a conversation I had with him, I was satisfied that strong denunciation of Turkish rule by him did not at all imply approval on his part of Russian aggression. India is not well represented in the House of Commons. Hardy[1] was sent to the India Office because they wanted a strong man to keep the Council in order. . . . I see nothing of that august body, except, of course, old Sir Robert Montgomery, and Rawlinson and Ellis, who are on the Royal Geographical Council, of which I am an unworthy, but very dutiful, member. . . . We flourish but very humbly, and I am a perfect model of economy, and *sometimes* go second class, but I hate it! . . .

May 30.—Bright's criticism on the move of the Indian troops[2] shows great ignorance of the real relations between England and India. We, out here, all think this move an excellent one, and we are much obliged to Russia for giving us a good excuse for strengthening our position in the Mediterranean. I am far from crediting Russia with all manner of designs against us, but I don't think a half-civilised country can be trusted to do exactly as she pleases, and I think we ought to lose no opportunity of maintaining our way to India. The safer it is, the less we shall have of scares in future. I am thought a hopeless Russophil out here by my friends, because I have never believed that war would or ought to come, and because I do not regret the downfall of Turkey. We have an old lady, a Miss Marianne North, staying with us for a couple of days; she is a cousin of Mrs. Philip Egerton, and we were asked by the Lieutenant-Governor to receive her. She travels all over the world by herself, without a maid even, and makes *oil* paintings of all the tropical flowers, trees, and scenery she can. Her paintings are to our eyes magnificent, and she has at present some five hundred on loan exhibition at S. Kensington. Her father was an M.P., and evidently they used to travel together, and now, as an English climate does not suit her in winter, she continues to move about, only spending a few weeks at a time in her London flat, which she keeps up. . . . She is no trouble in the house, amuses herself, and is entertaining to talk to, as she has seen so much and knows so many people. She is tall and spare; she was off

[1] Gathorne Hardy.

[2] To Malta.

at sunrise this morning to paint one of the gates of the city. . . . Her art is evidently her life, and I doubt not she is happier than most old maids who have nothing to do.[1]

June 9.—Thanks for sending the newspapers about the Edinburgh poisoning case. I have only had time to read the outline as yet. We have plenty of poisoning cases out here. Smyth and I had to confirm death sentences on three men the other day. They wanted to get rid of a certain enemy, so they cooked a dish of rice and poisoned it with arsenic. Then they got hold of a half-witted traveller, and told him to take it to a certain person in a distant village, and to say it had been sent by the priest of a shrine which the man-to-be-poisoned was in the habit of visiting. The unsuspecting victim received the dish, called the members of his family to partake of the holy food. Seven were poisoned, three died, and four recovered. The case was well proved. Indeed, the men confessed complicity, though each one tried to throw the greater part of the blame on his companions.

July 7.—Work continues very heavy here. . . . I require all my wits and more, and a great deal more than all my 'learning' to keep up to the mark. I am daily conscious of having much less 'learning' than my colleagues, though I do not find myself deficient to them in experience. Of course, many of the more intricate Civil cases are very difficult, and involve reference to books and branches of law which I have never heard of. I try to look wise, and to pick up the pieces as best I can afterwards. The truth is, I have had such a busy life in India that I have never been able to keep up a course of study, my daily cutcherry grind being more than enough to exhaust my energies. The Peshawur work was very same, and only served to prepare one for a small part of the duties here. I am never tortured and vexed and annoyed as I used to be at Peshawur, but nevertheless one has to work at high pressure, and it is difficult to be good for much after the day's grind.

[1] I will only add to the foregoing a recommendation to readers who feel interested in Miss North to read *Recollections of a Happy Life*, published in 1892, some years after her death, and to visit the collection of her paintings in Kew Gardens.

July 22.—Now, don't you think Disraeli has really managed this winding-up of the Eastern question remarkably well? I think he deserves great credit as an official, whatever he may be as a man. I have always thought that our position must be strengthened, for we cannot afford to be scared out of our lives whenever two half-civilised nations like Turkey and Russia choose to quarrel. I think the Cyprus move first-rate, and I believe this settlement will last our time, at all events. Of course, I don't mean to say that this is what the Ministry meant to do all along, but they have been guided by public opinion and the progress of events, and have taken good care, but not too much, of our interests.

SIR DOUGLAS FORSYTH TO G. R. ELSMIE.

76 ONSLOW GARDENS, *July* 2.

. . . I am spreading out my roots pretty firmly. I find that gradually it is possible to extend one's hold on City business. I have just got on to the Sind and Punjab Railway Board, and have one or two other pleasant little seats, and now I am nearly able to give a patient ear to the soft voices of alluring constituents. I hope there may be no dissolution of Parliament till the end of next year, and thus it is possible I may find myself on the hustings denouncing Gladstone, and pinning my faith to the Conservative cause. I have had one or two offers of seats, but have not quite definitely closed with either of them. I think I should like the life of an M.P., but shall only go in for it if I find I can afford it. . . . It is pleasant to occupy oneself in English and European politics. I dare say I should keep up a keen interest in Indian affairs, if I were in office. But you know how close all Indian officials are. The members of the Indian Council look on all outsiders as enemies to be deluded, and left at a distance, and consequently there is little inducement to me to trouble myself about what goes on in India, now that I have left the service. . . .

From the middle of August till the middle of October the Chief Court was closed on the Civil side, and by way of encouraging the judges not to take privilege leave, permission was granted to them to dispose of the current Criminal work at Simla. Accordingly, about the second week in August, we found ourselves, after an interval of ten years, back in Simla. The journey had now become a comparatively easy matter. We travelled to Ambala by rail, thence to Kalka by carriage, and from Kalka to Simla by tonga or hill pony-cart. In this way the time occupied was about twenty-two hours, a pleasant contrast to the journey of ten years before, when the only way of travelling from Kalka to Simla, a distance of say fifty miles, was on horseback or by dooli or dandy. We lived during the two months of semi-vacation in a small house called Marley Villa on the slope of Jakko. We found many old friends around us, notably Charles Grant (from the Central Provinces), Charles Bernard (at this time Home Secretary to the Government of India), J. B. Lyall (Settlement Commissioner of the Punjab), all men of my term at Haileybury. At Snowdon dwelt General Roberts, Quartermaster-General of the Army. At Barnes Court, General Peter Lumsden, Adjutant-General of the Army. The Lieutenant-Governor of the Punjab, Mr. Robert Egerton, lived at Oakover, and one of the first entertainments to which we were invited was a dinner-party given by his Honour, when the principal guest was Lord Lytton, the Viceroy.

D. SIMLA, *Sunday*, *August* 18.—Mr. Matthew [1] preached. It was a pleasure to listen to him.

[1] Whom we had heard and admired as Chaplain of the Fort Church in Calcutta in 1869. See p. 142. He afterwards became Archdeacon and Bishop of Lahore.

It was about this time that the difficulties which led to the second Afghan war began to be publicly known. The Amir, Sher Ali Khan, had received a Russian Mission at Cabul. The Government of India determined to send a counter Mission *viâ* the Khyber Pass. General Sir Neville Chamberlain, the Commander-in-Chief in Madras, was selected to be the head of the Mission. Captain Cavagnari was to be his second in command. Both of these officers arrived at Simla early in September to receive the instructions of Government. Sir Neville was the guest of the Viceroy, who gave several entertainments in his honour. I dined at Government House on the 5th of September. Dinner was followed by some more or less impromptu charades. Among the actors were Mrs. Richard Strachey, Mrs. Newmarch (formerly Miss Agnes Norman), Mrs. Scott Napier, and Mr. Meredyth Plowden. The last scene was a representation of Mrs. Jarley's waxworks, introducing the whole strength of the company. In describing Britannia, one of the figures, an attempt was made to hit off the political situation of the day, chiefly with reference to the movement of Indian troops to Malta, the Berlin conference, the appointment of Lords Beaconsfield and Salisbury as Knights of the Garter, and the impending Mission to Cabul. The following is a fairly accurate version of what was said :—

Mrs. Jarley loquitur.—'The last figure in the collection, ladies and gentlemen, is Britannia, the Pride of the Ocean. Hurrah for the Red, White, and Blue!

'They do say, 'owever, that the good lady has had her share of trouble just lately, owing to one thing and another. People laughed at her and said her nature was a commercial marine kind of one, and that she could only go sailing from one 'arbour to another, and was afraid to put her foot on dry land. But Lor' bless you, in a very short time she plucks up her spirits, sends for a few ounces of Indian curry powder, just to give a flavour to her Red mullets at Malta, plants one foot on the Dizzy heights of Jerusalem and another on Salisbury plain, and so mastering Europe, ties on a pair of bran' new garters, puts her arms akimbo, and says she's ready for any of 'em, and never felt so peaceable and honourable in her life. And now that she's got an excellent watchfire lit on (Lytton) her path, she's going to send her Grand Chamberlain to join a Rooshian tea-party at Cabool.'

This sketch of the state of affairs seemed to win the favour of the audience, and at a later period of the evening Lord Lytton said that he had been much amused by the 'gag'—his own expression. Sir Neville, from his fine personal appearance and many splendid qualities, was fully entitled to the epithet 'Grand.' I had had the privilege of meeting him several times before, when he was commanding the Frontier Force. The impression made was a lasting one, and his subsequent career was always followed with great interest. He died in England in 1902, having been appointed a Field-Marshal some years before.

SIMLA, *September* 16.—General Chamberlain and Cavagnari started from here a week ago, and I suppose have reached Peshawur. . . . The Russians in sending a Mission to Cabul have been guilty of a breach of faith. I think the question is really a military one. If we cannot defend India without outposts at Candahar or Herat, we must have them at all cost. . . Personally, I wish that we could afford to rest calmly in our present position, this side the hills, and fight the Russians or anybody else when they come. But the opinion of the majority seems to be that we cannot afford to wait. Certainly our relations with Cabul of late years have been most unsatisfactory, and nothing could be worse than the system of subsidising, and getting nothing at all in return.

D. September 23.—Considerable Cabul excitement, troops ordered to the Front, etc., owing to the Commandant at Ali Musjid having refused to let the Mission pass.

October 3.—I am glad to learn from the telegrams that the Russians have been explaining the reason of their demonstration. I suppose our Government is right in their determination to have more satisfactory relations with the Amir. He is a mad fool, but I hardly wonder at his being afraid of us. Military opinion seems to have been gradually coming round to the view that our present frontier is an unsatisfactory one, and difficult to defend. If this be true, we cannot afford to have a hostile Afghanistan next door to us. The English papers seem to urge an immediate advance, but the Government of India is supposed to be merely trying what a show of displeasure will do. . . . Troops are being moved forward daily to Kohat, Quetta, Dera Ghazi Khan.

In the middle of October we returned to Lahore. The Civil vacation was at an end, and full work was resumed in the Chief Court.

LAHORE, *November* 12.—We are all on the *qui vive* for the 20th, when it will be known whether the army is to advance or not. . . . It is out of the question that the Amir, after all we have done for him and this perpetually recurring Russian scare, should be allowed to sulk and absolutely refuse to have anything to say to us.

November 27.—The beginning of the war has been most triumphant, and I suppose the Amir will soon collapse. I agree more with Sir J. Stephen than with Lord Lawrence. The latter is very obstinate. It is absurd to my mind to say the Amir has been ill-treated. He has been spoiled by being made too much of; very few Orientals can stand it. The Cabul problem had to be solved sooner or later, and although Lord Lytton may have been wanting in tact in the way in which he brought on the crisis, there can be no doubt that he has been wise in firmly recognising from the first that our relations with Cabul and the Border tribes were very unsatisfactory, and that they could not continue in their then position many years longer. Lord Lytton understands principles better than he understands men. Of course it would be better if he understood both, but principles live longer than men. The great end to be accomplished is the laying the ghost of Russian intrigue and possible invasion. Very possibly it is only a ghost, but so long as we are utterly ignorant of what is going on in Cabul and Central Asia, we cannot tell what it is. I firmly trust we shall not annex Afghanistan, but we must have intimate relations therewith. The Viceroy's proclamation sets forth our grievances pretty clearly. We have given everything and received nothing. Sher Ali richly deserves his fate, and I have no pity at all for him. I am like Mr. F.'s aunt in *Little Dorrit*—'I hate a fool,' and Sher Ali is one. He is probably more or less mad.

At the end of November the Viceroy, Lord Lytton, and staff arrived in Lahore. He occupied New Park, which had now become the property of the Nawab of Bahawulpore.

D. December 5.—News of General Roberts's victory at the Peiwar Pass.

D. December 6.—Went to Mrs. Egerton's garden-party, where the Viceroy, Lady Lytton, and many others were. . . . News of opening of Parliament, etc.; all very interesting.

D. December 7.—Evening we had a dinner-party. Lady Browne (wife of Sir Sam Browne), the Colleys, etc. etc. . . . Telegrams very exciting. Letter from the Amir acknowledging ultimatum, etc.

D. December 14.—Dined at Government House to meet the Viceroy. E. sat next to Lord Lytton and enjoyed the conversation. I sat between Lady Browne and Mrs. Peter Lumsden and was very happy. Altogether the party was a success.

Some of the Viceroy's remarks are still remembered. He spoke bitterly of the criticisms made on his policy and conduct of affairs by Lord Hartington in the House of Commons, declaring that if the Liberal party came into power with Lord Hartington as a Minister he, Lord Lytton, would resign his office.

Meanwhile, on the advance of the armies under Generals Roberts and Browne, the Amir Sher Ali fled from Cabul and crossed the Oxus into Russian territory. Soon afterwards he fell ill and died on the 21st February at Mazar-i-sharif.

CHAPTER XVI

SECOND FURLOUGH

1879—1880

MR. JUSTICE LINDSAY having returned from leave, we left Lahore in the middle of January and went home on furlough.

We lived in London with our children for several months, meeting many of our Indian friends: Sir Robert and Lady Montgomery, Sir Douglas and Lady Forsyth, Sir Richard and Lady Pollock,[1] Mrs. Nicolls, and others.

D. April 28.—We dined with Miss North;[2] a pleasant party. Met Kinglake, the author of *Eothen*, Mr. Knox, late Marlborough Street Police Magistrate, Mr. Bentham, botanist, etc. etc.

At the end of June we moved to Linton, a country house in Aberdeenshire which we had taken for a year. A phalanx of children, governesses, and nurses accompanied us. The new life seemed to be congenial to all. The commodious and convenient house, the grounds or 'policies,' the large fruit, flower, and vegetable garden, formed a delightful contrast to the surroundings of our abode in South Kensington. The estate consisted of some twelve or thirteen hundred acres of fields and woods, while at a distance of six or seven miles lay about three hundred acres of moor, on the slope of the hill of Corennie, which

[1] Sir Richard Pollock had now finally left India.

[2] See p. 251.

were generally good for the yield of thirty to forty grouse and a sprinkling of hares. The Sauchen burn which flowed through the fields held a considerable number of small trout, the capture of a half or three-quarter pounder being an event remembered for many days. Our life at Linton, specially enlivened during the autumn by visits from our friends Sir Douglas Forsyth and Mr. Donald Macnabb, was practically undisturbed till news from the East suddenly engrossed all our thoughts. The following letter from Sir Louis Cavagnari was written by him on his way to Cabul and reached me on the 24th August.

It was in reply to congratulations on his appointment as Chief of the British Mission which, at the invitation of the Amir Yakub Khan, was to be established in Cabul.

SIR L. N. CAVAGNARI TO G. R. ELSMIE.

PEIWAR KOTAL, *July* 16, 1879.

So very many thanks for your kind letter of congratulations, which it gave me great pleasure to receive. I have been most fortunate from first to last in the late campaign, and it has been a matter of gratification to me to observe the general satisfaction the settlement with the Amir has caused. Of course the moment Yakub Khan left his capital to come and negotiate, peace in some form or other was certain, but my object was to obtain what the Government wanted, and at the same time make the Amir feel that he had been generously treated by us. He is or pretends to be very grateful to me personally, and I hope to work on his feelings after I get to Cabul. Of course there are difficulties to be contended with ; the most prominent are but those which every Frontier officer has had to face, viz. fanatical attacks. The pessimist politicians are inclined to predict all sorts of evils to come, but I am sanguine that they will prove to be false prophets, as they have been from the commencement of the war up to the signing of the treaty. I have had a fortnight up at Simla and enjoyed it very much. The Viceroy was very kind and complimentary to me, and I have been recommended for a K.C.B. (civil), which is a great deal more than I ever aspired to. He has advised me to be Sir Louis and not Sir Napoleon, as he said there could not be two Napoleons in the world. My only hope is that it won't degenerate into *Sir Lewis!*[1]

I am now on my march to Cabul, which I expect to reach on the 23rd. A force of all three arms escorts me to the Afghan frontier, and thence a couple of the Amir's regiments take me on.

I have been made Envoy and Minister Plenipotentiary, which will be more pleasing to the Amir than the Indian title of Resident, which every Native State fears to have lest his administrative arrangements are interfered with. The only part that is not as pleasant as I could have wished is the increased separation from my wife, but she is very good about it, and has behaved pluckily throughout.

I hope to have her back in India by the time the Amir visits the Viceroy. . . . I am to have the pay of a first-class Resident, Rs. 4166.10.8,[2] which will induce me to save some cash. I leave the Punjab Commission, and will be placed on the regular political list. I heard nothing definite about the Frontier separation scheme, but I think it will come on again in some form or other. I doubt much whether there will be a Chief Commissioner, as the scheme was found to be too expensive. . . .

Believe me, yours ever sincerely, N. CAVAGNARI.

D. September 7.—On going to Aberdeen heard the news of the revolt at Cabul, and of the probable massacre of poor Cavagnari and his companions. It is a most awful calamity. We tried to hope some might have escaped, but I can see no ground for hope.

D. September 8.—Thinking of little save Cabul and poor Cavi.[3] I cannot attempt to write what I think.

[1] Referring to Sir Lewis Pelly. [2] Per mensem.

[3] As many of his Frontier friends familiarly called him.

D. September 11.—Much thought about Afghanistan. The subject will not brighten, looks very black. . . . Cavagnari is a very great loss to the Government.

D. September 12.—Did little save read, write, and think about Cabul.

D. September 13.—Much reading of papers, concerning Afghan matters. Difficult to see a way out, but it is clear that an advance is imperative, and I suppose the future will unfold itself.

E. P. Henderson, Government Advocate, Punjab, to G. R. Elsmie.

Simla, *September* 7, 1879.

. . . We are all *crushed* by this heart-rending news from Cabul. Your letter containing those well-deserved words of praise of poor Cavagnari only reached me yesterday; and yesterday evening the news was known. It is simply heart-breaking. It seems that the ammunition of the little escort was stored elsewhere, and they had only twenty-three rounds per man; but that notwithstanding this, they defended the Residency for thirty-six hours against *ten* regiments, viz. three Herati and seven Cabul ones, till at last it caught fire, and they were all massacred *to a man*. The last news is that all the bodies had been recovered and recognised. Poor little Jenkyns, too; I am grieved for him. Lord Lytton is, I believe, much cut up about it. It is a great blow to him. Poor Cavagnari, what a loss he is! I am sure you will be most deeply distressed to hear of it. . . .

P.S.—There was a most extraordinary prediction of the massacre of Cabul in Wednesday's *Statesman*, the very day it occurred, *exactly* as it happened.

Sir Robert Montgomery to G. R. Elsmie.

India Office, *September* 23.

. . . I *think* you were rather an advocate for an advanced policy. But I may be in error. I should like your view on the present situation, and what we should do after avenging Cavagnari's murder. The announcement must have caused you great pain, and I doubt not you knew many of those with him, the European as well as the native portion. . . .

G. R. Elsmie to Sir Robert Montgomery.

Linton, *September* 25.

My dear Sir Robert,—In your letter of the 23rd, which I have just received, you write, 'I *think* you were rather an advocate for an advanced policy. But I may be in error. I should like your view on the present situation, and what we should do after avenging Cavagnari's murder.' This seems to give me an opportunity of writing down some of my Cabul creed, such as it is, and it is rather a relief to do so in this remote corner, where there are no 'experts' to talk to. Of course I read the papers, more especially the *Times*, regularly. I first began to think about Afghanistan in 1863, when you supplied me with the material for writing that short epitome of our relations with Dost Muhammed from 1854 till his death. All my natural instincts have always been against Russophobia. I altogether abominate the policy which led to the first Cabul war, and I must say I had great intuitive sympathy with the feelings which led Sir John Lawrence in 1854-55 to throw much cold water upon Sir Herbert Edwardes' proposals for more intimate relations with Afghanistan. However, Lord Dalhousie sided with Sir Herbert, and I suppose it must be admitted that in 1857 our renewed friendship with Dost Muhammed proved to be of great value. Sir Herbert laid great stress on this fact, but I suppose he would have admitted that the idea of an alliance with Afghanistan as a means of strengthening us against internal troubles, was not a very prominent one when he first proposed a treaty? I think, however, when this *ex post facto* justification of the new policy had taken place, it would have been impossible for us to rescind the treaty. We had made a fresh start, and we were bound to carry on the new policy to its legitimate results. Now, whether I am mistaken or not, Lord Lawrence never appeared to me heartily to recognise the fact that we *had* made a fresh start. He always seemed to desire to get back to the old position, or at all events to let the new policy virtually die for want of reasonable development. In my opinion, during the greater part of Lord Northbrook's Viceroyalty, our relations with Afghanistan, for all practical purposes, were in a moribund state, and instead of being any help to us, were a source of embarrassment. I don't think many Frontier authorities of note, either Native or European, were of opinion that matters could remain *in statu quo.* The policy of 'letting alone' our Afghan relations and of submitting to insults from the Border tribes had, I think, reached a depth where it could not, in the nature of things, remain. The Afghan Blue-Book shows this truth to have been so vigorously grasped by Lord Salisbury that he took the most extraordinary, not to say rash, plan of overruling suddenly the whole weight of Indian opinion, of opening direct communication with Sher Ali by means of two instruments altogether new to the work, who in my opinion set upon the task of forcing on a crisis in a method marked by the greatest want of tact conceivable. The deputation of Sir Lewis Pelly to Peshawur, to work independently of the Local Government and the local officers, was in my view the grossest of blunders, and to it I attribute in a great measure this second Afghan war. When Sir Lewis appeared at Peshawur it did not require words to tell the Afghans, from the Syud Nur Muhammad[1] downwards, that the English were divided in counsel. Just imagine the spectacle of an Envoy and Plenipotentiary, a complete outsider, from a Punjab and Pathan point of view, *living with Mr. Hughes the missionary*, acting in total independence of the Commissioner and the Local Government, ordered to commence operations by begging nearly the whole question, namely that of Residents in Afghanistan. In the nature of things, such an attempt *could* not succeed.[2] It utterly

[1] The Cabul Envoy who conferred with Sir Lewis Pelly at Peshawur.

[2] A Frontier official of great experience, at an interview with Lord Lytton in England, before the latter started for India as Viceroy-elect, said to his

failed, as it deserved. . . . I do not of course blame Lord Lytton individually very much, for how could he possibly know better? How was he to know by intuition that Pathans could only be managed by officers who understood their character? I blame the Home Government, who conceived the most rash project of carrying out a new policy in the teeth of the Indian authorities. It was impossible to do so, and the event has proved its impossibility. Now what I contend is that the Indian authorities, at all events, or the *local* Punjab authorities, if they had been taken the right way, would have been perfectly willing to do their utmost to improve our relations with the Amir and with the Frontier tribes. Much might have been done by conciliatory measures on our part, together with a clear manifestation of our strength and determination. I find, on looking over some old papers, that I wrote to you from Peshawur in October 1877 somewhat to the same effect, so that my present views are not new. I will give you some quotations from my former letter, merely explaining that when it was written, the general belief was that the new policy had been devised by Lord Lytton, whereas the Blue-Book now shows that he was a mere agent in the early stage. What I wrote had chiefly reference to the separation scheme, as at that time the Cabul negotiations had been kept secret, but I believe that my remarks would be applicable to the Cabul question as well as to that of the Frontier tribes, and the internal administration of our own Frontier territory. I make these quotations from my former letter. 'From all I can gather, most Frontier officers are far from thinking the present system perfect, and would be glad to see some changes which would lead to greater vigour being introduced into the administration generally. I have heard that the Viceroy complains greatly of the attitude of the Frontier officers, considering that they have shown no desire to help him. Very possibly they have held back, but if they have, it was because

lordship: 'Yes, sir, it is most desirable that we should have English agents at Cabul, Candahar, and Herat, and most reasonable to expect the Amir to agree to that—but he is not reasonable, and he won't agree, and if you press it there must be war.'

they did not know they were expected to come forward. They imagined, wrongly no doubt, that all the changes had been cut and dried, when Sir Lewis Pelly appeared on the scene as the chosen apostle of the new policy. They felt themselves to be condemned unheard for having obeyed their former masters. . . . The Viceroy's assumption of superior wisdom, accompanied by an ignorance of detail which manifested itself constantly, together with the unfortunate selection of Sir Lewis, generated more opposition than his actual policy did. I believe I am right in saying that the best Frontier officers would be glad to see some change . . . and they need not on that account be in any way credited with a desire to advance beyond our present border and get into Central Asian difficulties.' . . .

Now, when you say you think I was 'rather an advocate for an advanced policy,' I reply most emphatically that up to the time of Sir L. Pelly's appearance at Peshawur, I would have advocated nothing more than the improvement of our existing relations with the Amir. To do *something* would sooner or later have become absolutely necessary. We could not have gone on for an indefinite time with no better source of information than we had. Our relations with Sher Ali, instead of improving, were growing colder and more unsatisfactory every day. However, the whole aspect of affairs changed in 1878. We had broken with the Amir altogether, and in the month of July we found him entertaining a Russian Mission. I dare say it would not have done much harm to ignore that Mission,[1] . . . but I think it is clear enough that the majority of the English nation is at present very far from believing it to be consistent with common prudence to allow Russia to be supreme at Cabul. . . . That being the case, I don't see how we could have avoided making a counter move in August last year. Whether Lord Lytton and his officers displayed complete tact in the attempt to send the Chamberlain-Cavagnari Mission to Cabul is

[1] It has been said that if we had ignored it, the Afghans in time would have dealt with its members as they dealt with Sir Louis Cavagnari and his staff a year later.

open to doubt, but on the whole I am inclined to think Sher Ali behaved disgracefully and like a madman in refusing to receive us, and that it was impossible *at that stage* to avoid going to war. Although, therefore, I sympathise in a great deal that Lord Lawrence wrote last year, and though I could go on indefinitely in denouncing Lord Lytton up to and including the Pelly episode, I could never bring myself to think that we could with honour have avoided coercing the Amir and bringing him down from his pinnacle of Afghan pride.

As to whether we were wise or right in fighting for a *scientific frontier* is another question. My inclination is to believe that our old frontier was a good one, and that we could have held it against any possible enemy. But then I have no pretension to scientific military knowledge. Last winter's campaign, however, was commenced with the intention of bringing Sher Ali to his senses, and making a satisfactory settlement for the future. It was brought to an end when Sher Ali ran away and died, and when we had taken possession of the scientific frontier. I am afraid we stopped when our work was only half done, and before we had sufficiently impressed the Pathans with our power. At this distance one supposed (certainly not without a good deal of misgiving on my part) that Cavagnari and the Viceroy had good ground for believing in Yakub's[1] power to carry out his engagements. But events have shown that they were miserably deceived. I fancy, if the truth were known, the Indian authorities would gladly have gone on to Cabul, and have settled the matter thoroughly, but probably they were held back by the Government and public opinion at home. Cavagnari, brave and able fellow as he was, must have been carried away by the prominence of his position, and been led (against his judgment) by his desire to bring affairs to a speedy close. Both he and the Viceroy must have been in a most difficult position, bullied beyond measure by the screams of parties at home and orders from the Government. I can never believe that Cavagnari in his inmost heart was thoroughly satisfied with the settlement. . . .

[1] Yakub Khan, who had succeeded his father, Sher Ali, as Amir.

I do not see how we can hope to leave Afghanistan till we have established a strong government there.[1] I believe we can do so, if we spend enough of money and men. And England, who has put a Russophobist Government into power at home, must, or at all events *ought* to, pay the cost. There seems to be nothing now but to go ahead, to occupy the country with an army, to collect information, and then carefully and deliberately, without hurry, to decide on our future course. It is difficult to believe that a settlement can be arrived at for some time, two or three years perhaps. I doubt much whether the present Government will see the end of it.

I am really quite ashamed of the length of this letter. You will not have patience to read it. It is difficult to put all one has to say on such a subject into small compass, and I doubt not I have left my meaning obscure on many points. Perhaps you will let me explain myself verbally if I succeed in getting up to London next month.

Sir R. Montgomery to G. R. Elsmie.

7 Cornwall Gardens, S.W.,
October 4.

My dear Elsmie,—I received your memo. about Frontier and Cabul matters. . . . I liked your paper much, and there is little I did not agree with, and I am much obliged to you for it. The only point in which perhaps I did not join in with you was in the earlier stages. I gather from the extracts you sent me, and also from your letter to me from Peshawur, that you rather formed one of the party that wanted a change (*radical*) on the Frontier, perhaps, I should say, considered the old policy should be changed.

I quite admit that it is far from perfect, and was susceptible of improvement. But, after all, what would we give now (I mean before the Cabul outbreak) to have had the peace of olden days. I had a letter from the Punjab, describing the Frontier on the

[1] Abdul Rahman Khan was afterwards established as Amir, and he proved a strong ruler till his death.

25th August. It was in a blaze all along, and there were four expeditions in contemplation and the tribes threatened to attack us. During the whole of Davies's tenure of office (except the Kohat Pass matter brought on by Cavagnari) not a shot was fired for six years. When the Russians came I admit we had to advance.

Pelly's Mission had much to do with this, *added* to the occupation of Quetta, blockading the Frontier, withdrawing our Agent.[1]

This so irritated Sher Ali, that in desperation he received the Mission[2] with open arms. Then the tone of the official communication was enough to drive him more mad than he was. I am off to Paris for a fortnight, and only just scratch off these few lines before I go. I can only repeat I am much obliged to you for your letter. . . .—Yours very sincerely,

R. MONTGOMERY.

A few days after the letter just quoted was written, viz. on the 12th of October, General Roberts, who had started from Simla within twenty-four hours of the receipt of the news of the massacre, received the submission of the Amir Yakub Khan, entered Cabul with a splendid and triumphant army, and remained in possession of the city.

In the spring of 1880 we went to live in the town of Aberdeen. Home politics soon became an engrossing subject.

D. January 30, 1880.—In the evening to a Liberal demonstration at the Music Hall, where an address was delivered by Lord Fife, which was on the whole very good. He was followed by Lord Aberdeen, Grant Duff, Farley Leith, and others. I did not agree in much of the Foreign politics spoken, nor could I go in for the strong party vein, but the speaking was good and worth listening to.

[1] Our Native agent at Cabul.

[2] The Russian Mission.

D. February 7.—Had a long talk with Dr. Farquharson of Finzean, who is the Liberal candidate-elect for West Aberdeen shire; a pleasant and intelligent man.

D. March 9.—News of the Dissolution of Parliament.

D. March 17.—At 10 A.M. went to Sheriff Thomson's court, and was interested in hearing and seeing how work is done. Much easier and simpler for the Judge than in India. All routine taken off his hands. Criminal work was ridiculously easy. I think I could have got through it without any previous Scotch training.

D. March 25.—Went to the Sheriff's Small Debt Court, and was a good deal interested in what I saw and heard. Sheriff Thomson is very pleasant and does his work in good style,[1] but it is infinitely easier work than what we have to do in India; no comparison.

D. April 1.—Heard of the first day's elections, a wonderful turn of the tide towards Liberalism, which has taken every one by surprise. The Aberdeen election going on. It resulted in a victory for Webster (L.) over Shaw (C.) by about 4000 votes.

D. April 5.—Heard of Gladstone's victory at Midlothian. Will he take office? I hope not. . . .

D. April 6.—Dined out, meeting Dr. Farquharson. An interesting gathering. Immediately afterwards we went down to the Imperial Hotel, and heard that Dr. F. had been returned for West Aberdeenshire by a majority of over 1300. He made a speech. . . . Afterwards to the Northern Club, where there was a considerable gathering and a good deal of noise.

D. April 9.—Liberal victory still being carried on in a marvellous manner.

A Liberal ministry was then formed with Mr. Gladstone as Premier. Lord Lytton resigned, as he said he would.

D. April 28.—Lord Ripon, the new Governor-General.

D. LONDON, *May* 4.—Much pleased with the *Pirates of*

[1] At a later period Sheriff Thomson, who had resumed practice as a barrister, successfully defended the accused in the celebrated Tighnabruaich case.

Penzance. The Prince and Princess of Wales in the theatre with five children. Two of them, the young Princes, just home from the sea. We had a capital view of them.

D. May 9.—Dined with Sir Richard and Lady Pollock, when I met Sir Sam Browne and had some interesting talk about Afghanistan, etc.

D. May 14.—With Sir Douglas Forsyth to a reception at the Chinese Ambassador's. . . . The collection of people was well worth seeing, and the diamonds were indeed marvellous to my unaccustomed eyes.

D. May 16.—Called at Miss North's, but was told she had gone to Borneo!

D. May 26.—Dined at the Pollocks', where I met Lady Cavagnari and her sister. Very touching to see Lady Cavagnari with 'Patty,' the little dog who accompanied her husband to Cabul, and was probably the sole survivor of the massacre. She was found in the city by an officer,[1] and brought home to her mistress.

D. June 9.—To see Sarah Bernhardt in *Phèdre.* Very much pleased, enjoyed the play extremely. . . . Gladstone and his family in a prominent box.

D. ABERDEEN, *July* 28.—Appalled by reading in the evening paper of the complete annihilation of Burrows's force near the Helmund. Certainly a great achievement of Ayub Khan. Great disgrace to us.

D. July 29.—Thinking much of this fearful disaster in Afghanistan. Subsequent accounts, however, make it seem less of an annihilation, but I fear it must be very bad nevertheless.

D. July 30.—Afghan disaster appearing to be less serious than at first supposed, but telegraph to Candahar is cut, so it is impossible to be sure of what has happened or is happening.

D. September 3.—At 12.30 went over to the old town (Old Aberdeen) to be present at the unveiling of poor Jenkyns's[2] memorial in the vestibule of King's College.

[1] When the city of Cabul was occupied by General Roberts's army.

[2] See pp. 229-263.

William Jenkyns had been a student of the Aberdeen University. He took a high place in the Indian Civil Service competition. As already mentioned, he was serving at Peshawur at the time of the Pelly conference. I saw much of his judicial work and had formed a high opinion of his ability. Subsequently he was chosen to accompany Cavagnari to Cabul, where he perished in the massacre. The Memorial is a white marble tablet with a bust in alto relief. The inscription is in Latin and runs thus:—

GVL: JENKYNS, A.M.
COMES IND: IMPER:
NATVS ABERDON: A.D. MDCCCXLIX.
NECATVS AD CABVL A.D. MDCCCLXXIX.

EFFIGIEM SVPRA CERNIS PRAECLARI ILLIVS ADOLESCENTIS
HVIVS VNIVERSITATIS ALVMNI
QVI IN FVNESTA CAEDE LEGATIONIS BRITANNICAE AD CABVL
INTERPRETIS VICE FVNGENS
FATO MORIBVSQVE INSTAR PROXENI ILLIVS XENOPHONTEI
III NON. SEPTEMB. A.D. MDCCCLXXIX MORTE OCCVBVIT.

RARO EXSTITISSE TANTAM INDOLEM TAM MATVRAE VIRTVTIS OPINANTES
VOLVIT QVI TENDERE AD INDOS AVRORAMQVE SEQVI
AMICI LVGENTES POSVERE III NON. SEPTEMB. A.D. MDCCCLXXX.

Nearly a quarter of a century later, on the 20th July 1904, immediately opposite the Jenkyns Memorial, a bronze tablet with the following inscription to the memory of Field-Marshal Sir Donald Stewart was unveiled by General Sir Peter Lumsden:—

IN MEMORY OF

FIELD-MARSHAL SIR DONALD MARTIN STEWART, BARONET.

G.C.B., G.C.S.I., C.I.E., D.C.L. OXON., LL.D. ABERD.

BORN NEAR FORRES, MARCH 1ST, 1824. DIED AT ALGIERS, MARCH 26TH, 1900.

A STUDENT AND PRIZEMAN OF THIS UNIVERSITY, HE JOINED THE BENGAL ARMY IN 1841 AND SERVED WITH DISTINCTION IN FRONTIER WARFARE, AT THE SIEGE OF DELHI, THE RELIEF OF LUCKNOW, AND IN ABYSSINIA. IN THE SECOND AFGHAN WAR HE LED THE SOUTHERN ARMY TO CANDAHAR, AND LATER, DURING HIS GREAT MARCH TO CABUL, WON THE BATTLE OF AHMUD KHEL, AFTERWARDS ASSUMING THE SUPREME MILITARY AND POLITICAL COMMAND IN AFGHANISTAN. HE WAS COMMANDER-IN-CHIEF IN INDIA FROM 1881 TO 1885, AND ON HIS RETURN HOME HE BECAME A MEMBER OF THE COUNCIL OF INDIA, AND IN 1895 GOVERNOR OF THE ROYAL HOSPITAL, CHELSEA.

STRONG, BRAVE, GENIAL, EMINENTLY WISE AND JUST, FORGETFUL OF SELF, AND MODEST, DONALD STEWART DID WITH HIS MIGHT WHATSOEVER HIS HAND FOUND TO DO.

We left Aberdeen on our return to India in October, intending to be in London some time. My mother having died during our stay at Linton, the series of letters from which I have made so many quotations came to an end. My mother took a very keen and intelligent interest in Indian affairs, hence the fulness with which I wrote to her about my work.

D. LONDON, *October* 23.—On driving in an omnibus to Euston station, I found myself sitting beside Julian Robinson of the *Pioneer*. I had a talk to him. He did not recognise me, but I identified him and told him that I had met him twice before to speak to, first at Mirzapore in 1858, when I stayed in the same house with him and heard him preach as Government chaplain;[1] secondly, at Simla, in 1861. He was pleasant enough, and we had plenty to say about Afghanistan and the

[1] See note 2, p. 39.

like. On parting, he said I had the advantage of him and begged to be told who I was. I satisfied his curiosity and bade him adieu.[1]

D. Hôtel Bedford, Paris, *November* 4.—Forenoon, Donald Macnabb came for us, and then we all walked together to 65 Rue Miromesnil, where we had breakfast with Edward Prinsep.[2] He has a charming suite of rooms. . . . Then we went on to the Louvre and spent most of the afternoon amongst the pictures. Later, we dined with Macnabb at the Hôtel Continental, and thence went to the Comédie Française, where to our great delight we saw *Le Bourgeois Gentilhomme.*

D. November 10.—A very miserable day, in the train. We were to have arrived at Rome at 12.45, but, a few hours after leaving Pisa, we came to a break in the line, caused by floods. Had to leave our carriage and walk along with our things to another train. Then we got to a station, Corsetto, where we were detained for hours, could get no information. Eventually it seemed it was impossible to go on to Rome. We were taken back to Pisa and then Romewards *viâ* Florence, being thus nearly twenty hours longer in the train than we had expected.

D. Rome, *November* 11.—At last we reached Rome, not feeling very bright as we were much wearied, and, as I anticipated, our baggage with that of the other passengers had been left behind somewhere. At the recommendation of one of our fellow-passengers, Count Vanutelli, we went to the Hôtel Constanzi, and to our surprise, on going into the breakfast-room, we found Cordery[3] and his sister, the sole occupants. We had a friendly meeting, and the C.'s most kindly asked us to join them in going to the Vatican, St. Peter's, etc. This we were very glad to do, and felt compensated for all our worries. Had it not been for our accident we certainly should not have gone to the Constanzi. We were much impressed by St. Peter's and the Vatican pictures.

[1] We never met again.

[2] See pp. 158, 159.

[3] Mr. J. G. Cordery, a Punjab Civilian, afterwards Resident of Hyderabad, a distinguished scholar, who translated the *Iliad* and the *Odyssey* into blank verse.

Did not see the statuary. Of course our visit was very hurried, and our lost luggage weighed much upon us.

D. November 12.—About 8 A.M. started with Cordery and his sister to see what we could of ancient Rome, went to the Capitol, Forum, Arches of Titus and Constantine, Coliseum; a most enjoyable morning, very fine, and we had an excellent and undisturbed opportunity of seeing the ruins. . . . Afternoon, we went to the baths of Caracalla, greatly struck by the immense size of the buildings. . . . To our great relief, our boxes at last turned up, and we were able to arrange to start by night train for Naples. . . .

D. NAPLES, *November* 13.—Reached the Hôtel de Rome between 8 and 9 A.M. Soon after, drove to the San Carlo Opera House, of which we saw the vast interior. Then to the Museum, many pictures and much statuary, the latter appeared specially interesting and very well arranged. At 1 P.M. we started by rail for Pompeii, and spent the rest of the day on the excursion. Much delighted both going and coming (after dark) with the various views of Vesuvius and with the fire, smoke, and lava which were issuing from the crater. Pompeii is indescribable in a few words, save as in truth a City of the Dead making the strongest impression on the living. We were intensely interested, and had a very good guide, No. 58, who seemed thoroughly master of his subject; said he had been the Prince of Wales's and Lord Lytton's guide, and that the latter had presented him with a copy of the *Last Days of Pompeii.*

D. November 14.—Reached Foggia about 6 A.M., started for Brindisi at 11.30, travelled all day rather pleasantly along the coast. At one of the stations found ourselves drawn up alongside a train going northwards. Our window looked into a large Pullman's car in which we recognised familiar faces. To our astonishment the carriage contained General Sir Frederick Roberts and many of the principal officers who were returning with him from Afghanistan.[1] General Sir James Hills, Colonel

[1] *I.e.* returning from Afghanistan after Roberts's splendid march from Cabul and victory over Ayub Khan at Candahar.

E. Chapman, General Hugh Gough, etc. I sprang out of our compartment, shook many by the hand, some of our friends rushing from their carriage to greet E. Just managed to get back to my seat when the two trains started in opposite directions. We were on board the ss. *Thibet* in the early evening.

D. November 15.—On board the *Thibet.* About 7 A.M. the ship started. Lady Ripon, it appears, is on board. . . .

D. November 18.—Reached Port Said between 1 and 2 P.M., and were transferred to the *Cathay.* . . .

D. November 29 *and* 30.—On Monday E. was introduced to Lady Ripon. I was introduced on Tuesday; saw a good deal of General Biddulph.[1] . . .

D. December 1.—Reached Bombay early in the morning. The Viceroy came on board to receive Lady Ripon. Allen Johnson also came on board, and he told me I had been promoted to be Commissioner of Lahore.

From Bombay we travelled to Lahore without a halt, and I at once took charge of the Commissionership. We had great difficulty in finding a house to live in, but the Financial Commissioner, Mr. J. B. Lyall, was just about to go into camp. He was kind enough to lend us his house until we were able to secure one of our own.

[1] General Sir Michael Biddulph, K.C.B., etc.

CHAPTER XVII

COMMISSIONER OF THE OLD LAHORE DIVISION

1881

THE Lahore Division consisted at this time of three districts, Lahore, Gujranwala, and Ferozepore. The Commissioner was the chief Executive representative of Government within that area. He was the principal Revenue officer, the principal original Civil and Civil appellate judge. In the Criminal department he was the Sessions or Assize judge, and also judge of appeal from all first-class magistrates within the Division. As an example of the miscellaneous executive duties of a Commissioner, I may give the following instance.

I had only been a few days in charge of the Division, living in the small house which had been temporarily lent to us, when a telegram was handed to me from the Commissioner of Delhi, saying that Sir James Fergusson,[1] the Governor of Bombay, with a numerous staff would arrive in Lahore the following morning. Sir Robert Egerton, the Lieutenant-Governor, was absent from Lahore, travelling in camp in a remote part of the Province. The visit had been suddenly determined on. The task of arranging for the proper reception of his Excellency seemed almost impossible. My wife and I looked at each other in blank despair. In a few seconds,

[1] Who lost his life in the recent earthquake in Jamaica.

however, we remembered that our old home, New Park, now belonged to the Nawab of Bahawulpore, and was probably standing unoccupied, but fully furnished. I telegraphed at once to his Highness, asking permission to make use of it for the Governor's reception. A favourable reply came in a few hours. My wife and Mrs. Arthur Brandreth immediately proceeded to the store, where we had deposited a good deal of property on going to England two years previously. They unpacked glass, china, lamps and ornaments, and forthwith did their best to carry out the necessary preparations. The next day Sir James Fergusson and his suite arrived by train at noon. With a small gathering of European and Native gentlemen I met him at the railway station and drove him to the Bahawulpore house, taking the northern route round the City and Fort. My wife and Mrs. Brandreth received his Excellency. After luncheon, I drove Sir James to the City, where he visited the Fort, the great Mosque, Ranjit Singh's Palace and Tomb, etc. Later, we had a large dinner-party. Between eleven and twelve at night, his Excellency and suite returned to their railway carriages. Our sense of relief was great, and we wondered what we should have done had it not been for the happy thought of the Bahawulpore house. Next day we could not help a smile at the discovery that the Native guard of honour had used the lids of the wooden cases from which all our glass and china had been unpacked, as firewood; the result being that the return journey to the store ended in the breakage of many of the contents of the uncovered boxes.

Towards the end of January we started on a camping

tour through part of the Lahore and Ferozepore districts. As I rode along the Ferozepore road, a few miles from Lahore, I asked the Tehsildar, who was accompanying me, the name of a large village on the right hand which seemed to contain a number of unusually high old brick buildings. The reply was, 'That is the ancient town of Ichra, in comparison to which, in olden times, Lahore was an unimportant village; the tradition of Ichra's greatness has survived to the present day. The Benares Shroffs (bankers) still send their hundis (bills of exchange) addressed to "Lahore, near Ichra."'

On the 24th and 25th of January we were encamped outside the large town of Kasur, the headquarters of a magistrate, who at this time was a Muhammadan gentleman named Kadir Bukhs, with whom we took tea one evening. Kadir Bukhs showed me over the town, specially pointing out the schools, the carpet manufactories, and a public garden which had been laid out by and bore the name of his predecessor, Mr. H. W. Steel of the Civil Service, an officer whom I had never met, but who was at this time serving in the neighbouring district of Ferozepore. In describing the recent progress and prosperity of Kasur, I noticed that Kadir Bukhs frequently introduced the name of Mrs. Steel. To the energy of this lady many improvements in female schools were attributed, as well as the starting of sundry new weaving industries. We were somewhat surprised to hear so much about the work of an European lady from the lips of a Muhammadan magistrate. Turning to the latter, I said, 'Well, sir, you have told me much about what Mrs. Steel has done, what have you to say about

Mr. Steel?' Kadir Bukhs replied, 'Sir, Mr. Steel is an angel' (ek ferishta hai).

The Mrs. Steel referred to by the admiring Kadir Bukhs was no less a personage than the lady who has since astonished the world by her writings. Kadir Bukhs was the first to tell us of her talents, and I can only say that our own subsequent knowledge made us even more enthusiastic admirers of her genius than her Muhammadan eulogist.

D. January 26.—Marched or rather drove into Ferozepore. Roads wonderfully improved. Beautiful trees on road from City to Cantonments; great difference since I was here twenty-one years ago, but the station itself seems little changed. We put up in tents in the Sessions House Compound. Much work during the day, receiving Native visitors, etc.

D. January 28.—The Steels dined with us. Mrs. Steel very interesting; she is a sister of M'Callum Webster, whom I knew at Haileybury, and who died, it seems, about a year ago in Madras.

D. February 7.—Marched to Faridkote; met by the Raja.[1] Then drove with him in his carriage, E. going on by herself to our encampment. The Raja is not very demonstrative, but seems to mean well, and I liked him better the more I saw of him. Afternoon he paid me a formal call. . . .

D. February 8.—At Faridkote. The Raja entertains us most hospitably. . . . In the evening paid a return visit to the Raja. E. visited the Ránis. Altogether our stay in Faridkote has been a success. I like the Raja and am glad I have been here.

D. February 19.—Marched to Chunian in the Lahore district. On the way I went into the jungle and had rather an exciting stalk after ravine deer. I had a capital chance, but unfortunately my cartridge missed fire. Later, however, took a long shot, more than two hundred yards, I think. Anyhow, I put up

[1] Bikrama Singh, the son of Wazir Singh. See p. 80.

the two hundred yards sight, and to my great delight the deer fell. Turned out to be a female, but with good horns. The distance was so great *I* couldn't have distinguished her from a male.

D. February 23.—Went into Lahore by evening train and drove to a furnished house, which at last we had managed to secure.

SIR DOUGLAS FORSYTH TO G. R. ELSMIE.

76 ONSLOW GARDENS,
February 17, 1881.

. . . I like to think of you occupying my old place at Lahore. . . . It is to my mind now, calmly reviewing everything, the finest post a man can hold. Others may be more distinguished and give higher emoluments, but for influence, power of doing good, and for comfort, there is nothing equal to it. These are the words of a man who has had some experience, you 'll allow. Of course, I don't mean to say that if you had the offer of a seat in Council you would not find that infinitely preferable. But I am dealing with the ordinary run of appointments. Of course, at times, when the thermometer is above 100° and a furious dust-storm blowing, and Serishtadarjee[1] quietly informs you that ẹk aur hukm áp ka—khubr na kis tarah—Chief Court se mansookh hua,[2] or the Secretary to Government sends you a snub, you may feel inclined to chuck the whole thing over. But I would gladly submit to this and fifty times more, to be back again in my old place at Jullundur, and wish I had been tied there for life.

This is a sermon on contentment, is it not? . . . We are sorely anxious about Colonel Parker,[3] as he is rapidly advancing into the thick of the fight, and these Boers are awkward customers. It seems to me that Colley, the prize boy of the new school of military tactics, is no better than one of the old school. The question of the retention or abandonment of Candahar is now

[1] Native head reader.

[2] 'Another order of your honour's—don't know how—has been upset by the Chief Court.'

[3] Of the 92nd regiment—Sir Douglas Forsyth's son-in-law.

under discussion and is made a party matter. . . . I hope you will now and then attempt to resuscitate the memory of me in the minds of the old Lahorites who used to be my friends. But I suppose they are nearly all dead and gone by this time. Rai Mul Singh[1] used to be a great ally of mine and I believe is still alive. Sirdar Tara Singh is not a subject of yours, I fancy, but I dare say you may now and then see him. Please remember me affectionately to any of the old lot. . . .

Among letters received at this time I find one from Sir Donald Stewart, who had just been chosen to succeed Sir Frederick Haines as Commander-in-Chief. The letter should have been published in the Life of Sir Donald, but unfortunately its existence had entirely escaped my memory.

SIR DONALD STEWART TO G. R. ELSMIE.

CALCUTTA, *February* 22.

MY DEAR ELSMIE,—I am sure you think me a wretch for not replying to your kind letter of congratulation of 1st February.

The truth is that the pen is never out of my hand, and all my private correspondence is in arrears.

If I do not answer all the letters I receive, it is not from any want of courtesy, for no one appreciates the disinterested approbation of friends like yourself more highly than I do. The long illness of Lord Ripon threw back much important work, and now we are shoving ahead full power without much regard to the condition of our safety valves.

I quite remember our discussion about Afghan affairs. Somehow, I have always thought that the war was unnecessary. I object to our withdrawal from Kandahar, *not* because I think it is a place of great strategical value, but because I do not think one Government is justified in repudiating the pledges given by its predecessor. This my only reason for sticking to Candahar.

[1] See p. 149.

Although many great authorities think differently, I can see no advantage in occupying such an advanced position. Moreover, we should not be there five years before circumstances forced us to go to Furrah and Herat.

The Government is being dreadfully bullied at home about this subject, but I think they will not give way to clamour nor to any other sort of pressure. As I said before, I am opposed to their action because it disturbs that continuity which ought to be a marked characteristic of our rule in this country, and I feel all the more strongly on this point because I see a very distinct intention on the part of the present ministry to do anything that will discredit the other party. This is bad, very bad, but it is no less true. . . .—I am, yours sincerely, D. M. STEWART.

Towards the end of February came the news of the disaster at Majuba Hill. A letter to me from a friend contained the following passage, with which many men who had had opportunities of judging would have concurred at the time:—

The death of Colley and the massacre of his detachment has fallen upon us rather like a thunderbolt. He was always rash and always wrong, and wanted us to walk through Afghanistan with only a weak brigade. He has fallen into the destruction which his obstinacy nearly brought upon our army in Cabul. I am very grieved for Lady Colley.

The month of March was cheered by visits from Sir Hugh Gough and Mr. Donald Macnabb. We had parted from the latter in Paris. At that time Macnabb did not know that he was likely to return soon to India, but on our arrival in Bombay we found telegrams in the newspapers showing that he had been offered and had accepted the appointment of Governor-General's Agent at Quetta. Macnabb accordingly followed us quickly to India, but he soon found that his health had failed, and he doubted his ability to give full effect to the policy of Government on the Biluchistan Frontier. He therefore determined not to take charge of his new appointment and to resign the service.

The Deputy Commissioner of Ferozepore was, at this time, Major Grey, who was afterwards well known as Commissioner of Delhi and Resident at Bahawulpore. Major Grey was an officer of much energy. He made his mark in Ferozepore chiefly by extending the artificial irrigation of lands lying within the reach of small canals from the Sutlej. The benefit to the Jat cultivators was great and was fully appreciated by them. An intelligent native gentleman told me that many of the Jats accounted for Major Grey's zeal for irrigation in the following manner. 'This Major Grey Sahib must have been one of our ancestors in his former life, and must have suffered a great deal from want of water in the old days, when he was a Jat; so, after his death he thought of doing good to his children, and was therefore born this time in the house of a Sahib, and at last came to this land again and has done all this for our generation; otherwise why should a Sahib take all this trouble?'

D. June 13.—Began work in the Chief Court.[1]

Sir Robert Montgomery to G. R. Elsmie.

June 2, 1881.

I am only able to write a few lines to acknowledge your letter of 8th May and to say we are so glad that you like your position of Commissioner of Lahore, a post I once occupied. And when

[1] To which I had been appointed to fill a short vacancy.

I began, there was not a house[1] in the Punjab but the old Residency at Lahore, nor a road, nor a cantonment, nor any districts, thanahs or tehsils marked off, and no map, but the old Arrowsmiths' of one hundred years ago! Think of the change!

I fear you will be absorbed in the Chief Court. It has its good side, more pay and two months in the Hills, and we can't have everything. . . .

D. Week beginning June 26.—Rather a wretched week. Young Innes's[2] death from typhoid was followed on Wednesday by poor Ghafur's,[3] who succumbed to the after effects of cholera. We thought at first that he would recover, but, although he got over the early stage, he was too weak. He was a good servant, and we shall miss him much, *and* not easily replace him. . . . On Sunday we were shocked by hearing of poor young Bean's[4] death of cholera after eight hours' illness.

SIR DOUGLAS FORSYTH TO G. R. ELSMIE.

76 ONSLOW GARDENS, *July* 5.

I am ashamed to look at the date of your last letter. . . . I only wish the happy time had arrived, as surely it will come, when, instead of the barbaric system of using pen and paper, suited to such ancients as the Egyptians, or of the more advanced method of talking by telegraph or even telephone, both of which require a wire to be stretched from one end of the world to the other, a clumsy contrivance which our remote descendants five thousand years hence will class with the days of styles and papyrus, we, or ourselves reproduced in our second or third incarnation, shall communicate with each other in some ethereal and mysterious manner. Well, suppose such a time to have already arrived and then I cease all further apology, for I have, in the spirit, sent you fifty letters and have told you everything! So you know how we went to Spain and had a most delightful trip. . . . We saw the Alhambra and were quite charmed with

[1] O. course Sir Robert meant a house on an European plan.

[2] A young Civilian.

[3] One of our native servants.

[4] A young police-officer.

it. Then we went to Seville and enjoyed seeing splendid Murillos. After that we travelled to Madrid and feasted on Velasquez, Murillo, and all the first masters of painting. From Madrid we took a compartment in a Wagon-lit and came right through to Paris, passing through lovely country in the Pyrenees. . . . The object of our venturing so far from home was primarily to enable me to negotiate with the Portuguese Government the terms of a concession for the construction of a railway through Portuguese Indian territory. . . . I am now Chairman of this Railway Company[1] and have a secretary and a duftur,[2] and only want a jemadar and chuprassies[3] to fancy myself back in Lahore! I shouldn't be exceedingly astonished if I found my business required me to make a visit to India, but this is anticipating the future. At present I am qualifying for such a trip by gasping in tropical heat, which is all caused by 'that comet.' It is quite frightful. . . .

D. July 28.—Last day on Bench of Chief Court meanwhile. . . .

D. July 29.—Resumed work as Commissioner of Lahore.

D. August 8 *to* 21.—There is little to record from the 8th to the 21st August save the sudden and serious increase of cholera in the City and round about, which has caused much anxiety. . . First signs in the Central gaol about the 8th, after which the prisoners were gradually moved into camp, and up to date I have only heard of twenty fatal cases, but there must have been more. In the City and suburbs the reports have shown gradual increase of mortality from two or three per diem up to twenty-five or even over fifty. Now (21st) I think a slight change has taken place for the better.

D. August 28.—Cholera still bad. Every little improvement seems immediately followed by violent reaction.

D. September 10.—Cholera has not disappeared, but it has greatly declined, and is almost non-existent in Anarkuli.

D. Sunday, September 11.—Evening a great shock, from

[1] The Great Indian Peninsula.

[2] An office.

[3] A sergeant and messengers.

hearing by telegram of Colonel Millar, Deputy Commissioner of Gujranwala, being seized with cholera. Knowing that there was no Civil Surgeon there, I went off for Dr. Fairweather, Civil Surgeon, Lahore, and with him to the railway station. After much difficulty, arranged to send him on an engine to Gujranwala, but alas! as he was starting, another telegram came saying the poor fellow was gone. Most sad and grievous. . . . He was on the point of starting for Simla on leave when he was taken ill. Major Roberts arrived by train to relieve him half an hour after his death. . . .

D. September 17.—I have been living from day to day, and what I should have done without Justin M'Carthy's *History of Our Own Times* to read at leisure moments, I know not.[1] . . .

D. September 22.—Cholera really decreasing.

D. October 2.—Mr. Hughes, the missionary from Peshawur, dined with us. Talking of A. and B.[2] Mr. H. related that the young Khan of Hoti had said he would rather be hanged by A. than fined by B.

D. October 15.—A fresh vacancy having occurred, took my seat on the Chief Court Bench for the third time.

SIR ROBERT MONTGOMERY TO G. R. ELSMIE.

INDIA OFFICE, *November* 9, 1881.

I was very pleased to see your handwriting in your letter of the 9th October, and to know that you had got through the terrible time of sickness at Lahore. . . . By God's mercy you have been spared, and in future, with a seat in the Chief Court, you will get away during the unhealthy season, and though the work may not be so interesting as the Commissioner's office, still there is a compensating advantage of the Hills and higher pay. Colonel Millar's death happening at such a period was especially heart-rending to the family.[3] . . .

[1] My wife had by this time been obliged to go to the Hills.

[2] Two Frontier officers.

[3] A son of Sir Robert Montgomery was about to be married to Colonel Millar's daughter.

CHAPTER XVIII

JUDGE OF THE CHIEF COURT

1882—1884

RAI MUL SINGH called on me one day, and we talked about Sir Henry Lawrence. I gave Mul Singh the lead by saying, 'Henry Lawrence was a most kind and amiable man, was he not?' 'Yes, sahib, he had a very tender heart, but he often displayed anger and irritation when people attempted to trade on his good-nature. Sometimes even, when reasonable requests were made at inopportune times, or when he might be undergoing great anxiety, he would become "maghlub al ghasab" (overcome by anger), and turn indignantly on the applicant and order him out of the house. But if, on reflection, he thought he had been harsh or hasty, he would bid a messenger hurry after the petitioner to bring him back to have his prayer granted. So well known,' continued Mul Singh, 'was this characteristic of the great Sir Henry that in old days, when we saw him working himself into a rage, when perhaps too audacious a request had been preferred, we would say to ourselves, "Thank God, the storm (andhéri) is upon us, the air is black with dust, keep good heart, for, in a few moments, the Almighty will send down the beneficent rain and the earth will be fertile."'

D. March 25.—Spent in going over with E. to Amritsur in the Lieutenant-Governor's special train, to see him turn the first sod of the Amritsar and Pathankote Railway. Heat considerable, but everything was well arranged, and there was not much delay. . . .

D. March 30.—After dinner to the Montgomery Hall, where was held a conversazione in honour of Sir Robert and Lady Egerton. A great success on the whole; the music very good, singing most effective.

D. April 1.—Evening, to a conversazione at Government House, to meet Sir Charles Aitchison, who had arrived that afternoon to take over the Lieutenant-Governorship.

D. April 3.—Evening, E. and I went to the station to see Sir Robert and Lady Egerton depart. A large collection of people, and some enthusiasm.

Sir Douglas Forsyth to G. R. Elsmie.

76 Onslow Gardens, *March* 19, 1882.

I haven't heard from you or of you for an age. Whether it be my fault or yours, I shall assume the privilege of an old man to give a homily on the importance of exiles in India keeping up the 'touch' with England, and not allowing purely Indian official life to absorb all your thought and time. Men who neglect their English friends and fall into the Indian official groove find the greatest difficulty when they retire in getting anything like wholesome occupation, and generally rush into wild schemes for supplying fresh meat to the public or for extracting gold out of Providence mines, and end, of course, in ruining themselves and their families, or if they have expended all their energy, they lead a restless, aimless, querulous existence; whereas had they only kept themselves up to the time of day and had fresh communication with Old England, they would find themselves quite *au courant* with the busy life of London on their return, and could take directorships and chairmanships by the dozen. So you see how much you are likely to lose if you allow a musty old 'misl' [1] to be preferred in your own mind to an epistolary chat with me! You think of retiring early, I believe, and yet even were you fifty-five when you gave up the service, you would find yourself young enough among your contemporaries at home. I am no chicken, you'll allow, yet my colleagues on one Board call me 'the Bucha.' [2] Irreverent, I admit, but it will give you an idea to what ages people go on in business here. *You* may do the same. I find myself quite as busy as I ever was in India, and in fact have no time for calling or indulging in the ordinary gaieties of London life. . . .

In April, I was appointed permanently to be a Judge of the Chief Court. I had, however, previously explained to Sir Robert Egerton and Sir Charles Aitchison, the retiring and incoming Lieutenant-Governors, that I trusted that when a Commissionership with a Hill station or other suitable Executive post should fall vacant, my claim to it might be considered.

D. May 8.—A trying excitement in the morning; . . . the burning down of part of our stable and the thatched huts in the stable-yard. We felt much put out; a good deal of damage was done. However, when in the evening the news of the murder of Lord Frederick Cavendish and Mr. Burke came by telegram, we felt humbled and thought little more of our own misfortune. . . .

D. May 24.—Evening, we had a large garden-party for Natives and for Europeans. The Muhammadans ate refreshments prepared by Mangul Khan.[3] The Hindus were entertained by a sweetmeat-maker behind screens, and they seemed all pleased. Garden looked pretty, grass green, band played. . . .

This was the first party of the sort we had ever given.

[1] File of the vernacular papers in a case.
[2] The young one.
[3] Our Muhammadan butler.

It was a novel experiment in Lahore, but, according to the Native press, it was much appreciated by our guests.

D. July 14.—Much excitement owing to the telegrams regarding the Egyptian bombardment. In the end we must assume a position in Egypt, and unless difficulty arises from the Turkish direction, there will be no opposition from the rest of Europe apparently.

D. July 15.—Bombardment over; it seems a great pity that we haven't the troops to land at once.

SIR ROBERT MONTGOMERY TO G. R. ELSMIE.

Wednesday, July 12.

. . . I should like to know about the administration generally. How is it going on? any changes contemplated? How do you all like your new Lieutenant-Governor?[1] . . . If you go to Simla, tell me about the local politics and doings there. We are not impressed here with the wisdom of all that is generated there. I write generated, because great and momentous changes are proposed out of some one's brain, I don't know whose, and they are often deemed to be applicable to *all* India, without *all* India being consulted. . . . What appears to me is that whatever one man writes, all sign. There is an apparent want of independence, often in most vital and momentous questions. But I may be quite mistaken. I am sure they desire to do well, and none more so than the Viceroy. I should like your impression. . . .

D. August 12.—Arrived at Simla for the two months' semi-vacation. . . .

D. SIMLA, *September* 6.—We dined at Peterhof. . . . After dinner was taken up to talk to the Viceroy, Lord Ripon. H. E. spoke about the present position of the Chief Court.[2] . . .

D. September 16.—Excellent telegrams from the Secretary of State to Viceroy, telling of the capture of Arabi, Cairo, and the virtual close of the war. . . .

[1] Sir Charles Aitchison.

[2] Which was at that time in hopeless arrears of work. We were trying to obtain sanction for a fourth judge. *Now*, I believe there are six or more judges.

D. October 4.—First day of meeting of the Punjab Reorganisation Committee, consisting of J. W. Smyth, Colonel MacMahon, H. E. Perkins. J. B. Lyall, Mackworth Young, and myself.

D. October 11.—Last meeting of Organisation Committee, from 11 A.M. till past 6 P.M.; however, most of the recommendations were put into shape, and we had much discussion.

The chief change proposed was that the Commissioners of the Punjab should be reduced in number from ten to six, that they should be relieved of all Criminal and Civil judicial work, and that the territories under their administrative control should be greatly increased in area. This proposal was eventually sanctioned, and the new arrangement has lasted to the present day, save that the North-West Frontier province has now been separated from the Punjab.

D. LAHORE, *November* 8.—Went with J. B. Lyall to the railway station, to meet the Viceroy, Lord Ripon. At twelve, a levée at Government House. . . . Evening, to the Government House reception, where the Governor-General received an address and made a long speech on Local self-government, which made one think he protested too much. I doubt whether he knows very well what he is speaking about, and I prophesy that very little appreciable change on the face of affairs will result from the excitement about so-called self-government. There has never been any desire to check local self-government in the Punjab. Quite the reverse. The difficulties lie in the character of the people.

D. November 9.—Started for Peshawur on inspection duty.

D. November 10.—Reached Attock by rail at 3.30 A.M. A good view of the comet, which is still bright. Crossed to Khairabad, then on to Peshawur, arriving at 8.30 A.M. Railway very smooth and easy. Put up with Mr. J. G. Cordery, the Commissioner.[1] . . . On the whole, I felt low on returning to Peshawur and finding so few of the old people here.

[1] See p. 275.

This journey was a great contrast to my first journey from Lahore to Peshawur, ten years before. The railway had now been completed and opened, with the exception of the bridge at Attock.

D. November 11.—At Peshawur. To the city before breakfast with Mr. Beckett, the Deputy Commissioner. Then received a great many old Native friends.

D. LAHORE, *November* 18.—To the University Convocation, where Leitner[1] was made D.O.L.[2] and the Viceroy made a long speech. . . . The noise in the galleries was terrific, but I suppose the Viceroy enjoyed it as 'Statesmanship without Administration.' . . . Evening, the Kiplings came to dinner with their son.

The Kiplings here referred to were Mr. John Lockwood Kipling, Head of the School of Art at Lahore, and his wife, Mrs. Kipling, sister of Lady Burne-Jones and Lady Poynter. The son was a young man in his teens who had just arrived from England. He is now the celebrated author, Rudyard Kipling.

Towards the close of the evening, Mrs. Kipling told me that her son was bent on a literary career; that, while he had been at school at Westward Ho, he had written a variety of verses which seemed to disclose unusual power in a boy of his age. Mrs. Kipling went on to say that a collection of these verses had been privately printed in pamphlet form, and she proposed to send me a copy to read. The pamphlet duly came. I read it and returned it, having been greatly struck by the contents. In 1899 I was told that one of these pamphlets had been sold through Messrs. Sotheby for £117.

[1] The Principal of the Lahore College and Registrar of the Punjab University.

[2] Doctor of Oriental Literature.

SIR ROBERT MONTGOMERY TO G. R. ELSMIE.

7 CORNWALL GARDENS, *November* 7.

. . . We have the proceedings connected with giving Native magistrates full powers over British subjects. In time it would have come. But it seems to me as a child born out of due time. Mr. Hope made a modified proposal. This I should have preferred, but when a majority of the Viceroy's Council and *all* the local Governments approve of it, the Council here are helpless, and could not negative it; though, I think, not one of us really approved of it in its *entirety*.

Looking on at a distance the process in India now is like that of a forcing-house, and the Lieutenant-Governors of Provinces, more than ever the nominees of the Viceroy, adopt and even go beyond the advanced views of clever, inexperienced men in the Government. Of course there is the éclat of the Indian and English press. This, I often think, leads to measures being adopted, which those who have a single eye to the good of India would hesitate about, at any rate not force on. Your Viceroy seems to be very genial, a good speaker, very fond of making speeches. Such men are not always the soundest. . . .

I see that *he*, Lord Ripon, and Baring are bent on what is called, I suppose, *disestablishing* the Indian Church, reducing the chaplains by not appointing and filling up vacancies, and practically leaving *all* but the Military to make their own arrangements. Happily five of the Council are opposed. But the Liberal Government here would delight in such a proposal. . . . But still India is, I think, prospering, advancing rapidly; what will it be fifty years hence? Our Indian troops, owing to *Egypt*, have, for the first time, been really valued by the English public. They did well, and their representatives who came here raised the whole body in general estimation. . . .

The first note of interest which I find in 1883 was written about the middle of February, and refers to a proposed Act of the Legislature, embodying the policy of giving Native magistrates full judicial power over British subjects, mentioned by Sir Robert Montgomery in his letter of 7th November just quoted.

The Bill was somewhat unfairly known throughout India as the 'Ilbert Bill.' Mr. Ilbert indeed introduced it, but its main features had, I believe, been settled before he arrived in India. My rough note runs as follows :—

There is nothing big going on, with the exception of the fuss about giving jurisdiction to Natives over Europeans. This excitement has been gradually growing till it has assumed very considerable dimensions by to-day; indignation meetings being held everywhere. The better opinion says that Natives[1] care nothing for it. *Times*, etc., in great excitement thereanent.

My opinion on the proposed change had been called for by the Government, and had been given in 1882 as follows :—

It appears to me rather premature to alter a law which has just been passed[2] on such an important point. I am willing to admit, however, that it would be very anomalous to appoint a Native covenanted civilian to the charge of a district, and to deny him jurisdiction over European British subjects. I think that serious practical difficulties might arise if such jurisdiction were not given. I would therefore amend the law to this extent if it is in contemplation to appoint Natives to the charge of districts. But I would not go further in the meanwhile. I do not think any practical difficulty is likely to arise, for some time to come, from not giving Native Sessions Judges power to pass the high sentences on European British subjects as contemplated by section 449 C.P. Code. Cases of the kind are not very common, and I think no practical difficulty will arise from sending them

[1] *I.e.* Natives generally. Bengali Babus, of course, clamoured for it.

[2] The recently amended Code of Criminal procedure.

to the nearest Sessions Judge who is qualified under the Act as it now stands. . . . In a matter of this kind, I think, it is well not to forget the saying, 'festina lente.'

At a later time, when my opinion was called for on the so-called 'Ilbert Bill,' I wrote :—

I have little to add to the opinion given by me on the 31st May 1882, when this subject was first raised. I beg to refer to that opinion.

So far as the Punjab is concerned, I think I may safely say that no necessity whatever has as yet arisen for making the proposed changes in the law. We have no Native Civilian appointed by competition. We have one Native Assistant Commissioner, Muhammad Hayat Khan, C.S.I., who is not a member of the Civil Service. We have also four young officers appointed within the last two or three years, under the provisions of Chapter iii. Statute 33 Victoria. It will be a long time presumably before any of these officers is appointed to be a Magistrate of the district, or a Sessions Judge.

From a Punjab standpoint, therefore, I should much prefer to wait till we see what style of work these officers turn out, and how they conduct themselves generally, before we make such an important change in the law.

As far as other provinces are concerned, their local officers are in a better position than I am to say whether the necessity for a change has arisen or not. I confess I still adhere to the view that *all* Magistrates of Districts should have equal powers. I think the prestige and authority of Magistrates of Districts should not be lowered, and if Natives are to be appointed to be Magistrates of Districts, I would not deny them the powers proposed to be granted. But this view is based on administrative grounds only, and I have no sympathy, at present, with the proposal so far as it is founded on a desire to remove so-called anomalies, or to remove disabilities from individual officers, or from a class of officer.

I still think that no practical inconvenience whatever is likely to be felt from withholding these powers from Native Sessions Judges.

On the general question of the agitation which has been caused throughout India it is difficult to remain altogether silent, though, perhaps, opinions are hardly required on this point. Much of the excitement is probably due to an exaggerated idea of the practical effect of the proposed alterations. Nevertheless, the antipathy of non-official, and even of official, Europeans to such a measure is not unnatural.

All persons acquainted with the administration of Criminal justice in India are painfully aware how prone the more ignorant portion of the Native community is to bring false charges against persons to whom they bear a grudge, and to add to true charges against guilty persons, false charges against the friends and relatives of those persons. False evidence is easily procured, as we all know, and as counsel daily tell us when arguing criminal appeals. In a country where these things prevail is it to be wondered at if the European community fears the consequences of the removal of a single safeguard? Rightly or wrongly, European Judges are more trusted by their countrymen, and even by Indians, than Native Judges.

Allegations, false or true, are very commonly made against the trustworthiness of Native Judges, and in the Punjab applications are by no means uncommon by which the superior courts are moved to transfer Criminal cases from Native to European courts. I do not know that I have ever heard of an application for a converse transfer, viz. from an European to a Native court.

Under these circumstances it seems natural enough that, until the European community has had fuller opportunity of judging of the qualifications of the new Native civilians, the proposed change should be met with strong, and, perhaps, unreasoning opposition. Such changes must probably be eventually accepted. This is the view held by an ex-Punjab official of very high standing and of great experience, now in England, but that gentleman, in writing to me some months ago, said he regarded the measure as at present premature, as a 'child born out of due time.'

D. March 12.—Telegrams about the European British Subject Bill; all very interesting. The Bill will certainly be much modified, if not withdrawn altogether. The commotion is very remarkable.

Eventually, by Act III. of 1884, 'Jurisdiction over European British subjects' was conferred on District Magistrates only, with the proviso that the accused may claim that the trial shall be before a jury. That is the present state of the law.

Another mania which prevailed in 1883 was for the promotion of so-called Local Self-Government in the various provinces of India. The general tone adopted by the Supreme Government on the subject was to the effect that European officials, instead of encouraging the people to manage their own affairs hitherto, had done their utmost to suppress aspirations of the kind. This was certainly not correct so far as the Punjab was concerned. In giving my opinion on a draft Bill to make provision for 'Local Self-Government in the Punjab,' I wrote as follows:—

The general object and scope of the proposed law seems to me to be excellent, and I have full sympathy with a measure which appears to provide for a fair and legitimate expansion of the principles, rules, and laws which are at present in force in the Punjab in regard to the levy and administration of local funds and rates.

I am inclined, however, to deprecate the adoption of the proposed short title of the new law: 'The Punjab Local Self-Government Act.' This title does not strike me as a happy one. It does not convey to my mind any precise idea of its meaning. The new law will only affect a few of the matters which belong to the 'Government' of the province or the districts, and so long as the major departments of the Government remain under Imperial control, I think the adoption of the high-sounding title 'Local Self-Government' in regard to a few minor departments is both misleading and inappropriate.

Moveover, much that has been said and written in India during the last year regarding the policy of Local Self-Government has proceeded on the assumption that a *new* departure has been made, and that a *new* boon is being conferred on the people. However true this assumption may be in regard to those provinces of India of which I have no personal knowledge, I cannot for a moment admit that a new departure is being made in this matter in the Punjab. The draft Bill proposes what I regard as a reasonable and legitimate advance of the policy which has prevailed in this province during the twenty-four years I have served in it.

I have had the honour of serving under every Lieutenant-Governor who has governed the Punjab, and from the earliest year of my service I have been fully impressed with the belief that one of the chief principles of our administration, a principle insisted upon most strenuously by each successive Lieutenant-Governor, has been that of enlisting the co-operation of the people, and inviting them to take the initiative in all matters appertaining to local improvements, education, municipal government, the levying of new rates, and such like. . . . In proof of this, it is only necessary to refer to the annual reports, which will show how much has been done during the last quarter of a century in the matter of entrusting Native gentlemen with the exercise of Civil and Criminal powers, in appointing Zaildars or Honorary Police Officers, in promoting the old town-punchayats to be Municipal Committees, in constituting dispensary and district boards, and so on.

Even in the matter of 'election' to Committees, the idea is by no means a novel one in the Punjab. So far back as 1867, under the direct encouragement of the Government, many of the nominations to Municipal Committees proposed by me as Deputy Commissioner were based on the votes of the people most immediately concerned. For these and similar reasons, therefore, I deprecate the adoption of a title for the proposed law which, when taken with all that has been said and written in India on the subject of the so-called 'Local Self-Government,' seems to cast a slur on the past history of the Punjab, and I would suggest that some such title as the 'Local Rates Levy and Administration Act, 1883,' should be chosen instead. . . .

Sir Robert Montgomery to G. R. Elsmie.

India Office, *May* 7.

. . . Your memo. on self (local) government I entirely concur with. Local self-government has always existed in the Punjab. The new departure is going beyond the old line of not moving till localities were fitted for it. If you refer to the letter from the Secretary of State to the Viceroy, dated October 5, 1882, published in the Parliamentary Blue-Book, you will see, paragraph 2, that the Secretary of State distinctly lays down that the regulation of the government of India, dated 23rd May 1882, is asserted to be a 'farther extension of local government.'

I am told (rumour merely) that this has caused annoyance at headquarters.

The feeling, I think, here is, that it will be unsatisfactory if the district officer is not Chairman of the District Local Board.

The Ilbert Bill was most unfortunate. The Government will in future look very closely into any general sweeping proposals from India. Confidence in the wisdom of some has been shaken of late. I believe Lord Ripon to be most conscientious, and desirous of doing what is right. His advisers are more to blame, and few seem to be able to resist supporting what emanates from Simla.

I am glad to see you are independent in your opinion. It is a great thing for a Governor to have men who will write and speak unreservedly. . . .

At the beginning of July, my health forced me to take short leave, and I went to Simla so that I might join six weeks' privilege leave with the two months during which the Court held its sittings at that place. A good deal of leisure time was given to reading Lockhart's *Life of Scott*, which has always been a source of great pleasure to me. I find that I made the following extract as a testimony against those who deny Walter Scott's title to a high place amongst the poets.

On being requested to inscribe his name in the album of the Bell Rock Lighthouse, Scott penned immediately the following lines :—

'*Pharos Loquitur.*'

'Far in the bosom of the deep,
O'er these wild shelves my watch I keep;
A ruddy gem of changeful light,
Bound on the dusky brow of night;
The seaman bids my lustre hail,
And scorns to strike his timorous sail.'

On the 10th of August an interesting series of *tableaux vivants* was given at the theatre. Among the scenes were *Pygmalion and Galatea*, the garden scene in *Romeo and Juliet*, *The Boatman and Elaine*, *Titania and Bottom*, and so on. The following evening we happened to have a dinner party, at which the principal guest was the Maharaja of Kuch Behar. Whilst talking over the entertainment of the previous night, it suddenly occurred to me that it would be amusing to invert the positions of the principal characters of the scenes. I knew the Maharaja to be fond of fun, but I was not aware that he was a skilful musician. On my telling him the idea, he entered into it keenly and said the best help he could give would be an improvised musical accompaniment. So we rapidly cleared a space for the stage, collected some scratch dresses and properties, and showed Juliet serenading Romeo on the balcony; Elaine gracefully guiding the boat, with the dead boatman lying in state; Galatea sculpturing Pygmalion, etc. etc.; while His Highness the Maharaja fulfilled his promise of providing a musical accompaniment with perfect skill.

D. October 10.—Went to the Legislative Council Debate to see the Local Self-Government Bill (Punjab) passed. I believe the title is altered to 'Local Boards Bill,' and this is what I urged in my opinion. . . .

H.E. the Viceroy did the Council Presidency business in capital style.

An important subject occupied many of my leisure hours during 1884. Ten years previously I had made an unsuccessful attempt to bring about certain changes in the mode of Criminal Administration on the Peshawur Frontier. Now that I was serving on the Chief Court, cases from Peshawur, either on appeal or reference, were daily coming before me. The old difficulties, the old unsatisfactory mode of surmounting them, were forced upon my notice. Moreover, since I had written on the subject in 1873, I had had four years or more of personal experience of trying persons accused of violent crime on the North-West Frontier.

One day, on thinking about the subject, I determined to send for the records of all heavy Criminal cases which I had tried at Peshawur, and from them, to build up a solid body of fact which might perhaps induce the Government to face the question in real earnest. I carried out this plan by slow degrees, being greatly helped by Mr. Henry Rivaz, an English Barrister, and a member of the Punjab Bar, who was interested in the subject, and was glad to give me the benefit of his advice. My book was eventually printed, and submitted to Government. It contained no recommendations, but it marshalled a series of facts which eventually led to the adoption of even more stringent measures than I had ventured to hope would ever be sanctioned.

Another reminiscence of 1884, relating to a very different subject, may be held to be of some interest perhaps, when the subsequent careers of the persons principally concerned are recalled to mind. I have before mentioned that Mrs. Steel took a great interest in the cause of female education, and had probably done more to promote its advancement among Native women in the Punjab than any one else had done up to this time. The Government Educational Department fully recognised Mrs. Steel's talents and acquirements, and they occasionally invited her to examine groups of schools and to report on their progress. Early in 1884 Mrs. Steel was asked by Government to pay a visit to Lahore, and to make a special report on female education in that city. Mrs. Steel wrote to us and asked whether we would receive her during her stay in Lahore. We replied that we should be delighted to see her for as long as she pleased, provided that during her visit she would act in our drawing-room the principal lady character in a play called *Winning a Husband*, a quaint transpontine farce, originally produced in the early years of the century.

The principal character, 'Jenny Transit,' involves eight

changes of costume and personality. The plot is simple. An elderly romantic and pedantic bachelor has advertised for a wife. His sister and her friend, Jenny Transit, conspire together in sending answers from six or seven candidates. These candidates include a poetess, a lady of fashion, a French dancer, a rustic beauty, a pork butcher's widow, and so on, all of whom are impersonated by the clever Jenny. In the end, Sir Roderick discovers the plot and, fully appreciating the talents of the only candidate, falls at her feet. Mrs. Steel played one candidate after another with brilliant success. Another character in the piece was represented by Mr. Leslie of the Artillery. The principal member of the audience was Sir Charles Aitchison, the Lieutenant-Governor, whose concurrence in some of her educational proposals Mrs. Steel was most anxious to obtain. She made us laugh afterwards by saying that while in the character of the French dancer she was performing a *pas seul*, she could not help feeling that she might be accused of dancing with extra verve, in the hope of gaining a reward from the ruler of the country. Another member of the audience was Mr. Rudyard Kipling. Fifteen years later, Mr. Leslie recalled the old performance of *Winning a Husband*, and asked if we had been aware that the author of the short critique which appeared in the local paper was the now celebrated writer and poet.

I reproduce the notice inserted by the *Civil and Military Gazette* of the 21st of February 1884. It is interesting to read a genuine appreciation by Mr. Kipling (if indeed he was the writer) of Mrs. Steel as an actress, written before either of them had become candidates for public fame.

(FROM A CORRESPONDENT.)

Your dramatic critic wishes it to be known that he formed one of a distinguished and discriminating audience whose fastidious taste was gratified on Thursday night by a private performance of George Macfarren's comedietta, *Winning a Husband, or Seven's the Main*. Private theatricals, when they are good—and they are usually bad—have a charm of their own. Of much that constitutes that charm, however, it would be unbecoming to speak. But good acting, even though it be in a drawing-room, is considered a legitimate subject for public notice nowadays, especially when the names of the chief actors may be found—though not in that capacity—in the Army and Civil lists; and when some of those on the other side of the curtain rule a province, command a division of the army, or perform equally arduous though less remunerative duties. So I will not apologise further for saying that M. Louis Malgré[1] . . . played 'Sir Roderick Strangeways,' last night, to every one's admiration. There was a refinement in his romantic absurdities, an air in his affectations, which made the part delightfully sentimental and extravagant. The accomplished Signora Silva—whose versatility is a provincial byword—'exemplified the changeableness of human affairs'—including one's clothes and character—with a liveliness and skill which makes it seem almost incredible that talents so evidently meant for the capital should be given up to the districts. The Signora played the part of 'Miss Jenny Transit'; and the Protean Miss Jenny, in the play, sets herself to represent one after the other, Margaret MacMucklecanny, Miss Cornelia Clementina Clappergo, Lady Dorothea Dashly, Mrs. Deborah Griskin, Mademoiselle Antoinette Marosquieu, Bridget Buckthorn, and Lieutenant Thaddeus O'Transit. Mademoiselle Algé, who played the part of Lucinda, Sir Roderick's sister, fairly incurred the risk of publicity by the cleverness with which she showed conclusively that histrionic genius is hereditary; while as regards M. le Grand-Fusil, his

[1] The actors and actresses appeared in the playbills under stage names.

name is so well known in amateur theatricals as to make it almost unnecessary to say that as 'Davy' he was inimitable.

In the beginning of March we were delighted to receive a visit from Sir Douglas Forsyth, his daughter Miss Ethel Forsyth, and his brother Mr. William Forsyth, Q.C.[1] It was a great pleasure to see Mr. William Forsyth in India. He was much interested in the various sights of Lahore, and when he had exhausted them, his principal occupation was to accompany me to the Bench of the Chiet Court and watch the proceedings.

On the 3rd of March we gave a large garden-party for Europeans and Natives at which Sir Douglas was glad to meet many of his old friends. A few days later, he returned to England *viâ* Mooltan, Sukkur, and Karachi. At Sukkur he unfortunately met with a serious carriage accident, from the effects of which, I fear, he never thoroughly recovered. On reaching England, Sir Douglas wrote :—

> I especially thank you for giving me such opportunities of seeing my old friends. . . . It was a great treat seeing India again, but it is a treat which cannot be repeated, and now I feel there is nothing for me but to sit quite quiet on my perch till it is time for me to drop off.

At the beginning of July, my book, *Crime and Criminals on the Peshawur Frontier*, was published. A letter on the subject from a learned friend, who afterwards took a prominent part in amending the Frontier Criminal Regulations, ran as follows :—

> Many thanks for your book, which is very useful and instructive. An apt collection of facts tells you a hundred times

[1] See p. 150.

as much as any amount of ingenious generalisations. The state of things which your cases disclose remind me much of Icelandic society in the eleventh and twelfth centuries as depicted in the Sagas, and of the uglier times described by Thierry; . . . the same common motive for crime, quarrels about land and women, the same code of morality which makes killing a duty where the law is compelled to treat it as murder, the same view that when you can't kill your enemy directly, you may legitimately swear him to death. I have no doubt that equally close parallels may be drawn from more recent times in the out-of-the-way parts of Europe such as Corsica. What we are apt to put down as characteristics of a particular race and country are much more often characteristics of a particular stage of civilisation.

Towards the end of the year H.R.H. the Duke of Connaught, who had been commanding the Meerut Division for some time, arrived in Lahore with the Duchess. Their Royal Highnesses were the guests of the Lieutenant-Governor and Lady Aitchison at Government House. On the 20th December the Duke held a levée, and on one evening during the visit we were invited to meet their Royal Highnesses at dinner. My wife had the honour of sitting next the Duke, and was much struck by the trouble which H.R.H. had apparently taken to ascertain what was likely to interest the lady on his left hand and so to set her at ease. At this time the widow of an officer was staying with us. Her husband, who had lately died in a sad way as he was returning from the Zhob expedition, had served for some time under the Duke at Meerut. H.R.H. at once inquired for the widow in a most kind manner, spoke warmly of her husband, and afterwards kept up a pleasant conversation, seemingly without an effort.

I appear to have read about this time some lectures by our old Professor of Sanscrit at Haileybury, Monier Williams, of which I copied the following passage as worthy to be remembered :—

Perhaps the points that had impressed him most forcibly was that India was a land of surprises, contradictions, and anomalies which over-precise, over-logical and self-opinionated persons had better not select as the sphere of their lives' work.

CHAPTER XIX

COMMISSIONER OF THE NEW LAHORE DIVISION

1885—1886

A MARKED change in my position took place early in 1885. The report of our Simla Committee of 1882 had at length borne fruit. Commissioners had been relieved of their Criminal and Civil judicial work, Divisional Judges being appointed. At the same time the areas of the Commissionerships were greatly enlarged. The Lahore Division, which had previously consisted of three districts, now contained the Mooltan, Jhung, Montgomery, Lahore, Amritsar, and Gurdaspore districts. The charge of this newly constituted Division was offered to me,[1] and although the change of appointment involved a very material loss of pay, I accepted it, and in February took over charge.

SIR DOUGLAS FORSYTH TO G. R. ELSMIE.

January 30, 1885.

I am right glad to hear you have actually taken the step you have so long contemplated, and are once more in the more healthy line of the service. . . . Now you will have more leisure to write, and I should dearly like to be kept posted up in the chronicles of my old Division. Fancy being a Commissioner with no appeals or Civil work. Why, my dear fellow, that was the dream of my life, a perfect official paradise. I

[1] See p. 291.

should never have left the service had such good-luck befallen me! Last night visions of India passed rapidly before my eyes. I went to one of the M——'s[1] 'at homes,' and there saw old fossils, ancient crones who I thought had been dead and buried long ago. But there they were . . . and carried me back to nearly forty years ago. Well, it was pleasant to talk of the old days, and revive old acquaintances and friendships. . . .

My appointment as Commissioner was quickly followed by that of the very troublesome honorary office of Vice-Chancellor of the Punjab University. The Registrar of the University was the well-known Dr. Leitner, to whom no doubt the main credit of the early establishment of a University in the Punjab is due. Dr. Leitner was a notoriously difficult man to work with, and I was given to understand that the Government hoped I would be able to keep his idiosyncrasies within bounds. That the task was not easy may be inferred from the following note of what took place at the first University meeting which I attended :—

D. February 16.—To a meeting of the University Syndicate, which much resembled a bear garden. I presided as Vice-Chancellor, but could not do much to calm the Leitnerian storm. Leitner burst forth, and subsequently had to apologise.

Early in March I received an order to be present at the great Durbar at Rawul Pindi, where Lord Dufferin, the successor to Lord Ripon as Viceroy, had arranged to meet the Amir Abdul Rahman. This order involved a good deal of rapid preparation. A very careful selection of Native gentlemen of the Division had to be made with a view to their appearing at the Durbar as repre-

[1] Old Indian friends.

sentatives of Lahore, Amritsar, and other chief places of the Division. My wife and I reached Rawul Pindi on the 30th of March, and were the guests of Colonel Nisbet, the most hospitable Commissioner.

D. March 31.—Up at six A.M. . . . With Nisbet to the railway station; preparing to mount elephants in procession, but rain and wind coming on, procession was countermanded. Amir arrived punctually; was received by Lieutenant-Governor; drove away in a carriage. We had a pretty good view as he passed through the station. Portly man, dressed in black, lame, rolling gait. Home as best we could, dull wet day.

Rain to greet the arrival of a guest in India is regarded as a most auspicious omen. It is the welcome of Heaven to the blessed footstep of the stranger. In this case, the omen was, to say the least, portentous. The rain, which fell during the first two days of Abdul Rahman's visit to Rawul Pindi, may now be regarded as historic, and no one who experienced it and survives until now can have forgotten its abundance. The Amir, himself, was comfortably sheltered in one of the largest houses of the station. The Viceroy, the Duke and Duchess of Connaught, and the Commander-in-Chief were in tents.

D. RAWUL PINDI, *April* 1.—A very miserable day. We were all made fools of by the rain and wind. . . . In the afternoon . . . a great thunderstorm, followed by very heavy rain. This lasted all evening, going out impossible. After dinner word came from the Viceroy's camp that they were being washed out; so Nisbet had to offer his house, and we, to prepare to depart.

D. April 2.—Clouds cleared in the night, a splendid morning. . . . Paying visits in Viceroy's camp, etc.

D. April 4.—Day of the Punjab Durbar held by the Viceroy;

it went off remarkably well. All the Punjab durbáris, the Rajas, the Lieutenant-Governor, and other officials.

D. April 6, *Easter Monday.*—Out with Nisbet before breakfast to the neighbourhood of the Fort, where it had been arranged that the march past should take place. After breakfast we all went there, and took our position in carriages. At 11 the march past began; a great success it was. All the regiments crossed a railway bridge, when in front of the Amir and the Viceroy. Evening, I accompanied Mrs. Nisbet to the Viceroy's reception. I was asked to introduce Native gentlemen to Lady Dufferin and to the Duchess of Connaught, so had an opportunity of seeing them well, hearing them talk, etc.

D. April 7.—After breakfast, to the Review on the Khanna plain. Review very successful; afternoon, to a garden-party in the Viceregal Camp, a marked feature being an avenue of caparisoned elephants from the camp entrance to the Durbar tent.

D. April 8.—Day of the big Durbar. . . . Capital view of the Viceroy and the Amir, also of the Duke of Connaught, who sat on the Viceroy's left. Saw the presentation of the sword to the Amir, who said that by the grace of God he would therewith strike down any enemy of the British. . . . At 6 P.M. we managed to effect our escape from Rawul Pindi, being allowed seats in a special train.

C. E. Bernard (who was now Chief Commissioner of Burma) to G. R. Elsmie.

Rangoon, *March* 27.

. . . I think that you are quite wise to forsake the Bench and take to executive work. Your soul would have rebelled against indefinite more years of civil appeals in a horrid climate and without intermission. One great, very great advantage of executive employment is that, when one feels hipped, or out of sorts, or when (q.d.a.) one's wife is unkind, one can run out into the interior for change of air and to shake off vile humours.[1] . . . The merchants and the European community

[1] A vein of fun was often present in Charles Bernard's letters.

here made a great fuss about annexing Ava and smashing King Thebaw. The latter is not a very friendly or delightful monarch. But according to my lights he gave us no sufficient ground for interference; no doubt our trade suffered in consequence of his misgovernment; possibly his people might, at the outset, be happier under our rule than under his. But these facts and considerations gave us no real ground for annexation; so far as I can see, I think the trouble and anxiety in the Soudan, in the Red Sea, and on the Hari Rud, caused the Indian Government to forbear. If it had not been for these complications, I dare say there would have been a strong party in favour of 'going for' Thebaw, in these days when annexation is so much in the air. Then it is the nature of things for every Viceroy to differ from his predecessor. Lord Ripon was certainly against annexation; Lord Lytton was certainly for annexation; and in the nature of things the pendulum is bound to swing now to Lord L.'s views. . . . We are getting to our hottest weather here now; it was 93° in my study yesterday. Still, nights, mornings and evenings are cool. Even in the daytime the sun is bearable. Monday last, coming back from some forest inspections, I had walked nine miles in the morning over some rough hilly ground till 10 A.M., hoping to find my breakfast on the edge of the forest, and my pony to carry me into the railway station sixteen miles off. The breakfast was there; but the pony was dying; nothing else was to be had, except and with difficulty a bullock cart, which would have jolted fearfully over those tracks. So I had to walk the extra sixteen miles in the sun. I did not feel it much, except being thirsty and dusty; and was none the worse for the twenty-five miles in the heat.[1] Seeing that I am an elderly man of sedentary pursuits, I think this speaks well for the climate of British Burma.

The Assembly at Rawul Pindi was quickly followed by a visit of the Viceroy, Lord Dufferin, to Lahore. The

[1] But I fear that this and similar expeditions helped to undermine Bernard's strong constitution.

general excitement was rendered intense by the almost simultaneous arrival of the news of the affair of outposts at Penjdeh, between the Afghans and the Russians. This was the beginning of what has since been known as the Russian scare of 1885.

D. LAHORE, *April* 15.—A busy day. Maharaja of Cashmere arrived in the morning. Soon after his arrival, I had to go with the Financial Commissioner and others for 'mizáj pursi' (inquiry for health). At 1.45 Viceroy arrived from Rawul Pindi. Public arrival, uniform, etc. Evening, to a levée at Government House, not very entertaining; much interrupted during the day by applications for levée tickets.

The following day I was suddenly summoned to Government House in order to interpret between the Viceroy and certain Native gentlemen, whom His Excellency had decided to receive privately. This summons rather took me aback, as I had no idea which Native gentlemen were to be there, and it was more than possible that some of them might be strangers to me, as I had so recently rejoined the executive line. To my relief I found, on entering the room, that I was acquainted with all the visitors. I was shown up to the Government House drawing-room, where I found the Viceroy and an A.D.C The latter brought in the Native gentlemen one by one, and my duty was to introduce the visitors and to interpret the conversation. Some of them paid very fulsome compliments; so much so, that I felt bound to take His Excellency's orders as to whether the translations should be *literatim et verbatim.* One said that he had gone down to Calcutta to bid farewell to Lord Ripon on his departure for England; that Lord Ripon had said that he was about to be succeeded by a Viceroy who was infinitely superior to himself. The truth of this assertion, the visitor declared, had now been proved. Lord Dufferin smiled, and remarked that it was difficult to embark on a comparison of the merits of Viceroys.

Another gentleman said that Lord Ripon had been four or five years in India, but that Lord Dufferin in a month or two had drawn all hearts.

The most interesting of all the visitors was a fine-looking old man, Nawab Nawazish Ali Khan, the son of a refugee Afghan nobleman, who in process of time had become the President of the Municipality of Lahore, the Lord Mayor, in fact. The Nawab was one of the important personages who had been dwelling in tents during the Rawul Pindi Durbar. After preliminary greetings, Lord Dufferin directed me to express a hope that the affairs of the Municipality were prosperous. The Nawab replied that all was for the most part well, save that the city funds were suffering from too limited an income.

'Ah,' said H.E., 'tell the Nawab that I have dwelt in many parts of the world, have known many men and seen many cities, and there is no want among them which I have found to be more universal than the want of money; so I can fully sympathise with Lahore.' The old gentleman received this remark with evident satisfaction, and the conversation continued for a short time on subjects which I do not remember. When the Nawab had made his bow and was about to withdraw from the room, a sudden thought seemed to strike Lord Dufferin.

'Please call the Nawab back for a moment. Tell

him,' continued the Viceroy, 'that I hope and trust that money will pour into the coffers of the Lahore Municipality with the same abundance as the rain descended on us at Rawul Pindi.' The Nawab's face lighted up with infinite pleasure; he bowed low with the utmost grace, and departed.

D. April 17.—About noon I accompanied the Viceroy and an A.D.C. to return the visit of Maharaja Ranbir Singh.[1] . . . Immediately on re-entering his carriage, Lord Dufferin, turning to me, said, 'That man is a real gentleman.'

At 3 P.M. I went to Amritsar with H.E. and Lady Dufferin. They most kindly asked me to travel in their carriage.

During the journey Lord Dufferin referred at some length to the question of the expediency of allowing the Maharaja Dulip Singh to return to India.

D. April 17 (continued).—At Amritsar, the Deputy Commissioner received the party, and we had a most successful expedition to the Golden Temple. All took off shoes and put on slippers, and I don't think any humiliation was felt. Lord Dufferin was quite clear he would do it, and said he must bow in the house of Rimmon. I drove with Lady Helen Blackwood and Mr. Mackenzie Wallace, the Private Secretary. . . . After the city, returned to the railway station, dined with H.E. in his railway carriage, then returned to Lahore.

SIR DOUGLAS FORSYTH TO G. R. ELSMIE.

May 10, 1885.

. . . Of course, like all the rest of right-thinking men, I am quite frantic at the way Gladstone has humiliated England, and this does not add to the sweetness of one's temper! But I suppose things will come right in time. . . . I am going to

[1] Of Cashmere. The Maharaja was a perfect master of the best manners of an Oriental Chief.

Lisbon on the 24th for a few weeks on business, and shall be glad of the change and enforced rest, while at sea. . . . I take things more quietly, and am avoiding all extra work, except taking the Chair at a large meeting in Exeter Hall to denounce the traitorous *Pall Mall* and all unpatriotic Englishmen. The report now is that Lord Dufferin has resigned, and I should not be at all surprised. But Gladstone is keeping it as quiet as possible till he has got it all settled his own way, and then he won't care if his deceit is found out. I am thankful I am not in Parliament. I could not stand the lying and chicanery which go on in Politics. Pray give me the news of the Punjab. . . .

The Commissioner of Lahore was permitted to do his work at the hill-station of Dalhousie in the Gurdaspur district for the greater part of the hot weather. I had never been to Dalhousie before, and I was delighted to find myself about the middle of May in that beautiful place, built on its three hills of Bakrota, Téra, and Potrain. Towards the north arose a magnificent barrier of snowy mountains, and in a valley, about twenty miles to the north-east of Dalhousie, lay the headquarters of the young Raja of Chamba. The air of Dalhousie seemed to be particularly invigorating, and although but a quiet and sparsely populated place, it is, as a summer retreat, in many respects preferable to the larger hill-stations in the Punjab.

On the 30th of May we were awakened about 3.15 A.M. by a most disagreeable earthquake, which seemed to me, as I opened my eyes, to be accompanied by mysterious noise and light. The earthquake lasted fully half a minute, and was very severe. We felt sure that there must have been serious mischief somewhere, and a day or two later the newspapers enabled us to identify the shock which we had felt, with the disastrous earthquake which wrought great destruction in Cashmere.

During this season I saw much of General John (afterwards Sir John) Murray, who commanded the Lahore Division and made Dalhousie his summer headquarters. General Murray had been well known as Jock Murray, whose regiment, the 14th Native Cavalry, is still called Murray's Lancers. He was a most genial and humorous Scotchman, a charming companion whom it was always a pleasure to meet.[1] The Assistant Adjutant-General of the Division was Colonel George Wolseley,[2] brother of Lord Wolseley, who had just returned from service in the Soudan. He told me that on rejoining at Mian Mir he found the heat greater than in any part of Egypt where he had served.

A visit to Chamba in company with Colonel Marshall, the Superintendent of the State, and Colonel Harcourt, Deputy Commissioner of Gurdaspur, took place in the first week of September. The march from Dalhousie to Chamba is very beautiful; the first stage is along a riding path through luxuriant woods to Kajiar. Kajiar is a lovely green basin, with a small lake in the centre, surrounded by deodar trees, quite unique in my experience. At one end of the basin is a comfortable rest-house where we put up for the night. The next morning we rose early and rode, mainly down hill, some nine or ten miles into Chamba. We were met by the young Raja, Sham Singh, at the bridge over the Ravi. The

[1] Since the above passage was written many Native officers and other friends of Sir John Murray have built a dharmsala in the city of Delhi to his memory. It was dedicated recently by General Sir Alfred Gaselee.

[2] Afterwards General Sir George Wolseley, K.C.B., of the Western Command in India.

bridge was decorated, and we entered the little town on elephants. Later in the day we were taken to see a leopard hunt, but no game appeared. Afternoon, we paid a formal visit to the Raja, conferred with him on sundry matters relating to his State, and dined with him in his palace in half-native fashion. Next day we returned to Dalhousie. Early in October we were back again at Lahore, in good time to be on the outlook for difficulties which might be expected to arise at the forthcoming celebrations of the Muhammadan Muharram and the Hindu Duserah, the dates of which happened to coincide this year.

D. October 16.—Rather a disturbed day. Letter early in the morning from Clark[1] (the Deputy Commissioner of Lahore), saying that there had been a row in the city, and proposing an indent for troops. He came to see me. I agreed. Much excitement during day, shops shut, etc. Clark and police in the city. Afternoon, Deputy Inspector-General of Police and District Superintendent of Police came to suggest more troops. I agreed, telegraphed to Government, received reply later, saying I had full authority. A shower of telegrams in the night.

D. October 17.—Day passed quietly. Troops in the city; processions in the afternoon, no further fuss; good hope that all will go smoothly now. I am pretty clear that the mischief has been caused by attempts to arrange too much. Anxious during day, but fairly confident that all will go well.

And so it did; the conjunction of the two festivals was, of course, unusual, and could only recur again after a long period. The local police had been so anxious to prevent the rival processions from clashing, that they perhaps overdid their attempts at prearrangement. I had no

[1] Now Sir William Clark, Chief Judge of the Chief Court, Punjab.

objection to making a show of the troops. They had to come from the Mian Mir cantonment, six miles off, but so little did the Lahore townspeople see of Mian Mir and its soldiers that in my opinion they scarcely realised its existence, and as the event turned out, a mere parade of a few companies through the city was sufficient to calm down the rival religionists.

D. October 31.—I had to attend a University Syndicate meeting early. Indeed we have had one every morning since Thursday; however, to-day things waxed to a climax, and to the great relief of all concerned, Dr. Leitner resigned the Registrarship and withdrew. The Syndicate proceeded to make arrangements for carrying on the work.

D. November 13.—I went to the Lieutenant-Governor on University matters. He expressed himself satisfied with all that had been done.

D. November 28.—A weary day; University Senate meeting, with all the Leitner battle from 11 A.M. till close on 7 P.M. . . . However, Sir Charles Aitchison presided as Chancellor, and Leitner got but little of his own way and ought to consider himself suppressed, whether he is or not. . . . A notable battle of Armageddon in University affairs.

On the 2nd of December the University Convocation was held. It fell to me as Vice-Chancellor to deliver the address. I did so in Urdu, avoiding all controversial matters.

The following is the original English text of the greater part of my speech, which appeared next day in the local newspaper:—

The burden of my words will have to do with what wise men, from Socrates downwards, have regarded as one of the essential elements of the true attitude of a student—humility. It has been well said that the posture of humility is that in which alone the mind can grow in wisdom and power. Socrates 'professed to know this only, that he nothing knew'; that is to say, he knew the depth of his own ignorance. He knew that such things as he knew were infinitesimal in comparison to those things which remained unknown. In the presence of the Sophists, the professors of universal knowledge, Socrates assumed the position of one who knew nothing and who was ever seeking information. The ideal life of the student may be compared to that of a man blind from his birth, on whom the gift of sight is eventually bestowed. At first, as the film of darkness leaves his eyes, he will experience a sensation of dawning light. The light will strengthen, he will see moving forms, men as trees walking. Gradually his vision will become clearer. One by one the objects of this earth will be perceived by him—the birds, the beasts, the fishes, the insects, and the wonders and variety of the vegetable kingdom. Then with the aid of the microscope he will be enabled to see the minute and hidden marvels, which with his naked eye he could never have perceived or imagined. When night comes the mysteries of heaven will reveal themselves—the moon, the planets, the thousand stars. The telescope will lead his vision into greater depths; he will see the moons of the planets; looking deeper, he will perceive the fixed stars dividing themselves into pairs. Has he seen all now? Surely not; a still more powerful glass will resolve the Milky Way into myriads of stars, the number of which and the unfathomable depth beyond must convince him that the things which he has even now seen are but as drops in the great Ocean of the unseen. But though this will keep him humble it will not make him unhappy. No; he will rejoice when he reflects that there is ever before him a multitude of unseen marvels. He will rejoice that his hunger to see can never be fully satisfied, and so in the life of a student. He will begin with letters, go on to words, then to sentences, then to anecdotes, then to books; and if he is wise, he will find as he goes on how small his knowledge is in comparison to what remains to be acquired. But this will not grieve him if he is wise—on the contrary, it will be the source of his greatest delight. His life will be one of constant progress, with a bright past and still brighter future. He will not, however, boast himself of his learning, but, deeply conscious of its insignificance, will ever strive in humility and faith to acquire more. The student can indeed look forward, without apprehension, to his old age. He can continue to add to the treasure of his knowledge to the very last day of his life. Unfortunately, however, the attitude which I have attempted to describe is not the only one which we see among so-called students. Very different postures are often assumed by mere beginners, by boys and men who have climbed only a few steps on the ladder of learning. Their conduct causes the judicious to mourn and to say sadly, 'Knowledge puffeth up,' 'A little learning is a dangerous thing,' and so on. I am sure that there are many among us in the Punjab who would do well to ponder these words of the wise. Judging from some of the books that are written, the matter which we find in our newspapers, both vernacular and English, there is no doubt that many persons who are only possessed of a minimum of knowledge—just enough to make them dangerous guides—have been endeavouring to teach under the vain belief that they already know all. I was much struck the other day by the words of a venerable gentleman who had held a position in the Punjab prior to the annexation. He was speaking of the impatience of the younger men of the present day, who are over-anxious for the adoption of measures of so-called progress and advancement. He said: 'We old men are well pleased with such progress as is going on; we know how much progress has been made within the last forty years. We remember the scorching sun, the *dhup* of the time before annexation. These youths only know the *barsat* (the time of fertilising rain) of the British Government. They do not know the extent of the blessing they are enjoying, and are not thankful as we are.' There seemed to me to be much sense in the words of the old man; and I thought that if the youths to whom he referred had more knowledge and more of the posture of humility, they would perhaps be wiser, more patient, and happier. My advice then to you is, emulate the example of the wise Socrates in the matter. Let all who know a little be very humble when they think how much remains to be known; and let those who know much rejoice that the fields where they gather their treasures are unlimited. What a treasure all real students possess! When I talk to my friends of the time when I shall retire from the service and go back to live in England, some of them say: 'But what will you do?—you will be old—you will have no work—you will be miserable.' I reply: 'No; I love books, I love knowledge, I will continue to be a student so long as God will allow me the power of sight and keep my mind clear. There will always be new things for me to learn, new treasure to gather, and I have no fear that I shall become weary.' I think if you students have learned nothing more in your school or college than to love knowledge for its own sake, to be never weary in its acquisition, and after all to be able to say, like Socrates, that you know nothing in comparison to what you have still to learn, you have gained a treasure far above gold and jewels, which can never be taken away from you.

C. E. Bernard to G. R. Elsmie.

S.S. 'Peel,' near Ava on the Irrawaddy,
December 14.

. . . The expedition to Mandalay was a most striking and dramatic success. The capital was occupied, and Thebaw was deported within fourteen days of our crossing the border; and there was very little loss of life. There was some little cholera; perhaps thirty deaths among eighteen or nineteen thousand soldiers and followers. But much more than this might have happened in cantonments or on the march among a single regiment in peace time. From battle casualties our total loss is six or seven killed, and thirty to forty wounded in all.

But now the difficulty comes. The whole country is devastated by dacoits. All the unpaid, disbanded soldiers have taken to dacoiting. All around in every district as we come up the river we hear of dacoities on all sides. There must be thirty or forty every twenty-four hours. It will take a long time to get things into order. Of course, dacoity and misgovernment and oppression have been the rule in these parts for some years. But just now dacoity is very much worse than usual. We are getting police together; we are putting detachments of soldiers about, and the old officials are coming over to our side. Still it will be hard work to get matters straight. The fact that no decision has been taken for annexation or for any other policy makes matters all the more difficult. For the local officials know or think that, if they join with us too readily, they will be marked men, and will go to the wall under a restored Native Raj.

The big towns and villages along the Irrawaddy seem to be very prosperous and flourishing. You may form some idea of what the North Burma trade, even under Thebaw, was, when I say that the trade across our inland border, almost all to King Thebaw's realm, nearly equalled the total land trade of the rest of British Indian border from Kurrachee all round to Chittagong. I don't reckon in this comparison the railway material sent Quettawards, or the army supplies sent to and brought backwards from Peshin. Mr. O'Connor, in his India trade reports, in the most unblushing way treats this all as part of our external trade, and congratulates the Government on the increase. I, for my part, do not advise annexation. I think we can safeguard our trade and keep out French intrigue without taking any extreme step of this kind. I think we have enough territory; and we ought not to annex a nation merely because its king was unfriendly or cruel. . . .

These naval officers and bluejackets are capital fellows. They always seem so much more cheery than army men. My personal guard on board this ship consists of twenty-five bluejackets. They are always cheerful and never grumble; it is a treat to see them running round with the capstan hauling up the anchor. There are now five men-of-war in Rangoon, all of which have sent contingents to the Naval Brigade. These latter have had most of the work, for there was no opposition to the landing parties of soldiers at any place except Minhla, about forty miles beyond our border.

If Upper Burma were added to Lower Burma as a British province, it would be enormous, about two hundred and sixty thousand square miles, including the dependent Shan States. But the new province would not pay, and would be a loss financially for some eight or ten years at least. Lower Burma yields a surplus of ninety lakhs after paying for her garrison. Though our population is so small, the total revenues of British Burma are very nearly as large as the total revenues of the Punjab when you and I joined the province. . . .

The book *Crime on the Peshawur Frontier*, which I published in 1884, had been well received officially and by critics generally. Early in 1886 the Punjab Government determined to entrust a further inquiry into the subject to a committee, which was ordered to assemble at Peshawur. I was appointed President, with the following colleagues:—Colonel Nisbet, Commissioner of Peshawur; Mr. (now Sir Richard) Udny, Deputy Commissioner of Kohat; Mr. (now Sir Frederick) Fryer, afterwards Lieutenant-Governor of Burma; Mr. H. St. G. Tucker, Deputy Commissioner of Peshawur; Mr. A. H. Benton, Sessions Judge, Peshawur; Sirdar Umr Khan; and Mr. (now Sir Lewis) Tupper, who was also to act as Secretary.

The inquiry and consideration of the various questions for decision occupied us about a week. On one of the days a large body of Native gentlemen was called in to aid us in our deliberations. They assented to many of the proposals, and gave some very valuable and intelligent opinions. On the last day of the meeting we formally approved the final draft of the new Regulations which we proposed. The draft passed through the ordeal of the Local Government and of the Government of India, and was accepted almost in its entirety, and became law with, I believe, highly satisfactory results up to the present day. I will not weary the reader by giving details. Suffice it to say that before the New Regulations came into force, a person accused of murder could, as an alternative to being tried by the ordinary Criminal Courts, be brought before a Jirgah or Council of Elders of his countrymen, and sentenced to a moderate fine, for the realisation of which no proper machinery was provided. Under the new Regulations, such accused person, on being found guilty of murder by a Council of Elders, could be sentenced to seven years' imprisonment, such sentence being subject to confirmation by the Deputy Commissioner. Analogous enhancements of the powers vested in Councils of Elders will be found all along the line on comparing the old and new Regulations, but for my present purpose it is enough to say, pointing to the example given above, *ex uno disce omnes.*

Sir Douglas Forsyth to G. R. Elsmie.

1 Cranley Mansions,
South Kensington, *April* 2, 1886.

I was much cheered by the sight of your handwriting, and glad to get your news. The time will come to you, as it has to me, when you will cling tenaciously to the last link with India, just in proportion as that country recedes from your view. I am thankful that I was able to go out and take a look at the old scenes and old friends before I had entirely faded away from recollection. If I ever went again, I should soon find myself a stranger in a strange land, and yet, to my dying day, I shall always have the strongest affection for the dear old country compared with which England seems but an adopted land. . . . I could write a lot about politics, Indian and English, but it is a wearying subject. Here we are all astonished at Gladstone, and wonder what the end will be. In India you seem to have attained to a perfect Viceroy, and the utmost confidence is felt in him here. . . . The new Parliament has not brought any accession of strength to the Anglo-Indian M.P.s except Maclean, editor of *Times of India*, who has made a decided hit. —— imagines himself a success, but is voted by every one else an unmitigated failure. . . .

C. E. Bernard to G. R. Elsmie.

MAHLEIN, *May* 20.

. . . I am now on my way marching across from the Irrawaddy to the Sittang. No European has been the whole way since the war, though we have troops along the route and civil officers; but they came up from the two ends. I believe it would be safe enough to canter along with a few sowars. But I am travelling with a big convoy of supplies, one hundred carts, and an escort of six mounted European infantry, twenty-five European infantry, and fifty Native infantry. To-day ten sowars of the Madras cavalry have joined us. It is very slow work as carts can only go two miles an hour; the weather is hot; so for the sake of men and beasts we travel much by night. However, I sleep pretty fast on horseback, so I get on fairly well.

As yet we have had no sign of rebels or dacoits; and the country so far is much more in hand than tracts nearer Mandalay. But there is a big gang of several hundreds somewhere about twelve or fifteen miles to the N.E. of this; and places along our march of the next two days have been recently sacked and looted.

There are a good many troops about, but the country is big; and no troops except cavalry can move quick enough to catch these people, or at any rate to catch their leaders. They never stand nowadays to meet our troops, and flee before the smallest bodies. I hope that in about one year the country will be pacified and we shall begin to get our revenue in this year. The rebellions all over the place will make the occupation and annexation much more costly than was expected. . . . I expect to reach Rangoon about the 8th June or so; and then after a few days I shall return to Mandalay. At present I am enjoying a satisfactory rest from paper work and from telegrams, cipher and other. . . .

SIR DOUGLAS FORSYTH TO G. R. ELSMIE.

DUBLIN, *August* 15.

. . . Within the next few years, you in India are likely to have an exciting time, and I believe there *must* be serious trouble. These wretched Home Rulers may not be successful at present, but Lord Ripon has sown the seeds of disaffection which sooner or later must bear evil fruit. Russia, of course, is a standing bugbear, but I am thankful that we have had a respite, and we are taking advantage of the breathing time to make ourselves secure. But we have acted like idiots in allowing Dulip Singh to have a grievance unredressed and not securing a hold over his person. He has slipped through our fingers, and when the time comes, will probably prove a second Nana. And so we blunder on, but there is this consolation that, with all our blunders, we manage to keep the old ship afloat. . . .

In the first week of November the Viceroy and the Duke of Connaught visited Lahore and were invested with the degree of Doctor of Literature by the University. One of our guests at this time was Dr. Farquharson,[1] M.P. for West Aberdeenshire, whom we had known in Scotland, and who retained his seat in Parliament for more than twenty-five years.

D. November 2.—At 7 A.M. I had to meet the Nawab of Bahawulpore at the train and take him to his tents. At 9, in full uniform to the reception of the Duke and Duchess of

[1] Now the Right Honourable Robert Farquharson.

Connaught (at the railway station), and at 11 to Government House, while the Viceroy received in formal Durbar the Maharaja of Cashmere,[1] the Rajas of Jhind, Nabha, etc.

Afternoon, I had to go round with Lord Dufferin, Mackenzie Wallace, and others, while H.E. returned eight visits. The camps of the Chiefs were pitched on the plain between the Fort and the Ravi. The displays in the tents were well worth seeing. . . . Evening, a ball at the Montgomery Hall, a great crush, but it went off well. . . .

D. November 3.—Afternoon, the ceremony of the laying the foundation-stone of the Punjab Chiefs' College by the Viceroy[2] came off. . . . The arrivals of the various Chiefs were imposing. . . .

D. November 4.—A very busy day. University Convocation at 11. All went better than one could have hoped. . . . I escorted the Duchess to her seat, and H.R.H. said she was much pleased with the arrangements. . . . Then the conferring of degrees on the Viceroy and Duke took place. Afternoon, a very interesting investiture of Sir West Ridgeway with the K.C.S.I. Very well done at Government House. Lord Dufferin made an impressive speech. Afterwards a garden-party. Then at 9 P.M. I had to be at the railway station to see the Viceroy and Royal party leave.

The letter from which the following extract is taken reached me on the 6th November. It was the last I ever received from Sir Douglas Forsyth. I answered it on the following day, thus unconsciously closing a correspondence which had lasted more than twenty-six years.

SIR DOUGLAS FORSYTH TO G. R. ELSMIE.

ATHENÆUM, *October* 14.

. . . I don't like all these disturbances in India, but I hope the authorities are equal to the occasion. . . . I shall rejoice to

[1] *I.e.* Pratap Singh, the present Maharaja, who had meanwhile succeeded his father, Ranbir Singh.

[2] Who gave it the name of the Aitchison College.

see you if you do come home. But come with a light heart and *full* purse, if possible.—With affectionate remembrances, yours very sincerely,

T. DOUGLAS FORSYTH.

In December some time was spent in camp in the Lahore and Montgomery districts. The only note regarding this tour which seems worth preserving is the following:—

One day I had a long talk with a headman of the village of Chung on the Lahore-Mooltan Road. We spoke, amongst other things, about the state of crime in the district. I asked his opinion why crime went on increasing? He replied, 'Ap logon ne saccha mulk ke kānun jhutha mulk men jári kardya'; that is to say, 'You Sahibs have introduced into a false (speaking) country the laws of a true (speaking) country'; meaning, in other words, that our English methods had too quickly superseded the old native ones.

The year closed in gloom. On the 21st of December the news of Sir Douglas Forsyth's unexpected death reached me at Lahore.

A bright light in the home horizon was thus extinguished to the infinite regret of ourselves and many other friends to whom the loss was indeed an irreparable one. The references to Sir Douglas and the many extracts from his letters which are to be found in this book will, it is hoped, be welcomed by those who admired and loved him. His words seem to me to go far in revealing his delightful character. They show his indomitable energy, spirit of enterprise, unfailing courage, and great administrative talents. They illustrate the kindness and encouragement with which he treated his subordinates, while he himself was always modest and unassuming in his estimate of his own qualifications. Further they bear witness to his sympathy with and affection for the Natives of India, and show how greatly removed he was from the type of unsympathetic Civilian of whom certain unjust and ignorant critics wrongly suppose the great majority of the class to consist.

CHAPTER XX

FINANCIAL COMMISSIONER AND MEMBER OF THE LEGISLATIVE COUNCIL

1887—1888

THE beginning of the year 1887 is remembered in the Punjab by the uncertainty which prevailed regarding the selection of the next Lieutenant-Governor. Sir Charles Aitchison's time would expire early in April, and the question, Who would succeed him? had been answered in various ways. The candidates prominently mentioned were Sir Charles Bernard, Chief Commissioner of Burma; Sir Lepel Griffin, Resident at Indore; and Mr. J. B. Lyall, Chief Commissioner of Mysore. Finally, about the middle of January it became known that Mr. Lyall had been chosen. Gossip said that the Viceroy, Lord Dufferin, had been anxious that Sir Charles Bernard should be appointed, while the Secretary of State, Lord Randolph Churchill, was in favour of Sir Lepel Griffin. The controversy, if there was one, was closed by a compromise—namely, the choice of Mr. Lyall. A keen-witted Irishman is reported to have said that he had heard of a man falling between two stools, but that this was the first occasion in his experience of a man's rising from that position to a higher plane.

On Sunday morning, the 16th of January, I was awakened by a messenger, who brought from the railway station a letter purporting to come from the Governor of Bombay, accompanied by a hastily written pencil note. The former was from a Bombay Secretary to introduce Mr. and Mrs. Brassey and friends, who were about to travel in the Punjab. The pencil note was from Mrs. Brassey to announce the arrival of the party in their special train, and to say that they would be glad of any help that could be given them in seeing the sights of Lahore, but that they would make their railway carriages their headquarters. The Lieutenant-Governor being absent in camp, it fell to me to do what I could. I sent an order to Government House placing the Lieutenant-Governor's camel-carriage at the disposal of the travellers, and we invited the party to tea in our grounds that afternoon. They came, and proved themselves to be most interesting and pleasant guests. Next day the special train moved on to Peshawur, but returned on the following Friday, when we had the pleasure of receiving Mr. and Mrs. Brassey with their friends at a large garden-party at which many European and Native guests were present. A special reason for inviting Native gentlemen on this occasion was that the Hon. Maude Lawrence, the youngest daughter of the late Lord Lawrence, was one of the travellers. The welcome to Miss Lawrence was so enthusiastic as to cause some alarm to Mrs. Brassey, who, fearing that her friend was being mobbed, inquired anxiously if there was no danger for her in the midst of a crowd of natives. They were, however, only anxious to greet heartily the daughter of their old Chief.

The open-air gathering was followed by a dinner-party, which we thoroughly enjoyed. We had been surprised, not to say startled, by the unexpected advent of a somewhat formidable-looking phalanx of travellers, but when they left Lahore after dinner we were truly sorry to bid them good-bye. Mrs. Brassey was kind enough to present us with copies of two of her books, and some years afterwards a copy of *The Last Voyage* was sent to my wife by Mr. (then Lord) Brassey 'in memoriam.'

The day following the departure of the Brassey party we had a glimpse of two other interesting travellers from England. We dined quietly with Mr. Plowden to meet the Duke and Duchess of Manchester, who were journeying towards Quetta. The Duchess is now the Dowager-Duchess of Devonshire.

In February, leaving my wife in Lahore, I went to England on short leave in order to make certain arrangements in regard to the education of children. One of my fellow-passengers from Alexandria was Mr. Munro-Ferguson, M.P. for Leith Burghs. He had been on a tour in India with Lord Rosebery. We travelled through Europe in the same compartment of a Mann's car, and had much interesting talk. A few weeks later I met Mr. Munro-Ferguson on the steps of the House of Commons, when we exchanged hasty greetings. We have never come across each other since, but I was much interested when I heard of his marriage to Lady Helen Blackwood, who had been so much admired in Simla society.

During my short visit to England I met many old Indian friends, among whom I may mention Sir Donald Macnabb,[1] Sir Sam Browne, and my old colleague, Mr. Arthur Brandreth.

[1] Who had just been made a K.C.I.E.

D. March 14.—Had a long talk to Sir Robert Montgomery at the India Office, finding him kind and sympathetic as of old.

A few days later I dined alone with Sir Robert and Lady Montgomery, and we talked 'Punjab' for several hours.

My last interview with Sir Robert took place at the India Office on the 28th March, when I found him 'enthusiastically kind and warm to a degree.' It is no wonder that he had the power of inspiring affection and enthusiasm in others.

On the 4th of April, under the auspices of Dr. Farquharson, I paid a visit to the House of Commons, and was fortunate in witnessing what may be regarded as an historical scene—the Speaker, Mr. Peel, denouncing an unruly Member, Mr. Conybeare, in what appeared to me to be a very majestic and grand manner.

During my short stay at home I paid a hurried visit to Aberdeen and Edinburgh. In Aberdeen I met an old College friend who, since I had seen him last, had become a Government Inspector of Schools. He amused me by an examination story which, though new to me, may have been of more ancient date than I supposed. In a certain school in Scotland a subject of examination was the parable of the Good Samaritan. One of the questions asked was, 'Why did the Levite and the priest pass by on the other side?' 'Because,' said an examinee, 'he 'd (*i.e.* the man who fell among thieves) been robbit before they came.'

The day before I left London I was surprised to receive a telegram from the Punjab Government offering me the second Financial Commissionership, rendered vacant by the promotion of Colonel Wace to succeed Sir William Davies, the first Financial Commissioner. I accepted the offer, started on my journey, and reached Lahore at the end of April. The duties of my new office were both judicial and administrative; the former consisting chiefly of the disposal of final appeals in cases under the Tenancy Act; the latter, of the administrative superintendence of the Excise, Income Tax, Salt Revenue, Trade Statistics, etc. etc., of the Province. During a considerable portion of the hot weather the Financial Commissioners had their headquarters at Simla.

D. SIMLA, *May* 28.—Called up about 2 A.M. Heard much noise outside. This proceeded from our servants who were watching the Chota Simla Bazaar on fire. A great blaze; sparks falling in all directions and on our wooden roof. We were anxious about our house, which was within fifty yards of the Bazaar. I went up to the Financial Commissioner's Office, found preparations for safety of papers, etc., being made. The fire raged for hours; very little water obtainable. Wind rather high. Lieutenant-Governor and all manner of authorities on the spot, but little power to do anything. We didn't go to bed again till 5 A.M., much exhausted.

D. June 23.—I was one of a small dinner-party of eight men at Viceregal Lodge. Very pleasant. Lord Dufferin had not even an A.D.C. in attendance. I sat on his left. His conversation was very interesting, but the enjoyment of the party was somewhat marred by ——, who insisted on talking a great deal too much, and illustrated some of his points by rising from his chair and executing certain antics on the floor.

One morning in September Colonel Morton[1] came to

[1] Afterwards General Sir Gerald Morton, K.C.I.E., Adjutant-General of the Indian army and the General commanding the Dublin district.

consult me as to the style of entertainment which should be chosen for an evening party at Barnes Court. Something out of the beaten track of theatricals or music was wanted. I told Colonel Morton of the Scenes from Dickens twenty-one years ago. The result was that a mixed programme of *tableaux vivants* and Dickens's scenes was approved by Mrs. Lyall. Three of the scenes were to be 'Bob Sawyer's Party,' 'The Scene at the Portsmouth Theatre,' introducing the celebrated dance by the Infant phenomenon and the Savage, and 'Mrs. Gamp's Tea-party.' The principal tableaux were to be 'Queen Katherine's Dream' and 'Cleopatra in her barge.' The only lady in India believed to be competent to take the characters of Mrs. Raddle, the Infant phenomenon, and Mrs. Gamp lived some four hundred miles off in the plains. The difficulty was got over by Mrs. Lyall writing to Mrs. Steel at Muzaffargarh and inviting her to come up and pay a long visit to Barnes Court and take part in the performance. Mrs. Steel at first remonstrated with me for having suggested her for such an enterprise, but eventually she agreed, came up to Simla, and performed the characters allotted to her with triumphant success. On returning to the plains, Mrs. Steel sat opposite to an unknown lady at luncheon in a railway carriage. Conversation ensued in a friendly way until the lady, who had evidently been one of the guests at Barnes Court, paused, held up her hands, and exclaimed, 'Why, you are the Infant phenomenon!' Another difficulty in connection with this performance was the selection of a Pickwick. A certain secretary with a bland countenance and gold spectacles seemed the very man for the character. He absolutely declined to attempt it. We asked him to dinner and did all we could by way of persuasion, but our friend remained obdurate. A dance took place at the Viceroy's a few evenings later. Colonel Morton and I determined that we would walk round the room till we could see a likely man. For some time we were in despair. Suddenly, when we were looking on at a set of Lancers, we saw a gentleman advancing in the second figure with an amiable gait and smile. He wasn't in the least like Pickwick in the face, but we perceived a great field for 'making up.' We lay in wait for him till the end of the dance. To his honour, be it said, he became as clay in the hands of the potter, and he appeared in our scenes as Pickwick to the delight of Mrs. Lyall's guests. It only remains to add that the correctness of our eye for an all-round man has been proved by the facts that at a later period Mr. Walter Lawrence was chosen as Private Secretary by Lord Curzon, and Sir Walter Lawrence as Chief of the Staff during the Indian visit of His Royal Highness the Prince of Wales, in both of which rôles his success has become historical.

Our time at Simla came to an end in the middle of October. The rest of the year was spent at Lahore and in a rapid tour to some of the outlying Punjab districts, Muzaffargarh, Dera Ghazi Khan, Dera Ismail Khan, and Shahpur.

In the last days of the year telegraphic news reached Lahore of the unexpected death on the 28th December of Sir Robert Montgomery. Some weeks later I received particulars of the illness, which had only lasted about three days, from his son, James Montgomery.

Among his papers was found one in which he had made some notes on a few of his later birthdays. . . . The last entry of the

12th December 1887 is as follows:—'This is my seventy-ninth birthday. I have arrived at a great age. God's goodness and mercies have been continued to me. . . . I wish to express most truly and earnestly my sense of my utter unworthiness.'

And so passed away a most characteristic Punjab figure. I have tried to let him speak for himself in many of these pages, to show what manner of man he was. Many of his old subordinates and friends felt the loss most acutely, and would have joined in my opinion that, after John Lawrence, he was the greatest Lieutenant-Governor who had ruled the Punjab up to that time, and that we should not 'look upon his like again.'

At the beginning of 1888 Colonel Wace went home on furlough, and I found myself appointed to act for him as first Financial Commissioner. Later in the year I also took Colonel Wace's place as a member of the Legislative Council of India at Simla.

D. May 22.—Big dinner at Government House (in honour of the Queen's birthday). This was followed by a Levée, and then came the Investiture of Sir Frederick Roberts as Grand Cross of the Indian Empire.

D. May 24.—Ball at Government House. . . . Lady Dufferin magnificent with diamonds. Lord Dufferin in full uniform as a Lord-Lieutenant; dancing a good deal. I admire his pluck at sixty-two.

D. July 11.—At eleven I was at Viceregal Lodge and sat for the first time in the Legislative Council. Made a very short speech introducing a Tolls Bill.

D. August 8.—We went to dine at the new Viceregal Lodge.[1] I took in Lady Helen Blackwood. A dance afterwards. . . . The house is delightful, plenty of room, light excellent. . . .

October 2.—A very broken and disturbed day. Harvey James,

[1] Which had just been completed.

Secretary to the Legislative Council, came (to our house) soon after 8.30 A.M. and said it had been suddenly settled that I should introduce the Punjab Appeals Bill that day.

It was a terrible scramble. No time to write speech. Hurried over to Council, tried to get out of it, but to no purpose, so had to speak extempore and make the best of things.

I had had nothing to do with the drawing of the Bill, and had but the vaguest notion of its contents. However, Mr. James left the papers with me, to digest as well as I could before 11 o'clock. One of the chief objects of the Bill was to curtail the right of appeal in Civil cases.

D. October 25.—To Council at 11, having breakfasted with Mr. Scoble[1] and dovetailed our speeches. I made a speech on the Appeals Bill which was subsequently passed.

The speech was too long and in many parts too technical to be reproduced in full. I may, however, give an extract from it which describes the early Punjab system of Civil appeals, and shows why a naturally litigious people, with much of the Dandie Dinmont spirit in them, were not over keen to approve of a curtailment of their former right to carry their small disputes through a series of four courts.

My own personal experience extends from the year 1858, and I can remember that, until the establishment of the Chief Court in 1866, the pettiest decree in a small cause case could be appealed both on facts and law, first, from an Assistant Commissioner to the Deputy Commissioner, then from the Deputy Commissioner to the Commissioner of the division, and lastly from the Commissioner to the Judicial Commissioner sitting at Lahore. I have still a vivid recollection of a suit for the division of some seventy or eighty rupees on account of priests' fees brought by

[1] The Legal Member of Council, now Sir Andrew Scoble, K.C.S.I.

certain Brahmans against their rival co-sharers, which cost me considerable trouble to decide, and which excited so much party feeling that it was carried by the litigants themselves, without the aid of lawyers, through the various Appellate Courts I have mentioned, to the Judicial Commissioner. The justification of this liberal system of appeal lay in the inexperience of subordinate Courts, both original and appellate. When I arrived at my first station I had never been in a Civil Court in my life, but my Deputy Commissioner told me that I must immediately prepare to decide about a hundred civil suits a month, as there was no one else to dispose of them. Two or three days were given me to look through the records of cases decided by my predecessor, and to study Sir Richard Temple's Punjab Civil Code. I was then ordered to set to work and to make the best of it. In many instances *Appellate* Judges had to begin without much greater experience. Military officers were appointed direct from their regiments to be Deputy Commissioners, and civilians from the North-Western Provinces, who had never tried civil suits, either original or appellate, were appointed to be Deputy Commissioners and Commissioners in the Punjab, and were required to dispose of the work of Civil Courts, to which they had been previously unaccustomed. At this period the description of the appellate system quoted in this Council by the Honourable Mr. Ilbert, namely, that it was a 'sifting of cases through a succession of bad Courts in the hope that they will come right in the end,' was perhaps not altogether inappropriate, and it is easy to understand how the people of the country became thoroughly accustomed to the system of three appeals, first, to the head of the district; secondly, to the head of the division; thirdly, to the Judicial Commissioner at the provincial headquarters, and have been somewhat unwilling to part with a privilege which they valued.

On the first of November Colonel Wace returned from England. I relinquished my two acting appointments and reverted to the second Financial Commissionership.

Soon after our return to Lahore, Lord and Lady Dufferin paid a farewell visit to that place. On the 15th of November we dined at Government House to meet them. The following day, at a garden-party, their Excellencies bade their Punjab friends farewell and left the province for the last time.

In the spring of 1889 Mrs. Bishop (*née* Isabella Bird), the great traveller, came to Lahore. We met her there several times, and again, a year or two later, in Simla. She was a woman of very gentle manners, thoroughly feminine in appearance and ways. It was difficult to imagine that Mrs. Bishop could be capable of holding her own under all circumstances and of undergoing great fatigue and exposure in every variety of climate and weather. She had a very kindly face, a pleasant voice, and wonderfully clear and cultured speech. Our meeting at Simla was on Mrs. Bishop's return from Leh and the confines of Thibet. She told us that on coming back from the wilds, and meeting the first English face, she realised her rough appearance and could not refrain from tears. Mrs. Bishop did not speak much in private of her adventures, but seemed quite able to take up the threads of the topics of the day, though she must often have been cut off for long periods from all sources of news. She was an enthusiast about Mission work, and very anxious to obtain statistics and other facts regarding the progress of Missions in India. At her request we invited a lady connected with one of the great Missionary societies to meet her. Mrs. Bishop was full of eager anxiety to hear details of her work from the Missionary. The latter was equally anxious to learn details of her adventures from Mrs. Bishop. The result was a cross-fire of remarks and questions which resulted in neither lady gaining the information she wanted. This incident has recently been recalled to mind by the *Life of Mrs. Bishop*, in which an interview is described between her and Mr. Gladstone. In the latter case, however, the attitude of the two speakers was in contrast to that which we had observed at Simla. The traveller readily gave the statesman full details of the Kurdish atrocities amongst Nestorians, while Mr. Gladstone, in response to the traveller's inquiry, poured forth a stream of learned exposition of the true nature of the Nestorian heresy.[1]

We met Mrs. Bishop for the last time four or five years after we had left India. She came to deliver a lecture on Medical Missions in Aberdeen, to which we listened with great interest, her delivery being particularly good and clear. We had the pleasure of calling upon Mrs. Bishop at the house where she was staying. The contrast between her appearance and what it was when we had seen her last in Simla was great. No signs of the traveller remained. She was now an exceedingly well-dressed English lady. In the interval she had travelled through Persia from end to end and through part of Korea, enduring many hardships and facing wild and dangerous people. We found her charming as of old, and we met with a most kind welcome, but we were never able to accept her invitation to visit her in her home on the West Coast of Scotland.

On the 21st of March Colonel Wace, who had just come back to Lahore from camp, was reported to be ill. He rapidly became worse. On the 24th of March he died in the early morning and was buried in the Lahore

[1] *Life of Isabella Bishop*, p. 246. Murray, 1906.

Cemetery in the evening. The shock to the whole of the European community was very great, Colonel Wace being a highly respected officer, most amiable and kind-hearted. Officially he had a great reputation for his knowledge of the principles of Land Revenue Settlement.

Sir James Lyall, the Lieutenant-Governor, was in camp when Colonel Wace, in this sad and sudden manner, died at his post. Sir James at once returned to Lahore in order to ascertain full particulars of the occurrence, and to take steps for filling the vacant appointment. It will readily be believed that it was with very mingled feelings that I found myself, within a week of Colonel Wace's death, appointed to be first Financial Commissioner.

Towards the middle of May we were again in Simla for the hot weather. Lord and Lady Dufferin had meanwhile returned to England, and Lord and Lady Lansdowne reigned at Viceregal Lodge in their stead.

D. LAHORE, *November* 26.—University Convocation. Lord Lansdowne made a D.L.[1] He gave a good speech, not delivered in an eloquent way, but sensible and to the purpose, upholding knowledge for its own sake, and deprecating the cry for lower standards.

D. CAMP, *December* 14.—Marched into Loodiana; met by a great number of people, from Shahzada ——[2] downwards. . . . Loodiana much changed since I knew it thirty-one years ago. It is difficult to believe that so long a time has elapsed since 1858.

D. December 15.—Went to call on Shahzada ——. E. visited the ladies.

My wife gives me the following note of her recollections of the visit:—

The Shahzada and another native gentleman met me at the

[1] Doctor of Literature. [2] One of the pensioned Cabul Princes.

door of his house, and took me through an unpaved courtyard, and then up a rather steep and narrow earthen stair, to a large room furnished in a mixed European and Native style. Here, the Shahzada said, he received his guests. There were the usual chandeliers, wall lamps, highly coloured pictures, and a few arm-chairs. Small carpets were spread here and there over a mud-plastered floor. I was then taken to the next story, where two or three ladies, with hair very much oiled and brushed very smooth, wrapped in bright shawls or chádars, and wearing very full baggy silk divided skirts (?) received me. The room looked on to the roof of another building, and seemed to be a kind of landing or hall, with doors opening on two sides of it. There were four chairs ready placed; no other furniture did I see. I was told to sit next to the senior wife, an elderly lady of gentle face and manners. The talk was of the usual kind. How many children had I? had I a son? and so on. My knowledge of the language being limited, I doubt whether I spoke very correctly, but I could easily understand what was said. By this time the apartment had become full of women and children who crowded in through every door, some hiding their faces, many giggling and chattering, but there was no man to be seen save the master of the house, who sat gazing placidly at the somewhat noisy assembly. Turning to my elderly hostess I asked how many children she had, as a bright-eyed merry little boy rushed up to us with an air of independence which showed that *he* fully understood his position as a lord of creation. The lady replied, 'God has bestowed no son on me, but are not these all my children?' This was said with a glance and a tone, which, more fully than words, conveyed to my mind what sorrow and disappointment the gentle-eyed, sonless wife, with her gracious, dignified manner, had probably endured.

D. LAHORE, *Sunday*, *December* 22.—The Bishop preached morning and evening. In the morning, he said a good test of whether a name had been blotted out of the book of life was, 'Can you say from the heart the collect for the fourth Sunday in Advent?' I liked this way of putting it. Evening, sermon on the foolish virgins. He repeated Tennyson's 'Late, late, too late,' very finely.

The above extract leads me to add a few words to previous brief references to Henry James Matthew, who, by this time, had become Bishop of Lahore in succession to Bishop French. I have already mentioned how much we admired Mr. Matthew as a preacher in the Fort Church, Calcutta, in 1868-69, and how we became acquainted with him as Chaplain of Simla in 1878. On his becoming the first Archdeacon of Lahore under Bishop French, Mr. Matthew continued to be Chaplain of Simla, but he frequently visited Lahore as Archdeacon. During the years 1881 to 1886 our acquaintance with Mr. and Mrs. Matthew ripened into a strong friendship, which only came to an end on their deaths in 1898 and 1887 respectively. As Archdeacon, Mr. Matthew proved himself to be an excellent administrator and man of business. These qualities, joined with his great learning, and eloquence, and staunch Churchmanship, were recognised by both clergy and laity (official and non-official) throughout the province. When it became known that Bishop French was anxious to resign, it was a foregone conclusion that he would be succeeded by his Archdeacon. Indeed, if I remember rightly, Bishop French told me at Simla in 1887, that he had practically made it a condition of his retirement that Archdeacon Matthew should be his successor. Mrs. Matthew having died in England late in 1887, the consecration of the new Bishop early in January 1888 caused him more than ordinary strain. His wife was endowed with a great power of sympathy. She had a remarkable gift of music, and was an excellent organist. In every way she was a fitting helpmeet of a parish clergyman, and her co-operation would have greatly lightened the burden of a bishopric. Writing to me from London on the 5th January, Archdeacon Matthew said:—

> My consecration takes place to-morrow. . . . Under my present circumstances, the ceremony becomes a very trying one. It is at such a moment one misses to the full the presence of one who doubled all one's joys. I shall be surrounded by hundreds of friends to-morrow, for many have shown wonderful kindness in making long journeys to be present. . . . I hope to arrive in Lahore on the 17th of February, just possibly on the 16th, which would be a curious coincidence, as I landed in Calcutta, almost 21 years ago, on that day. I shall be formally installed in the Cathedral on Sunday, February 19th.

I need only add that while Bishop of Lahore, the highest expectations of his friends, and of all with whom he was brought in contact, were fulfilled, and his unlooked-for death in 1898, following a sudden seizure in the Cathedral after his last sermon, caused a grievous loss to the Diocese.

CHAPTER XXI

THE LAST YEARS

1890—1893

THE beginning of 1890 was marked by two events. First, the assembly at Muridki, some twelve or thirteen miles from Lahore, of a large Cavalry camp, and second, the visit of the Duke of Clarence—Prince Albert Victor of Wales.

The number of regiments collected at the camp was thirteen or fourteen. Sir Frederick Roberts, Commander-in-Chief, was present, his large camp being pitched in a convenient position not far from the scene of the manœuvres.

D. LAHORE, *January* 25, 1890.—Early to the station to meet Prince Albert Victor. He arrived soon after 8 . . . was presented. . . . After dinner, to a conversazione at the Montgomery Hall in honour of the Prince. A large gathering; address duly presented.

D. January 26.—About noon all of our party started for Muridki, where our tents had been pitched. . . . Evening, rode to the Cavalry camp.

D. January 27.—Rather a pleasant day at Muridki. Looking on at the Assault of Arms, with an interval for luncheon; met many friends. Chief there, and Prince Albert Victor. H.R.H. is visiting the Chief in a magnificent camp.

D. January 28.—The great day at Muridki. Rode out to the Parade ground before breakfast to see where we could have places for carriages. After breakfast we went out and had a fine view of the show. Some thirteen or fourteen cavalry regiments; the 5th Punjab Cavalry[1] amongst them. The march past and gallop across the plain in single line very fine. Then the Chief addressed the officers, who formed a semicircle around him, in a capital speech, delivered while he remained mounted on his favourite Arab.[2]

February 3.—We dined at Government House to meet H.R.H. Then came the big ball at the Montgomery Hall. . . .

In the month of February I made an interesting march through the Gujranwala District in company with Mr. Denzil Ibbetson,[3] the Deputy Commissioner. We travelled stage by stage *viâ* Hafizabad and Jalálpur to Chiniot, where we were met by Baron John Bentinck, the Deputy Commissioner of the Jhung District. The Baron was an interesting personality; a Dutchman, I believe, connected with the Portland family. He had come out to India some twenty years before, and eventually obtained a post in the Punjab Commission as an uncovenanted officer. He was a man of considerable energy and power of administration. His friends much regretted his retirement when it took place in the nineties, and still more his death in England in the year 1899.

D. CHINIOT, *February* 18.— . . . Evening, we rode to the river Chenab, and saw the rocky hills on either bank which Ibbetson happily called the 'Iron gates' of the Punjab. These hills in and around Chiniot, forming a gorge through which the Chenab flows, are a remarkable feature. The stone is a peculiar granite,

[1] In which was our eldest son.

[2] By name 'Vonolel,' after a Looshai Chief. More than seven years later, at the Jubilee of 1897, it was delightful to see Lord Roberts cantering down Pall Mall on the same spirited horse which he had ridden at Muridki.

[3] Afterwards Sir Denzil Ibbetson, K.C.S.I., Lieutenant-Governor of the Punjab.

mixed with clay slate, said to be of very old formation. Evening, we dined with the Baron and fared sumptuously. He had a most neat little repast laid out in his shamiana (shade tent) in the rest-house compound. Chinese lamps in the garden, altogether quite a fête.

From Chiniot we turned back marching direct towards Lahore *viâ* Shekhopura.

D. February 23.—Halted at Sukheki (from which we proposed to visit the rocky hill of Sangala, some thirteen or fourteen miles distant, believed to be the ancient capital of the Kathæans, the scene of one of Alexander's great battles). At 1 P.M. started for Sangala, drove in a mail-cart, and rode. Expedition altogether took some five or six hours. Distance thirteen or fourteen miles each way. Much interested in Sangala, which I fully believe to be the scene of Alexander's battle.[1] A reddish slaty rock, with many traces of old brick buildings. The palus or marsh near the base (just as described by Arrian). Height of hill, 218 feet; circumference, a mile. We went to the top and had a grand view of the *Bár*,[2] and of Chiniot and its rocks in the distance.

Our trip came to an end about the 1st of March, and was highly enjoyable as long as it lasted, but it afterwards appeared that we had gone through a part of the country where influenza of a serious type was raging. The result was, that before reaching Lahore, I experienced unmistakable symptoms of illness, which developed into influenza or dengue fever, and were followed by sequelæ of divers kinds, which forced me to take leave, to beat a retreat to Simla, and to remain on the sick list until well into May.

[1] Sir Charles Rivaz, however, tells me that the latest authorities have shown that the battle must have been much nearer the Himalayas.

[2] The well-known grazing jungle of Gujranwala.

After that I resumed work and remained at Simla for the rest of the season.

Before passing from the year 1890, mention may be made of a circumstance, which, though essentially personal to ourselves, may be regarded with some interest on account of its unusual nature. When we returned to India from furlough at the end of 1880, we left our ten children at home. In the decade which had elapsed, they had been coming to India in detachments. In 1883, our two eldest daughters arrived. In 1885, our eldest son joined the army at Dinapore. In 1888, our four youngest daughters, then mere children, came out. In 1889, our second, and in 1890, our third son joined their regiments in India. In the latter year we all spent Christmas Day together, and filled three pews in the Lahore Cathedral. I thought of Genesis xxxii. 10.[1] There were ten children, three grandchildren, and three sons-in-law. The Bishop of Lahore, writing to us on Christmas Eve, said: 'Now let me wish you and yours what you can hardly fail to have, a bright and merry Christmas. It is pleasant to think of you all united so far from England. I should think that very few have ever gathered in Lahore such a family party.' The gathering was broken up after two days, and has never again been collected together.

D. LAHORE, *January* 13, 1891.—At 11 A.M. to the railway station; a bright day. The Czarewitch and Prince George of Greece, with suite, arrived. Followed (by order) their cortège to the Fort, Mosque, etc., through the city to Government House. . . . Afternoon, went to see sports, at which H.I.H. was present.

D. January 14.—We dined at Government House to meet the Czarewitch. E. was taken in by Prince George of Greece, who

[1] 'Now I am become two bands.'

spoke excellent English, and was very pleasant. . . . Later we went to a conversazione at the Hall.

These brief extracts relating to the visit of the present Emperor of Russia to Lahore may be somewhat enlarged from memory. We had an excellent view of the Czarewitch, on the evening of the dinner-party, as he walked through a long vista of rooms attended by his host, Sir James Lyall, and followed by their respective staffs, to the drawing-room, where Lady Lyall and a large number of guests were assembled. The appearance of His Imperial Highness was not imposing. He seemed to be short in stature, and his expression was grave and devoid of brightness. As he stood under the arch, at the entrance to the drawing-room, two of the principal lady guests were presented to him, after which H.I.H. at once turned and led Lady Lyall to the dining-room. The atmosphere of the evening was distinctly serious and dull. It was easy to imagine that H.I.H. was aware of the rumour which had been circulated during the day that Nihilists had followed him even to Lahore.

Later in the evening the Montgomery Hall was densely packed with Native Princes and Nobles, magnificently dressed, who were eager to offer their salutations to the heir to the Russian throne. H.I.H. looked anxious and very grave. The crowd was great, though under perfect control and supervision. The Imperial visit went off without any contretemps, but we all sighed a sigh of relief when the last salute was fired and we realised that the Czarewitch had left Lahore in safety.

In February and March we made a very pleasant camping tour in the Mooltan and Muzaffargarh districts through country which was for the most part new to me. Starting from Lahore by railway, we found our tents pitched at Channu, about fifty miles east of Mooltan. From Channu we marched northwards to the river Ravi, where I inspected the canal works at Sidnai. From Sidnai we marched through Mooltan to Shini. At Shini we crossed the river Chenab to the Muzaffargarh district, returning thence to Mooltan *viâ* Alipur, Khangurh, and Muzaffargarh. This tour was one of the few in my experience which fulfilled the old ideal of an Indian official's life in camp. The march was accomplished in the early morning before breakfast. From about eleven o'clock till three or four in the afternoon, troops of Native visitors were received and the current office work disposed of. In the afternoon, for two hours or more, I went out gun in hand. For the most part in the Punjab such expeditions would be fruitless, owing to the scarcity of game; but, in the Muzaffargarh district, there is a good deal of marshy ground with streams which, during the cold weather, are the haunt of many species of wild duck, while the grassy jungles in the neighbourhood of the swamps hold a fair supply of black partridges.

Perhaps the most interesting feature of our march was the remarkable straight reach of the river Ravi, called the Sidnai reach. Higher up in the neighbourhood of Lahore, no river course could be more tortuous than that of the Ravi. In the neighbourhood of Sidnai, however, the river flows for about ten miles in a perfectly straight line. The breadth is about three hundred yards and the scene is made beautiful by the fact that the banks are clothed with trees, mainly palms and pepuls (*Ficus indica*). The local tradition gives the following explanation of the straightness of the Sidnai reach. In ancient times, a

G. R. Elsmie
1891.

certain god espied a beautiful goddess seated at some distance from him on the bank. On his hastening towards her the goddess took fright and ran down stream along the bank. As the river course zigzagged greatly, the goddess was soon lost to view. The god, full of rage and disappointment, ordered the river to become straight. On this the Sidnai reach was formed, and made further concealment impossible.

D. SIMLA, *Sunday, June* 7.—Mr. Winter preached for the Delhi mission, and preached very well and in a really interesting way. Afternoon, I went to the Town Hall to hear Dr. Pentecost hold forth, but I was not agreeably surprised. A vulgar American with plenty of flow of tongue; he gave us a series of sensational anecdotes which effectually quenched any desire to hear him again. I went on to Christ Church and heard Mr. Macduff, and concluded that both he and Mr. Winter were better worth hearing, by a long way, than Dr. P.

In the month of December, after a lapse of nearly thirty-two years, I revisited the subdivision of Mithunkote or Rajanpur, where I had served as Assistant Commissioner in 1859. I travelled by train from Lahore to Khanpur below Mooltan, thence by mule carriage to the river Indus, rowed across in a comfortable English boat, and was met on the other side by Captain Powney Thompson, Assistant Commissioner, and many Native chiefs and gentlemen. The Mithunkote which I knew had, in the interval, been entirely swept away by the river. I was taken to see a large wheat-field, which was supposed to cover the site of my old house and garden. Absolutely nothing remained of the old town and station. The new town of Mithunkote, where I now put up, is some four miles inland, and bears no resemblance whatever to its predecessor. The next day we visited Rajanpur, the headquarters of the Assistant Commissioner and of a Punjab Cavalry regiment.[1] Captain Thompson received me in his house, which I soon discovered was the old dak bungalow of which I laid the foundation in 1859. It was the first European house built in Rajanpur, but great improvements and enlargements had been effected since I saw it. I was interested to find that the two orderly messengers of the Assistant Commissioner, who had served under me, were alive. One of them, Gulan by name, still occupied his old post. The other, Jowahia, was a pensioner, and lived in the town. Imam Buksh, the chief of the Muzáris,[2] was still at the head of his tribe, having meanwhile been created a Nawab and a K.C.I.E. His son, Behram Khan, was deputed by his father to visit me, the old gentleman himself being ill and almost entirely blind.

Miran Khan, Chief of the Dreeshaks, who in 1859 was a youth under the Court of Wards, was still living, and I was glad to renew acquaintance with him. The Mithunkote-Rajanpur country, which had been famous in 1859 for its wild duck and partridge shooting, could still present a fair show of small game. I was not able to go out duck shooting, but my old orderly, Gulan, arranged two expeditions against the partridges, with the result that I bagged thirty-three brace of blacks and three brace of greys, which I thought a very fair result indeed. On inspecting the Assistant Commissioner's office I went into the record room and called for the papers of two or three old cases which I dimly

[1] Rajanpur had taken the place of the old cantonment at Asnee.
[2] See p. 67.

remembered to have dealt with thirty-two years before. In one of these, a murder case, I had discharged the accused in January 1860. It was the same case that is referred to in the extracts given at page 66. On looking at the papers in 1891, I made the following note regarding my handywork at the age of twenty-one.

Record full; I am sure the conclusion was right. The record contained a good deal of rather absurd indignation on my part against village head-men and others for suppressing evidence.

Young officers are somewhat apt to suppose that evidence is suppressed when, in truth, crimes having been committed with skill, no evidence exists which could be produced. Zeal in demanding evidence from the police and head-men not unfrequently results in the subornation of false witnesses.

I returned to Lahore before Christmas, and on the last day of the year we were present at a large dinner-party given by Sir James and Lady Lyall at Government House to as many of the members of the Punjab Commission and their wives as happened to be present in Lahore. These 'Commission' dinners, as they were called, were a very enjoyable feature during Sir James Lyall's time as Lieutenant-Governor, and I was glad to be permitted to propose the health of our host and hostess and to offer them the warm thanks of their guests.

D. January 15, 1892.—A cable slip to say that the Duke of Clarence has died. . . .

D. January 20.—All offices, etc., closed on account of the funeral of the Duke of Clarence. Afternoon, we all went to the Cathedral, where there was an impressive service, the Bishop preaching with much good taste and excellence.

D. January 30.—Bernier said that the great Moghal could only be said to be a wealthy monarch 'in the sense that a treasurer is to be considered wealthy who pays with one hand the large sums he receives with the other.' (How true of many with nominally large incomes.)

Starting from Lahore in the last days of January, we spent nearly the whole of February in a camping tour through the Delhi and Rohtak districts. The railway carried us from Lahore to Delhi in one night. At Delhi we found our tents comfortably pitched amongst trees near the Commissioner's house, Ludlow Castle. We marched from Delhi to the Kutub and encamped in some open ground not far from the Minar. This gave us an excellent opportunity of seeing, at our leisure, the Kutub enclosure, of ascending the Minar, of examining the ancient Hindu remains, the iron pillar, etc. Next day early, we went to Toghlakabad, the ancient fort and city of the Toghlak dynasty. A grand ruin. We specially noted the very quaint tomb, surrounded by an extraordinary battlemented wall.

We marched back to Delhi, visiting on our way the tombs of Humayan, Nizamudin, and Jehanara. We were much interested in the fine view of Purana Killa, which we passed on the right, taking note also of Ferozeshah's city and Asoka's pillar on a height. From Delhi we marched into the country, travelling as far as was possible along the side-path of an old canal. On the evening of our first day we were much interested in watching all that we could see of the conjunction of Jupiter and Venus. When the planets became visible, they were situated thus **, the conjunction having taken place at 4 P.M.

Our march does not call for lengthened description,

but nevertheless, from an Indian point of view, like our Mooltan march of the previous year, it was ideal. Beginning with the two or more hours' journey before breakfast, work and receiving Native visitors occupied me from 10 A.M. till 3 or 4 in the afternoon. After that came an evening shooting excursion. We were back in Delhi on the 25th of February and in Lahore on the 26th. The total of my game bag was one hundred and fifty-six head, viz. two black buck, seventy-seven ducks, forty-eight snipe, three black partridges, thirteen grey, three hares, and ten sand grouse.

The time had now arrived when a change of Lieutenant-Governors was to take place. On the 26th of February a large Ball was given at the Montgomery Hall, in honour of Sir James and Lady Lyall. The next day, the Punjab Commission gave a dinner to Sir James in a large tent in Anarkuli, while my wife gave a ladies' party to Lady Lyall at our own house. On the 2nd of March, Sir Dennis Fitzpatrick, the new Lieutenant-Governor, and his daughters arrived, and on the 5th, Sir James and Lady Lyall left Lahore for Bombay.

Before the appointment of Sir Dennis Fitzpatrick had become generally known, friends both European and Native had often expressed surprise because I seemed to have no expectation of succeeding Sir James Lyall. Though I had risen through all the grades in the Province to the office next to the Lieutenant-Governor, I had spent my best years in exclusively judicial posts, and I had never served as a Chief Commissioner or a Resident in other parts of India. It was not likely, therefore, that I should be thought of as in the running, when the services of Sir Dennis Fitzpatrick were available. A Member of Council at Simla, speaking of the subject, said that a man who, like Sir Dennis, had had a distinguished career in the Punjab, had then been a Secretary to the Government of India, and had acted as Chief Commissioner of the Central Provinces, of Mysore and of Assam, and as Resident at Hyderabad, and had done well all round, must practically be without a rival when the Lieutenant-Governorship of his old Province fell vacant.

In the middle of March I travelled to Kohat on the Frontier, where there were one or two questions relating to the Excise administration which required investigation and decision on the spot. My wife and two daughters accompanied me. We travelled by rail from Lahore to Khushálgurh on the Indus, driving in mail-carts the remaining thirty-one miles to Kohat. After a four days' stay, we travelled to Peshawur, *viâ* the Afridi Pass. The journey was no light undertaking for ladies, but it was successfully accomplished in about nine hours. Starting before 5 A.M. we drove to the foot of the Kotal, the high ridge at the Kohat end of the Pass. Thence the ladies were conveyed in dandies or carrying chairs, while I rode on horseback. We followed the rough track for some four and a half hours through the Afridi country. This brought us to Aimal Chabutra, a police post on the Peshawur side. There we were met by a very primitive phaeton in which, at a slow pace, we drove into Peshawur. I was glad to be there once more. I received visits from many old Native friends, and bade them good-bye. The journey back to Lahore, which occupied about twenty-four hours, was entirely by rail, bridges over the Indus, the Jhelum, the Chenab, and the Ravi having been finally completed. The contrast between this journey and our first journey from Lahore to Peshawur in 1872 was great. To travel the three hundred miles in a comfortable railway carriage without a single change was different indeed from the weary progress in a post-carriage extending over five days.

By the middle of May we were again at Simla, feeling that our remaining days in that pleasant place were numbered.

D. June 24.—Surprised by a note from Sir Alexander Miller (Legal Member of Council) saying he was authorised by the Viceroy to offer me the first nomination to the Legislative Council under the new Act, and that I should be gazetted in about a week unless I declined.

D. August 11.—Rode to Council. . . . The Council has many bald heads; I counted six—Viceroy, Chief, Barbour, Crosthwaite, Brackenbury, self, against Hutchins,[1] Fitzpatrick, Miller. . . .

D. September 22.—It is settled that at the end of the Simla time, I am to go on privilege leave and to join the Council at Calcutta on the 2nd of January, retiring in February.[2]

D. October 6.—We dined at Viceregal Lodge. Rather a pleasant party, the Chief and Lady Roberts there; Lady Lansdowne looking charming in pearls and diamonds and white satin. I suppose this is the last time we shall dine at Viceregal Lodge. . . . . E. was on the Viceroy's left, and seemed to have plenty of pleasant talk. . . .

D. October 17.—We all dined at Barnes Court. A farewell dinner given by Sir Dennis Fitzpatrick to E. and myself. Hutchins', Badcocks, Mackworth Youngs, etc., etc. Some thirty-four in all. Sir Dennis proposed our health in a very hearty way, and spoke very warmly of us. I thought my reply

[1] Sir Philip Hutchins, K.C.S.I. See p. 7.

[2] Under the thirty-five year rule.

was poor, but I was harassed by the dread of being tedious, and I said little that sounded satisfactory to myself. I decided that it was easier to propose a toast than to return thanks.

Our last days at Simla were in the first week in November. My wife and one daughter went down to Lahore to pack up and make preparation for our final departure to England. Another daughter and I left Simla *en route* to Naini Tal *viâ* Ambala, Saharanpore, and Bareilly to Katgodám. Thence we drove for two hours in mail-carts, along a beautiful road, not differing much in character from that which ascends from Kalka towards Simla, but wider, more wooded and prettier in every way. Entering Naini Tal at the east end of the lake, we travelled on by dandy and hill pony till we reached our destination, 'Ardwell.' Naini Tal at once struck me as a place well worth seeing, larger than I had imagined, but the lake smaller and not so imposing. One day we had lunch with Mrs. Rivett Carnac, daughter of Sir Henry Durand,[1] whom I had often met at Simla. The table was placed out of doors on a sort of terrace, close to the house, commanding a grand view of the snow. Then we walked from one vantage point to another, getting splendid views. Another day, I was delighted to meet and talk to Mr. William Kaye, Member of the Board of Revenue, a fellow termsman at Haileybury, whom I had not seen for many years.[2]

D. NAINI TAL, *Sunday*, *November* 20.—The church is really very pretty. After service we looked at the windows, brasses, etc., which are worth seeing; the landslip memorial especially,

[1] And wife of Mr. Rivett Carnac, C.I.E., Opium Commissioner.
[2] See p. 33.

with its singularly appropriate inscription: 'And the Lord Himself buried them in the valley.'

On the 23rd of November, having travelled down the hill with my daughter, Mrs. Holderness, we arrived at Lucknow, and put up in the Secretariat quarters in the Dár-ul-shufa. The same afternoon we drove to the Victoria Park and witnessed the unveiling of a statue of the Queen, by Sir Auckland Colvin, Lieutenant-Governor of the North-West. There I met General Robert Low, whom I had known so well as a subaltern at Murree in 1863, when, in our amateur theatricals, he used to play the *ingénues* to my middle-aged ladies. General Low was now commanding the Lucknow Division. Later in his career, as Sir Robert Low, he was Commander-in-Chief in Bombay.

D. LUCKNOW, *November* 26.—Paid a preliminary visit to the Residency. Found poor Jim Shepherd's[1] grave, near that of Sir Henry Lawrence.[2] All the grounds and surroundings in first-rate order. It will take me some time to understand all thoroughly, but I am glad to have come here, merely to see the scene of the prolonged contest of 1857. Felt much moved.

D. December 4.—Afternoon, drove to the Alam Bagh, where we saw Havelock's tomb, an obelisk; a very lengthy inscription, too much so, and very goody-goody. A great contrast to the simple inscription on Sir Henry Lawrence's grave. Nothing to see at Alam Bagh, save the little cemetery, the ruins of a garden-house, and the surrounding wall.

D. December 7.—At noon, started from Lucknow for Cawnpore. Arrived about three, and went for a drive round the

[1] A son of my uncle, John Shepherd; he was in the Bengal Light Cavalry, and was shot by one of our own sentries during the siege.

[2] See Gubbins's *Mutinies in Oude*, page 268.

station, visiting the Memorial Church, the massacre ghát, Memorial well and gardens. General feeling that of much depression. All is sad here, no redeeming point. The garrison did not hold out as at Lucknow. The screen and angel figure over the well are fine, and one cannot but admire the calm triumph over terrible disaster. Returned to the train and travelled on to Agra.

D. AGRA, *December* 8.—We took a carriage and went to the Fort. Very fine; I remember it indistinctly in 1861-62. Somewhat same style as Delhi, but more varied and interesting. Then on to the Taj, which is as glorious as ever. It was worth coming to Agra to see it again. The ground in very good order, trees lovely. I could go there often and often. Then we drove through the station, and later, after dinner, between 10 and 11, we went to see the Taj by a $\frac{5}{8}$-moon. There was hardly enough light, and though I admired much, I was somewhat disappointed. We should have been energetic and gone the previous night when the moon was brighter. However, we were amply repaid for coming to Agra by what we saw. The Taj is one of the few sights of the world which entirely come up to one's expectations. The defect, if any, seems to be the absence of a background.

D. December 9.—A day to be remembered. I had felt lazy about going to Futehpur Sikri; however, after breakfast we had a good carriage and drove out, taking luncheon with us. A very pleasant, shady drive of twenty-two miles. . . . The place is far grander than I anticipated, and more interesting. The red sandstone delightful; we practically had it to ourselves, and walked and travelled all over it. Panj-mahal, Mosque, Diwan-i-Khas, etc. etc. Futehpur Sikri, though not equalling Pompeii in interest, comes within the same category. . . .

D. December 10.—At Agra. . . . Afternoon, we drove to see the old cemetery in the Agra Civil lines. Rather interesting Armenian tombs. Tomb of Hessing, etc.; then on to Sikandra (Akbar's tomb), which is very fine, though not nearly so impressive as the Taj and Futehpur Sikri. Went to the top, delighted with the marble tracery work. . . . Left Agra between 12 and 1 at night and returned to Lucknow.

D. LUCKNOW, *December* 25.—To the Residency. Saw the Tykhanas (underground rooms), which are of great extent. They sheltered many women during the siege.

D. December 30.—Reached Benares about 10 A.M., drove to a ghat, where we went on a large barge and rowed along the ghats for a short time. The buildings above the ghat were fine, but on the whole we were disappointed. We did not attempt to do the city; back to our railway carriage at the station and went on to Calcutta.

D. December 31.—Very fast journey during the night; reached Howrah (opposite Calcutta) soon after 5 A.M. Drove to the flat which we had secured in 37 Chowringhee.

D. CALCUTTA, *Monday, January* 2, 1893.—At 7 A.M. we went to see the New Year's Day parade. . . . An invitation came for me to dine at Government House; the big New Year's Day dinner. Before dinner, in the Government House drawing-room, Sir Philip Hutchins told me I was to be a C.S.I. After dinner, was sent for by the Viceroy, who congratulated me, and said he had written, but letter must have crossed me. 'Blessed is he that expecteth nothing.' I certainly expected nothing. . . .

FROM THE VICEROY.

GOVERNMENT HOUSE, CALCUTTA,
December 30, 1892.

MY DEAR ELSMIE,—Your name will appear in the New Year's Day *Gazette* for the honour of a C.S.I. Accept my hearty congratulations. I hope it will be agreeable to you to carry away this mark of the appreciation with which your long and honourable services are regarded.—With best wishes to Mrs. Elsmie and yourself, I am, my dear Elsmie, yours sincerely,

LANSDOWNE.

D. January 5.—We went to the State Ball at Government House. . . .

D. January 12.—At 10.30 A.M. started for Government House. Council at 11. Room fine, large picture of Warren Hastings with very expressive eyes looking down on us. Motto, *Mens aequa in arduis*, and he certainly looks calm, though anxious. A good deal of business. Hutchins made two long and good speeches, introducing Criminal Security and Surveillance and Emigration Bills. I introduced the Punjab Government Tenant's Bill in a short speech which I had all ready. Rather enjoyed the business. . . .

D. Sunday, January 15.—We all four went to the Cathedral to be present at the Consecration of Bishop Clifford (Bishop-elect of Lucknow). Some eight or nine Bishops of the Province were there. . . . The Bishop of Lahore preached the sermon from the forty-fifth Psalm, seventeenth or eighteenth verse, but was not heard to advantage. We sat in the middle of the Cathedral and lost many words.

D. January 16.—We dined at Government House (an Episcopal dinner-party). We hoped that E. would be taken in by our Bishop, and that I should take in Mrs. Clifford (wife of the newly consecrated Bishop and sister of Charles Bernard), and so it was. . . .

D. February 1.—Up early to the Currency Office to see the arrival of the Austrian Archduke, wonderfully clothed in red pants, blue coat, green spreading plume. . . . Evening, E. and I dined at Government House. E. went into dinner with Mr. Justice Norris, and enjoyed talking to him. I took in Mrs. Merritt, wife of the American Consul. . . . Dinner-party about eighty. . . . We had an excellent view of the Archduke and suite.

D. February 2.—To Council for the last time. My small Bill was passed with an amendment suggested by Sir Alexander Miller at the last moment. Rather a scramble to get it in. . . . Afternoon, the Chief, Lady and Miss Roberts came to say good-bye to us. Very nice of them; we had a friendly chat. Evening, dined at Belvedere to meet the Archduke.

D. February 4.—To the great crush at Government House

to meet the Archduke. Had an excellent opportunity of saying good-bye again to the Chief and Lady Roberts. Said good-bye to Lady Lansdowne. . . . We never got near the Viceroy, so shall have to leave without bidding him good-bye or saying a word of thanks.

D. February 6.—Last day in Calcutta. Dined with Mr. and Mrs. Stuart, Mrs. S. being sister of my old Haileybury friend, George Lang.[1] At night went on board the s.s. *Rosetta.*

D. February 8.—At anchor at the mouth of the Hooghly till about twelve, when we steamed on; passed a lightship in the afternoon. Said lightship signalled for us a telegram of farewell from our friends the George Rivazes in the Punjab. I suppose the message had been forwarded by the P. and O. Office, Calcutta, by wire to the ship. Anyhow it was a novel and pleasant experience to get such a telegram at sea.

And so, within some four days of the completion of thirty-five years' service, I left India and forthwith became a pensioner.

[1] See pp. 30-36.

APPENDIX

CROWN *VERSUS* (1) KHALIL ; (2) DILDAR ; (3) BOSTAN

CHARGES { MURDER—AGAINST NOS. 1 AND 2.
ABETMENT OF MURDER AGAINST NO. 3.

This was a very characteristic case. Sháhdád Khán of Hund, a Chief whom I knew well, and who had often acted as an assessor in the Sessions Court, was murdered while kneeling at prayers in a mosque. He made the task of discovering his murderer a very difficult one by declaring with his dying breath that he had turned round and *identified twelve members of a band of murderers.*

JUDGMENT.—*30th October* 1876.

SHÁHDÁD KHÁN, Khán of Hund, was assassinated in the village mosque about 9 P.M. on the 3rd July 1875. He was engaged at the time in the *khuftán* prayers. The assassin chose the moment when the whole congregation were prostrated with their heads on the ground to deliver a well-planted blow with a dagger on the Khán's right side. The mosque is a small one, described by the Inspector of Police (witness No. 11) as being about the size of the room in which this Court is held, *i.e.* about 30 ft. × 20 ft. The worshippers, of whom there were only about twelve, stood in two lines ; the Imám being in front alone, leading the devotions. In the line immediately behind him were eight men, including the Khán. In the second line were four boys. The plan attested by witness 11 has been most carefully prepared, and gives a very clear idea of the scene in the mosque, and of the surrounding lanes, *hujras*, walls, and gates of the village. I am helped to make this remark by my own personal knowledge, having spent a day in camp at Hund in 1873.

The mosque being a small one, it appears that the spot where the Khán was praying could not have been much more than fifteen feet from the small opening in the back wall, used as an entrance. A lamp or *chirágh* was burning in the mosque building.

Immediately on being stabbed, the Khán fell over against the man on his left hand, crying out that he had been wounded. The alarmed congregation broke off from prayers and followed the Khán, who, staggering towards the entrance, sank down at the place where the shoes had been left. The question which this Court has to decide is, whether the Khán or any of his companions identified with sufficient accuracy any or all of the accused rushing from the mosque down the lane towards the east. It is obvious that to do so could not have been easy. The night was dark. Only a dim lamp was burning at the upper end of the mosque; the enclosure was small. The assassin had only to retreat about five paces ere he got into the lane. His back only would be seen by the people in the mosque. Moreover, it appears from what all the witnesses say, that a certain amount of time elapsed before the worshippers arose,—very short it must have been, but still they appear to have waited till the Imám gave the signal to break off. So that the wounded Khán, who had fallen on his side, was actually the first to rise up and to reach the shoes. A few only of the men who were in the mosque profess to have seen and identified any of the assassins. The statements of most of these having varied considerably since they were examined on the following day by the Tahsíldar-Magistrate, it is necessary to compare with the greatest care the accounts given by them at the various stages of the inquiry. The principal, and, *primâ facie*, the best witness in the case is one Jáfar, a distant cousin and brother-in-law to the Khán. He, with the village chaukidár, made the first report at the Thánah of Utmán Bulák, about 11 P.M. the same night. He said that five men had been seen running away, out of whom Khálíl (accused 1), and Dildár (accused 2), had been identified by him, Jáfar, Said Ali, Sher Zamán, Akhtarai, etc. He added also that the Khán had himself identified these two men, and that it was quite possible that the remaining three might have been dentified by some one. Although Hund is only a few miles from the Thánah and Tahsíl, the Deputy Inspector and Tahsíldar did not reach the spot till the next morning after dawn. The delay has not been satisfactorily explained.

The Tahsíldar recorded the evidence of Jáfar fully. The witness adhered generally to what he had said at the Thánah, but, as was to be expected, gave additional particulars. He admitted that he had only seen the backs of two men going out of the door, but had, nevertheless, been able to identify them. He added that he, with Akhtarai, Sher Zamán, and Said Ali, had gone twenty paces in pursuit, and that the five assassins had run to the east and escaped out of the village by the south or river gate. He tried to account for no real attempt to arrest the assassins having been made by saying that there was much anxiety felt on behalf of the Khán, and that the pursuers were afraid of the murderers.

Before the committing Magistrate, on 27th July, Jáfar dropped all mention of *Akhtarai*, whom the Police inquiry had proved not to have been in the mosque at all. A man *Sháhwali* was substituted for Akhtarai, and Jáfar asserted that Said Ali, Sher Zamán, and Sháhwali had pursued further than he had, and on returning said they had identified the third, fourth, and fifth assassins as Mír Afzal, Akbar, and Bostán (accused 3).

In the Sessions Court, Jáfar has added several particulars to his former statements. He has explained fully how much deliberation there was in his rising from his knees, thereby unconsciously weakening his story. He has also admitted that he only ran five or six paces from the mosque; but he tried to strengthen his evidence by declaring that accused 1 and 2 had, in their fear of being arrested, turned round their faces towards him and enabled him to identify them thoroughly by the light of the lamp. He also added that the Khán, in sending him to report, did not tell him to take any names, but said he had recognised his assassins and would himself name them when called upon. The demeanour of this witness in the Sessions Court was fairly satisfactory save when making manifest exaggerations, such as in giving the account of the assassins turning their faces towards him. The next witness to identification is Sher Zamán (No. 3). He, too, began before the Tahsíldar by naming Akhtarai as one of the four worshippers who ran towards the mosque door following the Khán, but he emphatically denied that any one had pursued the assassins, and was absolutely positive that he himself had not. He said that all had stood by the Khán. Nevertheless, Sher Zamán declared that he had identified three men who ran out of the mosque as accused 1, 2, and 3, and had seen two others (not identified) standing outside.

Before the committing Magistrate this witness, Sher Zamán, said he *did* run out of the mosque; that he identified four men by sight, viz. accused 1, 2, and 3, and Akbar, and a fifth as Mír Afzal by voice. He added that he had actually laid hands on Dildár (accused 2). Sher Zamán dropped all mention of Akhtarai before the committing Magistrate and Sessions Court. His story in the two Courts was much the same, save that before the Sessions he did not mention Mír Afzal. His demeanour was, as noted at the time, 'very far from satisfactory,' and considering it, and the many variations in his stories, I should be extremely reluctant to accept his evidence as worthy of credence. The third witness to identification is Said Ali (No. 4). Before the Tahsíldar this man said that he and Jáfar had pursued the assassins for twenty paces, whom they saw from behind and recognised as accused 1, 2, and 3.

Before the committing Magistrate Said Ali stated he had identified a fourth man as well, viz. Mír Afzal, whom he had actually laid hold of, and that he had been knocked over by accused 1 and 3. He explained that he had been ashamed to mention to the Tahsíldar his futile attempt to arrest Mír Afzal. Before the Sessions Court he said much the same, adding that on returning he openly proclaimed his having identified four men.

The fourth witness to identification is Sháhwali (No. 5), who was apparently substituted for Akhtarai after the first day or two. Before the Tahsíldar, Sháhwali admitted having run some twenty or twenty-five paces with Said Ali and Jáfar, in the direction supposed to be taken by the assassins, but denied that they had seen any one. He said the Khán said that he had identified 'his criminals.' Before the committing Magistrate, Sháhwali greatly expanded his statement. He declared that he identified the three accused and Mír Afzal, and had actually seen them seized by the other witnesses. He said he had been afraid to speak in the first instance. In this Court Sháhwali has declared that he recognised three only—not having seen Dildár, accused, at all.

These may be said to be all the witnesses to the alleged identification; inasmuch as the prosecution, represented in this Court by Muhammad Amír, Inspector of Police, virtually lays no stress at all on the dying declaration of the Khán in which he professed to have identified five men inside the mosque and seven outside. Any more palpably false statement could hardly be conceived. Indeed, it seems naturally to suggest the remark, that it is no matter for surprise that the man who was capable of making it with his dying lips, should have had scores of enemies and should have been assassinated by some one or other of them. To suppose, however, that a band of twelve men would have gone together to effect a treacherous assassination of the kind described is altogether inconsistent with probability.

The calendar contains the names of the four boys who stood in the third row, but the prosecutor only called one of them. These boys had, in the first instance, denied having seen any one, though they were the most likely, *primâ facie*, to have been first on the alert.

The boy Gharíb (No. 9), who has been examined, professes now to have identified accused 3 and Mír Afzal as they retreated in a westerly direction, *i.e.* in the direction opposite to that said by the other witnesses to have been taken by the assassins. It is clear that, if this boy's story is true, the main theory of the prosecution is false; but the boy's demeanour was highly unsatisfactory, and, as the Magistrate had discredited him and his companions, I think the prosecutor did right not to call the remaining three.

I propose now to examine the evidence of the other persons present in the mosque, whose statements have been recorded. The chief of these is Fazl-i-Ahmad, the Imám, apparently a very straightforward and respectable man. The prosecutor has tried at various stages of the proceedings in this Court to make me believe that this man declines to give a tittle of evidence against any of the accused, simply through fear. I am bound to say that I can find no proof in the record that this assertion is true. In the first instance, it appears that the Khán and his friends kept back from the Tahsíldar and Police the fact that Fazl-i-Ahmad had been the officiating Imám, so that we find no trace of his having been questioned till the 8th July. His brother, Muhammad Sádik, was made to declare to the Police that he had been the Imám, and the explanation offered is that the Khán ordered him to say so to prevent Fazl-i-Ahmad being dragged before the Courts. This seems hardly a satisfactory explanation. The prosecutor did not adopt it, but asked the Court to believe that the Khán kept back this man because he knew him to be *afraid* to tell what he had seen and heard. But it is obvious that a third explanation may be given—the more especially if Fazl-i-Ahmad can be accepted as a truthful witness, viz. that he was kept back because every one knew he would not tell an untruth.

Now, on looking through the record, I fail to find that Fazl-i-Ahmad ever *denied* having been Imám. He kept silence certainly till he was questioned, but when questioned he admitted the fact of his presence freely.

The evidence given by this man in the Sessions Court is so important that I quote it almost in full :—

'I was Imám, and conducting prayers at the time of the murder. The Khán at first mentioned another because he wanted me to stay with him. There were seven men and four boys saying prayers. We were all in *Sijda* (prostration). Suddenly, as I was lifting my head, I heard a noise behind me. I did not hear the Khán's voice. I broke off the prayers and looked round and saw that some of the men who had been praying were out of the enclosure. Some were round the Khán, where the shoes were, about six paces behind me. The Khán, in answer to my inquiry, said: "Thieves have killed me." He hadn't fallen. Muhammad Sádik and others were supporting him. He showed where his wound was. He said: "Take me home; I cannot wait." Then we took him home, about eighty paces off. He begged me to stay with him. I stayed accordingly, till morning. He did not tell me how it happened; he was in pain. He took no names. I was occupied in taking care of him and in tending the wound. Many people came and went, *but I did not hear any one take anybody's name that night.* Jáfar certainly came in and went rapidly to report. He said nothing in my hearing about having recognised the assassins. *No one until morning said that any one had been recognised.* I have been Imám for four years. My ancestors were Imáms before me. I was a great friend of the Khán. There were no secrets from me. In the mosque, there was a small *chirágh* burning. It lighted the courtyard, but had any one been in the doorway, with his back to me, there would not have been enough light for me to identify him; but if he had turned his face I might have done so.'

Now, it is clear that if Fazl-i-Ahmad's statement is to be relied upon, it must be regarded as almost fatal to the prosecution. As far as demeanour in this Court is concerned there can be no question that Fazl-i-Ahmad appeared to be far more worthy of credit than any of the witnesses whose evidence I have already analysed, and I incline much more to believe him than any of the others. Passing on to the evidence of Muhammad Sádik, brother of Fazl-i-Ahmad, we find him in the first instance falsely asserting to the Tahsíldar that he was the Imám, joining the others in saying that *Akhtarai* was one of the worshippers who pursued the assassins, but denying that he himself had seen any one running off, and omitting to say that the Khán or his companions had taken the names of any of the accused.

Before the committing Magistrate, Muhammad Sádik substitutes Sháhwali for Akhtarai, and asserts that the pursuers returned and at once named five men—accused 1, 2, and 3, Mír Afzal and Akbar. It may here be remarked, that if they did do so, it is most extraordinary that Jáfar should not have mentioned all of them at the Thánah.

In this Court, Muhammad Sádik (No. 6) gives a very confused statement, the most important point in which is that he now omits all mention of Akbar as one of the men recognised by Mír Zamán, etc.

The next witness is Chirágh Sháh (No. 8), an old man who now gives an account so totally different from what he gave in the first instance as to be hardly worth notice.

Mahammad Said (No. 11 of the calendar) was not called in this Court by the prosecutor. It is, however, necessary to refer to his previous statement, because I find that the Magistrate, in his committing order, mentions this man as corroborating Jáfar's statement regarding the identification at the time of Khálíl and Dildár. He doubtless did so in *cross-examination* before the Magistrate, but if his previous statement before the Tahsíldar is referred to, it will be found that he distinctly said the pursuers had taken no names on their return. That part of the evidence for the prosecution which relates to the finding of a knife outside the village and the identification of the assassins beyond the wall has been virtually withdrawn, and very rightly so, I think, judging from the manifestly false statement of Habíb, whom I called merely to see whether anything could be made out of this part of the case. Of circumstantial evidence against the three accused there is practically very little or none. The Magistrate has been at immense pains in going through several scores of old cases which tend to prove the enmity existing between the Khán and the various persons accused in this and the Magistrate's Court. But I must confess myself quite unable to understand the necessity for so much investigation of the past history of the parties, and I am very clearly of opinion that the time expended in the examination of these papers has in no way been repaid by the result, while the delay entailed in the committal of a case, which, when divested of all irrelevant matters, simply turns on the credibility of certain eye-witnesses, who were forthcoming at once, is much to be regretted. The value of promptitude in dealing with such a case seems greatly to have been lost sight of by the Magistrate, and, however much I may admire the great perseverance and pains bestowed on the inquiry, I am constrained to say that whatever may be the result of the trial, they were out of proportion to the task in hand, and I cannot admit that there was anything in the case which necessitated the delay of nearly eleven months from the date of the crime till the date of committal. With regard to the motive, which may have actuated the accused, it may readily be conceded that according to Pathán ideas, they had an ample one. This is hardly denied by the accused themselves. The Khán had had a long series of litigation with Bostán (accused 3), the last phase of which took place at Mardán on July 2nd, the very day before the murder, when, in an execution of decree case, Bostán, exasperated by the persistence of the Khán, manifested through his legal agent Azízulla (witness No. 7), burst into a rage and declared in open Court that if he had had a knife he would have killed himself or Azízulla. It is an undue straining of words to say, as the Magistrate does, that this declaration was tantamount to a threat to stab the Khán, for it is quite possible to suppose that Bostán believes the agent to have been the Khán's chief adviser in pressing his case, and may, at the moment, have been specially enraged at some word or gesture used by Azízulla. It cannot, therefore, be admitted as a logical consequence that when Bostán said he would like to stab Azízulla, he thereby indicated an intention of stabbing the Khán who was not present. Yet, at the same time, it is perfectly possible that, exasperated by the steps taken to eject him from his house in the execution of decree case, he hurried home bent on vengeance, and did thereon take steps to have the Khán assassinated. But, however easy it may be to imagine that Bostán should adopt such a course, there is not a tittle of evidence to show that he did so, save that the Khán was stabbed on the evening of the 3rd July, and that on the 4th some men said they had seen Bostán running away from the scene of the crime.

Take away the direct evidence of these witnesses, and it seems perfectly impossible to fasten the guilt on Bostán from the mere fact of the existence of bitter enmity and of the scene in Court at Mardán, the previous day, the more especially as it is admitted by the prosecution that many other persons were at the time plotting the Khán's murder. So that after all I find myself thrown back on the evidence of the identification at the time, which, after weighing and analysing it to the best of my ability, I find myself quite unable to accept as a sufficiently trustworthy basis for the conviction of the accused of a capital crime. When the various statements of witnesses 3, 4, and 5 are carefully examined and tested by comparison with those of Fazl-i-Ahmad, the Imám, and the other men who were present, I think they must all be rejected as worthless. *Primâ facie*, it is far more probable that the assassin or assassins of Sháhdád Khán were not recognised as they darted away into the darkness, than that the alarmed worshippers, who could see their backs only, clearly identified them.

The only witness whose story I have some hesitation in rejecting is Jáfar, who, as far as appears from the records, has been fairly consistent throughout. But he is a near relative of the Khán, and his story is entirely opposed to that of the Imám Fazl-i-Ahmad, who struck me as the more truthful of the two. The strongest argument that can be put forward in favour of Jáfar's story is contained in the committing order of the Magistrate, and I will quote it in full:—

'One consideration which leads me to credit the evidence is that accusation has not been made against any of the *Khán Khel* themselves of having been the actual assassins. A Hindustáni syce has been accused as the principal, and the descendant of a Hindu renegade as his companion. This is so unlike the usual procedure in these cases, where the actual assassin, if a man of low birth, is frequently not named, but the supposed instigator of the deed is. . . .

'In the present case, the relatives of the deceased Khán, even if accused 1 and 2 suffer the highest penalty of the law, will not, from an Afghán point of view, consider themselves revenged by the blood of a syce for that of a Khán, and this is a consideration that ought not to be lost sight of in weighing the evidence for the prosecution.'

This argument would carry greater weight if Khálíl and Dildár were men not ordinarily likely to be charged with the crime, but a reference to previous records shows that the Khán and his friends would very probably suspect both of them of having a hand in a deed of the sort. At the very time the murder occurred, an application for security to keep the peace towards the Khán, to be taken from accused 1 and 3, was pending before the Magistrate, and it is much to be regretted that circumstances prevented final orders being passed on this application at an earlier period.

And I find that the accused Dildár, who is a dependant of accused 1 and 3 and a noted bad character, had been punished for a grievous assault on one of the Khán's relatives, and had been released from prison in 1874. On his release the Khán submitted a detailed recommendation to the Magistrate in which Dildár's misdeeds were fully set forth, and a prayer made that security should be taken from him, as a very dangerous person. All this renders it very natural that Khálíl and Dildár should be accused merely on suspicion, while Bostán, of whose return from Mardán the Khán and others may have been ignorant, was not charged until the next day, when it became known that he had come back.

However that may be, Jafár's evidence cannot but lose much of its value when the recklessness of the Khán in accusing *twelve men* and of his son in trying to implicate *nineteen*, is taken into consideration. By the wicked extravagance of these statements, it must surely be admitted that the Khán's family have forfeited all their right to obtain justice in our Courts. At the conclusion of the trial I expressed my opinion to this effect to the son Azád Khán, telling him that if the real murderers of his father escaped justice either in this or in a higher Court, the fault would lie with those who had attempted to strengthen the case with manifestly false evidence. The two assessors were divided in opinion, one accepting generally the evidence for the prosecution, the other rejecting it and declaring that the identification of the assassins in the manner alleged was not only *primâ facie* improbable, but impossible. This man evidently thinks Dildár guilty from the general complexion of the case, not from the evidence. He would therefore act as one of a Council of Elders would, and give him a slight punishment. My own final opinion is that Jafár *may* be speaking the truth, but I am not sufficiently satisfied that he is to enable me to convict the prisoners on his statement. 'It is ill work,' as remarked by the Chief Court in one of last year's cases, 'convicting on evidence like' that which has been adduced here.

For these reasons, I concur with the assessor, Abdul Azíz Khán and, acquitting the accused, direct that they be set at liberty in respect to the charge on which they have been tried.[1]

[1] The committing Magistrate informed me some time after my order had been pronounced, that he had been disposed to recommend the Government to appeal from the acquittal, but that further information which he had obtained led him to believe that these accused did not actually take part in the assassination.

INDEX